Enlightenment 2.0

Enlightenment 2.0

Restoring sanity

to our politics,

our economy,

and our lives

Joseph Heath

HarperCollins*Publishers*Ltd

For Andrew

Contents

Introduction

Head versus heart

The National Mall in Washington, D.C., is one of the world's great boulevards. Officially designated a national park, its tree-lined expanse runs from the Lincoln Memorial in the west to the Capitol in the east, punctuated by the Washington Monument almost square in the middle. It provides a grand setting for America's great national institutions, museums, and memorials, and it is where over 24 million tourists come every year to bask in the glory that is the United States of America.

It is also where a great many Americans come to complain about their government.

There have been thousands of rallies, great and small, over the years, but in October 2010, the National Mall was the scene of perhaps its most peculiar event to date. On the day before Halloween, close to a quarter million Americans gathered, not for civil liberty or equal rights, and not to oppose the war or support the troops. Instead, they rallied for sanity.

Led by Jon Stewart, host of the satirical news program *The Daily Show*, the rally was intended as a call for more reasoned discussion in American politics, outside the cacophony of partisan extremism that dominates America's news media. And while Stewart insisted that the rally was not a partisan event, it was widely interpreted as a response to the Reclaiming

Honor rally hosted two months earlier by then Fox News personality Glenn Beck. Intended or not, the Rally to Restore Sanity[1] quickly turned into a mass protest against the extreme craziness that had erupted on the American political scene after the election of Barack Obama.

It was the first time, perhaps since the French Revolution, that *reason* had become the object of large-scale political mobilization in the West. This says a lot about the changes that have occurred in American political culture in the past few decades.

The big tent of the American right has always sheltered its share of crazies, particularly gun nuts and religious conservatives, but in recent years they have been joined by the anti-tax Tea Party movement, the birthers (who deny that Obama was born in the United States), the truthers (who believe that the collapse of the World Trade Center towers was an inside job), and a dog's breakfast of antiscience denialists who believe in neither evolution nor global warming and who are highly suspicious of much else besides. There came a point, however, when the sideshow began to take over center stage. Americans woke up to find that their political system was increasingly divided, not between right and left, but between crazy and non-crazy. And what's more, the crazies seemed be gaining the upper hand.

Consider the case of Glenn Beck, who is a conspiracy theorist in the classic mold. Before he finally lost his TV show on Fox News, Beck used to draw elaborate diagrams on a chalkboard, sketching out the "connections" he saw between various people and trends, all part of a vast secular socialist conspiracy aimed at robbing Americans of their birthright. It was all so stereotypical—as though someone had put in a request to central casting for a "nut" to do political commentary. Higher-ups at the network may have seen it as pure entertainment, but millions of Americans took it quite seriously.

Popular awareness that something was going quite wrong in America probably came in 2005. That was the year the comedian Stephen Colbert coined the term *truthiness* to describe the growing abuse of appeals to emotions or "gut feelings" by politicians in lieu of arguments based on reason, evidence, or even fact. According to his inspired definition, a claim is "truthy" when it *feels* true, even though it may not, strictly speaking, *be* true. As Colbert said in an interview at the time, feeling had now triumphed over objective truth: "It used to be, everyone was entitled to their own opinion, but not their own facts. But that's not the case anymore. Facts matter not at all. Perception is everything."[2]

Since 2005, the syndrome that Colbert described has, if anything, become more virulent. The 2012 primaries for the Republican presidential nomination, for example, became almost otherworldly, the discussion and debate increasingly unhinged from reality. Rick Santorum, who was the only person able to mount a serious challenge against the eventual nominee, Mitt Romney, at one point made the following series of claims (against the specter of government rationing of health care):

> In the Netherlands, people wear different bracelets if they are elderly. And the bracelet is: "Do not euthanize me." Because they have voluntary euthanasia in the Netherlands, but half of the people who are euthanized—ten percent of all deaths in the Netherlands—half of those people are euthanized involuntarily at hospitals because they are older and sick. And so elderly people in the Netherlands don't go to the hospital. They go to another country, because they are afraid, because for budget purposes, they will not come out of that hospital if they go in there with sickness.[3]

What is astonishing about this sequence of claims is that almost everything in it is false—and not just false, but fantastic, made-up, disconnected from reality. The only thing Santorum said that is true is that the Netherlands permits physician-assisted suicide. Needless to say, no one is subject to involuntary euthanasia (i.e., murder) in the heart of Europe.[4] The statistics are all false. The detail about the bracelets is completely imaginary. And there is no evidence of elderly Dutch people traveling to other countries for fear of being euthanized at their local hospital. It was as though Santorum were living in a parallel universe, where the facts were what he wanted them to be (and happened to support his paranoid, apocalyptic, ultra-rigid brand of Christianity).

Furthermore, he seemed not to realize that the Netherlands was a real place, where people might hear what he said and hope to set the record straight. The Dutch were actually quite upset about the lies that were being told about their country in America. Yet when pressed by a Dutch reporter to explain Santorum's comments, his official spokesperson—amazingly— refused to retract or apologize for Santorum's claims. She defended him on the grounds that Rick "says what's in his heart."

Sometimes the jokes write themselves. In this case, it was as though the Santorum campaign got their talking points from Colbert. Their defense, in a nutshell, was that even though the candidate's claims were not true, they were nevertheless *truthy.* Simply pointing this out was satisfactory, from their perspective; no apology or retraction was necessary.

¶

The same year that Colbert coined the term *truthiness,* a short essay written by the philosopher Harry Frankfurt, entitled "On Bullshit," became an international sensation. The essay was actually more than twenty years old and already widely known among academics. But when the press reissued it as a stand-alone volume, it clearly hit a nerve with the public, who propelled it onto the *New York Times* bestseller list for twenty-seven weeks. It was not so much that people enjoyed Frankfurt's writing—indeed, it is not clear how many people actually cared to read through and follow the argument. What mattered more was that Frankfurt had given a name to something that everyone had already noticed but didn't have a way of talking about. (As he put it in the opening lines, "One of the most salient features of our culture is that there is so much bullshit. Everyone knows this."[5])

Frankfurt's important contribution was to have distinguished between lying and bullshitting. What characterizes the bullshitter is that, unlike the liar, who at least maintains the pretense of telling the truth, the bullshitter has simply opted out of the truth-telling game. There is no pretense with the bullshitter. Although producing ordinary declarative sentences that would normally be evaluated under the categories of truth and falsity, the bullshitter is not even trying to say something that sounds true. (In a subsequent contribution to the genre, Laura Penny picked out the phrase "your call is important to us"—repeated ad nauseam to callers on hold—as quintessential bullshit.[6] It's not just unbelievable, it's *inherently* unbelievable. If your call was important, then you wouldn't be on hold.)

In the same way that truthiness has become central to our political discourse, there has also been a significant rise in the amount of bullshit. Lying for political advantage, of course, is as old as the hills. What has changed is that politicians used to worry about getting caught. Lying also requires some effort—you have to come up with something that, if not exactly true, at least sounds true. But there came a point when politicians discovered that if you simply kept repeating the same thing over and over again, a lot of people would come to believe it regardless of whether it was true or not. And in a democracy, what the majority believes is much more important than what is actually the case. As a result, many politicians dropped even the pretense of trying to tell the truth.

There are many examples of this new attitude on display, but one of the most striking occurred in the fall of 2012, when the Conservative government in Canada decided to accuse the opposition New Democratic Party of supporting a carbon tax. Anyone who had been paying attention knew this to be not only false, but the opposite of true. The NDP probably *should* support a carbon tax, given its left-wing, environmental sympathies. And yet one of the more controversial aspects of its platform has been its vocal opposition to carbon taxes. During the 2008 federal election, when the Liberal Party of Canada actually ran on a carbon tax platform, the NDP upset an enormous number of environmentalists by opposing it. And in British Columbia, the only jurisdiction in Canada that has actually implemented a carbon tax to date, the NDP has consistently threatened to repeal it if elected. (The federal NDP's official policy is in support of a cap-and-trade system, the same policy that the Conservatives supported and campaigned on during the previous two elections.[7])

If the Conservative accusation had simply been put forward as an argument, then of course it would have been quickly dismissed. What the Conservatives decided to do instead was to have every member of Parliament on their side use the phrase "carbon tax" (or better yet, "job-killing carbon tax") on almost every occasion that anyone rose to speak, regardless of the topic, and claim that the NDP supported it. This went on literally for weeks, to the point where one journalist described it as the "death by talking point" strategy.[8] In a breach of parliamentary tradition, not to mention decorum, they also had their backbenchers recite the same talking points during their members' statements—made during a fifteen-minute period before the beginning of Question Period, when members are entitled to rise to make a statements to the House of their choosing (traditionally used for tributes to deceased constituents or to announce events in their ridings).[9]

The Canadian print media, not being quite as supine as their American counterparts, immediately denounced the carbon tax claim as a "lie" and roundly condemned the tactic for its political cynicism. Yet this did not deter the Conservative government from following up with a nationwide radio and television advertising campaign repeating the same false claim about NDP support for carbon taxes.

The accusation was bullshit, in the technical sense of the term. Relentless bullshit, however, creates something of a dilemma for those being subjected to it. In a sense, all that the NDP could do was deny that it supported a carbon tax. But it's very difficult to do this without yourself using the phrase "carbon tax." So what the average person hears is simply "carbon tax, NDP, carbon tax, NDP, carbon tax, NDP, carbon tax . . ." And that's precisely the point. Pretty soon "low information" voters were probably saying to themselves, "The NDP, aren't those the guys who support a carbon tax?" That was, in any case, the Conservative ambition. It was a classic instance of what is now routinely called a "post-truth" political strategy.

¶

Some people like to find "balance" whenever discussing politics, to see the left and the right as mirror images of one another. When it comes to attitudes toward truth, however, there are clear differences. Democratic Party politicians in the United States may manipulate, exaggerate, and lie, but they are not unhinged from reality. When they debate policy, they still make some attempt to discuss the actual issues. The debates between Barack Obama and Hillary Clinton on the subject of health care during the Democratic primaries in 2008, for instance, provided a fairly reliable sense of what each candidate actually intended to do with that file. At no point did it degenerate into the sort of display that has become commonplace among Republicans, with each contender competing against the others to say how many government departments he would close down upon being elected—when no one could believe for an instant that any them would do any such thing.

The difference is that conservatives have become enamored of the idea that politics is ultimately not about plans and policies, it's about "gut feelings" and "values." Elections are decided by appealing to people's hearts, not their heads. So, for example, when a Republican candidate says that he is going to "close down the Department of Energy," he doesn't really mean that he is going to close down the Department of Energy and fire all of its employees. After all, the U.S. Department of Energy is responsible for maintaining the nuclear reactors in U.S. military submarines, among other things. What it really means to say that you'll close down the Department of Energy is just "I feel very strongly that the federal government hates oil companies, and I want to change that." The objective is to communicate your *feelings,* not your thoughts.

This privileging of visceral, intuitive, gut feelings is central to the movement known as "common sense" conservatism, which has become a powerful force everywhere in the Western world, not just the United States. The central characteristic of common sense, according to Republican communication strategist Frank Luntz, is that it "doesn't require any fancy theories; it is *self-evidently* correct."[10] To say that it is self-evident is to say that it is known to be correct without argument and without explanation. Thus, making common sense the core of one's political ideology amounts to a pure privileging of intuition over rational thought, of "gut feeling" over deliberation, and of heart over head. Indeed, one can see in Luntz's description the explicit downgrading of rationality. Common sense is independent not just of "theories," but of "fancy theories"—the kind proposed by effete East Coast intellectuals. The crucial thing about fancy theories is that you can feel free to ignore them, precisely because they are fancy. You don't have to worry about the actual content of what the person is saying.

The phrase "common sense" itself has of course been test-marketed, and picked because it maximizes positive resonance. Who doesn't like common sense? And yet it is also quite apt at describing the most important unifying idea in contemporary conservatism. If the plan that you're proposing needs to be explained, then it's not common sense. If it doesn't *sound* right, then it's not common sense. And if it requires some sort of data or study, then it most certainly isn't common sense.

Part of the popularity of this brand of conservatism is that it generates a set of incredibly powerful *electoral strategies.* Appealing to the gut rather than the head plays well on television, not to mention on talk radio. Indeed, the major channel through which this American style of conservativism has spread is not its intellectual expression, but the hiring of Republican *cam-*

paign strategists during the off season. (Tellingly, Conservative governments in both Canada and the United Kingdom have made significant use of Republican campaign strategists.) This is what explains the otherwise mysterious fact that conservatives—supposedly the guardians of old-fashioned values like honesty and forthrightness—have been the most aggressive at employing "post-truth" political strategies. It's because these coincide with their political ideology.

According to the "common sense" conservative view, most of the problems in the world today are caused by intellectual elites, who chronically overestimate their ability to understand and control the world. It is these so-called experts who built the public housing projects that became magnets for crime, initiated the "war on poverty" that created an epidemic of welfare dependency, introduced the trade policies that led to the evisceration of U.S. manufacturing, negotiated the treaties that undermined U.S. military supremacy, introduced the environmental regulations that destroyed the competitiveness of U.S. industry, brought in the education reforms that left American children unable to read and write, did all the hand-wringing and second-guessing that led to the loss of the Vietnam War, and promoted all kinds of feminist ideas that undermined parental authority, producing several generations of rude and disrespectful children. If these overeducated elites with their fancy college degrees had just spent a bit more time listening to their "heart," rather than their "head," and stuck to good old-fashioned traditional values, then none of this would have happened.

Perhaps the highest-profile defender of this view is *New York Times* columnist David Brooks, whose recent book *The Social Animal* is essentially an extended defense of truthiness. Brooks draws on a vast repertoire of social science and psychological research to show that what we call "rational" thought is nothing but an elaborate self-deception, that the real forces driving our decisions are unconscious instincts, dopamine levels, and pheromone trails. We are, in Brooks's view, nothing but the sum of our biases. Our best response, then, is simply to relax, go with the flow, and embrace what our "gut" is telling us. There is no truth, only truthiness, and so we should not aspire to anything greater. We certainly should not try to achieve anything too ambitious, like improving the human condition.

The difference between conservatives and liberals, in Brooks's view, is not that liberals are more rational or more committed to thinking things through. It is simply that they are more self-deceived. They think they're being rational, when in fact they're being just as emotional and intuitive as everyone else. This self-deception would be harmless except that it tempts them to hubris. They overestimate their ability to anticipate, to control, and to change the world. This leads them to engage in expensive, futile schemes to improve the human condition, which usually leave everyone worse off than they were before. The modern welfare state, according to Brooks, is essentially a consequence of this sort of social engineering: "We've reformed the education system again and again, yet more than a quarter of high-school students drop out, even though all rational incentives tell them not to. We've tried to close the gap between white and black achievement, but have failed. We've spent a generation enrolling more young people in college without understanding why so many don't graduate. One could go on."[11] What Brooks thinks we need in order to avoid these pitfalls is a frank embrace of the "deep wellsprings of human action," the intuitive, nonrational form of thinking that is the province of the unconscious.

The idea that conservatism is grounded in a deeper understanding of human nature, or at least one less tainted by self-deception, has been echoed by psychologist Jonathan Haidt, who claims that "*Republicans understand moral psychology. Democrats don't.*"[12] In *The Righteous Mind*, Haidt argues that human morality is based on six innate "social receptors,"[13] which he compares to taste buds. The central argument between liberals and conservatives, he claims, is that conservatives value all six of the basic moral intuitions, whereas liberalism is based on a lopsided emphasis on only three of them—and often only one or two. Liberals put a huge amount of emphasis on harm reduction and fairness while downplaying the concerns that animate many other moral codes, around the world and throughout history, such as purity, obedience, and loyalty. This is, he argues, a narrow and truncated conception of morality. (He compares it to a restaurant that serves only sweet food, or only salty food, with no attempt to provide any sort of variety.)

Seen from a broader perspective, there is, of course, a reason that liberals are not so keen to go with their instincts. The first half of the twentieth century was arguably the most catastrophic in the history of Western civilization, beginning with two almost unimaginably destructive wars and culminating in the development of a nuclear standoff that came rather close to destroying all of humanity. The lesson many people took away from all this is that there are certain instinctual forms of human behavior that may be harmless when deployed in small-scale societies but that become disastrous when applied at the level of modern, technologically advanced, large-scale nation states. Group loyalty begets nationalism; obedience to authority encourages totalitarianism. And purity? The suggestion that it should be restored to pride of place in our system of values seems particularly obtuse in the wake of the Holocaust.[14] What recent history has taught us is that we need to *repress* certain instincts. This is true not only of obviously antisocial tendencies, such as the way that we are tempted to enjoy cruelty, but also of pro-social instincts that give us particularistic loyalties, such as concern for our family, friends, and ethnic group.

Haidt ignores this concern because, fundamentally, he doesn't believe that there is any standpoint from which we can make the decision to repress our instincts. He agrees with Brooks that rational thought is essentially an illusion. He compares the relationship between reason and intuition—or conscious, explicit thought and the unconscious—to a rider mounted on an elephant: "The mind is divided, like a rider on an elephant, and the rider's job is to serve the elephant."[15] In his earlier research, Haidt became well known for having argued that, in moral judgment, the "emotional tail" wags the "rational dog." When people make moral judgments, they do so almost instantly, as an immediate emotional reaction. It is only afterward that they make up reasons to justify this reaction. The reasons, however, are not doing any *work*. They mainly serve as window dressing, and as a way of pressuring others to share our judgments. *Reason is actually just rationalization.*

Rather than serving as the foundation of Western civilization, in Haidt's view the "worship of reason" is "one of the most long-lived delusions in Western history." It is not just mistaken, but also politically dangerous: "The rationalist delusion is not just a claim about human nature. It's also a claim that the rational caste (philosophers or scientists) should have more power, and it usually comes along with a utopian program for raising more rational children."[16] All of this needs to be rejected, according to Haidt, so that we can get back to our roots. (Lest anyone accuse him of being a conservative, he goes on to some rather '60s-tinged talk about the power of ecstatic dancing, and its ability to put us in touch with deeper sources of the sacred.[17])

Haidt presents these arguments as an apologetic for modern American conservatism, based on the discomfort he evidently feels with the narrow-mindedness and self-satisfaction of many American liberals. Brooks presents his arguments as a defense of conservatism, although he writes in the tone of someone who is somewhat appalled by the florid irrationalism of the American right but nevertheless feels obliged to put the best face on it he can. What they share is the conviction that a politics that appeals to the heart rather than the head is not just more successful on the campaign trail, it is also more authentic, more true to human nature. Liberalism is based on delusions of grandeur, on hubris. Modern psychology, by taking us down a notch, exposing the weakness of rationality, helps to free us from this delusion.

And yet there is an obvious disconnect between this psychological theory and the way that history has unfolded over the past two thousand years. The world that we live in today is both unnatural and highly unintuitive. The three major institutional features of our society—the market, representative democracy, and human rights—were all innovations that, at the time they were adopted, struck people as being completely crazy, absolutely contrary to human nature (which is why they were rejected throughout most of human history). It is only through a long, patient process of reasoning, debate, and experimentation that they were tried and shown to be successful. Our society is the product of the Enlightenment—of the arguments and theories that came to prevail during that period. (As Pierre Manent has observed, the political history of ancient Greece and Rome "can be related without referring to 'ideas' or 'doctrine.'" The same is not true of modern societies, where the basic governing philosophy was "conceived and chosen *before* being implemented." This is why, in our political systems there is "something essentially deliberate and experimental, that implies a conscious and 'constructed' plan."[18]) We enjoy the life that we do because, over the long slow course of human history, certain *arguments* eventually came to prevail over human passions.

To propose the restoration of instinct to supremacy is to attempt to undo all of these great achievements. The question is, how to respond?

§

Adbusters magazine styles itself as "the journal of the mental environment." For nearly twenty years, it stuck largely to publishing advertising parodies, promoting its annual "Buy Nothing Day," and selling "anti-consumerist" running shoes. All that changed, however, in the summer of 2011, when the magazine produced an eye-catching poster calling for the occupation of Wall Street. The idea caught on, so that on September 17, 2011, the Occupy Wall Street movement was born. Protestors set up an encampment in Zuccotti Park in Lower Manhattan, and copycat occupations quickly sprang up across North America (many of which lasted all fall, and well into the winter).

In the media frenzy that followed, aging radicals across America dusted themselves off and stood up to declare the Occupy movement to be the second coming of the 1960s. Less starry-eyed observers could see that the movement would have incredible difficulty translating its enthusiasm into concrete political action. It's one thing to rage against the privileges enjoyed by the top 1 percent, quite another to figure out how to do anything about it. *Adbusters,* to its credit, pushed the participants to agree on "one demand" that they could put forward, but members of the various movements that had sprung up under the "Occupy" banner balked.

Many commentators suggested that the Occupy Wall Street movement might become the left-wing equivalent of the right-wing Tea Party movement. This certainly would not have hurt. In the winter of 2010, when the Dodd-Frank bill—the United States government's major legislative response to the 2008 financial crisis—was being debated in Congress, the airwaves were dominated by the Tea Party, while the financial services industry was spending $1.3 billion lobbying against the stricter provisions of the bill.[19] The left, meanwhile, sat on its hands. There was simply no organized pressure group pushing legislators to enact stricter regulation. Democratic politicians, facing no countervailing pressure from the left, predictably caved to the interests of Wall Street on numerous points.

The Tea Party movement, sparked just two years earlier by an off-the-cuff rant by CNBC commentator Rick Santelli, had at the time been incredibly successful at steering the entire agenda of political debate in America to the right.[20] In the 2010 midterm elections, it managed to get thirty-one affiliated members elected to the House of Representatives. More importantly, by staging successful primary challenges against Republican incumbents, it was able to scare a solid majority of sitting Republican legislators into catering to their demands. This was an important factor in the inflexibility that Republicans exhibited during Barack Obama's first term of office.

By contrast, the Occupy movement has seen no such success. Far from electing any legislators under the "Occupy" banner, it has not even succeeded in applying any sort of effective pressure on elected Democratic politicians. The movement has, of course, had many defenders, willing to offer the usual excuses—that the movement refused to be "co-opted" by participating in mainstream democratic politics, or that its participants were anarchists, refusing to have any truck with existing power structures. But this is obviously sour grapes. If the inability of the Occupy movement to achieve any political gains whatsoever for the left in America is not a stunning political failure, it is at the very least a huge missed opportunity. Democratic politicians would find it easier sticking to their guns if they could even *claim* to be under some pressure from the left, regardless of whether it were true.

Why this difference in outcome? Why is the right so much more effective than the left, particularly in America? How was it able to take the catastrophic failure of deregulated markets and turn it into a powerful social movement against government? It will be a central contention of this book that the problem is not just that the left missed its opportunity, or that it was inarticulate, or that its leaders were craven. Rather, there is a fundamental asymmetry between right and left that comes to the fore in times such as these. Progressive social change is inherently complicated, difficult to achieve, and requires compromise, trust, and collective action. It cannot, therefore, be achieved on the basis of "heart" alone—it also requires a huge amount of "head."

Collective action also requires institution building. Undermining collective action is, by contrast, much easier to do. Since the primary function of government in modern societies to solve the most intractable collective action problems, anti-government activists have an inherently easier time of it than pro-government activists. The Tea Party had no trouble translating the rage and frustration of its members into concrete political action. Tax resistance, for example, can be framed in a number of highly intuitive, viscerally appealing ways (e.g., "They're taking your hard-earned money!"). The case for paying taxes, on the other hand, is difficult to present in a way that gets anyone excited. This is not an accident. The logic of taxation—the reason why markets fail to provide certain goods, so that the state must do the job instead—is something you work out in your head, not something you feel in your heart.

There are many examples of this. Consider the phenomenon of road rage, a modern ailment that is no doubt an expression of the frustration that drivers feel being stuck in traffic for hours on end on hopelessly congested roadways. The solution to traffic congestion is well known: it involves a combination of mass transit and road tolls. And yet car drivers go ballistic whenever anyone suggests this, because it looks like taking money away from *us* and giving it to *them* (specifically, "freeloaders"). Explaining the logic behind it is somewhat complicated: the total number of cars on the road is not a fixed sum, and many people don't have to drive; if you give them an incentive to take mass transit it will result in less congestion for those who do choose to drive. No one has ever found a way of explaining this in an intuitively compelling way. So right-wing politicians can collect votes from angry commuters by vowing to end the "war on the car," then use this as a mandate to scale back public transit. The result is worse for everyone, including drivers, but trying to get that idea to stick has proven incredibly difficult.

Needless to say, trying to do something about the distribution of wealth and opportunity in America is also going to be extremely complicated. Occupying a park near Wall Street does nothing to diminish the power of the great investment banks. It is possible to change the way that banks operate and to punish them for their misbehavior, but this is all accomplished through *regulation*. And to demand action on that front, one must know what to demand. Figuring that out requires getting involved in a lot of boring, nitty-gritty details. Yet who among the occupiers had the patience to work out the ins and outs of capital reserve requirements or credit default swaps, or the difference between an exchange and a clearinghouse? Even something as simple as redistributing wealth from the rich to the poor quickly gets complicated, involving boring debates about the tax code (the treatment of capital gains, the alternative minimum tax, etc.).

The problem with the Occupy movement was not that it lacked good *slogans*. The difference between the Tea Party and the Occupy movement is that the Tea Party's slogans were also its policies, and so the Tea Party had an easier time motivating its followers to get involved in the political process in order to make very specific demands of their representatives. The problem with Occupy is it they never got beyond slogans—and not for want of trying. It's because the type of changes its participants wanted were *intrinsically* more complicated, more controversial, and could not so easily be derived from its slogans.

All of this lends support to the idea that progressive social change is going to require more than just a new set of policies; it will also require a change in the mental environment, so that a more reasoned discussion of policy questions has a chance of taking place. And yet that change, should it occur, is unlikely to come about through the type of interventions that *Adbusters* undertakes. Like the Occupy movement, *Adbusters* exhibits a "fight fire with fire" impulse, wanting to confront its opponents on its own terms. It figures that if advertisers use clever tricks to persuade you to buy things, it will use the *same* clever tricks to persuade you *not* to buy things. Unfortunately, there is only so far you can go with that. Hitting the streets to resist global capitalism lends itself to graphical treatment; bolstering oversight of the securities industry does not.

If the mental environment is dominated by propaganda, it is not obvious that producing counterpropaganda will improve things in any significant way, just as when someone is yelling, yelling back at him may not be a useful way to respond—it may just increase the noise level. To bring about real change in the mental environment, a more fundamental transformation may be required. We may need to change things so that the voice of *reason* can prevail, so that a more dispassionate, informed, civilized debate can take place. The only problem is, we seem to have no idea how to do this.

¶

One of the most striking things that could be observed at the Rally to Restore Sanity was a desire on the part of many to change not the *content,* but rather the *tone* of political debate in America. Many of the signs, for example, criticized the practice of comparing political opponents to Hitler ("Obama is not Hitler, Glenn Beck is not Hitler, Hitler is Hitler"). Others called for less anger ("Use your inside voice," "I'm with reasonable") or to dial down the rhetoric ("Honest, I don't mind paying my taxes," or "France seems nice enough"). Some people even complained that the protest seemed to have become a rally to restore politeness rather than a rally to restore sanity.[21]

And yet there is a connection between politeness and sanity. One of the things that has been noted about those on the American right is that they always seem to be very angry. Furthermore, anger sets an emotional tone that seems to *work* for certain kinds of political views but not for others.[22] This is particularly obvious on talk radio, where the more effective hosts spend a significant portion of their time trying to get their listeners worked up. This sort of anger is clearly not politically neutral. Anger makes people more receptive to some viewpoints than to others. Seen through the lens of common sense conservatism, it is easy to see why this is. Anger works for this particular brand of conservatism because angry people aren't thinking with their heads, they're going with their gut. This makes them more likely to trust "common sense" solutions—ideas that are familiar and intuitive—and to mistrust the fancy talk of liberal intellectuals (or any argument with more than two steps to it).

What the polite protesters understood is that people must be in the right frame of mind in order to think rationally. When people are angry, you need to get them to calm down before you can talk to them. And yet one might wonder what it is about rationality that makes it incompatible with anger. Why do strong emotions prevent us from thinking straight? These are all questions that it would be nice to have some answer to if we wanted to develop a strategy for "restoring sanity" in our culture. Unfortunately, there is no off-the-shelf concept of "reason" or "sanity" that we can pull down and put to use to answer these questions.

Indeed, it is a bit rich for the progressive left to all of a sudden want everyone to calm down and start thinking rationally. From the '60s counter-culture through '70s feminism and '80s postmodernism, the "left" seemed united in the conviction that "rationality" and "truth" were part of a plot to impose a hegemony of white, heterosexual male thought on anyone who dared to be different. Over the course of the twentieth century, the left was not a particularly faithful friend of either science or reason. It's difficult to turn around and rally for "sanity" after films like *One Flew over the Cuckoo's Nest,* which convinced an entire generation of American liberals that the whole concept of "sanity" was nothing but a plot perpetrated by "the sys-tem," designed to control those who challenged mainstream beliefs. (In a more highbrow vein, Michel Foucault became the darling of the postmod-ern intellectual left by claiming that "reason" was able to assert its suprem-acy only through the invention of the asylum, where all those who refused to bow down before its dictates could be locked away out of sight.[23])

Indeed, the current mood within the liberal academy remains one of intense antirationalism, motivated not only by political ideology, but also by the last several decades of research in psychology, which have shown that we are all, in general, much less rational that we take ourselves to be. Literally dozens of major books have been published in the past decade, echoing the same theme: that we are fundamentally not rational animals.[24]

Part of the motivation for this wholesale assault on reason has been that economists, throughout the twentieth century, maintained a dogmatic adherence to a peculiarly narrow concept of rationality, one that denied any status to moral principles or rules.[25] Because their most important mathematical models depended on this conception of reason, they were extremely reluctant to acknowledge any evidence that contradicted it. So they often went to great lengths to deny the fact of human irrationality. (This tendency reached its most absurd heights in the work of Chicago economists Gary Becker and Kevin Murphy, who argued that addiction was part of a perfectly rational, consistent consumption plan.[26]) Many noneconomists found this incredibly frustrating, and so went a bit over-board in their efforts to show how implausible the economic conception of rationality was. (Many also found the model to be morally repulsive, which made the debates a lot more heated than they otherwise would have been.)

It is important, however, to recognize that the economists' conception of rationality was never widely accepted in the social sciences. Furthermore, because these debates generated a certain amount of overstatement, many people were left with the impression that "reason" is not a valid psychological construct. It is often suggested that "science" has somehow proven that there is no such thing as reason, or if there is, that it plays little or no role in guiding our judgments or behavior. And this in turn has been taken as vindication of the current state of politics, with its flagrant irrationalism. Our degraded public discourse and demagogic politics are portrayed as simply an expression of the human condition, not the result of choices we have made. Those who complain are simply victims of rationalist self-deception.[27]

"Science" has, in fact, proven no such thing. What psychologists have shown is that we have two rival control systems—reason and intuition—which frequently conflict in vying for control of our judgment and behavior. The extent to which one or the other prevails is determined by characteristics of the individual and of the environment that she finds herself in. It is true that the old Enlightenment view of reason—as a divine spark, the purest part of the soul, able to govern and lead us to a life of perfect freedom and autonomy—has been permanently discredited. Reason is a lot more fragile than we thought, a lot less capable, and a lot more dependent upon its social and cultural environment. This environment, however, is one that we have created. This means that if our political views are irrational and our elections are decided by naked emotional appeals, then that is a *consequence* of decisions we have made. It is the world that we have built, and that we must take responsibility for. It is also a world that we might seek to change.

¶

Suppose we were to take seriously the idea of restoring sanity, creating a return to reason in politics. Suppose we wanted to advance the Enlightenment agenda of freeing humanity—not just the educated elite, but the *mass* of humanity—from ignorance and superstition. Suppose we wanted to restore order, so that the "rational dog" could wag the "emotional tail" once again. How would we go about doing that? The first Enlightenment project appears to have stalled. How can it be restarted?

This book outlines a program for a second Enlightenment, or Enlightenment 2.0. The "2.0" is a reference to Web 2.0, a term that was coined in 2003 to describe a number of important changes in the development of the internet. I use the expression here not because it is trendy and high-tech—by now Web 2.0 is old hat; people have moved on to 3, 4, and 5.0. I use the expression because the shift in thinking that I would like to recommend in how we think about rationality resembles in several important respects the shift in thinking that marked the transition to Web 2.0.

In the early days of the internet, people treated it like a giant library. In order to access the content, the assumption was, some central authority would need to survey it all and organize it. This was the approach that early firms like Yahoo! took. The approach taken by Google, on the other hand, represented a fundamental shift. Rather than trying to organize all the content into a single system, Google looked at how users of the internet themselves were organizing it. Its now-famous "pagerank" algorithm, which remains at the heart of the Google search engine, gave websites a score based on how often they were linked to by other web pages. It then used this information to determine what content was more or less interesting and relevant to search users. This marked a shift away from central authority toward a decentralized, social model of content organization.

The central flaw in the concept of reason that animated the eighteenth-century Enlightenment is that it is entirely individualistic. Reason was thought to be contained entirely within the brain of the individual.

The result was a lack of attention to what was going on in the individual's environment, both physical and social. The development of a new Enlightenment requires the recognition that reason is both decentralized and dispersed across multiple individuals. It is not possible to be rational all by yourself; rationality is inherently a collective project. This is precisely why we need a *politics* of rationality.

The first part of this book sketches out this new approach to the understanding of reason—as it has emerged from the work of philosophers, psychologists, sociologists, and linguists over the course of the past century. It acknowledges the limitations of reason and the power of intuition, but it also explains clearly why reason is indispensable. Reason may not be all that powerful, but it is the only tool that has allowed us to escape from tens of thousands of years of hand-to-mouth existence in small-scale tribal societies. Civilization—by which I mean complex, organized societies based on extensive systems of mutually beneficial cooperation among genetically unrelated individuals—is not something that comes naturally to people, and it is not something that we would ever arrive at by following our instincts. It is a highly artificial construct, based on a *rational* insight into the way that the human condition can be improved.

The second and third parts of the book use this new understanding of rationality to explain how the current environment of irrationalism came about and what can be done to change it. Once we recognize that reason is both social and environmental, this knowledge can help us to understand why the first Enlightenment project failed, and also why our current social and media environment is making it so difficult for the voice of reason to be heard, in either our personal lives or the public sphere. It can also give us a new set of strategies for change.

Consider again Haidt's image of reason being like a rider perched on the back of elephant. In his view, the rider can't do very much to actually control the elephant, so if he feels the beast beneath him starting to go one way, he is better off just holding on tight and leaning in the same direction. There is a lot to be said for the essential metaphor—reason is not that powerful when it comes to our ability to straightforwardly overpower intuition. But a crucial piece of the picture is missing in Haidt's scenario. Imagine that the rider also has the ability to hop off and rearrange things on the ground, in order to redesign the environment the elephant is moving through. This opens up a whole new world of possibilities. Now if you want the elephant to go left, rather than ineffectually kicking him and yelling at him to go in that direction, you can just hop off and put something that he's afraid of on the right (perhaps a mouse?). Once you get back on, you are controlling the elephant—it's just that you are no longer doing so directly. Your control of the elephant may be environmentally mediated, but it is still control, and ultimately that is what counts.

Once we begin to examine the structure of human reason, it becomes obvious that we rely on these sorts of environmental manipulations all the time. Most of us would be unable to get anything done without them. By using them more carefully, we can enhance our decision making as consumers, as voters, as citizens, and as private individuals. But in order to get there, we need to invest a *lot* more energy in thinking about how to make our social environment work for us, rather than against us.

It is also important to recognize that there are no simple villains in this case. It does no good to blame "the media" or "advertising" or "greedy corporations" for contaminating the mental environment. What we are facing instead is a long-term process of cultural change, in which innovations that exploit people's cognitive biases have a better chance of surviving and being reproduced than those that do not. As a result, we wind up with an environment that over time forces us to expend more and more effort in order to think and act rationally. Fixing this is not going to be easy. So far, however, we have been handicapped by an inability to even understand the problem correctly. Developing a better understanding of reason is the first step in learning how to develop effective collective strategies for restoring it.

Part I

The Old Mind and the New

*Modern psychology has shown that reason is far
less powerful than it was once thought to be. To the
extent that it functions at all, it does so because we
have discovered work-arounds for the flaws in the hardware
that has been provided to us by evolution. This is
the correct observation at the heart of the conservative
critique of rationalism. And yet modern psychology
has also shown that certain problems can be solved
only by reason. While reason may not be perfect,
we have no choice but to work with what we have.
Civilization depends on it.*

1. The calm passion

Reason: its nature, origin, and causes

Anyone who has ever taken an aptitude test with an "analytical" section will undoubtedly have encountered little word puzzles such as the following:

> *The Marriage Problem:*
> Bill is looking at Nancy, while Nancy is looking at Greg.
> Bill is married. Greg is unmarried.
> Is a married person looking at an unmarried person?
> Answer: A) yes, B) no, C) cannot be determined.[1]

If you are like most people, you will get this question wrong the first time you try to answer it. The obvious answer is C, "cannot be determined." This is what our intuitive, rapid problem-solving system tells us. How do we arrive at that conclusion? Through a style of pattern matching. We are looking for a married person looking at an unmarried person. So we take the first couple: Bill is looking at Nancy. Bill is married, but we have no idea whether Nancy is married or not, so there is no match. Now we take Nancy looking at Greg. Greg is unmarried, but again, we have no idea about Nancy, so there is no match. Bill looking at Greg *would* be a match, but Bill isn't looking at Greg, so we get no matches. Response: We can't say.

27

In order to answer the question, we would need to know Nancy's marital status.

This is how we tackle the problem when we are being less than fully rational.[2] There's a problem, though. Indeed, just walking through the steps, the way I did in the paragraph above, explicitly articulating how the pattern-matching approach works, will make the problem stand out for many people. (Hint: Do we *really* need to know whether Nancy is married?)

Now consider what a solution to this problem looks like when you use the rational part of your brain. We know that Bill is married and that Greg is not. We do not know whether Nancy is married. Yet there are only two possible states she can be in. The first is that she is married, the second that she is unmarried. Now, suppose that Nancy is married. Is a married person looking at an unmarried person? Yes, Nancy is looking at Greg. Now suppose that Nancy is unmarried. Is a married person looking at an unmarried person? Yes, Bill is looking at Nancy. So it doesn't matter whether Nancy is married or not. Under either state, a married person is looking at an unmarried person. The correct answer to the question is A ("yes"). This is actually quite obvious, from a rational point of view. But it is also unintuitive, which is why people tend to get it wrong on first pass.

§

The term *reason* traditionally refers to a particular mental faculty, one that is associated with a distinctive *style* of thinking. David Hume famously described reason as a "calm passion,"[3] and a degree of detachment and distance from immediate circumstances is a hallmark of the rational style. But perhaps the more significant feature of rational thought is that it can be made fully *explicit*. To the extent that we are reasoning, we are fully aware of what we are doing and we are able to explain fully what we have done— hence the connection between the faculty of reason and the practice of *giving reasons*, or argumentation and justification. For any particular claim, we must be able to explain what *entitles* us to make it and we must be willing to acknowledge what it *commits* us to.[4]

This provides the basis for the traditional contrast between reason and intuition. An intuitive judgment is one that you make without being able to explain why you made it. Rational judgments, on the other hand, can always be explained. This doesn't make intuitive judgments wrong or defective; it just means that they are produced by a different sort of cognitive process. Malcolm Gladwell helped to popularize this distinction in his book *Blink*, using a number of very striking examples. One involved a forged statue and a group of art historians, many of whom were convinced that the piece was inauthentic but who were hard-pressed to explain why. Something about the statue just felt wrong. According to one of these experts, the first word that came to mind when he saw the (supposedly ancient) statue was "fresh." Another said that the statue "felt cold," as though he were seeing it through a pane of glass.[5]

These judgments were clearly the product of *cognition*—in fact, they were the product of very sophisticated expert judgment, a system of discernment built up over the course of decades of experience. But they were not rational judgments. Why? Because the experts themselves had no access to the basis of these judgments. They could not explain what exactly it was about the statue that triggered the reaction.

We make this sort of judgment all the time. Look at a photo of a young child, maybe five years old. Is it a boy or a girl? In most cases you can easily tell. Yet how do you form that judgment? What exactly is it about a boy's face that makes him look like a boy, not a girl? Most of us would be hard-pressed to say. Judgments of age are similar. How do you tell the difference between an eighteen-year-old and a twenty-five-year-old? The judgment is intuitive, not rational. We can go back afterward and try to figure out how we made the decision, but the basis of that decision is not available to consciousness as we are making it. What intuitive judgments provide us with are simply the *outputs* of a set of cognitive procedures.

Rational judgments, on the other hand, are based on reasons—considerations that the American sociologist Harold Garfinkel described as "detectable, countable, reportable, tell-a-story-about-able, analyzable—in short accountable."[6] With a rational decision, we have conscious access to the inputs and the decision procedure, as well as to the output. If the experts assessing the statue had been able to point to an aspect of the technique, the material, or the style and show that it was anachronistic, this would have provided a basis for rational judgment. Like Sherlock Holmes solving a crime, they would have been able to explain precisely how their process of deduction had unfolded. But they weren't. They just *knew*, without being able to say *how* they knew.

Rational thinking is slow and onerous, which is typically why we try to avoid doing it. The "marriage problem," however, shows us why it is nevertheless indispensable. One might be tempted to think that that first time we tried to solve the problem we simply made a mistake but that the second time, when we looked at it more carefully, we got it right. This idea—that the mistake is attributable to what psychologists call *performance error*[7]—is highly misleading. Our brain, according to this view, is like a cigarette lighter that sparks but sometimes fails to produce a flame, so we shake it a bit and try again. In fact, our brain is more like a bureaucracy or a customer service center, which strives to solve every problem at the lowest possible level. It is only after we have tried and failed to solve a problem using frontline resources that we decide to kick it up to a higher level, and maybe get management involved in the decision making.

In other words, the first time we look at the problem, we typically use a limited set of cognitive resources to produce an answer. Specifically, we try to solve it using a fast, intuitive pattern-matching approach. It is only after finding out that the answer is wrong that we go back and bring additional resources to bear upon it (the mental equivalent of calling a manager). This is when reason becomes engaged. When we decide to concentrate more carefully on the problem, our motive for doing so is not to eliminate a source of error, but rather to facilitate the operation of this new set of cognitive resources. We are, in effect, kicking it up from an intuitive to a rational level. The need to concentrate is just a sign that we are bringing these new resources online. The reason we are forced to do so is that some problems cannot be solved simply by using an intuitive thinking style.

The thought process that leads to the correct solution to the marriage problem has five characteristics that are widely recognized as the hallmarks of rational thinking:

1. Working out the solution requires *explicit linguistic articulation*. Many people will look at the problem and very quickly come to the intuitive, incorrect conclusion, without any explicit awareness of how they got there. It just seems to them that the answer must be indeterminate. When told that the correct answer is actually "yes," they may stare at the problem blankly for a while. It is only by explicitly talking their way through it— either to themselves or out loud—that they are able to see the rationale for that answer. It is only the very odd person who is able to come to the correct conclusion without any explicit awareness of how he or she got there. (Consider another problem: "Everyone is prejudiced against prejudiced people. Nancy is prejudiced against Bill. Is Greg prejudiced against Bill?"[8] The correct answer is "yes," but very few people can see why without talking their way through the problem, step by step.)

2. It requires *decontextualization*. The mistaken response to the marriage problem starts with the tendency to think about it too concretely. We imagine that in order to solve the problem, we need to know some fact about the world: namely, whether Nancy is married or not. We fail to realize that there is a more abstract fact that, alone, is sufficient to resolve the problem: namely, that Nancy is either married or unmarried. Seeing this more abstract fact and its relevance requires an insight into the logical structure of the problem, which in turn requires abstraction from the specific

information that we have been given about Bill, Nancy, and Greg. This is a major difference between intuitive and rational thinking. Intuitive thinking relies upon contextual information to solve problems—often supplementing existing knowledge of the problem with additional information that might seem relevant. Rational thinking moves in exactly the opposite direction, stripping the problem of contextual details in order to get at elements of structure.[9]

3. It makes use of *working memory*. The chain of reasoning that leads to the correct solution requires us to hold an intermediate conclusion in what psychologists call working memory.[10] To see what this is, consider how you go about solving a long multiplication problem in your head. For simplicity, consider 8 times 23. Most people don't have the answer to this memorized, and so need to work it out. The standard procedure for doing this is to break it down into two smaller problems. First, multiply 8 by 3 to get 24. Then multiply 8 by 20 to get 160. All you have to do now is add up 160 and . . . what? At this point you have to pull the 24 back out of memory to get the answer of 184. That place where you put the 24, while you were working out the second part of the problem, is your working memory. It's called that because, first, you are using it as part of an ongoing computation and, second, you will dump it some time shortly after you're finished. That may seem simple enough, but there is a very widespread consensus among cognitive scientists that rational thought processes depend crucially on this working memory system.[11] The pattern-matching system fails to solve the marriage problem because it moves through, making pair-wise comparisons, looking for a "hit" on the pattern it is scanning for. Failing to find one, it concludes that the problem is unsolvable. The rational solution requires first considering what follows from the assumption that Nancy is married, storing that in working memory, then considering what follows from the assumption that she is unmarried, retrieving the first result from working memory, and integrating the two. (The "prejudice" problem

is similar. In order to get the correct answer, you need to first figure out the crucial intermediate conclusion, that Bill is prejudiced against Nancy, then use that as a basis for further reasoning.)

4. It is capable of *hypothetical* reasoning. The intuitive problem-solving system likes to work with facts; it is no good at handling suppositions. The marriage problem forces us to construct a hypothetical scenario ("Suppose Nancy is married") then figure out what follows from it. Furthermore, we know that the supposition underlying at least one of the two scenarios is false (Nancy is either married or she is not, but she cannot be both). Thus one of the two scenarios is not just hypothetical, but counterfactual. Only reason can deal with these sorts of constructs.[12] Intuition is useful when it comes to thinking about and responding to the real world, but whenever we need to think about some possible world (including the negation of the real world), we need to use the rational part of our brain. This means that we need to use reason in order to engage in contingency planning ("What if Plan A doesn't work?"), strategic thinking ("If I do this, then she may do that"), modal reasoning ("That's not necessarily true"), and, most importantly, so-called deontic moral reasoning ("He ought to pay her back").

5. It is *hard* and *slow*. Thinking rationally is difficult, which is why most of us try to avoid doing it until absolutely forced. As we shall see later on, there is a good reason for this—you are basically making your brain do something that it was never designed to do. Much of this difficulty is a consequence of the fact that rational processing is slow, relatively speaking, and cognitively demanding, primarily in terms of attention. Maintaining this sort of attention involves inhibiting or controlling all sorts of other thought processes, which in turn involves significant self-control. This is why it is so hard to think clearly when you're in a rush, or when there is a lot of distracting noise or competing stimuli. (One sure way to irritate other people when they are trying to count is to stand beside them and shout out

random numbers. They are bound to lose their place. Yet our own brains are constantly doing the same thing to us: "I'm hungry," "Look at that bird!" "I'm itchy," "It's been a while since you checked your email," etc.)

¶

The picture that emerges from this is of a mind that is capable of two very different styles of thinking. At one extreme, we have fully reflective, rational thought. This style of cognition is linear, conscious, and explicit, requires attention, and has access to working memory. On the other extreme, we have completely automatic, "modular" systems, which are fast, unconscious, and implicit and can run in parallel (since they require no attention and do not make use of working memory, several tasks can be performed at the same time).

The classic example of mental modularity is our capacity for facial recognition. You see a person, you instantly recognize him as familiar (even if you can't quite put your finger on who he is or where you met him). The cognition is triggered automatically by the visual stimulus (at no point do you get to decide whether to run your facial-recognition program on people—you can't stop it even if you want to). You might be hard-pressed to say exactly what it is about him that is familiar, or how you recognized him. Furthermore—as we know from trying to program computers to do facial recognition—an astonishing amount of extremely complicated visual processing must be going on. Not only are faces very complex, but they are seen from different perspectives and angles, not to mention that they change over time (for instance, people's noses and ears get longer as they age). Yet people are able to recognize each other in all sorts of different circumstances and after years of separation. Thus the processing must be happening very quickly, much faster than anything we can reproduce in consciousness.

The facial-recognition program is also domain specific, which means that it is by and large good for only one thing. For example, while we are very good at recognizing individual faces, we are very bad at recognizing individual trees. A person who spends a lot of time in the woods and worries about getting lost might want to become better at recognizing trees (say, by remembering slight differences in the patterns on their bark). Unfortunately, whatever portion of our brain we use to recognize faces can't be redeployed to this task (the best we can do is to try to find "faces" in the bark). The domain of this competence is innately specified. This is what leads many cognitive scientists to describe these sorts of intuitive processing systems as part of the "hardware" of the brain.

One other feature of our facial-recognition program is that, because it is triggered and runs automatically, it doesn't require any attention on our part. It also doesn't seem to make use of any shared or central resources: there is nothing to stop this program from running at the same time that you are doing other things. When someone you know walks into the room, you recognize that person immediately, regardless of what else you happen to be doing at the moment. It's not as though you have to wait until you're finished before turning your attention to the task of deciding whether you know this person. Thus many psychologists have argued that these cognitive competencies are modular, in that they are self-contained and self-sufficient and in that they can run *parallel*, which is to say, at the same time without interfering with one another. Supporting this contention is the fact that some people suffer from a condition called *prosopagnosia*, which is a specific impairment in their ability to recognize faces. What is striking about this condition is that pretty much all of these people's other visual and cognitive competencies are unaffected. This lends support to the description of facial recognition as a module that can be added to or subtracted from the brain without really affecting other systems.

The style of cognition associated with rational thought is quite different. Not only is it slow, domain general, explicit, and demanding in terms of attention, but it has a completely different *structure* from what is going on at the level of intuition. Reason is what computer types call a *serial processing system.*[13] Unlike a parallel system, which can do many things at the same time, a serial system can do only one thing at a time. This produces an obvious weakness: it gets bottlenecked at the central processor, and so can run very slowly. The advantage, however, is that it can chain together a coherent sequence of operations in a sustained fashion, in order to produce what we refer to (revealingly) as a "train of thought." Indeed, the kind of argument analysis involved in solving the marriage or the prejudice problem, which involves generating intermediate conclusions then using these as the basis for further inferences, is a perfect demonstration of how serial processing works. The central weakness of parallel processing is that it lacks this sort of focus and coherence. It's like dividing up a writing assignment between ten people, having each person do one section independently, then pasting it all together. The job may get done faster, but it's unlikely to hang together as a coherent piece of writing. If the task happens to divide naturally into ten different topics, then the approach may work. But if the goal is to produce an argument, where what gets claimed in one section depends upon what is decided in some previous section, then the job simply can't be broken down in this way, with the different sections being written simultaneously. They need to be written in order, preferably by one person, even though this arrangement will make things go a lot slower.

The fact that serial processing gets bottlenecked is actually one of the features that psychologists can use to distinguish rational from nonrational processing in the brain. One technique they use is called *cognitive loading.* Investigators start by giving a person a mental task to complete that involves the use of working memory (say, memorizing a list of five words). They then interrupt that person and give her a second mental task (say, doing some arithmetic or tracking the movement of an object). When that task is finished, the person is instructed to return to the first. Investigators look to see if the interruption has caused any degradation of performance (how many of the five words can the person still remember?). Since working memory space is extremely limited, asking the person to do something that involves reasoning (such as mental arithmetic) will typically result in weak performance. Asking the person to do something that can be handled intuitively, on the other hand (such as visual tracking), has no impact on performance. The processing occurs "parallel" to the rational task that is being performed.[14]

The view that we have two rather different cognitive styles is referred to as *dual process theory*, although that suggests a somewhat oversimplified picture of how the mind works.[15] Many of the things that we learn explicitly can, through practice and repetition, become "second nature" to us, and so no longer require any attention (think of positioning one's fingers on the frets of a guitar, or shoulder-checking before changing lanes while driving). And many of the heuristics that we use when engaged in intuitive cognition can be introduced into the rational sphere, in order to provide us with shortcuts that we can take in our reasoning.[16] (This is arguably what is going on when we produce the incorrect solution to the marriage problem.) Thus a lot of performances are hybrids, in which we are making use of the two different styles of cognition simultaneously and to varying degrees.

For our purposes, it doesn't really matter whether we want to call these different processing systems. What is important is the general characterization of reason that dual-process theory suggests—that reason is serial, language dependent, explicit, and that it has access to working memory. Because of this, the *style* of cognition that it supports is quite different from what goes on elsewhere in the brain.

¶

Sigmund Freud left an indelible mark on psychology by arguing that unconscious, intuitive cognition played a much more important role in everyday life than Enlightenment rationalists had believed. But he made the mistake of characterizing the unconscious as being too much like a human agent. He used "us"—our conscious, rational selves, the part that is available to introspection—as a model for thinking about "it." Thus he treated the unconscious mind as having complex desires and relatively unified drives. It is no accident that as Freud's theories slowly drifted into popular psychology, the unconscious id came to be described as an "inner child." Modern cognitive scientists, on the other hand, are more inclined to describe the unconscious as an "inner Martian."[17] Why? Because the style of thinking that goes on there is *extremely* foreign to us. As the philosopher Daniel Dennett has observed, we actually find it easier to understand how computers work than we do our own brains.[18] This is because computers were designed, from the ground up, to be serial processing machines. The operations of a parallel processing system, on the other hand, are not something that we have introspective access to. We therefore find them confusing to think about.

The extent to which we misunderstand our own thinking was powerfully impressed upon cognitive scientists by early attempts to produce artificial intelligence systems. Computers are extremely good at doing things that people find very hard, like adding up numbers, solving equations, performing tasks in sequence, and remembering things. By the late 1960s, even the most primitive calculators were able to put seasoned engineers to shame. How long could it be, people figured, before computers start doing *all* of the things that we do, and doing it all much better? The famous HAL 9000 computer, from the movie *2001: A Space Odyssey*, was supposed to have been built in 1992. And yet here we are, over two decades later, still using *keyboards* to communicate with our computers, because computers can't even transcribe spoken language properly, much less understand it. What went wrong? On the technology side, nothing. It just turned out that much of the stuff we find really easy to do—like recognizing faces, or even objects; learning a language and talking to others; figuring out when someone is joking, or bluffing, or making a mistake; walking without falling over—are actually incredibly hard to do. The only reason we think they're easy is that our brains take care of these tasks for us, and don't really keep us posted on what they're doing or how they're doing it. (Protein synthesis is also very complicated; luckily, our cells take care of it for us, without requiring any sort of active intervention on our part.) It's only when we try to reproduce explicitly what our brains are doing implicitly that we realize how little we understand about our own cognitive systems.

The history of chess-playing computer programs provides a marvelous illustration of this. Every so often there will be a new "man versus machine" match, typically presented as though the honor of humanity were at stake and the "rise of the machines" near. What is astonishing, however, is not that the computer sometimes wins, but that any human being is able to beat even a mobile phone at chess.[19] Why? Because even though we find chess to be extremely hard—which is why an aura of genius surrounds "grandmaster" players—mathematically it is a very simple game. It actually belongs to the same family of games as tic-tac-toe, because it is finitely solvable.[20] This means that there is a single correct way to play it—a "solution," if you will. The only reason the game is interesting to play is that the solution is too large or complex for anyone to work out (much the way tic-tac-toe is for four-year-olds). It is only when the match moves into the endgame that a portion of the solution becomes apparent. So playing chess requires a lot of hypothetical thinking, of the form "if I do this, then he will do that, then I can do this, which will stop him from doing that," and so on. This is exactly the sort of reasoning that humans find very hard and computers find very easy. As a result, it was not long before chess-playing computers were developed that could analyze millions of branches of the decision tree in order to pick out an optimal move. And yet humans were still beating them!

This led scientists to study more carefully the thinking habits of human chess players, in order to figure out how they were doing this. What they found, to their surprise, was that grandmaster chess players actually investigate a surprisingly small number of branches of the decision tree.[21] The reason they tend to win is that this process of in-depth investigation is preceded by a heuristic pruning of the decision tree, guided by an intuitive sense of what seem to be the most promising moves or of what sort of position they want on the board. Significantly, no one is able to articulate how this initial pruning is done. It is all based on "feel." It is driven, in other words, by intuition (probably pattern recognition, built up through decades of practice and exposure to games). Thus human chess-playing is a hybrid performance, involving both intuitive and rational thought. To this day, no one has ever succeeded in reproducing the intuitive style of thinking in a computer, simply because we don't know how it is done (despite the fact that we ourselves do it). Instead, chess-playing computers continue to rely upon brute-force rational methods—trying to search more and more of the solution tree. Deep Blue, for instance, which attracted considerable attention when it first beat Garry Kasparov, was able to examine 200 million positions per second and had access to an enormous database of positions and past games. The current champion, Hydra (described by some as "the chess monster"), is a hybrid software-hardware parallel system running on a huge cluster of workstations in Abu Dhabi. The fact that this much computing power can be deployed without yet achieving the "final, generally accepted, victory over the human"[22] is a monument to the power and sophistication of nonrational thought processes in the human mind.

❡

Whenever one sees a practiced expert in action, whether it be a grandmaster playing chess, a doctor sizing up a patient's symptoms, or a basketball player setting up a play, one is witnessing the seamless integration of intuitive and rational styles of thought.[23] Unfortunately, this is very far from the norm. What we encounter more often is a conflict between the two styles of cognition. Indeed, it is precisely because they conflict so often that we are inclined to talk about different *systems* of thought, rather than just two components of a single system. Call it head versus heart, brain versus gut, or reason versus emotion, we are all familiar with the experience of being "of two minds."

Here is how one contemporary cognitive scientist, Jonathan Evans, describes the phenomenon:

> I define "mind" as a high-level cognitive system capable of representing the external world and acting upon it in order to serve the goals of the organism. The two minds hypothesis is that the human brain contains not one but two parallel systems for doing this. Animals, according to this view, have but one system corresponding to the "old mind" in human beings. Humans have a second "new" mind, which coexists in uneasy coalition with the first, sometimes coming into direct conflict with it.[24]

This "two minds" phenomenon is actually quite puzzling and, over the years, was responsible for a lot of speculation. It probably explains why most religions posit two distinct realms, the physical and the spiritual. Human beings are typically regarded as the point of intersection of these two realms, so that despite having physical bodies and desires (like animals), we are also thought to have immaterial souls (like angels or spirits) that can survive the destruction of the body. This is then appealed to as an explanation for the qualitative difference between us and other animals. The immortal soul corresponds to the "new mind," the higher cognitive faculty that no other animals have.

There are plenty of things wrong with this view, but there is one point on which is it right. There is something genuinely puzzling about the "rational part of our soul," or the "new mind," precisely because of the discontinuity one sees between human and animal cognitive competencies. To see this, consider what happens when one takes the standard approach and substitutes "evolution through natural selection" for "God" in the explanation of how we came to be rational. The "old mind" has the fingerprints of evolution all over it. Indeed, it has *exactly* the sort of structure that one would expect to see in a cognitive system that was the product of piecemeal natural selection. The "new mind," however, is in many ways the opposite. Explaining it in evolutionary terms, therefore, creates something of a puzzle.

The fundamental thing one needs to understand about evolution is that it is a tinkerer, not a designer. It works through a process of small, incremental steps. It's governed by the same principle as the children's game hot-warm-cold, in which you hide an object then try to guide a blindfolded child to it by calling out "You're getting warmer" when she moves closer to it and "You're getting colder" when she moves away. If you just blindfolded her and tossed her in the room, she would never guess where the object is. But if you provide her with feedback after every step, she can quickly find her way—even though each time she moves, she is still just guessing where to go.[25]

Evolution is the same. Coming up with a four-chambered heart is highly improbable, just like finding an object while blindfolded. But through a series of small steps, each of which constitutes an improvement over the last, one can construct amazing things. Starting with a two-chambered heart (fish), one can add a third chamber (amphibians), a third with partial separation (reptiles), and finally arrive at a full four chambers (birds and mammals). Each step represents an improvement over the previous step ("You're getting warmer!"), so evolution is able to produce a very complex structure that would never have been hit upon out of the blue. Of course, even then it takes an almost unimaginably long time for these processes to take place (with the heart, over 500 million years).

Because of this, evolution has something of a signature style when it comes to the design of organisms. First, it is *extremely* conservative. It doesn't do radical makeovers or system overhauls. It never goes back to the drawing board. Once it hits on something that works, even if it doesn't work that well, it sticks with it. This is why, although there seems to be extraordinary variety in the forms of life on earth, when you look more carefully, you can see an astonishing *lack* of variety. Go to a good natural history museum and you can see skeletons of 50-million-year-old mammals that have almost the same body plan as you have. You don't even need to know any anatomy—you can just look at each bone in the skeleton then feel for the corresponding bone in your own body. The same is true at a cellular level. The fundamental mechanism that your body uses to store energy, for instance, is shared with not only the rest of the animal kingdom, but with plants as well. Once nature hits on a good trick, it is extremely reluctant to throw it away.

Because of this conservatism, nature is full of designs that are incredibly inefficient. To see why, imagine trying to guide a child through a *maze* using the standard hot-warm-cold rules—so that you call out "You're getting warmer" whenever the child moves physically closer to the exit. The chances of succeeding are practically zero. Why? Because the child is almost certain to wander into a dead end. Once she gets there, she will get stuck, since the only moves available to her will be ones that make her "colder." Indeed, one can imagine a situation where the only way to get out of a dead end would be to take a complex set of backward steps, each of which takes the child *farther* from the exit. Nature has exactly the same problem. One can easily wind up with arrangements that are only satisfactory, and yet possible improvements cannot be reached, because getting there would first require a series of backward steps.

The mammalian body plan provides a wealth of examples. Obviously, it is "good enough" for most purposes—the fact that it has remained almost unchanged since the Eocene suggests that it is actually quite successful. And yet for *us* it has some huge problems. Most of these are related to the fact that it is not a good design for bipedal locomotion. In particular, the backbone is not well designed for weight bearing. If you want to support something heavy, it makes sense to have it rest on big, thick, solid long bones—such as one can find in our *legs.* The way our limbs and back are organized makes sense for a four-legged creature, but no sense at all for a two-legged creature. (Having a single post supporting one's upper torso is crazy, the biological equivalent of transporting something on a unicycle instead of in a wagon.) Similarly, for an upright stance, it would be much better for our knees to bend backward (the way our ankles do). Unfortunately, we're very unlikely to develop an extra backbone or reverse the direction of our knees. Developmentally, making these changes would require big alterations, and getting there would require several backward steps. Thus we are stuck with the generic mammalian body plan, which specifies one backbone and knees with the hinges on the front. The best we can do is try to avoid knee injuries and learn to live with back pain.

The conservatism one sees on display in our bodies is present in our brains as well. (Actually, if you think your body is badly designed, wait until you see what the brain is like!) Take, for example, the hiccup. It is an involuntary action consisting of sharp inhalation "followed by a closure of the glottis."[26] It is caused by a distinctive pattern of electrical stimulation originating in the lower brain stem. It is also completely useless. At least *in humans* it is useless. What is striking, however, is that almost the exact same breathing pattern can be observed in amphibians, and in them it does serve a useful purpose. For tadpoles, this motion is what allows them to switch between lung and gill breathing. Interestingly, several of the tricks that we use to stop hiccups (such as breathing into a paper bag, or taking a deep breath and holding it) have also been shown to inhibit gill breathing in tadpoles (exposure to carbon dioxide, or stretching of the chest wall). Crazy as it may sound, this suggests that when you hiccup, what's really going on is that an (evolutionarily) old part of your brain is trying to switch you over from lung to gill breathing. The physical machinery needed to carry out this instruction disappeared hundreds of millions of years ago, but there was no need to get rid of the electrical control system. And so there it remains, going off every so often, a glorious artifact of our evolutionary prehistory.

Hearing about the hiccup, one naturally wonders how much other leftover junk there is cluttering our minds. The answer is "a lot." The basic approach that evolution seems to have taken, when it comes to the structure of the brain, is that rather than getting rid of old stuff, it has simply layered the new stuff over top of it, then given the newer control systems some capacity to override the older ones when needed. As William Hirstein puts it, "It is a truism of neurobiology that throughout our evolution the brain grew outward from the brainstem by adding and enlarging structures to what already existed, rather than replacing or eliminating existing structures."[27] This is why we have a huge number of partially redundant systems in the brain, even for relatively straightforward operations like processing visual input. It also explains why people really do "regress" when they become disinhibited (through alcohol consumption or brain damage) and the "lower" functions acquire more control over behavior.[28]

Thus the brain has all the signs of having been put together piecemeal, over a very long period of time. One can see evidence of this in a number of different areas of cognitive function, such as memory. Unlike a computer, which has a single, well-organized memory system, all fully indexed and classified, we have at *least* three different memory systems, localized (sort of) in different parts of the brain. We know this because some people suffer from selective memory impairment—they lose all long-term memory but retain their short-term memory, or they lose all knowledge of facts but can still remember all of the skills they have acquired.

When it comes to problem-solving competencies, our intuitive judgment system seems to have the same piecemeal quality. At one level, our mind seems to be nothing but a grab bag of tricks, put together to solve very specific problems—such as how to tell people apart, in order to separate those you know from those who are strangers. Furthermore, many of our fast, intuitive problem-solving capacities have the same rough-and-ready quality that one sees throughout the natural world. They offer solutions that are good enough for all practical purposes. The reason for this is not hard to find. When it comes to any problem-solving competence, there is always going to be a trade-off between speed and accuracy. Furthermore, each will be subject to diminishing returns. The first 10 percent gain in accuracy can be achieved with minimal loss of speed; the next 10 percent gain, however, requires a slightly greater loss, the next an even greater loss. In an environment where being eaten by a predator is an everyday risk, the value of rapid decision making is likely to begin to outweigh that of increased accuracy long before perfect accuracy is achieved. One should therefore expect evolution to generate problem-solving systems that *never* produce exactly the right answer except when it is trivially easy to do so.

Reason stands as an exception to this rule, which is why it presents something of a puzzle. But with respect to our intuitive problem-solving capabilities, the trade-off between speed and accuracy has almost always left its mark. This is why, throughout much of the cognitive science literature, the intuitive problem-solving system is often called the *heuristic* system. Heuristics are basically rules of thumb, or shortcuts, used to solve problems when you can't be bothered to work out the correct solution. (A classic example in everyday life is the "rule of 72" used to calculate compound interest: "72 divided by the rate of return equals the number of years it takes for an investment to double in value." This doesn't give you exactly the right answer, but it's an answer that is close enough that you almost never have to do the real calculation.)

Our brains are chock-full of these shortcuts and tricks. For instance, we all come equipped at birth with a system of "intuitive physics" that allows us to anticipate the trajectory of moving objects. (Some rather clever experiments have shown that even newborn babies react differently to objects that are coming toward them, depending upon whether the object is on a collision course or not.[29]) This system of intuitive physics is very powerful, but it is also based on heuristics, which means that it sometimes produces the wrong answer. In particular, it has a huge bug when it comes to anticipating the trajectory of dropped objects. Intuitively, we distinguish between thrown objects and dropped objects. With thrown objects, we take into account both the force that is acting on the object and the effects of gravity. With dropped objects, however, we look only at gravity, and so assume that they will go straight down. As a result, when an object *that is already in motion* is dropped, we ignore the existing motion and assume that it will go straight down.

It's easy to see this in action. Put some children in front of a video game that requires anticipation of ballistic trajectories, such as Angry Birds, and they will instantly pick it up. They don't have to study the game carefully to figure out where things are going to land, they just *know.* Put them in front of a combat flight simulator, however, where they are required to bomb a target on the ground, and they all get it wrong. They wait until they are directly over the target before releasing the bomb, failing to realize that the bomb is going to continue moving forward at the same initial speed as the aircraft while it descends. (One can see the same mistake in children's drawings of airplanes dropping bombs, which inevitably show the bomb descending in a straight line.) This is a remarkably persistent error, one that even large numbers of university students studying physics and engineering have been known to make.[30]

But what else should one expect? Our brains are a product of evolution. There is no reason to expect to find the laws of Newtonian—much less quantum—mechanics inscribed in our subconscious. The environment of evolutionary adaptation didn't require early human hunters to go on bombing sorties, or even to drop rocks from moving objects. As a result, the expectation that dropped objects will go straight down was good enough for all practical purposes. Exceptions to the rule would have been sufficiently infrequent or inconsequential that there would have been no survival advantage to be had from the development of a more nuanced system of intuitive physics.

The discovery of these cognitive shortcuts in the early 1970s spawned a truly gigantic literature on "heuristics and biases" and their role in human judgment. The most important contributors were Amos Tversky and Daniel Kahneman, who had a peculiar genius for designing scenarios that would cause our cognitive heuristics to misfire. They were able to show that in a vast number of different areas, our brains weren't really *solving* the problems posed—or at least weren't working out a proper solution—but were actually just guessing, using very clever techniques that could be relied upon to produce the right answer most of the time under standard conditions.

This research has received an enormous amount of attention, particularly among people like David Brooks, who are keen to show that human rationality is hopelessly compromised—that we are nothing but the sum of our biases. Yet seldom does anyone stop to ask how we are able to discover our own biases. If our brains are the product of evolution, and if evolution produces all sorts of "good enough" problem-solving capacities, how did we ever acquire the capacity to reflect upon our capacities and discover that they are less than perfect? The only way to detect a broken instrument is by comparing it to one that isn't broken. But what do we have to compare ourselves to? It's all well and good to show that our intuitive judgments of probability, for instance, are out of whack when compared to the axioms of probability theory. But where does our capacity to grasp and apply the axioms of probability theory come from?

An unreasonable answer to this question would be simply to say, "Oh well, that evolved too." There is no doubt that it evolved. But it is very unlikely to have evolved in the same way as our other cognitive abilities. Obviously, when we correct our intuitive judgments of probability or of motion, we are using our capacity for explicit, rational thinking. The problem with reason, from an evolutionary perspective, is that it lacks all the usual characteristics of the "adapted mind."[31] Most importantly, it is domain general, which means that it can be applied to solve problems in any area. And yet in every other area of cognition, and in every other species, evolution has clearly favored cognitive adaptations aimed at solving very specific problems.[32] Furthermore, given how much more difficult it would be to evolve a domain-general problem-solving system, compared to a collection of domain-specific ones, there simply is not enough time for such a system to have developed within the human lineage. Evolutionary theorists often talk about how "exquisitely adapted" particular organisms are relative to their environment. And it's true, there are some exquisite adaptations out there. But these usually take millions of years to develop. Ants, for example, exhibit an astonishing array of complex social behaviors. But ants have also been on this planet, in pretty much their present form, for 140 million years. This means they've had time to work out all sorts of fancy adaptations. Modern humans, by contrast, branched off from the rest of the *Homo* lineage only about 250,000 years ago. The idea that between, say, the dawn of *Homo heidelbergensis* and rise of *Homo sapiens*—a period of maybe a half million years—we managed to evolve a completely new type of cognitive system, from scratch, which allows us to produce absolutely precise answers to any sort of question we might care to ask, is completely implausible.[33]

To see the problem, consider the case of mathematical ability. Human infants appear to come equipped with two innate modules for dealing with numbers.[34] The first (called the *subitization system*) allows us to deal with small numbers and to tell at a glance the difference between sets of one, two, and three objects. So if you show a small child two balls, cover them with a handkerchief, then add a third ball, the child will notice the difference when you pull the handkerchief off. But if you put five balls under the handkerchief then add a sixth, the child won't notice. The second module allows us to guesstimate with respect to the size of large groups. So a child will be able to see—again, at a glance—that a pile of twenty is more than a pile of thirty balls. This module cannot do fine discriminations, though, so a pile of twelve and a pile of thirteen will be treated the same.

One of the most striking things about these two modules is that they are shared with other primates. Chimpanzees and baboons, in particular, have been shown to possess *exactly* the same discriminatory capabilities. There is every reason to believe that our competencies in this area were inherited from a common ancestor (and thus constitute part of the "old mind"). At around age four, however, the time when children acquire advanced linguistic competence, they begin to develop new abilities. In particular, they develop mastery of the counting procedure and begin to integrate it with their innate competencies. Chimpanzees, on the other hand, even those who have been taught to sign, seem to be incapable of taking this step. They can be taught the signs for one, two, and three, but then they treat "three" as being equal to "anything greater than two." Teaching them the number four involves unlearning this understanding of three, but then they simply come to understand "four" as "anything greater than three." In order to teach them the number five, one must start all over again, unlearning this understanding of "four." Each new number must be taught through the same arduous process. At no point does the chimpanzee ever "get it," the way human infants do. They learn numbers the way we learn the names of objects. They can list the names, but at no point do they ever learn the procedure that we call *counting*.

Some evolutionary psychologists have been inclined to explain this by saying that humans have a third "mathematics module," which allows us to do all these advanced calculations. This could be true, but consider how implausible it is. In terms of sheer computational power, the two innate modules that we share with other primates are fairly pathetic and, furthermore, have undergone no obvious improvement in the past five million years. (How hard would it be to expand our range a bit, so that instead of being able to count up to three intuitively, we acquired the ability to count to four, or maybe even five?) And yet, at the same time as nothing was going on in either of these two modules, we somehow acquired—from scratch—a brand-new module, which no other animal has, that allows us not only to count to infinity, but also to understand fractions, decimals, vectors, limits, negative numbers, irrational numbers, imaginary numbers, transcendental numbers, and much more? It makes no sense.

The idea that we have one module for counting to three and another module for "all the rest of mathematics," and that these both came about through the same *kind* of natural selection, is completely unbelievable. First of all, there can be little doubt that both the subitization and the guess-timation modules evolved in order to do what they do. In other words, they were selected for precisely because of the fitness benefits that came from being able to carry out these sorts of discriminations. With the rest of mathematics, on the other hand, one can be quite certain that the underlying cognitive system was not selected for because it would facilitate the development of calculus, analytic geometry, or linear algebra—since these came about only within the scope of historical time. Even something as simple as counting to one hundred has no obvious fitness benefits (and if it did, why wouldn't one see modification to the small numbers module?). Thus we can be fairly certain that the ability to do mathematics in the way that we do is a byproduct effect of whatever cognitive adaptations happened to make it possible. In other words, the ability to do mathematics cannot have evolved in order to allow us to do mathematics; the fact that we acquired this ability must be just a happy coincidence.

The same argument can be generalized across other cognitive domains. There is simply no advantage to be had in building a single cognitive system that can be used to figure out the gravitational constant of the universe, build a machine to catch neutrinos, unlock the secrets of life on earth, assess counterfactual probabilities, or think about what to serve for dinner next Thursday.[35] It is difficult to imagine what sort of environmental challenge could require the construction of a system that flexible. Furthermore, such a system would simply be too overpowered relative to both the nature and the scale of the challenges facing our ancestors in the environment of evolutionary adaptation. It would be like putting a full-scale AI into a Roomba.

This leads us inevitably to the key conclusion: our capacity to reason must be a byproduct of adaptations that were intended to achieve other goals. In other words, *our primate brains aren't designed for rational thought.*[36] The "rational part of the soul," far from being the pinnacle of creation, turns out to be just an accident, a strange little offshoot in an otherwise unpromising lineage.

This helps to explain one thing: why thinking rationally is so *hard*. Dennett describes the conscious, rational mind as a "serial virtual machine implemented—inefficiently—on the parallel hardware that evolution has provided for us."[37] The key word here is *inefficient*. The mind simply didn't evolve to support the sort of linear, explicit processing that is the hallmark of rational thought. Furthermore, there hasn't been enough *time* for it to develop the adaptations that would greatly facilitate or enhance this style of thinking. Thus the way that your brain feels after writing an exam is like the way your back feels after a long day spent lifting boxes—neither was designed for the task that it is being asked to perform.

This is of enormous importance when it comes to updating the ideals of the Enlightenment. Reason is not natural; it is profoundly *un*natural. At the same time, it is the only thing that allows us to escape from the strait-jacket of our animalistic minds. So while it has the potential to free us from the state of nature, there is no reason to expect this process to be easy. The great thinkers of the first Enlightenment tended to believe that once prejudice and superstition were overthrown, reason would naturally take their place, without any sort of slippage or backsliding. We now know that this isn't true. But more importantly, we know *why* it isn't true.

§

So what is the adaptation that created all of these astonishing byproduct effects? Many cognitive scientists (and, for what it's worth, philosophers) believe that the answer is *language*.[38] Indeed, an increased appreciation for language and its importance in human cognition has been at the center of the most important conceptual revolution in our understanding of the mind since the beginning of the modern era. Throughout most of history, it was simply assumed that our minds came fully equipped with the ability to formulate complex thoughts all on their own. Beliefs were thought to be like pictures in the mind, images of things we have seen. Language was something that came along later, when we began to feel the need to communicate these ideas to one another. The universally shared assumption was that a human being could be fully rational all on her own, without ever having spoken a word to another person.

A number of developments began to chip away at this consensus over the course of the nineteenth century. Philosophers, in particular, realized that beliefs had a lot more in common with *sentences* than with pictures.[39] (Take, for instance, a belief like "The Battle of Waterloo was fought in 1815." What would a picture of that look like? How about "The ball is not red"?) Psychologists began to notice that all sorts of advanced cognitive abilities—including counting and arithmetic[40]—start to show up in children only *after* they have acquired mastery of a language. And linguists, analyzing the structure of syntax and grammar, began to establish connections between the formal operations we use to construct complex sentences and the operations we use to construct complex thoughts and arguments.

The net consequence of all this was an almost precise inversion of the traditional order of explanation. Rationality had always been taken to precede language. Now it began to look as though language preceded reason, or, more specifically, as though our ability to string together a set of thoughts into a coherent sequence—the centerpiece of serial processing—was a byproduct of our ability to produce a set of sentences in sequence. Language, according to this view, evolved primarily because of its role in facilitating communication. The adaptations needed to get it off the ground were well within the reach of the "old mind." Yet once a more complex system of communication developed, particularly one with the type of grammatical structure that ours has, it provided the basis for a new style of computation.[41] Thus the development of language produced significant cognitive benefits, leading to the type of thinking that we associate with the "new mind."

For example, one of the most basic uses of language is that it can be used to tell other people what to do. Not only can you tell people what to do, but you can give them a series of instructions in sequence, with the expectation that they will carry them out in the order specified. What is more, this tool can be used not just to control others, but to control the self as well. A set of self-directed imperatives is basically a *plan*. Mental rehearsal of actions—talking your way through them in advance—has been shown to improve performance. Thus we start by ordering people around and being ordered around, but in the process we acquire a new tool for controlling and planning our own actions.[42] As the psychologist Lev Vygotsky wrote, "the most significant moment in the course of intellectual development, which gives birth to the purely human forms of practical and abstract intelligence, occurs when speech and practical activity, two previously completely independent lines of development, converge."[43]

Rational thought, according to this view, is essentially a form of inner speech. When you listen to small children talking, they are not merely expressing their thoughts. You are literally hearing them think.[44] It is only over time that they develop the capacity to inhibit the physical motions, to compress the speech, and thus to think silently, to themselves. This process of internalization can be observed in other domains as well. In China, one can sometimes see older merchants doing extraordinary complex arithmetic "in their heads," without the benefit of any external devices. If you look carefully, however, you may see them making slight motions with their fingers. This is because they were trained using an abacus. After using one for long enough, they develop a clear enough picture of the device in their mind and a feel for where the beads would be, so that they no longer need the actual physical device. The slight movement of the fingers is the only remaining trace of the external origins of the competence.

In early twentieth century, Vygotsky and his colleague Alexander Luria were able to detect a similar process of internalization in children learning to write, but this time with speech, rather than with an abacus. Noticing that there was a "constant buzz" of quiet speech in a class of young students learning to write, they suggested that half of the class be allowed to whisper to themselves but the other half be instructed to hold the tip of their tongue between their teeth.[45] The second group suffered a significant degradation of performance. On the other hand, simply being asked to hold their teeth together or clench a fist had no such effect. It was suppression of the tongue movements specifically that generated a degradation of performance, because it prevented them from vocalizing, and therefore led to a greater number of mistakes.

All of this suggests that talking is actually the primitive form of thinking—or, more specifically, it is a developmental precursor to the form of explicit, conscious thought that is the hallmark of rationality. By the time we become adults, the process of internalization is so complete that we imagine that we always had the ability to think silently, "in our heads." There are times, however, when the earlier form breaks through. It is not unusual, for instance, to see someone who is struggling to follow a set of complex instructions stop and read them out loud to himself. Indeed, people often resort to self-directed talk when they are having difficulty exercising self-control, maintaining attention, or even just carrying out a difficult processing task. (Various psychological studies have shown that asking people to explain their thinking out loud as they are completing a task typically *improves* performance, rather than impairing it.[46] This is the opposite of what should occur if talking were a fundamentally different process from thinking.)

While language can be used to enhance self-control, it also allows us to think in a different way.[47] One can see this quite clearly when small children, having mastered the counting procedure, are suddenly able to perform feats of mathematical reasoning that are qualitatively different from anything else found in nature. The dominant view is that our grammar enables this, because it permits recursion—the familiar process of embedding one clause within another.[48] As anyone who has programmed a computer knows, recursion is hugely important and incredibly powerful. When you say something like "I wish that he wouldn't do that," it may seem like just a boring old sentence, but in fact you're doing something that your "old mind" can't do. By embedding one sentence ("he wouldn't do that") within another ("I wish that . . ."), you are constructing a recursive function. Embed yet another sentence in it, resulting in, say, "I wish that he wouldn't do that thing that he does with his finger," and you suddenly become the most powerful computational system in the natural world. This is why chimpanzees can't count and we can. They treat numbers as names, associated with groups of objects. We understand them in terms of a *function,* which can be applied to itself again and again, in order to produce an infinite sequence of numbers. This is what gives us the ability to do "all of mathematics."[49]

It is this foundation in language that also explains the two features of rational thought that were identified at the beginning of the chapter as fundamental. First of all, rational thinking is explicit. What this means, in effect, is that the sequence of steps that we go through in order to arrive at some conclusion can be put into words. With intuitions, we can usually state what the final judgment is, but we cannot articulate how we got there. The fact that rational thought is *already* linguistically formulated explains why we are able to articulate it so precisely and easily. It explains why we are, as the philosopher Michael Dummett put it, able to communicate these thoughts in language "without residue."[50] There is nothing that remains unexpressed when we have finished articulating a rational train of thought. "Thought," Dummett writes, "differs from other things also said to be objects of the mind, for instance pains or mental images, in not being essentially private. I can tell you what my pain is like, or what I am visualizing, but I cannot transfer to you my pain or my mental image. It is of the essence of thought, however, that it is transferable, that I can convey to you exactly what I am thinking."[51]

The second major feature of rational thought is its universality. Reasons that are good for one person are presumptively valid for all persons. It is not difficult to see why, if one keeps in mind that language is essentially public. In order to function as a means of communication, language must work according to a set of rules that are, if not identical, at least broadly similar for all persons. This means, however, that the same rules that govern public speech are also going to govern private rational thought. As a result, arguments that we find compelling are likely be found compelling by others, in a way that private intuitions or feelings may not.

This is why, even though people's brains are very different, and even though some people have remarkably different abilities in different areas, people all *reason* in very much the same way. Although the metaphor is slightly misleading, there is something to be said for thinking of human reason as akin to a software application that runs the same way on different hardware platforms (or a website that looks the same in any browser). With men and women, for instance, there are very significant differences in brain chemistry, physiology, and development. And yet clear-cut sex differences in cognition show up only in peripheral, modular systems (such as spatial rotation of objects or the ability to detect slight changes in the environment). For all the hype surrounding differences between the male and female brains, it is actually extraordinary how little difference there is in the way that men and women *reason*.[52]

For a long time, the discovery that rational thought depended on language, and not the other way around, was thought to have relativistic consequences. Indeed, a lot of postmodernism, and the associated assault on reason, was nothing but an early overreaction to these findings. When the dust settled it became apparent that, far from the evidence supporting relativism, the opposite was true. There are many different languages in the world, which means that there will be many different flavors of thought. And yet one of the striking features of these languages is that they are all basically intertranslatable. We have yet to encounter a language that is not learnable by someone willing to make the necessary investment of time and energy. Thus there is no tension between the idea that reason depends upon language and the idea that it possesses a universal structure.

§

The idea that our minds have different "parts," partially redundant and often conflicting, is one of the oldest and most troubling claims in the history of philosophical reflection on the nature of thought. Modern cognitive science has gone some way toward piecing together the puzzle. According to the "dual process" view, we have two different styles of cognition, distinguished by the following characteristics:

System 1: Intuitive, heuristic
Unconscious, automatic
Rapid, computationally powerful, massively parallel
Associative
Pragmatic (contextualizes problems in the light of prior knowledge and belief)
Does not require the resources of central working memory
Functioning not related to individual differences in general intelligence
Low effort

System 2: Rational, analytic
Linked with language and reflective consciousness
Slow and sequential
Linked to working memory and general intelligence
Capable of abstract and hypothetical thinking
Volitional or controlled—responsive to instructions and stated intentions
High effort[53]

In order to assess the prospects of a new Enlightenment, we need to understand more clearly the strengths and weaknesses of the unglamorously named "System 2." The great thinkers of the first Enlightenment tended to dismiss System 1 entirely, treating it either as nonexistent or else as inferior to reason. We now know better. Indeed, the pendulum has swung so far in the other direction that many people think System 2 is an illusion—that what we call "rational thought" is a sham, either hopelessly mired in biases or consisting of post hoc rationalizations. The reality is somewhat more prosaic. Reason is far less powerful and autonomous than it was once taken to be, yet it is still indispensable for certain forms of cognition. Evans sums up the state of play with admirable simplicity: "In terms of quantity, the analytic system can meet very little of the cognitive demands on the brain but in terms of quality it can do things that the heuristic system cannot."[54] The central question then becomes: What can reason do that intuition can't?

2. The art of the kluge

On the haphazard construction of the mind

In 1792, as the French Revolution entered its most radical phase, the Catholic church was outlawed by the central government and replaced by a new, secular cult, dedicated to the celebration of "Reason and Philosophy." Notre Dame Cathedral, in the heart of Paris, was stripped of its Christian furnishings and transformed into a Temple of Reason (complete with an "altar of Liberty" and an inaugural procession that ended with the appearance of the "Goddess of Reason").

The example was soon imitated across France. In 1794, at a ceremony held to inaugurate the new Temple of Reason in Châlons-sur-Marne, one observer provided a written account of the procession.[1] The most interesting part is his record of banners that hung from the carts and wagons that made up the parade. The picture that emerges provides an uncomfortable sense of the darker forces that were at work in French society at the time.

It started out innocently enough: "Reason guides us and enlightens us," read one pennant. "Prejudices pass away, reason is eternal," read another.

Interspersed with these noble sentiments, however, were some rather more sinister suggestions. One cart contained a group of French soldiers wounded in combat, with a banner reading "Our blood will never cease

60

to flow for the safety of the fatherland." A bit farther on, a call to arms: "Destroy the tyrants, or die."

Another cart displayed a group of wounded enemy prisoners. "They were very mistaken in fighting for tyrants," read the banner.

The most disturbing, however, belonged to the local "surveillance committee," the group responsible for rounding up and executing "counterrevolutionaries" in what would eventually come to be known as the Terror. Their banner read simply, "Our institution purges society of a multitude of suspect people."

In the end, the Goddess of Reason didn't quite merit the faith that was being shown in her. First of all, despite being "eternal," reason manifestly failed to deliver order and stability to French society. Since the revolution, the French state has gone through somewhere between ten and seventeen constitutions, depending on how you count (compared to, say, the United States, which is still on its first). France is currently on its Fifth Republic, but it has also been, since the revolution, a monarchy, an empire, a military dictatorship, and a Nazi client state—a procession of political arrangements that made the *ancien régime* look rather decent by comparison.

Apart from all that, the French Revolution also marked the appearance on the political scene of a certain sort of ruthlessness—indeed, murderousness—in the use of state power that was to be reproduced time and again over the course of the twentieth century. Many innocent victims were sacrificed on the altar of Reason. This is a legacy that defenders of the Enlightenment impulse must contend with. Robespierre had unwisely suggested that revolutionary leaders should "guide the people by reason and repress the enemies of the people by terror."[2] The question is whether the second half of this was just an unnecessary flourish or whether it bore some internal connection to the rationalist temperament. At very least, before calling for a second Enlightenment, we need to understand how the first one could have gone so horribly wrong. To say that "they weren't rational enough" is not an adequate response. What grounds do we have for thinking that we are any more

61

rational now? We need to face up squarely to the weakness and limitations of reason and to recognize that the desire to rebuild all of society along "rational principles" is misguided. Only then can we redefine the Enlightenment project in such a way as to make it not just workable, but also more likely to improve the human condition.

❡

There are many things that we are naturally well equipped to do; unfortunately, reasoning isn't one of them. The ability of our brains to sustain rational thought is an example of what evolutionary theorists refer to as *exaptation*—where something that evolved in order to serve one purpose gets co-opted to perform some other.[3] The classic example is feathers, which seem to have evolved in order to provide insulation and warmth, and only later became used for flight. Human design and engineering is full of this sort of repurposing as well. Consider the Nigerian student who acquired brief internet celebrity by building a helicopter from discarded car parts.[4] It worked, but not very well, simply because none of the components had actually been designed for the purpose to which they were being put.

Human reason has a lot in common with a helicopter built from car parts. As Daniel Dennett observes, "many of its most curious features, and especially its limitations, can be explained as the byproducts of the *kludges* that make possible this curious but effective reuse of an existing organ for novel purposes."[5] Dennett accentuates the word *kludge* (nowadays more often spelled *kluge*) here because it is the crucial concept. The term is commonly used by engineers, mechanics, and computer programmers to describe a solution to a problem that gets something to work without really fixing the underlying problem.

Programmers often have to resort to kluges when trying to debug software. Suppose, for instance, you write some subroutine that takes a number as input, performs a complicated calculation on it, and then spits out another number as output. Everything is working fine, except that for some reason, whenever it receives the number 37 as input, the subroutine does something strange and produces the wrong answer. After spending hours staring at the code, trying to figure out why it's not working properly, you give up trying to fix it. Instead, you just figure out manually what the right answer should be when the input is 37. Suppose it's 234. You then add a line of code at the beginning that says something like the following: "Take the input number and feed it to the subroutine, unless that input happens to be 37, in which case just send back 234 as the answer."

This is a kluge.

There are several components here that are essential. Most importantly, it *works,* in the sense that it causes the larger program to perform correctly even though the subroutine is still broken. It is also massively inelegant. If anyone else saw your code and figured out how you "fixed" the problem, you would be embarrassed. And finally, the underlying problem is still there, and so is likely to resurface on other occasions. (Suppose your code gets integrated into a larger program, and other people start using your sub-routine without realizing that they need to make this special exception for the number 37. Then the bug shows up again.)

Rational thought is made possible by an enormous collection of kluges. We tend not to realize this, simply because we have become so used to the way our minds work that we never stop to think about it. The psychologist Gary Marcus, however, has produced a sizable catalog of them (in a book appropriately titled *Kluge: The Haphazard Construction of the Human Mind*).[6] Consider, for example, the way human memory works. When people design information storage and retrieval systems, they usually use what's called a *location-addressing* system. The most familiar example of this is a library. Each book is given a number before it is put on a shelf in the stacks. This number is the "address," and it tells you the location of the book. Each address is entered into a central registry (what some of us still call, anachronistically, the "card catalog"), along with an indication of what can be found there. This makes retrieving things easy: to find a book, you just get the address from the catalog, go to the location it points to, and pull the book from the shelf.

This system is the most efficient way of storing information for subsequent retrieval, as witnessed by the fact that computer memory is organized in exactly the same way (with a set of locations, each identified by a unique address). Unfortunately, this is not the sort of memory system that was given to us by evolution. Marcus refers to the system we have as "contextual memory," and it has a number of quirky features.[7] Most importantly, it is not systematically searchable, but is instead triggered by various sorts of stimuli, usually coming from the immediate environment, and is linked together by chains of association.[8] For instance, many people will have had the following, familiar experience: you go to another room—say, the kitchen—to get something, but when you get there you can't remember what it was you came to get. Try as you might, you simply can't remember. If you go back to the spot where you were standing when you decided to go to the kitchen, all of a sudden the memory comes back again. Why? Because the memory is cued by the environment. When you see your desk you think, "Oh yeah, I wanted a cup of coffee." But the kitchen doesn't evoke that memory.

In many ways, our memory is like an old-fashioned "closed stacks" library, where you're not allowed to go in and look for the book yourself but instead have to give a little slip of paper to a librarian, who goes and gets things for you. Even worse, though, you often can't persuade the librarian to get the book that you want. Suppose instead that the librarian watches over your shoulder as you go about your business then runs off and fetches some book that he *thinks* you might find useful. Unfortunately, he has an unhealthy preoccupation with sex, violence, and food, and so often comes back with books that are not only unhelpful, but actually make it difficult for you to concentrate on what you're doing. (Also, the stacks are in complete disarray, being the result of a partial merger between three or four older collections. Many of the books have also been destroyed, with the library having only a low-resolution scan left. So the librarian has to print up a new copy for you whenever one of these books is needed. Each time he does this he "cleans things up" a bit—unbeknownst to you—rewriting text that is too fuzzy, filling in the blanks, or adding in some details that he thinks might have been missed in the scan.[9])

This is what we live with. There are, of course, good evolutionary reasons why the mammalian memory system would develop in this way (particularly if you think of our bodies, including our brains, as survival machines built to preserve our genes). It puts the highest-priority information at our fingertips, right when we are more likely to need it. Instead of having to search through our memory ourselves, we have what computer types call an "intelligent agent," who sorts through it for us, quickly and without taxing central resources. So we get rapid updates with useful information, like "That guy has a mean temper," or "Your brother was killed by a creature that looks a lot like that," or "Last time you ate one of those you were sick for days."

Unfortunately, the intelligent agent in question was programmed by our genes, not by us, and so its concept of important is not quite the same as *our* concept of important. When studying for an exam, the most important thing to *you* might be memorizing the periodic table, while your memory system is interested in anything but. And so your mind wanders, typically to things more closely related to survival and reproduction. Deleting things was also (apparently) not an important priority, given that the whole system was designed to work for only thirty years or so. As Pascal Boyer has observed, rather poignantly, the experience of grief is closely related to the fact that we lack the ability to delete the file on people after they have died, and so the librarian continues to prompt us with memories that are no longer relevant to the actual world.[10] We have no way of making him stop, except the passage of time, which weakens many of the associations.

The entire system would be completely unworkable were it not for the fact that we have discovered all sorts of clever ways of tricking the librarian into getting us things that we want and ignoring things that are irrelevant. In particular, we've figured out how to make it *look* like we're doing something, without actually doing it—enough to trick the librarian into going and getting us what we need. We've also noticed that the librarian tends to show up with more than just one book; he brings along extra material that he thinks might be related, based on patterns of association. So we have discovered that through repetition, or by putting things together into a narrative, or by otherwise building associations, we are able to enhance our recall.

And then, of course, there is language. Luckily for us, the librarian doesn't distinguish between the sound of a bird, a crackling fire, or a falling tree and the sound of a spoken word—any of these can cue a host of memories. Similarly, he does not distinguish between the visual pattern of a leaf, an animal, or a cloud and that of a written word. Thus we can use language to manipulate the librarian, creating a set of triggers that are decoupled from the immediate environment. You can retrieve a picture of an elephant just by seeing the written word *elephant*.

We also learn how to translate information into different modalities, to get it into a format in which it can be more easily remembered. An unfamiliar name may be impossible to remember as a sound pattern, but easy once you learn how to spell it. A Chinese character may be impossible to remember as an image, but easy once you've learned the stroke order with your writing hand. A list of objects may be impossible to remember as a list, but easy once you learn to imagine a room with all of those things in it. These are all different ways of coaxing better performance out of our memory system.

The important point is that none of these little tricks fixes the underlying problem, which is that our memory is not well designed to support rational cognition. But it is what it is, and we can't fix it. So we develop work-arounds, or kluges. Everyone has his or her own little bag of tricks, some of them better than others. There are some people who have great memories, such that one suspects that their brains just work better than everyone else's. But if you look more carefully, you can see that a lot of people with great memories actually just have a better bag of tricks.

❡

Suppose that one day you are abducted by aliens. You wake up on their ship strapped to a gurney. You notice that they are about to perform a series of horrific experiments on you, ending with a dissection that will most certainly bring about your death.

"Wait," you cry out. "Stop!"

The alien scientist comes by, looks at you, and says, "Why should we stop?"

Pausing only briefly to acknowledge his surprising mastery of spoken English, you say, "Because it's wrong to torture other intelligent species."

"What intelligent species?" says the scientist. "Surely, you're not referring to yourself."

"Yes, I'm referring to myself," you say. "I'm really smart."

"No, you're not," says the alien. "You can't even do mathematics."

"Yes, I can," you say.

"Okay, then tell me, what's 78 times 43?"

"No problem. Do you have a pencil and paper? And could you unstrap my arms?"

The alien looks puzzled. "Why do you need a pencil and paper? Can you answer the question or can't you?"

"Yes, I can answer it, I just need a pencil and paper."

"Where I come from, we use our *brains* to do mathematics. You do it in some other, alien way?" says the alien.

"Sure. Untie me and I'll show you."

Moments later, equipped with a pencil and paper, you quickly work out the answer (3,354). And just to make sure you don't wind up back on the gurney, you solve a couple of quadratic equations, derive some second-order derivatives, and sketch out Cantor's uncountability proof.

"Wow," he says. "You guys really can do math. What a strange species. How were we supposed to know that your brains require pencils in order to function correctly?"

At this point you realize that the alien has fallen victim to a very fundamental misunderstanding of how the human mind works. He thinks that your mind is housed entirely in your brain, and that your capacity to reason is based entirely upon the biological substratum of your cognitive system. So when you said that "you" were good at mathematics, he thought that you meant "you" in the sense of "your biological brain," whereas what you really meant was "my biological brain plus something to write with and something to write on"—an easy mistake to make. And if you think about the mind strictly in terms of the brain, then he was right: humans are not a particularly intelligent species. When you abduct people—separating them entirely from their environment and from the artifacts they have developed that both augment and transform their computational abilities—then they're not that smart. The peculiar genius of the human brain, however, lies not in its onboard computational power, but rather in its ability to colonize elements of its environment, transforming them into working parts of its cognitive (and motivational) system.

This misunderstanding of the human mind is actually quite common. Consider again Dennett's characterization of the rational mind as a serial virtual machine "implemented on the parallel hardware of the brain."[11] The serial processing system is actually implemented not just on the hardware of the brain, but on portions of the environment as well. (In philosophy this is known as the *extended mind thesis*; it has been articulated and championed most forcefully by Andy Clark.) Dennett acknowledges that the mind often has to "offload" some of its memories onto the environment.[12] The picture here is of the brain being like a CPU in a computer, while the world serves as a hard drive. Yet the role that the pencil and paper play when we are doing long multiplication would clearly be classified by any computer scientist as part of CPU function, not storage. This is even more obvious in the case of an abacus, where you are actually doing no math at all in your head, just moving your fingers in certain patterned ways, like playing a guitar. The computations are not just being *stored* outside your brain, they are being *done* outside your brain. Yet is there any important difference between the neophyte working an abacus and the older merchant who has "internalized" the device so that he need only twitch his fingers to work out the sums?

There is a close analogy to this in the way that we think about our body. Where does our body stop and the world begin? Our inclination is to think that our body is a collection of cells, distinguished by the fact that each one contains the same collection of human DNA. There is a sense in which this is true. And yet one's body, in this sense, is not a *functional* unit. The living breathing body that you walk around with is actually an extremely large colony of organisms, in which nonhuman cells outnumber human cells by at least 10 to 1. (The National Institutes of Health in the United States have recently launched the Human Microbiome Project, as a successor to the now complete Human Genome Project, in order to catalog and sequence the nine hundred or so species of microorganism that we normally carry around with us.) Some of these organisms are parasitic, but many are symbiant species. Digestion, in particular, would be impossible without all the helpful bacteria that populate our gut. A purist might want to say that, technically, all these bugs are not part of "you." The point, however, is that "you" are not functional without them, since your body has coevolved with them. We have no trouble saying that "you" digested your last meal, without getting picky about which parts of the process were done by which members of the colony. Furthermore, even though your gut basically "offloaded" certain tasks onto the bacteria, the entire process is still one that we are happy to call "digestion."

For the same reason, we should be perfectly comfortable calling a certain process "thought" even when portions of it are offloaded onto environmental systems. In the same way that your digestive system includes a population of bacteria, your "cognitive system" includes a lot of what Clark calls environmental "scaffolding": pencils, letters and numbers, Post-It notes, sketches, stacks of paper, internet searches, and, most importantly, *other people.*[13] These are not merely passive storage systems; they are *moving parts* in our processes of rational thought.

The most obvious examples of environmental scaffolding involve our memory system, which is, as we have seen, especially ill suited to the type of tasks that we would like it to perform. Working memory, in particular, is not only the central bottleneck in any serial processor, it is an area in which our biological brains perform particularly badly.[14] Most people cannot remember a seven-digit phone number for long enough to hang up their voice mail and dial it. (And, of course, the reason that most of us can't multiply 78 by 43 without a pencil and paper is that we can't keep the four intermediate products in memory for long enough to be able to add them up. This is, when you think about it, rather pathetic.) The central virtue of a writing system or an abacus is that it overcomes this limitation. Once the marks are made on the page or the beads are arranged in a certain position, they stay put, so that we can shift our attention to other things and come back to them later. The result is a massive increase in computational power.

This sort of "solution" to the limitations of our working memory system is the perfect example of a kluge. After all, writing things down doesn't fix the underlying problems with our working memory system, it simply allows us to work around them. Rational thinking, as we have seen, is made possible through an extensive system of kluges. Although many of them rely upon aspects of the environment, there is no useful inside/outside distinction to be drawn. Some kluges are environmental; some are psychological. Many more start out being environmental and later *become* psychological, through internalization. The important thing to recognize is that human reason is not merely "enhanced" by these environmental kluges, any more than human digestion is "enhanced" by the presence of intestinal flora. It *depends* upon them. In fact, psychologists have shown that a huge amount of human irrationality can be provoked by taking people out of their usual environment and putting them into a situation where they lack all of the scaffolding that they normally use to make decisions. Indeed, the typical psychology study, in which students are escorted into an empty room, seated in front of a computer, and then left alone in silence to answer a series of questions, is not all that different from an alien abduction. It's no surprise that people perform poorly under such circumstances, since our biological brains are not very good at reasoning all by themselves.

Imagine that, in order to abduct people, the aliens used a teleportation device that screened out all nonhuman DNA, so that when you arrived on the spaceship you were perfectly cleansed of all other organisms. You might enjoy being a couple pounds lighter, but unfortunately, your body would immediately start to malfunction in all sorts of ways (intestinal disorders, vitamin deficiency, skin infections, etc.). After several days, the aliens might look at you and wonder how humans manage to survive at all—we seem totally dysfunctional. But the mistake is on their side. No wonder you don't work properly: they abducted only a part of your digestive system when they left all the bacteria behind, just like they abducted only a part of your rational mind when they left your pencil and paper behind.

¶

As we have seen, the central advantage of a serial processing system is that it is able to chain together a sequence of operations, in which the content of what comes later depends upon what was determined earlier. This is what allows it to *reason*. This advantage, however, comes with a disadvantage. A serial processor, by its very nature, does one thing at a time. The world, unfortunately, often demands that we do more than one thing at a time. The only way that a serial processor can handle this is by taking turns, doing a bit of one task, then a bit of another, then returning to the first and doing a bit more. There is a huge bottleneck here, which in turn creates an extremely complex optimization problem. How much time should be allocated to each task? In what order should the tasks be performed? Unfortunately, the way that our biological brains try to solve this problem is very far from ideal, mainly because they are not adapted for serial processing.

To see what an optimal solution to the problem looks like, consider how multitasking is achieved in a computer. Multitasking—the ability to run several applications or processes simultaneously—is actually an illusion. The computer is doing only one thing at a time; it is just alternating very quickly between them. In order to manage all this, the operating system has something called a *scheduler,* whose job is to ration CPU time between all of these different processes. Apart from having an algorithm that it applies in order to determine task sequence, the scheduler has two special powers. The first is the power of preemption—if a process is taking too long, the scheduler has the power to interrupt it and move on to other things. Of course, since not all tasks are equally important, each task is assigned a priority level, and preference is given to high-priority tasks. The priority system, however, gives rise to potential abuse. What is to stop unscrupulous software designers from making their programs run faster, by assigning them urgent priority levels when the tasks they seek to perform are of only moderate importance? To avoid this problem, the scheduler exercises a second important power, which is the ability to control the priority level. The highest priority levels are completely controlled by the system, so that programs must ask for permission in order to be assigned a high level. The scheduler also reserves the right to reassign priority levels if it finds that certain processes are hogging CPU time or taking too long to finish. It can also terminate them at will if it feels that they are misbehaving, are no longer useful, or have crashed.

The reason this is worth knowing is that the problems posed for a computer by the need to multitask are *exactly* the same as the problems posed for a human. Our intuitive judgments are generated by a parallel processing system, which is capable of genuine multitasking. With explicit, rational thought, on the other hand, we are limited to one task at a time. The human equivalent of CPU time is *attention,* and as we all know, you can pay attention to only one thing at a time. (People who consider themselves good at multitasking in the realm of explicit cognition sometimes think that they are performing multiple tasks simultaneously, but in reality they aren't. They are simply shifting their attention from one thing to another. Furthermore, despite thinking of themselves as good at multitasking, there is some evidence to suggest that what they actually are is bad at concentrating.[15] They multitask only because they are easily distracted, as a result of which they tend to perform worse on *all* tasks when compared to those who have a more "plodding" style.[16]) Because of the bottleneck it creates, attention must be carefully rationed, in the same way that CPU time in a computer is rationed. Our scheduler, however, lacks some of the characteristics that a good system should possess. First, it has only limited powers of preemption and, second, it doesn't seem able to reassign priority to tasks. As a result, we wind up using all sorts of kluges in order to keep things running with at least a semblance of order.

There is general agreement among psychologists that attention is metered out through a system of *competition* between stimuli. At any given time, your brain is inundated with potential information. (Timothy Wilson estimates that our brains are receiving about 11 million discrete bits of information per second, of which no more than 40 can be consciously processed.)[17] Thus an enormous winnowing must occur. If you think of just your own body, there are usually several dozen spots on your skin that would like to be itched, some muscles that are slightly uncomfortable and would like you to shift your weight, a rumble in your stomach that is asking to be fed, a cut or bruise that is generating a slight pain, a roughness in your throat that would like you to cough, a fuzziness in your head that could be remedied with a short nap . . . The list goes on and on. When you're doing something engaging, such as watching a good movie or playing tennis, all of these impulses get ignored. They don't actually go away—they are still running processes—they simply lose out in the competition for attention. They get no CPU time. You notice them only when you start to do something slightly *less* engaging, like sitting quietly and reading a book. Then all of a sudden you find yourself scratching and shifting around, falling asleep, or even remembering things that you had been forgetting to do. This is because low-priority tasks are finally managing to break through into consciousness and attracting a bit of attention to themselves.

Surprisingly, there don't seem to be any stimuli with an automatic override in this system. Pain, for example, doesn't have any sort of dedicated channel, but rather has to compete on all fours with other stimuli in order to get noticed. This explains the well-documented phenomenon of soldiers in combat (or, less dramatically, athletes in competition) suffering serious injuries but not noticing the pain until things start to calm down.[18] It is also amazing what people are able to overlook when they are paying attention to something else. In one particularly famous experiment, subjects were shown a video of students in different-colored shirts passing around some basketballs, and were asked to count the number of times that someone wearing a white shirt passed the ball. Halfway through the video, a woman in a gorilla suit walked through the shot, stopped and thumped her chest, and walked off. Afterward, subjects were asked how many passes they saw, and then whether they had seen anything unusual in the video. Almost half of all subjects said no, and in fact had no recollection of the woman in the gorilla suit at all. When shown the video again, some insisted that it was a trick, and that the investigators must have been showing them a different video.[19]

It's not clear which is more bizarre: not noticing that your leg has been blown off while you're under enemy fire or not noticing a person in a gorilla suit right in front of your eyes, simply because you're trying to count. Either way, we have an amazing ability to ignore things. Unfortunately, we also have very little control over it. Part of the reason we find it difficult to believe that people could fail to notice traumatic injuries is that we have all had the experience of *trying* to ignore pain and failing. This is because we are powerless to reassign priority levels to stimuli the way that a multitask scheduler does. So we often find ourselves unable to ignore a nagging pain or an unwanted thought or the sound of a car alarm nearby, despite the fact that concentrating on these things serves no useful purpose. We therefore resort to kluges—often we try to distract ourselves, generating an alternate stimulus powerful enough to outcompete the annoying stimulus, thereby leading us to disregard it.

Our powers of preemption are also limited—although not entirely nonexistent. Many people who have suffered a traumatic brain injury, especially to the frontal lobe, exhibit perseveration, which is basically an inability to terminate thought processes in an appropriate and timely fashion. They find themselves unable to stop thinking about something, unable to move on to a new topic of conversation, and unable to abandon unsuccessful problem-solving strategies. While the symptoms in these cases are pathological, they are in many ways just an extreme version of a difficulty that we all face. If you keep track of your thoughts over the course of a day, you'll find that you are subject to an enormous amount of what psychiatrists call *unwanted ideation*—things you have difficulty stopping yourself from thinking about. It could be an irritating comment made by a co-worker, a video game you were playing yesterday, an anxiety related to your children, or a sexual image or fantasy. Straightforward inhibition of such thought processes is very difficult, and so most of us rely upon kluges—we try to think of something else, something more distracting, in order to drown out the thought we are trying to get rid of.

For most purposes, the system that we have works well enough. The mere fact that our brains don't straight-up crash is a significant accomplishment (software engineers have yet to invent an uncrashable computer system). Yet for certain tasks, particularly those that require a great deal of concentration, we start to bump up against design constraints. While certain complex reasoning tasks are highly rewarding (say, plotting out an elaborate revenge against a hatred rival), others are far less so. Consider the task of reading a textbook. Imagine that the information is presented in a dry, factual format, without the benefit of amusing anecdotes and alien abduction scenarios. Imagine that the benefits of learning the material are nonobvious and far removed in time (suppose you're reading it just because you feel it is something you should know). Many people find it absolutely impossible to concentrate under these conditions. They can read for no more than five minutes before other thoughts begin to intrude and eventually take over.

The problem is that the task you're trying to perform generates an incredibly low level of stimulus and therefore easily gets trumped by almost anything else that comes along. Because we are unable to directly control our thoughts, we need kluges. Some of this may involve making what we are doing seem more exciting, but the standard basket of strategies involves manipulating the environment in such a way as to make everything else *less* exciting. The first thing you need is to be alone. Then you need a place that is quiet: no music, no irritating noises. It's also good to have an environment that is familiar: nothing new or interesting to attract your attention, just the same old chair, with the same old lamp. And obviously, you need to get rid of anything that is even vaguely reminiscent of sex (since at least half the population finds sex second only to pain in its ability to command attention). It also helps to be healthy, fed, and well rested.

Think of these as the seven kluges of highly effective people. There are some environments in which it is literally impossible to think. The most basic trick when trying to concentrate is simply to close your eyes, an expedient that we all resort to at one time or another. It is important to recognize that this is, in its own way, a kluge. We cannot control our attention directly, so we resort to a second-best solution, which is to block out one of the channels through which our environment impinges on consciousness.[20] Unfortunately, there are many tasks that cannot be completed with our eyes closed. The next-best way to enhance our ability to think is to create an environment that is conducive to thinking. As Clark put it, one of the central features of human cognition is that "we build 'designer environments' in which human reason is able to far outstrip the computational ambit of the unaugmented biological brain."[21] When you walk into someone's office or study or even car—wherever that person does his or her thinking—you are typically entering one of these designer environments.

It is important to understand that these environments are not just ones in which we happen to feel most comfortable, like in a house set at room temperature. Our body temperature stays pretty constant, regardless of what the temperature in the room is—the only impact of the ambient temperature is on how much energy it takes to maintain a constant body temperature. Thinking, however, is not like this. Unlike body temperature, which you can maintain all on your own, concentration is not something that you can maintain on your own. Your biological brain simply lacks the tools needed to accomplish this. And yet concentration is absolutely fundamental to the task of reasoning. And so we try to achieve it through manipulation of the environment. To understand the relationship between your brain and the surrounding world, it is better to think of yourself as being like a cold-blooded creature, whose metabolism actually slows down and eventually stops altogether as the outside temperature drops. When lizards bask in the sun or retreat to the shade, they are using the external environment as a way of achieving an optimal body temperature. This is how our brains use the environment: we fiddle with it in order to get ourselves thinking right. We are like cognitive ectotherms.[22]

¶

These examples are all intended to illustrate Dennett's claim that our brains are extremely inefficient when it comes to reasoning. The philosophers of the first Enlightenment inherited from both the ancient Greek and the medieval Christian traditions a view of reason as a tiny island of perfection in a sea of corruption and decay. Reason was regarded as a direct imprint of the divine intelligence, and therefore as possessing the same perfections— unity, order, simplicity, and goodness. The central mistake made by early Enlightenment thinkers lay in their failure to break with this tradition.

They adopted a theory of reason that was not only untrue, but in many ways the opposite of what is true. Far from reflecting a divine intelligence, the structure of human reasoning systems is below even the (already low) standards of evolutionary "design," because it is not adapted for the job it is currently being asked to perform. When you hear the word *reason,* you should think not of angels beating their wings, but rather of homemade Nigerian helicopters.

Seeing things in this light allows us to better understand the failings of the first Enlightenment. The partisans of reason assumed something like an "anything you can do I can do better" stance toward *all* the products of the human spirit. Their goal was to *replace* tradition, authority, and intuition with the exercise of pure reason. This is one of the factors that made rationalist politics, from the very beginning, incline toward revolutionary politics. One can see this most clearly in the rise of social contract theory, an approach to thinking about political questions that was shared almost universally by first-generation Enlightenment thinkers. This theory invites us to imagine a "state of nature" in which there are absolutely no institutional constraints or rules: no state, no laws, no economy, no educational system, and in many cases not even the family. It then says, "Suppose you could rebuild all of these institutions, from the ground up, from scratch—how would you do it?" From this intellectual sweeping away of existing institutions, it was not such a great leap to a sweeping away in practice. Thus from the French Revolution through to the communist revolutions of the twentieth century, there was a widespread desire to rebuild both state and society from scratch, in accordance with rational or scientific principles.

To be fair, it should be acknowledged that by the middle of the eighteenth century, "reason" had accomplished a number of astonishing revolutions in the realm of scientific belief. Theories that had been held unchallenged for millennia had been completely overturned. Thus the general authority of tradition had been greatly eroded. Intuition tells us that the earth must be standing still; otherwise, we would fly off it. Yet Copernicus had shown that it moves. Aristotle said that there can be "no motion without a mover," and for thousands of years everyone had deferred to him. Yet Isaac Newton showed that it is only *change* in motion that requires explanation; objects in motion will continue that way until stopped.

For Europeans, who had spent centuries believing that their own civilization was inferior to that of the ancient Romans and Greeks, this sudden discovery of massive error in the ancient worldview created an enormous crisis of confidence, not just in ancient belief systems, but also in ancient institutions. Worship of ancient wisdom—Aristotle in particular—came to be seen as a major *impediment* to the progress of knowledge. It was not so great a leap to imagine that deference to ancient institutions—the church, the monarchy, Roman law—might be an impediment to progress as well. And of course, there were all sorts of problems with these institutions. Abandonment of the principle that the king and his subjects must share a religion, for instance, represented a major advance.

Yet there was considerable overreach in the Enlightenment project. Reason wound up being assigned all sorts of tasks that, in the end, it simply was not powerful enough to perform. At the same time, because partisans of the first Enlightenment conceived of reason in purely individualistic terms, as something that works away inside the brains of discrete persons, they wound up inadvertently dismantling much of the scaffolding that reason requires in order to function correctly. As a result, they kneecapped reason just as they were sending it onto the field to face a much larger and more brutish opponent. It is no surprise, then, that rather than improving various social institutions, in many cases they wound up making things a lot worse.

Psychologist Gerd Gigerenzer has an amusing story that illustrates precisely the trap that early Enlightenment thinkers fell into. It concerns a baseball coach who, frustrated that his outfielders were missing too many catches, became convinced that it was because they were running too slowly, taking too much time to get to the ball. And it's true—if you look at baseball outfielders, they often run at something much less than top speed when they are moving toward the spot where a pop fly is about to land. The coach decided that if the players simply ran to the spot more quickly, then they would have an easier time making small adjustments to improve their chances of catching the ball. So he gave them a set of new instructions on how to catch fly balls: look and see where it's going to land, run as fast as you can to get there, then look up and make whatever adjustments are required in order to catch it. Unfortunately, when the players tried to follow these instructions, they found that their ability to catch the ball had been completely undermined. They wound up standing nowhere near where the ball was going to land.

Why is that? Intuitively, anyone can sense what the problem would be. Imagine that you're standing around the outfield, slightly bored, enjoying the nice summer day. Suddenly there's a pop fly. You look up into the sky, and you see the white baseball moving against the clouds and the sun. You know it's your job to catch it. But how do you know where it is going to land? The answer is, you just *know*. Even people who are terrible at actually making the catch know—they usually manage to get to the general vicinity of where it is going to land. If you close your eyes and imagine the baseball, you can even *feel* what needs to be done in order to catch it. And what you know, in your body, is that adjusting your running speed is part of how you do it. That's why you see baseball players slowing down and speeding up as they move toward the ball.

What they're doing, in fact, is following a very simple heuristic. The mathematical calculations involved in figuring out where a flying baseball is going to land are much too difficult for us to carry out in real time. What we use, instead, is a simple little shortcut, which Gigerenzer calls the *gaze heuristic*. The rule is something like this: "Adjust your running speed so that your angle of gaze to the baseball remains constant."[23] If you follow this rule with a descending ball, you will initially start out running slowly, then gradually speed up until, as if by magic, you arrive at the ball just as it comes level with your head. (The rule for positioning yourself with respect to an ascending ball is slightly different, but just as simple.) If you override this heuristic by fixing your running speed—the way the coach wanted his players to do—the trick no longer works, and so you're likely to wind up nowhere near the ball at all.

The coach here exemplified—on a very small scale—the hubris of modern rationalism. He took a form of behavior that he didn't really understand, examined it superficially, noticed a few details that didn't make sense to him, and said, "Okay, stop what you're doing, it makes no sense, I have a new system that will be much better." He ignored the fact that baseball players have been doing things this way forever; he simply assumed that he knew better, and that there was nothing to be learned from intuition or from the accumulated wisdom of ages. He then presented his own, "more rational" solution. Yet the mere fact that something can be done does not mean that it can be done rationally. The coach put into place a system that completely failed, that was far worse that what it replaced. In his quest to improve things, he wound up breaking them.

This is a script that has been replayed countless times, often with far more serious consequences. The literature on development aid, for instance, contains literally thousands of stories of Westerners showing up and messing things up: replacing inefficient local irrigation schemes with large-scale projects that don't work at all; pressuring farmers to switch their seed, only to find that the new crops won't grow; bringing in complex equipment that breaks down and can't be repaired; clearing vast areas of forest, only to provoke large-scale soil erosion. Here is an example, taken almost at random from the literature:

> In Malawi's Shire Valley from 1940 to 1960 British officials
> tried to teach the peasants how to farm. They offered the
> standard solution of ridging to combat soil erosion, and were
> at a loss to understand how Malawian farmers resisted the

tried-and-true technique of British farmers. Unfortunately, ridging in the sandy soils of the Shire Valley led to more erosion during the rainy season, while exposing the roots of the plants to attacks by white ants during the dry season.[24]

There is an interesting parallel between these two examples. The first—catching the baseball—involves overestimating the power of reason by underestimating the effectiveness of nonrational cognitive systems. The second—choice of farming techniques—involves overestimating of the power of reason by underestimating the power of evolutionary processes in society. If farmers in Malawi are not able to offer a sophisticated explanation for the soil management practices that they use, there is a temptation to regard these practices as irrational, unjustified, "merely traditional." And yet people have been farming in the Shire Valley for thousands of years. Chances are their soil management practices are reasonably well adapted to the local environment. Furthermore, the chance that a total stranger is going to be able to walk into this complex ecology and figure out from first principles how things should best be organized is quite remote. And yet time and again, this is precisely what rationalists have done.

Modern conservatism was born as a reaction against this sort of Enlightenment hubris. It is well summarized in G. W. F. Hegel's powerful yet opaque pronouncement that "the real is rational." What Hegel meant was that if you look hard enough, you will find that there is usually a reason for the way that things are, even when the way that things are seems to make no sense. People may not be able to *say* what this reason is, and in the end it may not be the best reason, but you need to understand what it is before you start fiddling with things, much less breaking them down and trying to rebuild them. Thus the conservative temperament was born, as a defense of tradition against the tendency of Enlightenment rationalism to take things apart without knowing how to put them back together again, much less improve them.

In this respect, the core of the conservative critique was absolutely correct. The question is, once we acknowledge this, is the only alternative to fall back into an uncritical acceptance of tradition? Or is it possible to use this insight as the basis for a more successful form of progressive politics?

3. The nuts and bolts of civilization

Where conservatism gets it right

Many things that appear to be the product of intelligent design are actually the product of evolution. This is true not just in the realm of biology, but in human culture as well. For instance, no one just sits down and designs an airplane—or at least, not one that flies. Every airplane in the sky today is a descendant of the first successful airplane, fashioned by the Wright brothers in 1903. The process through which these primitive airplanes evolved into modern ones bears a remarkable resemblance to biological evolution.[1] First, there is variation: throughout the nineteenth and early twentieth centuries, literally hundreds of different "flying machines" were created: gliders, kites, dirigibles, ornithopters, and fixed-wing craft. Eventually, someone hit upon a solution to the key problem—which was not actually getting the machine into the air, but rather controlling it once it was up there.

Second, there is inheritance and differential reproductive success (in this case through imitation). After the first successful airplane design was established, a process of piecemeal refinement began. Other inventors copied the basic three-axis control system and wing plan used by the Wright brothers but then made small changes of their own (substituting, for instance, ailerons for wing warping as a way of controlling roll). From that day forward, anyone planning to design an airplane, rather than starting

84

from scratch, began with an existing design that worked, then made changes. A clear pattern of "descent with modification" was established.

Of course, the key difference between cultural and biological evolution is that change in the biological sphere is blind; it comes about by accident. This is sometimes the case in the domain of culture, but more often modifications that arise in culture occur because people are developing intelligent solutions to outstanding problems. Thus cultural evolution is *guided* in a way that biological evolution is not.[2] What makes the process similar to biological evolution is that despite each specific modification being the product of individual intelligence, these modifications eventually accumulate to the point where the artifact as a whole could never have been a product of individual intelligence. It doesn't matter how smart your engineers are—no one can sit down and design an Airbus A380 from scratch. And yet people do design Airbus A380s. They are able to do so precisely because they do not have to design them from scratch but are able to build upon the work done by previous generations.

Now if you can't design an aircraft from scratch, why would anyone think you could design a *society* from scratch? People are considerably more complicated and less predictable than mechanical parts. And yet these were precisely the pretensions of social contract theory. Idealists and visionaries were encouraged to imagine themselves in a state of nature, with no settled institutions, and then ask themselves what they would rationally agree to accept by way of constraints on their freedom. What sort of economy would they choose? What form of government? What sort of judicial system? Why not reorganize the family as well? Enlightened critics of society spent their time sketching rational utopias without, however, taking seriously the question of whether people could ever be persuaded to live in this way.

¶

In his justly famous critique of the French Revolution, Edmund Burke argued this sort of social engineering is doomed to fail. Successful institutions are built piecemeal, over time. "The work itself," he argued, "requires the aid of more minds than one age can furnish."[3] The model that Burke had in mind was, of course, the English system of government, which, rather than having been created from scratch through the adoption of a written constitution (in the Enlightenment style), was the result of parliamentary conventions, royal prerogatives, and judicial rulings, as well as laws and treaties, adopted and modified over the course of centuries. While offering exemplary stability, the British system is not obviously inferior to any of the constitutions produced through intentional design. Indeed, it remains the most widely copied system of democratic governance in the world (far more so than the American, which no one has ever seen fit to copy, and which Americans themselves do not even try to reproduce after having brought about "regime change" in other countries).

When one looks at a democratic political system, it is easy to see that it has an incredible number of moving parts. Creating a democracy involves much more than just letting people vote for their leaders. Successful democracies are also characterized by the rule of the law, the separation of powers, judicial protection of individual rights and liberties, competitive political parties, freedom of assembly and debate, an independent and free press, and a variety of deliberative and consultative processes (hearings, royal commissions, committee inquiries, etc.), not to mention a set of practices that are widespread but not universal, such as bicameral legislative bodies and constitutional review of legislation. Furthermore, the way that these parts are put together is different in every single country, largely in response to differences in national culture, institutions, and informal social norms.

This is why it is so difficult, especially for outsiders, to create democracies in previously nondemocratic countries. Not only are there a lot of moving parts, and not only do the parts function differently in different cultural contexts, but we don't even have a satisfactory theory of what makes the parts work together properly in our own society. Indeed, if one looks up "democratic theory" to see what political scientists have to say about democracy, one will find that the field is sharply divided into three separate camps, each wedded to a different theory of what makes a democratic society democratic.[4] So "reason" is not much use when it comes to bottom-up design. If our own political institutions were somehow to disappear overnight, along with our precise memory of how they were organized, we wouldn't know how to rebuild them from first principles. Is it any wonder then that we have such difficulty exporting the model to other countries? (Indeed, it takes a special sort of nerve for Westerners to lecture other nations about the virtues of democracy when our own experts can't even agree about what institutions and practices are essential to democratic governance.)

What Burke was reacting against, in the French Revolution specifically and in Enlightenment thinking generally, was the massive downgrading of tradition. The mere fact that people can't "give reasons" for a particular arrangement doesn't mean there *are* no reasons. In many cases, the way that things are is the product of many small adjustments that have been made over the years. Thus there may be an enormous amount of accumulated wisdom embedded in traditions and institutions, even if no one is able to articulate exactly what that wisdom is. If we insist on rebuilding everything from scratch with each new generation, then it is impossible to engage in any sort of cumulative learning process, whereby each new generation makes a slight improvement to what it has received then hands it down to the next.

Consider Thomas Jefferson's proposal, made in 1789, that all laws—up to and including the United States Constitution—should automatically expire after thirty-four years. His reasoning was a classic piece of Enlightenment rationalism. "No society can make a perpetual constitution, or even a perpetual law," he wrote. "Every constitution, then, and every law, naturally expires at the end of thirty-four years. If it be enforced longer, it is an act of force, and not of right . . . This principle, that the earth belongs to the living and not to the dead, is of very extensive application and consequences in every country, and most especially in France."[5]

The consequences of implementing such a proposal would be catastrophic, precisely because it seeks to eliminate the mechanism that allows for evolutionary change within our institutions. Imagine every generation having to refight every battle that was ever fought over legislation, not just about abortion, the death penalty, social insurance, and civil rights, but even over habeas corpus, private property, and freedom of conscience. There are many, many issues that we rightly regard as settled but that could easily fail to pass a free vote if they were put forward today as proposals. The recent normalization of torture in American political culture, along with the development of a significant pro-torture faction within the Republican Party, provides an instructive lesson in this regard.

Although many conservatives defend their local traditions merely out of a fondness for the content of those traditions, Burke's argument has an entirely different structure. In Burke's view, a general presumption in favor of the status quo is important because, when combined with a willingness to tinker and adjust, it makes processes of *cumulative* improvement possible. If everyone insists on reinventing everything, we'll never get anywhere, simply because no one is smart enough to understand all the variables and grasp all of the reasons that things are done exactly the way they are. Instead of trying to change everything at once, it's better to take things more or less as given, change *one* thing, then wait and see what happens. This is, of course, not really a full-blooded defense of tradition. It is more a species of neotraditionalism.[6] It is a *rational* argument in favor of deferring to tradition. As such, it does not claim that tradition is always right or that we should honor and obey our parents and elders in all matters. It says that in specific instances, reason is likely to do a bad job at figuring things out, so we may be better off relying on evolutionary processes.

When is reason likely to be bad? One area in which it is certain to be weak is in dealing with very complex systems, where it is difficult to trace causal connections, or when there is a long delay between intervention and outcome.[7] Consider, for example, the task of raising children. Anyone who starts out reading parenting books, in order to see what the "experts" have to say, will quickly discover that the experts completely disagree with one another about pretty much everything. Even something relatively simple, like how to deal with picky eaters, is subject to completely contradictory advice. Some say you should never force children to eat anything, or they will be traumatized and suffer for the rest of their lives. Others say that many foods are acquired tastes, so you should force your children to eat. But how many times, before you give up? Some say three, others say five, others say dozens. And should you bribe them with dessert? Some say yes, others say no.

We're not talking about a complicated question here, like how to get them into Yale. We're just talking about how to get them to eat vegetables. The reason the advice is so contradictory, however, is that questions involving nutrition are complicated—often too complicated to admit of controlled experimentation. Furthermore, the feedback loop is extended in time, making it difficult to track the consequences of different policies. And finally, kids are different, so some are likely to respond in different ways than others. Basically, given the constraints of resources and time, it's impossible to figure out. How then do most people handle the problem? By doing whatever their parents did.

This is why most people are conservatives when it comes to raising their children (and perhaps why raising children turns many people into conservatives). Most of the big experiments of the twentieth century in "alternative" childrearing and "alternative" education were either ridiculous failures or else made little difference to the way children grew up. As a result, most people today practice descent with modification. They take the way that they were raised by their own parents, modify it slightly to eliminate the parts they most disliked or that they think were most counterproductive, and then go with that. There is considerable wisdom in this approach, simply because "reason" is unlikely to do better than tradition in this area.

¶

Children talk to themselves a lot. If you listen carefully to what they're saying, it's actually quite interesting. Not so much in terms of the content, but in terms of what they are trying to accomplish. This is because a significant fraction of the talk—in some circumstances more than half—is aimed at controlling their own actions. Furthermore, the talk is not just about how best to get things done (for example, a child doing a puzzle, saying, "Does this piece fit? Maybe turn it . . ."). A lot of it is aimed at achieving self-control (for example, a child repeating to himself "Don't cry, don't cry" when he is upset). Children talk to themselves when, as psychologist Laura Berk put it, they need "to take charge of their own behavior."[8]

We have already seen how the internalization of this capacity leads to the development of rational self-control. Unfortunately, like everything else about human reason, the implementation leaves much to be desired. As we all know, just making up your mind to do something doesn't automatically lead to getting it done. Our ability to control our own behavior is far from perfect. Of course, the fact that we have any control at all is something to be thankful for. One of Jane Goodall's fabulous observations was of a chimpanzee who, having discovered a cache of uneaten bananas, clamped his hand over his own mouth in an attempt to suppress his own cries of excitement.[9] He wanted to avoid attracting the attention of others to his discovery, but unlike humans, chimpanzees don't have the cortical brain structures required to suppress these vocalizations internally.[10] So he opted for the kluge of holding his own mouth shut.

If you look at how human self-control works, a lot of what we do is not all that more sophisticated. The ideal, of course, is of the individual able to exercise complete control of his actions through internal willpower—the monk or the buddha, the individual who has overcome all of his more primitive desires and impulses and is able to carry though any plan that he adopts without resistance. For this paragon of self-control, "thinking makes it so" in the practical realm. Most of us, however, rely on an enormous amount of environmental scaffolding in order to get things done. In the same way as we build designer environments that enhance the computational abilities of our biological brains, we also build environments that allow us to exercise rational control over the behavioral impulses of our biological brains.[11]

The "old mind," as we have seen, lives in the present. It acts on the basis of what are called *occurrent psychological states*—things that you are feeling *right now*. One of the central functions of rational thought is that it allows us to formulate and pursue long-term goals. In order to do so, however, we must constantly inhibit and override automatic behavioral impulses arising from these occurrent psychological states.[12] In other words, we must resist temptation. Yet our ability to resist temptation through brute force—simply saying "no" to ourselves—is very limited.[13] Most of us rely instead upon an extensive bundle of tricks, which we use to get ourselves to do things that we ourselves know to be best.

For instance, one way of defeating temptation is to recognize that it is extremely time-sensitive. A lot of tempting things are tempting only when they are right at hand. A snack is very tempting when you only need to reach into your desk drawer to get it, not so much if you have to run out to the store. Checking your email is very tempting, but not if you have to turn on your computer and wait a couple minutes while it boots up. Because of this, we can often arrange things in advance—at a time when we are not having any self-control issues—so that certain things will be less tempting. For instance, if you exercise control over what you buy when you are in the grocery store or the liquor store, you don't need to exercise as much self-control when you are back home. This is true even with highly addictive behaviors, such as smoking. Many pack-a-day smokers will smoke a pack of cigarettes a day regardless of whether the pack contains twenty or twenty-five cigarettes.[14] (One proposed strategy for reducing the damage done by smoking is to reduce the number of cigarettes in a pack.) Part of this is no doubt psychological, but part of it must also have to do with the fact that many smokers buy their cigarettes one pack at a time, and so starting up a new pack requires a trip to the store.

If you take a look at any of the designer environments people create for themselves, you can see that they contain a huge amount of both cognitive and motivational scaffolding. With respect to motivation, the objective is to make certain kinds of activities either easier or harder at certain times.[15] Many writers, for example, prefer to work on an old computer, one that is extremely slow. Because word processing is so undemanding, almost any computer will be able to carry out work-related tasks at a reasonable speed. Try surfing the internet, however, and the whole system will slow to a crawl. This delay is just long enough to eliminate the lure of instant gratification that the internet usually presents.

Naturally, if we were creatures of pure reason, none of this would be necessary. Because we are not, we rely heavily upon systems, both environmental and social, in order to keep ourselves on task.

❡

Perhaps the most fundamental insight that reason has to offer—the one that really allows us to rise up out of the muck and slime of our evolutionary prehistory—is that we have a powerful interest in cooperating with one another. There are many circumstances in which *everyone* can be made better off by having everyone exercise some restraint in the pursuit of their individual interests. Cooperation, therefore, involves setting aside one's self-interest in order to do one's part in promoting the collective interest.

Consider, for example, the practice of lining up to escape from a burning building.[16] Initially, this may seem odd. After all, if the building is actually burning down, what is the point of the queue? It seems like an excessive preoccupation with orderliness to expect people to line up under such circumstances. The reason for it, however, becomes clear when one looks at what happens when people do *not* line up, as often happens with fires in nightclubs. When everyone rushes the exit, the doorway can become blocked, people are trampled, and typically *fewer* people wind up escaping from the building alive than would be the case if an orderly queue had been maintained. And so it makes sense to accept a compromise. Rather than taking a gamble between the best outcome (pushing your way to the front) and the worst outcome (getting trampled by someone else), everyone accepts a second-best outcome (waiting patiently in line), on the grounds that it offers a better expected outcome. This is what we call *cooperation*. By not pushing other people, you diminish your own personal chances of getting out alive, but you also increase everyone else's chances of getting out. When everyone does the same, the overall outcome is better for everyone, including you.

People figured out a long time ago that most of "justice" and "morality" has exactly the same structure.[17] There are many circumstances in which it is in our interest (narrowly defined) to assault, murder, slander, lie, fornicate, shirk, cheat, and steal. Nevertheless, we are all more or less better off if everyone more or less refrains from doing these things. While each of us gives up the advantages that can come from acting in this way, what we get in return is the reasonable assurance of not being at the receiving end of such behavior. Of all the pragmatic arguments in defense of justice, this is easily the oldest on the books, having been articulated with exemplary clarity by Plato in *The Republic*.[18]

Despite this insight, however, motivating ourselves to act cooperatively can be an extraordinarily difficult task. Even though we know that we're all better off if everyone follows the rules, the free-rider incentive is always there, dangling in front of our noses, creating a constant temptation to defect. Enlightenment rationalism suggests that as soon as people see the superior benefits that come from cooperation, they will just naturally fall into line. A lot of anarchist schemes, in particular, are based on the assumption that if everyone can see that something is in everyone's interest, then people will be naturally inclined to do what it takes to make it happen. In reality, getting people to do their part in a cooperative scheme can be very difficult.

And yet, given the incentives that exist to act uncooperatively, it is interesting to observe that instances of straight-up antisocial behavior are less common than one might expect. How often do you see someone just ignore a queue and push their way to the front (and not because they're from a culture where "single pile" is the norm, but because they genuinely don't care what other people think)? Even incarcerated criminals who have engaged in flagrant violations of the rules seldom admit to having done so out of naked self-interest. Indeed, the way self-interest undermines cooperation is typically not by overpowering it directly, but rather by biasing people's beliefs so that they adopt self-serving justifications for their crimes.[19] One famous study showed that convicted embezzlers often defended their actions on the grounds that they had merely "borrowed" the money, with every intention of paying it back; or that they had acted out of higher loyalties, to their family for instance; or that they were punishing the firm for its corruption, stealing money that was itself stolen; or that their actions produced no harm, since the amount was too small for anyone even to notice; and so on.[20] These are not just rationalizations: it is by adopting such views prior to committing the act that the criminal convinces himself that he is still a decent, perhaps even good, person, and therefore that it is permissible for him (it's usually a him) to break the rules.

The second tendency that works to undermine cooperation is the fact that people retaliate against one another. Whenever you get a reasonable-sized group together in any cooperative project, there will always be a few who refuse to play along (often because of the availability of the rationalization that because the group is so large, it doesn't matter if they defect). But then seeing a few people defect, others get upset and say, "I'm not going to play along if she doesn't." If the interaction is repeated, this will tend to erode cooperation over time (contrary to the expectation of standard economic theory, which says that repeated interaction should make it easier for people to cooperate, often it has the opposite effect, by setting off self-reinforcing cascades of mutual recrimination and punishment).[21]

The problem is that our intuitive responses are all geared toward supporting limited cooperation in the context of small-scale societies—such as were found in the environment of evolutionary adaptation. We have a set of "tribal social instincts" that make us naturally inclined to cooperate with family and friends but, beyond that, tend to serve as more of a hindrance than an aid.[22] For example, the retaliatory impulse, which is particularly well developed in humans, is highly effective at discouraging free-riders in small-scale communities, where everyone knows everyone else's name and can keep track of who is doing what. The love of gossip is often thought to serve a similar function. And yet in large-scale, anonymous interactions, these two proclivities start to have the opposite effect. As the number of cooperators increases, the chances that someone will defect, even if only by accident, increases proportionately. Under these circumstances, an over-weened retaliatory impulse is simply incompatible with the requirements of ongoing cooperation. It is more likely to generate unending cycles of tit-for-tat retaliation, like a blood feud, than it is to promote cooperation. Furthermore, gossip can greatly amplify the impact of bad behavior, making it seem as though defection is more common or more problematic than it actually is. Thus forms of behavior that are quite effective at promoting cooperation in small groups can make it all but impossible to achieve the same effect in large groups.[23]

So what do we do? We use kluges. We trick ourselves into cooperating with one another by exploiting *other* cognitive biases, turning them against one another. For example, we all suffer from a powerful in-group bias when it comes to cooperation. We don't mind sticking our necks out a bit for other people, as long as we feel that the beneficiary is "one of us." And if helping one of us requires harming "one of them," then so much the better.

Luckily for us, the way that we identify the other person as one of us can easily be manipulated. The in-group bias remains very powerful, even when we know that the distinction between "us" and "them" has been drawn arbitrarily. In one particularly famous experiment, Henri Tajfel and his colleagues started by showing subjects a series of paintings by Paul Klee and Wassily Kandinsky, then divided them up into two groups, depending on which painter they preferred. Subjects were then instructed to play a game, in which they could choose to act cooperatively or selfishly with any of the other players. The game was designed so that everyone would be better off if everyone acted cooperatively but each individual had a free-rider incentive to act selfishly while still receiving the benefits of the cooperative acts of others. Thus everyone had an incentive to act selfishly, but if everyone did that, everyone would wind up worse off. What Tajfel found was a strong tendency for subjects to act more cooperatively than usual toward members of their own group (e.g., the Klee-lovers) but less cooperatively than usual toward members of the other group (the Kandinsky-lovers), even though the game itself had absolutely nothing to do with art and art preferences. People took the arbitrary division of the population into groups and used it as a basis for heightened solidarity within the group, combined with heightened antagonism toward those who were not members.

This result should come as no surprise, since we have been using the same trick for thousands of years to increase the level of social solidarity within institutions. Having a common enemy makes people more likely to cooperate with one another. This disposition is sufficiently well established and manipulable that we often try to invent an enemy, or create an artificial one, in order to get people to act more cooperatively within large "impersonal" organizations. A simple strategy, used in bureaucratic institutions everywhere, is to divide people up into teams or work groups and then pit them against one another. One can see this strategy in the popular "house" system used in secondary schools, as well as "colleges" in universities. (These institutional arrangements are direct descendants of the system of *curia* and *collegium* established in ancient Rome, used to bring greater cohesion to the republic and, later, the empire.) It responds to a fairly simple organizational challenge. Primary schools in North America and Europe are typically rather small, so that students within a cohort all know each other by name. This means that basic "tribal" instincts are enough to maintain a reasonable level of social cohesion. Secondary schools, on the other hand, are often several times larger, easily exceeding the size of the largest ancestral village. As a result, informal mechanisms of social control begin to fail. Interactions become a lot more anonymous—for example, teachers will often not know the names of most students in the hall. This creates the potential for both alienation (students may have difficulty "fitting in") and antisocial behavior (vandalism, theft, etc.).

The most popular solution to all this has been permanently etched into popular consciousness by the Harry Potter books ("Ten points for Gryffindor!"). You take the students and arbitrarily divide them up into groups and give them a complete set of tribal markers, including a catchy name, a special color, a homeroom, and maybe even a crest. You then stage a set of completely artificial competitions between the groups (for example, instituting a weird "point" system that doesn't seem to generate any tangible reward). This promotes a huge amount of antisocial behavior *between* the groups but greatly enhances social solidarity *within* each group. The trick then is to set things up so that the uncooperative behavior is confined to largely symbolic activities that have no real-world significance (for example, quidditch matches) while the cooperative, pro-social behavior that occurs within the groups helps individuals to achieve genuinely significant goals (for example, studying and understanding course material, or defeating the dark lord).

This is a classic kluge. We can't fix the underlying problem, which is that individuals in large groups become alienated and so start to act less cooperatively (they become less likely to volunteer for jobs that need to be done, they are more likely to steal or vandalize public resources, they form fewer close ties with fellow group members, and so on). If people were perfectly rational, their willingness to cooperate would be determined entirely by the benefits of cooperation; the number of other people in the cooperative scheme would not matter. Motivationally, however, this is difficult, and so reason must resort to subterfuge in order to get its way. We therefore promote cooperation by creating artificial groups then using the "red versus blue" mentality this creates to promote greater solidarity. In many cases we don't even do this intentionally—the practices have simply arisen through a process of cultural evolution. As Peter Richerson and Robert Boyd put it, "social innovations that make larger-scale society possible, but at the same time effectively simulate life in a tribal-scale society, will tend to spread."[24] The division of the population into small "parishes," for example, was essential to the stability of European societies before the rise of the modern state.[25]

This phenomenon is also well known to those who study the military—which faces a particularly acute motivational challenge, since it must create a social environment in which soldiers are willing to follow orders that will foreseeably result in their own death. This is why the platoon, or squad, is the focus of the most intense social bonding. As the sociologist Edward Shils observed, soldiers care surprisingly little about "the total symbols of the military organization as a whole, of the state, or of the political cause in the name of which the war is fought." What they care about is their immediate comrades. "The soldier's motivation to fight is not derived from his perceiving and striving toward any strategic or political goals; it is a function of his need to protect his primary group and to conform to its expectations. The military machine thus obtains its inner cohesion . . . through a system of overlapping primary groups."[26]

Thus the military strives to create a real community—a "primary group"—that can serve as an object of intense loyalty and identification. On top of that, it adds several layers of what Benedict Anderson called "imagined communities."[27] So the organization of soldiers into small groups is accompanied by a hierarchy of larger units, such as divisions, up until the different services—army, navy, air force—that constitute the military as a whole. The objective is to promote interservice rivalry in largely symbolic areas, as a way of generating intraservice cohesion in areas where cooperation is most important, such as on the battlefield.

An even more dramatic example can be found in the division of the entire world's population into separate nations (again, with tribal markers: a flag, a national anthem, military parades, etc.). This creates the illusion that we are all members of a club, or members of the same tribe, even when we're not. No one has ever succeeded in constructing a modern nation-state without cultivating precisely this sort of collective illusion among its people. And it had not been for want of trying. Rationalist political movements have always been contemptuous of nationalism, precisely because it motivates people through an appeal to irrational biases. Communists, in particular, believed that the international solidarity of working people would overcome the forces of "bourgeois nationalism"—hence the long-standing persistence of the "socialist international" (a sentiment immortalized in the lyrics of "The Internationale": "Reason thunders in its volcano / This is the eruption of the end / Of the past let us make a clean slate"). And yet, when push came to shove, not one communist nation was able to forgo the collective benefits of nationalism. This became particularly evident at times when the need for collective action was greatest. (This is why the Second World War is still known, in the former Soviet Union, as the "Great Patriotic War," and why "The Internationale" became its de facto national anthem.) Liberal democratic societies are no different; they are all highly nationalistic. This is not surprising, since democracy also makes significant demands on citizens, in terms of the level of cooperativeness it requires (voting, accepting defeat when your party doesn't win, paying taxes, refraining from political violence, etc.). So it is not surprising that there are a lot of tricks underlying the practice of democracy, tricks designed to get people to behave themselves.

The Nazi philosopher Carl Schmitt exposed the dirty secret on nationalism, in 1927, when he argued that the central function of the modern state was to divide the world into "friend" and "enemy."[28] Warfare was central to the mission of the state, he argued, because it constituted the mechanism through which this distinction was preserved. The risk, of course, with this sort of thinking is that things may get out of hand, and that the negative consequences of intergroup rivalry will start to undermine the positive benefits of intragroup solidarity. The First World War provided a set of instructive lessons about how nationalism can generate war even when there is nothing in particular to fight about. The Second World War provided a more dramatic lesson, showing how destructive war could become when engaged in by modern nation-states able to mobilize their entire populations. Most people now agree that it is better to see these energies channeled into competition in the Olympic games or the World Cup of soccer.

Unfortunately, because of the success of these kluges, we sometimes tend to overestimate our own abilities. When it comes to large-scale cooperation, we humans have clearly exceeded our programming. We have become what biologists call an *ultrasocial species,* despite having a set of social instincts that are essentially tailored for managing life in a small-scale tribal society. It's crucial to recognize, however, that we have not accomplished this by reprogramming ourselves or overcoming our innate design limitations. We have accomplished this in large measure by tricking ourselves into feeling as though we are still living in small-scale tribal societies, even when we are not. Unfortunately, the trick works so well that we sometimes forget that we're using it, and so imagine that we can create large-scale systems of cooperation based on nothing more than our rational insight into the need for such institutions. This invariably leads to disappointment.

Consider, for instance, the problem of global warming. This is a very straightforward collective action problem. If everyone continues to burn fossil fuel, then the increase in global temperature will produce outcomes that are much worse for everyone. And so we all have an incentive to limit emissions. Yet the incentive to cheat on any such agreement is enormous. Hence the need for cooperation on a global scale. Unfortunately, there are almost no instances in recorded history of humanity as a whole agreeing to cooperate to solve a problem and then carrying through on that intention. The only mechanism that we have to solve big problems like this is the nation-state, but one of the major devices that states use to motivate their citizens to cooperate is rivalry with other nations. This makes genuine global cooperation very difficult to achieve (particularly when the issue is one where the public at large will be noticeably affected, and so the cooperative scheme cannot be implemented through elite consensus alone). There are, simply put, no assurances that we are capable of cooperating with one another to resolve problems of this scale. Instead, the free-rider incentive will bias cognition, leading large segments of the population simply to deny that there is a problem. And individuals will get locked into retaliation, refusing to do anything until others have made amends or done their fair share. All of these forces conspire with one another in such a way as to guarantee that nothing will be done to correct the problem.

It is a standard trope of science fiction that human history will continue on through a series of bloody and destructive wars until first contact with an alien species is made. It is then, and only then, that planetary unity will be achieved, a world government will be formed, and humanity will takes its place in the stars among the "advanced" races in an interplanetary civilization. There is an insight here that it so commonplace, its significance is in danger of being overlooked. Human beings are able to work together best when they have an enemy to fight against. Until we have a common enemy, or at least an "other," we cannot all be friends. The major advances in human civilization over the past fifty years have probably come from our ability to domesticate this impulse. We have learned to create *symbolic* rivalries, so that we can get the benefits of enhanced solidarity while stopping short—for the most part—of actually killing one another. But we should not kid ourselves about how much we have achieved. Our civilization is built on a kluge, one that works well enough for the moment but that might easily fail us someday.[29]

§

Perhaps the most disconcerting finding of twentieth-century social science was that most of what we like to think of as "morality" is actually not in our heads, but depends upon environmental scaffolding as well. This comes as a surprise to many people, particularly those who are inclined to think of "conscience" or some other type of "inner voice" as the wellspring of morality. In fact, when it comes to acting morally, we rely to an inordinate extent upon social cues—in particular, the behavior, expectations, and sanctions of others—in order to decide what to do. This is easy to prove; all you have to do is put people in a situation that generates the wrong cues, then wait and see what they do. What was discovered, in a series of now classic social psychology experiments, is that the average person is capable of perpetrating great evil under such circumstances.

Historically, there was a tendency to think that criminals and sinners were somehow "degenerate," that there was some sort of physiological or psychological difference between them and the average person. With the development of the social sciences in the late nineteenth century, in particular with the rise of psychology, some doubts about this hypothesis began to arise. Many criminals are moderately more impulsive than the average person, but beyond that there is very little to distinguish the psychological profile of a typical prisoner from a member of the general population (of comparable age, gender, and social status).[30] Thus early criminologists found themselves having great difficulty pinning down any one trait or combination of traits that could plausibly be thought to be responsible for criminal conduct.

The real crisis of confidence, though, arose as the scale of Nazi crimes during the Second World War became widely known. What many researchers found so extraordinary was the level of complicity of large segments of the population—including, but not limited to, members of the military—in policies that one would think anyone in their right mind could immediately see to be evil. If one looks at soldiers assigned to work in death camps, for instance, it is surprising to learn that very few suffered any disciplinary action for refusing to perform their duties.[31] It is even more surprising to discover how few such refusals needed to be dealt with. The Nazis encountered a very large number of organizational challenges, particularly in the later years of the war, but apparently convincing large numbers of soldiers to spend their entire day systematically murdering defenseless civilians was not one of them.

The circumstances in this case were admittedly extreme. But as the full implications of what had happened during the war began to sink in, psychologists started to wonder whether a similar phenomenon could not be reproduced on a smaller scale. This is what motivated Stanley Milgram's famous experiments on "obedience to authority."[32] Milgram tricked experimental subjects into thinking that they were being asked to deliver an increasingly powerful series of electric shocks to another subject. No threats were involved. When subjects expressed reservations about the experiment—which increasingly they did, as the "victim" screamed louder and louder and began to plead for mercy—they were simply told that "the experiment requires that you continue." Although initially skeptical about people's willingness to comply under these conditions, Milgram discovered, to his surprise, that more than two-thirds of subjects were willing to administer the shocks up into what they believed was the lethal range.

Milgram's experiments were focused on authority relations and the willingness of people to obey orders. But an almost equally famous experiment, carried out by Philip Zimbardo in 1971, the "Stanford Prison Experiment," examined the way that roles and role expectations determine people's behavior.[33] Zimbardo took a group of students and divided them arbitrarily into a group of "prisoners" and "guards," then set them up with appropriate props and cells to create a mock prison. The students, however, took to their roles so completely that within two days a riot had broken out, guards were imposing sadistic punishments, and several "prisoners" had to be removed from the experiment as a result of emotional trauma. By day six, both sanitary and moral conditions had degenerated to the point where the entire experiment had to be called off. (Lest it be thought that experimental subjects were merely play-acting, it should be noted that neither Milgram's nor Zimbardo's experiment can be reproduced in a modern setting, because—ironically—modern research ethics protocols would not permit them. This is because many of the participants became extremely distraught after the experiment had ended, thinking back about the way that they had behaved. They were, in effect, traumatized by the discovery that they could behave so immorally, with so little prompting.)

Less dramatic experiments have consistently confirmed the finding that people rely, to an inordinate degree, on their social surroundings as a way of patterning their behavior, so it takes only modest encouragement to get them to behave immorally. Student cheating is one area that has been particularly well studied, simply because psychologists have such easy access to large populations of undergraduate students.[34] What researchers have found is that large majorities of students can be induced to cheat, or to refrain from cheating, through very small environmental adjustments. If the professor seems unconcerned about cheating, students will be more likely to cheat; if students think that other students are cheating, then they will be more likely to cheat; and so on. What the students are responding to in these cases is not just opportunity, but also perceived social signaling. While personality differences have been studied extensively and have been shown to have some impact on the decision to cheat, situational factors—most importantly, perceptions of "peer behavior"—have been shown to be far more important.[35]

Although the great thinkers of the Enlightenment disagreed profoundly about the nature of morality—some thought that it was a product of reason, others that it was based on emotion—they all agreed that it was to be found somewhere inside the head of the individual. Thus they thought that the violence in human history was a product of ignorance, prejudice, and tradition. Get rid of tradition, they thought, let people decide for themselves how to act, and all will be well. What they discovered, to their dismay, is that tearing down social institutions, or even changing them too quickly, can create a sort of moral disorientation, wherein people really do lose their sense of what is right and wrong. This usually ends badly. Sometimes society dissolves into a state of alienation, selfishness, and criminality. More often, people gravitate toward charismatic authority—someone who promises a new set of rules, better than the ones that came before. Whether these rules are in fact better is a crapshoot. When they are not better (think Robespierre, Stalin, Mao), the consequences can be catastrophic, because the mechanism that adjusts individual behavior to social expectations can create systems of highly organized immorality (such as the bureaucratized mass killing that became such a characteristic feature of the twentieth century).

This is why, despite what Christopher Hitchens and others have claimed,[36] if you had to choose between reason and faith based purely on body count, it's not obvious that reason would come out ahead. There is no question that the most murderous regimes in the twentieth century were either explicitly atheistic (the Soviet Union under Stalin, China under Mao) or difficult to classify (Germany under Hitler). This is a bit of an unfair comparison, though, simply because people with completely unscientific beliefs tend not to be very good at building weapons—precisely for that reason—and so aren't able to kill each other quite as effectively. Christians and Muslims spent several centuries doing all they could to annihilate one another, the only thing that kept them from succeeding was the fact that they had to do it manually, one person at a time.

What we have learned, however, is that when you release people from the yoke of tradition, they don't automatically gravitate toward greater freedom and equality. It's perhaps not so surprising to discover that people use a variety of environmental kluges in order to motivate themselves to act morally. The shocking discovery is that we all rely quite heavily upon our environment in order to *judge* moral questions as well. Even when we have the rational insight that we should act more cooperatively, our willingness to do so depends very heavily upon our expectations about what others will do. If everyone else is taking bribes, then we assume that it is "no big deal" to take a bribe and, furthermore, that it is pointless as an individual to refrain. And if everyone else is torturing prisoners and killing civilians, then we tend also to assume that it is "no big deal" to torture prisoners and kill civilians.

Thus morality is best thought of not as something that lies within our hearts or our heads, but as a complex cultural artifact, that gets reproduced and modified over time, and that "lives" primarily in the interactions between individuals. Strip that away and people really can become quite unhinged.

§

Samuel Johnson once observed of a dog walking on its hind legs that even if it is not done well, "you are surprised to find it done at all." Similarly, the fact that a creature such as ourselves, capable of rational thought, should have evolved through natural selection is a remarkable thing. (After all, if the adaptive advantages were obvious, or if the pathway were direct, then we would expect evolution to have produced dozens of different species with our type of intelligence. Being able to *see* has obvious advantages, which is why the eye is thought to have evolved independently at least ten different times. The advantages of being able to *reason* must be considerably less obvious in order for it to have evolved only once.) The fact that we can reason at all makes us rather extraordinary; that we are able to do it *well* would be expecting far too much.

Thus it is unsurprising to find that our capacity for rational reflection and for rational control of our behavior is underpowered. The "new mind" is cobbled together out of bits of the old.[37] This is why reason has no hope of ever being able to "go it alone"; it simply does not have the computational power or efficiency. The central weaknesses of reason are easily enumerated: it is slow, requires a lot of effort, and suffers from limited attention, a working memory bottleneck, and unreliable long-term memory.[38] Unfortunately, we are easily lulled into *thinking* that reason is much more powerful than it is because we ignore all the environmental scaffolding and kluges that we have constructed over time in order to assist it in its operations. Indeed, if pressed to identify the one most powerful feature of human interaction with the environment, people often mention our ability to use tools, such as hammers and levers. The more powerful phenomenon, which typically goes unnoticed, is the way that we employ elements of our environment to augment our own cognitive powers. Just as the blind man begins to feel the end of his cane as an extension of his fingertip, so we lose track of where our own minds stop and the environment begins. Trivially, we think that we can do mathematics, while forgetting that we are unable to do so without pencil and paper. More significantly, we forget the contribution that thousands of years of human culture and civilization have made to our ability to accomplish almost anything. In particular, we assume that we are able to engage in productive, peaceful cooperation with one another while we ignore how terrible the human track record is in this regard and how much we currently depend upon the institutional arrangements that have been painstakingly built up over time. Even our ability to avoid patently self-destructive behavior is heavily dependent upon the environment that we find ourselves in.

There have always been people of conservative temperament, but conservatism as a political philosophy was born as a reaction against Enlightenment rationalism. In the beginning, it was clearly a defense of *tradition* against reason. This was the correct insight at the heart of Burke's critique of the French Revolution. We have a lot of social arrangements that seem quite arbitrary. Some of these are meaningless relics of the past. Some of them, however, are essential kluges, without which we would be unable to sustain our achieved level of civilization. ("Never tear down a fence," conservatives like to say, "until you know why it was built.") Utopians and rationalists going all the way back to Plato have found institutions like the family, for example, to be a constant source of irritation. The family seems so arbitrary, so inefficient, and often serves as a more powerful object of loyalty than the state. And yet all attempts to "abolish" the family and create some system of collective childrearing have been a disaster. More recently, attempts to abolish nationalism have been equally unsuccessful, even when existing national borders are known to have been drawn in a completely arbitrary way (consider the fate of "pan-Arabism" in the Middle East).

Despite this kernel of truth, however, it is easy to get carried away by the conservative critique. In some respects, tradition may be the accumulation of generations of wisdom, but in other respects it may simply be the accumulation of generations of prejudice.[39] One need only consider traditional attitudes toward women. Furthermore, there is a big difference between drawing attention to the limitations of human reason and glorifying its opposite. Yet what has happened to conservatism in recent years, particularly in its American variants, is that it has become a defense not of tradition against reason, but rather of *intuition* against reason. The origins of this transformation are somewhat complicated, but its consequences are clear. While there is much that is sound in our intuitions, there is also much that is faulty. Reason may not be as powerful or as capacious as the first generation of Enlightenment thinkers supposed, yet there remain many things that only reason can do. Understanding clearly what these are is the only way of advancing the progressive agenda that found its first, flawed expression in the French Revolution.

4. When intuition goes wrong

and why we still need reason

Malcolm Gladwell has done more than anyone to familiarize people with the amazing power of rapid cognition and intuitive judgment. His book *Blink* starts with a series of extraordinary tales in which people perform seemingly superhuman cognitive feats, all in the blink of an eye and without even being able to explain how they are able to do it. We meet Vic Branden, the tennis pro who can tell just by looking when a player is about to double fault; David Sibley, the birder who can identify a rare sandpiper at a glance from over two hundred yards away without ever having seen one in flight; and Bernard Berenson, the art historian who could instantly spot a fake without being able to explain how he did it.[1]

And yet as the book goes on, the discussion begins to shade over, almost imperceptibly, into a treatment of cases where intuition, far from providing us with unusually acute insights, actually goes horribly awry. The most dramatic example that Gladwell presents involves the shooting of Amadou Diallo, in which Brooklyn police officers completely misinterpreted a suspect's movements and wound up firing forty-one shots at him. Strangely, Gladwell seems not to notice the tension that this creates. Because of it, the book as a whole winds up being rather confusing. The take-home message seems to be "Rapid cognition is awesome! Except when it isn't!" But

Gladwell never gets around to asking the crucial question: How do we *know* when it isn't?

For instance, Gladwell makes a great deal out of a study by Nalini Ambady and Robert Rosenthal that shows that undergraduates watching a thirty-second silent video clip of a course instructor in action provided evaluations not all that different from those of students who had been in the course for an entire semester. The researchers concluded that "not only do we possess the remarkable ability to form impressions of others . . . but, perhaps more remarkably, the impressions that we form can be quite accurate!"[2] The wisdom of ages is thereby overturned. It turns out that you *can* judge a book by its cover.

But before one rushes into a wholehearted embrace of rapid cognition, a more thorough review of the psychological literature may be in order. That's because there is also a lot of psychological research showing that the impressions we form can be remarkably *persistent,* even when they are not accurate. For example, in a classic experiment, Jerome Bruner and Mary Potter showed subjects a series of slides, starting with an image that was completely out of focus and then slowly bringing it into focus.[3] Those who were shown the blurriest slides at the beginning took the longest to figure out what the image was. This is because they typically formulated incorrect hypotheses about it and then continued trying to fit the visual evidence to this preconceived idea. Thus Bruner and Potter were able to produce the remarkable spectacle of a person staring at what was, rather obviously, a picture of a fire hydrant—a picture that anyone, upon walking into the room for the first time, would undoubtedly recognize as a fire hydrant—and not being able to tell what it was!

This is a phenomenon called *belief persistence,* and it systematically biases human cognition, often with catastrophic consequences. Many oncologists can tell as soon as a patient walks into their office that the person has cancer. Yet an enormous amount of misdiagnosis also occurs because doctors form an initial hypothesis then cling to it for too long, ignoring the contrary evidence as it accumulates. Indeed, much of the old folk wisdom about first impressions is intended either to stop people from becoming victims of this bias ("Don't judge a book by its cover") or to help them avoid being victimized by this tendency in others ("You never get a second chance to make a first impression"). What the Ambady and Rosenthal study might just as easily have been taken to show is that students seldom get around to revising their initially formed beliefs, even over the course of an entire semester. The novelty of the research lies only in the finding that these first impressions are formulated more quickly and with fewer data points than anyone had ever suspected.

The question is, how are we supposed to tell what we are dealing with? Is rapid cognition amazingly prescient in this case, or is it, rather, the source of a very troublesome cognitive bias?[4] Actually, it doesn't even matter what the answer is. What matters is how we go about determining the answer. That's because *the only way to answer this question is to think about it rationally.* Therein lies the crucial difference between reason and intuition. Both faculties have their limitations and strengths, but reason is able to reflect upon and discern its own limitations, through things like controlled experimentation, whereas intuition is not. We have no intuitive grasp of the limits of our intuitions—on the contrary, the heuristic that we use to judge the reliability of our own intuitions is demonstrably flawed.[5] (Indeed, intuition has been described as "that strange instinct that tells us we are right, whether we are or not."[6]) Furthermore, intuition is incapable of self-correction. It just keeps applying the same bag of tricks, without any awareness of whether they are working or not.

To put this claim into slightly more technical language, the crucial limitation of intuition is that it is incapable of metacognition.[7] It solves problems, but it cannot think about how it goes about solving problems. This is not surprising, since there is considerable evidence to show that language is what makes metacognition possible.[8] This is why reason, as a language-dependent faculty, is capable of discovering its own limitations, and therefore of avoiding problems that it isn't good at solving. It is also why reason is able to rewrite its own script, so that it can stop making mistakes once it figures out what they are.

Of course, this is not to say that reason is great when it comes to discerning its own limitations or correcting its own faults. Indeed, the history of reason has been largely one of overconfidence and overreach. Many of the failings of the first Enlightenment came from a failure to appreciate the limitations of reason, and the conservative backlash epitomized by Edmund Burke served, in this regard, as a useful corrective. Facing up to our own shortcomings will always be a tricky job. The crucial point is that reason, whatever its shortcomings, is the only faculty capable of doing this job *at all*. So even after recognizing its limitations, we are still left with the conclusion that it is better than the alternative.

A lot of what has been written about the unconscious in recent years—from Gladwell to David Brooks—has a slightly reverential tone to it. Brooks gushes over how the unconscious is "200,000 times" more powerful than the conscious mind.[9] The unconscious is seen as a mysterious system of thought with untapped potential. This is perhaps inevitable, simply because the most fundamental feature of the unconscious is that *we don't know how it works*. The reason we don't know how it works is that we have no introspective access to it (which is, of course, precisely why it's called *the unconscious*). As a result, solutions get presented to us out of the blue, as if by magic. But that's precisely the problem. Because we don't understand how the unconscious works, we can't tell if it's working *properly*. And as we have already seen, the unconscious likes to take shortcuts. Almost every solution it offers is the product of a mechanism that was deemed good enough for practical purposes in the environment of evolutionary adaptation. Because we don't know when and where corners have been cut, uncritical acceptance of our intuitions is guaranteed to generate a steady stream of nasty surprises.

This is why reason must, in the end, be supreme—not in the sense that it must decide every question, but in the sense that it must decide how every question is to be decided. Reason must be the ultimate arbiter of when we listen to intuition and when we choose to inhibit or suppress our intuitive responses. No matter how astonishing and impressive the performances of the unconscious may be, and no matter how crippled and biased our meager powers of reasoning may be, the very possibility of progress in human culture and society depends upon the performance of our rational faculties. It is therefore worth reminding ourselves of the many ways in which our happiness depends upon our ability to reason.

§

Brooks talks about the unconscious as though it were a magical organ, or what he calls a "hidden oracle."[10] The unconscious "produces more creative links and unlikely parallels" than the conscious mind, he argues, because it can "take in many more factors."[11] It produces "a different sort of knowledge," that which "is produced over time, by an intelligence that is associational—observing closely, imagining loosely, comparing like to unlike and like to like to find harmonies and rhythms in the unfolding of events."[12] It has bestowed gifts upon us ranging from the creativity of Picasso to the technical wizardry of Silicon Valley. "If there is a divine creativity," writes Brooks, "surely it is active in this inner soulsphere, where brain matter produces emotion, where love rewires the neurons."[13]

This is vulgar romanticism. Relying on our gut feelings and intuitions gave us 200,000 years of hand-to-mouth existence in hunter-gatherer societies, riven by blood feuds, incessant tribal warfare, periodic famine, an average life expectancy of thirty, and polygamous marriage based on what anthropologists now refer to, euphemistically, as "wife capture."[14] If we let the unconscious have its way, that's what we would get all over again. There's a reason that civilization collapses into barbarism, and not the other way around.

It is important never to forget, when thinking about the unconscious, that each of the modules that are employed by System 1 cognition are adaptations, designed to solve specific problems that arose in the ancestral environment. The fact that they are direct adaptations means that, fundamentally, they don't work for *us,* they work for our genes. They were selected because they helped our genes to leave behind more copies of themselves. This is why our unconscious has such an unhealthy interest in sex and violence and why it is so relentlessly nepotistic and parochial. Reason, being an exaptation, is what allows us to achieve the "robot's rebellion" of formulating and pursuing our own goals and projects with some degree of independence from what our genes might like us to achieve.[15]

Recent work in moral psychology has generated an avalanche of books purporting to show that humans are, as one author put it "Born to be Good" (or that we are, as others put it, "The Moral Animal," or "Good Natured").[16] This is all very flattering, but not exactly true. Although human beings do have a number of adaptations that are obviously geared toward enhancing sociability, these adaptations are all, without exception, geared toward enhancing sociability within small-scale *tribal* societies, not large-scale societies with extensive networks of cooperation among genetically unrelated individuals. Humans are more innately altruistic and cooperative than other primates (which is actually not saying much, given how vicious and aggressive most primates are). But we are also powerfully biased in favor of friends and family, and retaliatory toward others. These dispositions facilitate certain forms of cooperation, but they also sharply limit its scope. So while it is true that humans are naturally suited for social life, it is absolutely untrue to think that we are naturally suited for the kind of social life that most of us currently find ourselves enjoying. Biological evolution gave us barbarism. Civilization is built on a set of strategies that have evolved or been designed to overcome the limitations of our tribal social instincts.

One of the characteristics of humans that distinguishes us from other animals is that even prior to the development of advanced technology, we managed to occupy a huge number of ecological niches, mastering different environments and subsisting on completely different diets. Much of this is due to our cognitive sophistication, in particular our ability to learn. It is crucial to understand, however, what sort of cognitive architecture underlies this learning system. The reason that psychologists find the "blank slate" idea, handed down from John Locke, so frustrating is that it dramatically understates the nature of our accomplishment. According to the blank slate view, the human brain starts out as a completely generic learning mechanism, then accumulates experience until it learns how to cope with the world. The reality is quite different. What we have, in fact, is a very rigid mind, like most other mammals—one that is specifically adapted for life in a particular environment, that of a small-scale tribal society on the temperate African savanna. We escaped from this by developing a more flexible language-based reasoning system, layered over top of our learning mechanism—a system that is only partially independent but that is capable of *inhibiting* these preprogrammed responses and substituting intentionally planned, learned behaviors. In other words, we acquired the ability—with varying degrees of success—to veto the proposals coming from our "old mind" and to suppress many of the behavioral impulses it generates, so that we can adjust to new environments without having to evolve a whole new set of dispositions.

This is why reasoning is such a tricky and demanding business. As Jonathan Evans puts it, "heuristic and analytic processes often seem to *compete* for control of our behavior."[17] More dramatically, psychologist Keith Stanovich has described us as having "a brain at war with itself."[18] If we were actually born as blank slates and learned everything from the ground up, then our dispositions, intuitions, and instincts would be perfectly aligned with the requirements of both our social and physical environments. We would not experience mental conflict. We would not be bombarded with bad ideas coming from the unconscious, and we would not be having to constantly veto our initial impulses. Unfortunately, that's not how things are. Instead, we must learn to bite our tongues, sit on our hands, count our calories, control our tempers, set aside our prejudices, keep an open mind (and a civil tongue), forgive and forget, think of the children, wait our turn, look at it from the other person's perspective, take cold showers, and perform thousands of other little acts of inhibition and self-control that make up the daily life of a civilized human being.

When exercising this sort of vigilance, what we need to be on the lookout for in particular are cognitive "misfires." These occur when heuristic responses that *usually* produce the right answer fail to produce the right answer, because the situation is somehow atypical, or different from the environment of evolutionary adaptation. Because many of the heuristics that we use involve rather clever tricks, it is easy to forget how dumb these sorts of behavioral systems can be. The same goes for animals—they often seem to behave intelligently when you see them in a standard environment. It's only when you change the environment that the deceptiveness of these appearances is revealed.

For example, think of a birdbath, of the sort that many people have in their backyard. Birds will land in the shallow pool of water then flick the water with their beaks, throwing it onto their back and wings. Watching this, you can't help but think, "Isn't that nice? The bird is taking a bath." But then another bird lands on a marble tabletop right next to the birdbath. Something about the reflection on the shiny surface seems to have caught its eye. She then proceeds to go through exactly the same motions as the other bird, who is in the water. This time you think, "What is she doing?" The answer is, she's "taking a bath," in exactly the same way that the other one is. Except the second bird is the victim of a cognitive misfire. These birds appear to use the visual impression of a shiny flat surface as a way of identifying water. Standing in this "water" triggers the bathing routine. The fact that there's no water on the marble tabletop simply fails to register.[19]

Why do birds make this mistake? Because there were no sheets of polished marble in the environment in which they did most of their evolving. In an environment free of human artifacts, the reflective surface of a body of water was quite distinctive, and so a crude water-recognition heuristic worked well enough. Furthermore, the consequences of getting things wrong were not particularly serious, and so again, the crude heuristic worked just fine. (There were also no plate glass windows or wind turbines in this environment, which is why birds fly into windows and windmills. But here the consequences of misidentification are sufficiently deadly that we may expect to see the evolution of more fine-grained heuristics among birds within a reasonably short period of time.)

Unfortunately, our brains also use some heuristics that are just as crude. Perhaps the most celebrated is the so-called availability heuristic, first identified by Amos Tversky and Daniel Kahneman as part of their now-famous "heuristics and biases" research program.[20] Tversky and Kahneman came across the availability heuristic while trying to figure out how people make estimates of frequency (and, therefore, of probability). Suppose a tourist were to stop you on the street and ask you a question, like "These maple trees are beautiful. Are they common around here?" The proper way to answer this question—the way that a computer would answer the question—would be to do a thorough search of your memory. Take some representative sample of the area: perhaps the neighborhood where you live, or the route that you walk to work. Count the trees, classify each one by species, and figure out what percentage of them are maples. Unfortunately, we don't have a memory system that is searchable like this (or that keeps a precise image of what the trees in our neighborhood look like). We have no choice but to ask the notorious librarian. But surprisingly, when we do ask the librarian, he comes back with an answer almost right away. Not only that, it's a pretty good answer.

What Tversky and Kahneman were able to show, however, is that the librarian isn't really doing a proper search either. He's using a trick. What he does is scour through the stacks to find a single instance of the item that he is being asked to recall. (In this case, the first clear recollection of a maple tree.) He then uses the ease or speed with which he was able to retrieve an instance (that is, its "availability") as a basis for estimating frequency—the principle being that the more maple trees you have in your neighborhood or on your way to work, the easier it should be to remember one. Thus we use availability as a *proxy* for frequency—the two are strongly correlated, but the former is easier to figure out than the latter, and so the former is used *instead of* the latter as the basis for judgment.

This is a very clever solution to the problem posed by our unsystematic and unreliable memory system, but at the same time, it's easy to see that it has the potential to go awry. Most obviously, because it is easier to remember exciting events than boring ones, it leads us to dramatically overestimate the occurrence of exciting events. This is probably the single most important source of the irrational fears that we all, to some degree, fall victim to.[21]

The biggest problem is that our intuitive judgment system has no error-correction mechanism. Even once we've read Kahneman and Tversky and figured out that we are likely to overestimate the frequency of exciting events, there is no way to reprogram the librarian or change the way the system works. In the same way that an optical illusion doesn't go away even after we have figured it out, the availability heuristic produces cognitive illusions that won't go away. The net result is that we have a buggy system that we can't fix and can't replace. So what do we do? Ideally, we work out an explicit model of how that system works in order to figure out when it is likely to go wrong. This will allow us to put our trust in the heuristic most of the time, but then override it—and try to work out a proper, non-heuristic solution, using explicit resources—when we suspect that the answer will be wrong. For example, it's easy to recognize our own tendency to overestimate the dangers of air travel, simply because when a plane crashes, the event tends to be rather horrific, and so remains lodged in our memory. We can use this knowledge to veto our intuitive urge to panic whenever we feel the bump of the landing gear being raised after takeoff. We can try to remember that the number of times we've seen something in the media is not an accurate reflection of how many times it occurs in the world, and so on.

Unfortunately, because of the basic architecture of the human mind, the irrational impulses and intuitions that we need to veto never really go away. Archaic structures don't get rebuilt; they simply get layered over with new structures, which have as part of their function the inhibition of behavioral impulses coming from the old ones. It isn't like the case of mistaken factual beliefs, which get replaced by new ones as soon as we discover the error. Faulty intuitions keep showing up, again and again. This is why, as Robyn Dawes puts it, "all sorts of irrationality—whether individual or social—that we thought had been relegated to the dustbin as a thing of the past keeps returning to haunt us in both our waking and sleeping hours."[22] The achievements of human reason—up to and including the creation of complex civilization—are always tenuous. We are constantly in danger of backsliding, of falling victim to the cognitive illusions that ruled the mental lives of our ancestors.

¶

There was a time, one might suppose, when our intuitive judgments were by and large sufficient, and when the rational "veto" over these reactions would seldom need to be exercised. Reason could fall asleep at the switch without catastrophic consequences. Unfortunately, in large measure due to the success of this rational override, the need for rational control has *increased*. This is because we have, through intentional control and planning, changed our environment in millions of different ways, so that heuristic decision-making processes that once worked tolerably well begin to misfire more and more often. In a sense, reason creates the demand for its own services by building a world where, increasingly, people *must* act rationally in order to succeed.

Consider, for example, the "availability heuristic." It is designed to calculate frequencies based on observation of *actual* events, which stands to reason, since the ancestral environment was a world almost entirely devoid of images. The only way to see the same thing over and over again was for it to actually *happen* over and over again. In this sort of environment, your brain would be quite right to infer, based on repeated exposure, that such an event is common. Yet in the modern world, much of what we see are recorded images. Our experience of reality is mediated by the media. There are many things that we feel we are quite familiar with but that we have never actually witnessed. We have simply seen images and recordings of them. Because of this proliferation of images, we are able to watch the same event multiple times even if it has only ever happened once. The older parts of your brain, unfortunately, don't necessarily know the difference, and so can be misled into thinking that certain things are very common even when they're not. The mere fact that some events are likely to be reported in the media while others are not is capable of completely misleading us.[23] Furthermore, many of the images we see on television and in movies are so vivid that they are even capable of producing false memories.[24] It is only rational oversight that allows us to keep straight what is fictional and what is real.

Stanovich refers to this as the "sodium vapor lamp" problem—an unnatural environment causes our heuristics to misfire.[25] Anyone who has ever had to search for their car at night under a sodium vapor streetlight will understand the phenomenon. Sodium vapor lamps use relatively little power, which is why they are favored in outdoor settings. Unfortunately, they also put out a very unnatural profile of light—one that is almost monochromatic, in contrast to the full spectrum that we get from the sun. This not only makes everything look yellow, but also makes it difficult to tell other colors apart (sometimes even making it difficult to find one's car).

We call this light "unnatural" because the specific pattern of spectrum that it is made up of does not occur naturally on planet earth. This is not to say, however, that there is no variation in the pattern of spectrum that does occur naturally. The pattern of spectrum in the light that comes to us from the sun is actually quite different at different times of day, because of the way that it gets filtered by the earth's atmosphere at various angles of incidence. Thus, in principle, objects *should* appear to us as being of different color at different times of day. What is strange, therefore, is not the fact that objects appear to change color under a sodium vapor lamp, but rather that objects do *not* change color over the course of the day, as the spectral profile of the natural light coming from the sun changes.

As it turns out, color constancy is an elaborate illusion, perpetrated upon us by our brains. Our *eyes* can see the difference between the way an object looks in the morning and the way it looks in the evening. However, our brain likes to feed us information on a strictly need-to-know basis, and it figures that we don't really need to know this—that seeing objects change color over the course of the day would just be confusing and would distract us from more important tasks. So our brain tweaks the data stream, adjusting the image so that color constancy is preserved. (This is how standard color illusions work—how we can be made to see black as white, blue as green, and so forth. By manipulating the surrounding visual field, the illusion tricks the brain into tweaking the data stream when in fact it shouldn't.)

What is striking about the illusion of color constancy is that it shows our brains to be exquisitely adapted to the precise range of visible spectrum that occurs naturally on earth. It is an amazingly sophisticated arrangement. And yet, as soon as you create an unnatural profile of spectrum, the way that a sodium vapor lamp does, this exquisitely tuned instrument simply doesn't work. It is designed to do something incredibly complex, but it does only one thing, in only one way, and it has no flexibility. A slight change in the environment can therefore cause it to fail completely. As we will see, this is the general problem with the intuitive style of cognition. The "simple heuristics that make us smart" in one situation can also make us incredibly stupid in others.[26]

Planners and architects have an excellent term that they use to refer to the world of offices, homes, vehicles, roads, and tools that we interact with: the *built environment*. The term is apposite, since that's exactly what most of us interact with most of the time—not a natural environment, of trees and meadows, but one that is entirely artifactual, which is to say, a product of human construction and design. The tree that you see was planted there by someone, for some reason. The amount of available lighting in the room was calculated by someone. The chair that you sit on, the bed that you sleep in, the cup that you drink from, even most of the sounds that you hear are all the product of thousands upon thousands of choices made by individual human beings.

Some of these choices lead to the creation of environments that imitate the natural world, but many more do not. As a result, psychologists such as Stanovich have argued that the modern world—the built environment—resembles a gigantic sodium vapor lamp. Many of our intuitive problem-solving strategies, no matter how clever they may have been in the environment of evolutionary adaptation, simply fail to work properly in an artificial environment. As a result, our ability to rely on these judgments to navigate the world is severely diminished. Unfortunately, our general approach to the world is one of cognitive miserliness. We try to solve problems at the lowest possible level, using cognitive resources that require the least attention and effort. Stanovich refers to this preference for the least demanding forms of cognition as the "fundamental computational bias" of the human mind.[27] This is what accounts in part, he says, for the increased need for education in modern societies:

> A large part of education can be viewed as an attempt to develop controlled processing styles that override the fundamental computational bias and thus enable learned rule systems to operate on decoupled representations . . . The need to override the fundamental computational bias in order to pursue normative rationality increases in a technological, knowledge-based society. Because postindustrial societies increasingly create more and more decontextualized information-processing environments (insurance forms, HMO rules, graduation requirements, taxation statutes), the cogni-

tive environment of present society—and the environment of the future—puts a premium on the ability to selectively override the fundamental computational bias.[28]

This is not in itself such a terrible thing. Many of the changes we have made in our environment—the changes that require a shift toward more "controlled processing styles"—are changes for the better. What it illustrates, however, is the madness of thinking that we can do without reason, or that it is somehow overrated.

¶

On some days, it is difficult not to think of reason as a faculty that largely interferes with our ability to have a good time.[29] The well-known phenomenon of "choking," for instance, occurs when a person starts to think too hard about something that she should be able to do automatically, unconsciously. Yet while it is no doubt true that there are certain activities that can be ruined by overthinking them, just doing what comes naturally is, in most cases, a recipe for an unhappy life. It is well known, for instance, that just eating whatever you want produces short-term satisfaction but long-term misery. From a dual-process perspective, this is easy to understand. Even though we have a lot of flexibility in what we eat, there is a huge physiological component to what we like and dislike, how much we eat, and so on. (Consider, for instance, the very specific food cravings and aversions that many pregnant women experience.) Thus we make a lot of intuitive judgments about food, many of which wind up, in the modern world, being misfires.

Foods like sugar and fat have very high caloric value but were extremely hard to find in the environment of evolutionary adaptation. Thus our brains follow a simple "eat as much as you can" rule when dealing with these food sources. This rule was perfectly adequate in an environment where these things were rare. But that is no longer the case. Because of this huge change in the environment, we are now in a situation where we must constantly override our basic impulses. Our failure to do so is reflected in the enormous transformation that has occurred in the diet of people in wealthier nations. Every year the average American eats 195 pounds of meat and 199 pounds of grain, but an astonishing 152 pounds of added sugar, as well as 75 pounds of fat and oil.[30]

Compounding our difficulties, in the case of food, is the fact that our choices almost always have a "short-term pain for long-term gain" structure. The pleasures of eating are available immediately, while the disadvantages occur only in the relatively distant future. Intuition, unfortunately, has what might be described as a "presentist" bias. It is concerned with what is going on right now, and is in many ways not even capable of *representing,* much less thinking about, what will happen in the future. Trying to remain healthy by controlling one's diet creates a conflict between a "hot" psychological state, often arising from an immediate environmental stimulus, and an entirely mental construct, namely, a hypothetical future state of affairs. The latter is, unfortunately, not available to intuition. It is posited by *reason* as the most likely consequence of the course of action being contemplated. Of course, reason has a certain number of kluges that it can use to trick the intuitive judgment system into taking the future into account. We can try to visualize the future, imaging what it would be like to be obese or to contract diabetes. We can even try to build up mental associations between, say, glazed donuts and images of bariatric surgery or morbid obesity. These are all tricks designed to take elements of the future and bring them into the present—by generating mental simulations that the unconscious mind may mistake for the real thing. The reason that we must resort to these psychological tricks is that intuition does not *automatically* weigh future misery against present satisfaction, but rather concerns itself entirely with what might generously be described as the "near term." Although we have many thoughts about the future, we do not really have a *feel* for it.

This presentist bias can lead us astray, in ways both subtle and gross, when dealing with choices that have effects over time. Some of the more subtle effects are involved in the phenomenon that Daniel Gilbert refers to as *miswanting*.[31] Our intuitive judgments are based on a naive attitude toward present desires, in the sense that intuition tends to take them at face value. We assume that what we want *now* is what we are going to want in the future, and that the strength of our desire for something *now* is predictive of how happy we will be when we get it. As a matter of fact, our desires are surprisingly adaptive, while our happiness level is surprisingly stable. We have no intuitive feel for this, however. Because we rely too much on our intuitions in this department, we tend to make very bad predictions about what we will want and how we will feel in the future. Both Gilbert and Timothy Wilson have argued, persuasively, that we would have a better chance of making ourselves happy if we were to give up on introspection entirely—forget about how we feel—and observe our own behavior with scientific detachment.

One experiment that reveals this bias in a particularly elegant way was done by a business school professor, Itamar Simonson.[32] Simonson told students that he would be providing them with snacks at every lecture over the course of the term, and that they would have a choice of what they wanted: chips, chocolate bar, crackers, and so on. With one group, he asked them to fill out a form at the beginning of the term, specifying which food item they would like to have each week. The second group was allowed to choose each week, at the beginning of class, what to have. He found that members of the second group tended to choose the same item, week after week. They simply picked their favorite snack. Many members of the first group, however, mistakenly treated the problem as though they were being offered all the snacks at the same time, and so introduced variety into their choices. They would choose a chocolate bar the first week, and maybe chips the second, instead of simply picking their favorite item and sticking with it. This sort of variation makes sense in the short term, because we tend to get tired of any single food item. But over the course of a week, whatever satiation we may feel at having eaten a chocolate bar will fade away entirely. Thus receiving a bag of chips the following week doesn't feel like a welcome relief from the tyranny of chocolate bars; it simply feels like a second-best option.

Wilson and Gilbert refer to this as a failure of "affective forecasting."[33] Even when our feelings change in very predictable ways, we routinely fail to incorporate this into our planning. Consider, for example, the choice many people make between a small house in the city, close to work, or a larger house in the suburbs, with a longer commute. Studies have shown that people adapt very quickly to their spatial surroundings, so that the sense of enjoyment associated with the larger house will quickly fade away.[34] Commuting through traffic, however, is something that people have great difficulty adapting to. Perhaps because the annoyances change from day to day, most people continue to find commuting a source of daily frustration and stress, even after living with it for a long time. As a result, many people make the wrong choice when it comes to housing, because they fail to anticipate that the way they feel about the costs and the benefits *now* is likely to be different from the way that they feel about these costs and benefits in a few years.

Perhaps the most destructive feature of the way in which we are naturally inclined to think about the future is the attitude that we have toward the passage of time itself. Humans, like every other animal, exhibit impatience, which means that we are often willing to accept a smaller benefit that we can get right away over a larger benefit that is available only after some delay. We dislike delay, and so in order to be willing to defer satisfaction, we need to be compensated with some larger reward. Another way of articulating this is to say that benefits are worth less to us in the present the further removed they are from us in time. On the flip side, this means that we are also less worried about costs, the further removed they are from us in time. Unfortunately, we tend to apply this discounting of future costs to our own dislike of delay. As a result, we treat a delay of a given magnitude as less of a big deal the further removed it is from us in time. A delay, however, is a delay, and so as the future comes closer to the present, we tend to change our minds about what we want. This creates what psychologist George Ainslie calls a "warp" in the way that we think about the future, and, left unchecked, it can literally destroy any chance at happiness you have ever had in life.[35]

Ainslie has a very simple example that he uses to demonstrate the phenomenon. Suppose that you are given a choice between a check for $100 that can be cashed right away and a check for $200 that can be cashed only in two years. Most people opt for the $100. Suppose then that you are offered a choice between a check for $100 that can be cashed in six years and a check for $200 that can be cashed in eight years. In this case, many of the same people will take the $200 check. The underlying thought—to the extent that there is an underlying thought—is that having waited six years to cash the check, another two years will not be such a big deal. But two years is two years. Six years from now, the choice between the check that can be cashed in six years and the check that can be cashed in eight years will have become identical to the choice between a check that can be cashed right away and a check that can be cashed only in two years. So the person who chooses $100 right away but $200 in eight years can be expected to change his mind about the value of the $200 check sometime during that six-year period.

What Ainslie has mapped out is a pattern that is extremely familiar to us all. It is called temptation. When both the smaller-sooner and a larger-later reward are off in the distant future, we may decide to be patient and hold out for the larger reward. But as time ticks by, the smaller reward begins to look more attractive. And when it is available *right here and now,* it often becomes irresistible. Thus the passage of time can generate preference reversals followed of course by regret when we no longer are able to achieve the larger reward.

This "warp" in the way in which we evaluate the future has the potential to create an enormous amount of misery. Ainslie argues that an extraordinary range of "bad habits" can be attributed to temporally induced preference reversals, starting with common problems like staying up late at night or compulsively checking a social network for messages, extending to more problematic forms of short-term thinking such as saving too little for one's retirement or putting off a colonoscopy, all the way to life-destroying addictions. What these forms of behavior all have in common is that they involve a short-term preference reversal that leads us to choose the lesser good simply because the satisfaction it provides is more immediate.

As far as bugs in our hardware go, this warp in the way that we deal with the future is a genuinely massive problem. Not only is it responsible for untold hardship, but it is extremely difficult to overcome or work around. Furthermore, our attitudes toward the future might not have mattered all that much in the environment of evolutionary adaptation, when average life expectancy was probably less than thirty years. But as we extend the human lifespan further and further, our near total lack of intuitive skills for dealing with the future, combined with a strong presentist bias, becomes increasingly troublesome. We expect people to save for their retirement, exercise regularly, eat a healthy diet, floss their teeth, avoid smoking—the list goes on and on. All of these are psychologically unnatural forms of behavior: they require a rational override of our intuitive impulses. In the same way that our bodies were not designed to last very long, neither were our brains, and so we simply do not come equipped with the "onboard" resources required to manage a long lifespan. Thus not only is reason absolutely indispensable, but it is becoming more and more indispensable as the environment in which we live becomes increasingly unnatural.

5. Thinking straight is hard to do

Pitfalls and challenges for the new Enlightenment

One of the downsides of being a philosopher, I've discovered, is that you get a fair number of unsolicited communications from people in cults, who are hoping to discuss their "philosophy" with you. These days my inbox is cluttered with messages from Falun Dafa (or Falun Gong)—which is a fairly harmless organization, except that they made the mistake of having spooked the Chinese government (just by being *organized*), and now suffer genuine repression. This has probably had the effect of making them more popular than they otherwise would have been. Their core ideology is an amalgamation of traditional Buddhist meditative practices with an elaborate alien mind-control theory. According to founder Li Hongzhi, the development of science and technology is an alien plot, designed to foment war and destruction among humans so that aliens can seize our bodies, replace people with aliens, and so on.[1] The details are, quite literally, crazy. But like all cults, the question is how so many thousands (or in this case, millions) of non-crazy people could come to believe it.

One of the astonishing things about Falun Dafa is just how *standard* it is, in every aspect. It's an absolutely generic cult, instantly recognizable as what it is to anyone from anywhere in the world. It's not crazy with Chinese characteristics, it's just plain old crazy, like the common cold of mental

Joseph Heath

infections. Reading through their literature, you get the sense that someone has been following a universal instruction manual on how to build a cult. How do you attract followers? Option number one: tales of miraculous healing! Sure enough, the other day I received a Falun Dafa email that included this testimonial:

> I have witnessed and heard of many stories about the wonders of reading "Falun Dafa is good." Ms. Liu, a villager in Tangshan City, is sixty-nine years old. Last year she was diagnosed with colon cancer. The doctor told her, "You are elderly and your blood pressure is too low. Quit seeking treatment. Go home and eat whatever you like." Her third youngest sister practices Falun Gong. She visited her and taught her to practice Dafa by reciting "Falun Dafa is good." Ten days later, Ms. Liu completely recovered and the late stage colon cancer disappeared. What is the most miraculous thing was that she looked like a young girl and became so beautiful. That's Falun Dafa's Divine Power. Master Li is absolutely superior to Jesus Christ! Falun Dafa saves people. Falun Dafa solves everything.

If this sort of thing sounds familiar, that's because it is. It turns out that there is something like a universal instruction manual for getting people to acquire false beliefs. As Pascal Boyer has shown, some fanciful stories are easier to get people to believe than others.[2] Human reasoning is subject to a number of very specific biases, and to the extent that a belief system is able to exploit these biases, it may be able to successfully reproduce itself. This is why the belief systems of cults and the "arguments" used to support them have a certain depressing familiarity. They all occupy the same ecological niche. Like a virus that is able to avoid detection by the immune system, some irrational beliefs are able to withstand whatever scrutiny most people are able to bring to bear upon them, because they exploit certain characteristic flaws in our reasoning. (Of course, the mechanism that generates the belief system is evolutionary, not intentional. Mental illness alone generates thousands of crazy preachers and belief systems, and of those, only a small fraction are able to attract followers. The belief systems that become widespread are ones that happen to exploit cognitive biases in a way that shelters them from rational scrutiny.)

Consider the story of Ms. Liu from Tangshan City. There's a lot going on in this email, but the most prominent feature of the story is that it exploits what psychologists refer to as *confirmation bias*. When considering a hypothesis, people have a tendency to look only for positive evidence that is consistent with the hypothesis, while failing to ensure the absence of evidence that is inconsistent with the hypothesis. They fail to "think the negative." Between Ms. Liu's recovery and the divine power of Falun Dafa, two pieces of information are missing. First, what would have happened if she *hadn't* recited "Falun Dafa is good"? For example, what are the chances that the cancer diagnosis was simply mistaken? Or if she had cancer, what are the chances of spontaneous remission, or even just not dying for a long time? Second, how many people suffering from terminal cancer who recite "Falun Dafa is good" *fail* to recover? Many people don't ask these questions, simply because it doesn't occur to them, or they don't realize that the story alone provides absolutely no support for the hypothesis without this missing information. Failure to appreciate confirmation bias is actually one of the hallmarks of "superstitious" thinking. (For comparison, consider this: When she was younger, my wife's relatives used to make her drink a "growth potion" that they had obtained from a herbalist, full of bark, leaves, and nasty chicken parts. They all agreed, however, that at age twenty she was a bit old to be drinking it, since the potion seemed to work best on teenagers.[3])

¶

There is a temptation when reading about these cognitive biases to think of them as the sort of thing that explains why *everyone else* is stupid. Diagnosing them in oneself is a lot more difficult. Daniel Kahneman describes this in terms of the "futility of teaching psychology." Students read about all sorts of experiments describing all sorts of pernicious errors and biases, then simply "exempt themselves" from the obvious conclusion that they themselves are just as biased.[4] In part this is because of the mistaken belief that bias can be detected through introspection (and so just knowing about a bias would be enough to provide immunity from its effects). In part it is a result of another well-known cognitive bias, which is that most people vastly overestimate their own abilities in every area of life.[5] Freedom from bias is just another one of those areas. Psychologists refer to it as the *bias blind spot*.[6] It's easy to lament the superstitiousness of Chinese peasants. With ourselves, on the other hand, it's a different story.

Take me, for example. I am a university professor, teaching in the Department of Philosophy. In order to get there, I both studied and taught logic, argumentation analysis, and probability theory. I'm also by temperament a bit of a rationalist. Kids started calling me "Mr. Spock" in grade three. From there I went on to chess club, computer programming, and, finally, logic and philosophy. I've also read extensively in the psychological literature on cognitive biases—enough, for example, to know what confirmation bias is and how it typically manifests itself. And yet one day, not that many years ago, I found myself falling into the most elementary trap, in a test used to detect confirmation bias. Here is how it goes.

The test was designed by Peter Wason, who had a peculiar genius for inventing problems that would cause people's reasoning abilities to go haywire. It goes something like this:

> *Experimenter:* I am going to present you with a series of
> three numbers, and you have to try to guess the rule that

generated them. Before deciding, you may ask me three questions. Your questions must have the following form. You give me a set of three numbers, and I will tell you whether or not they are an instance of the rule.

Me: Okay, fun! Sounds a bit like Mastermind. I used to be really good at that.

Experimenter: Your first set of numbers is: 2, 4, 6.

Me: Wow, that's easy. This must be the warm-up phase. Okay, how about: 6, 8, 10?

Experimenter: Yes, that is an instance of the rule.

Me: Um, okay. How about 22, 24, 26?

Experimenter: Yes, that is an instance of the rule.

Me: Okay, this is stupid. I don't even need the last guess. Let's try 100, 102, 104?

Experimenter: Yes, that is an instance of the rule.

Me: All right, the rule is 'Three even numbers in order.'

Experimenter: No, that is not the rule.

Me: Come again?

Experimenter: That is not the rule.

Me: Then what is the rule?

Experimenter: The rule is "Any three numbers in ascending order."

Me: You're telling me that 3, 5, 7 satisfies the rule?

Experimenter: Yes.

Me: 2, 67, 428 satisfies the rule?

Experimenter: Yes.

Me: Oh my God, I'm an idiot.

This is how I learned to take confirmation bias seriously.[7] When asked to formulate an hypothesis and evaluate it, I quickly jumped on the first pattern that I saw, and then proceeded to look exclusively for results that confirmed my theory, without trying to falsify it. Once I got it into my head that they were even numbers in order, it never occurred to me to suggest a sequence of odd numbers, with the aim of eliciting a "no" response. I completely failed to "think the negative."[8] In fact, I can clearly remember pausing just before asking the third question, not being sure what to ask, thinking that I had exhausted all useful questions. I was even a bit puzzled by the fact that I had been given three questions to ask when obviously I only needed one or two.

This is a big enough deal that it's worth dwelling on for a moment. Figure 5.1 provides a little graphical representation of the set of sequences that satisfy the actual rule ("any three numbers in ascending order"), along with the subset that satisfies the more restrictive rule that I guessed ("three even numbers in sequence"). These are both contained within an even more gigantic set—not shown—that contains all possible sequences of three numbers, in any order whatsoever. When presented this way, we can begin to see how extraordinary it is that I confined all my guesses to the contents of the small circle. Even if I was convinced that the rule was "three even numbers in order," a seemingly obvious way of checking this would be to guess a sequence of odd numbers, with the intention of generating a "no" response. (After all, a "no" can be just as informative as a "yes.") Had I tried this—guessing wrong on purpose—I would of course have been surprised to discover that I hadn't in fact guessed wrong, and that there was this enormous, unexplored territory just outside the realm of hypotheses that I had been considering. And of course, had I continued my attempts to guess wrong, I would have discovered an even larger territory just outside that . . . Why not guess a set of numbers out of sequence, in order to see whether that is essential to the rule?

Figure 5.1. The 2, 4, 6 problem

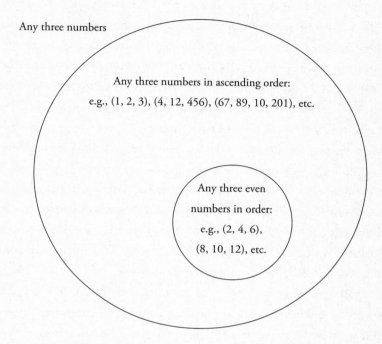

Any three numbers

Any three numbers in ascending order:

e.g., (1, 2, 3), (4, 12, 456), (67, 89, 10, 201), etc.

Any three even numbers in order: e.g., (2, 4, 6), (8, 10, 12), etc.

What is particularly striking about this test of confirmation bias is that it reveals more than just wishful thinking. It's one thing to know that people look only for supporting evidence for their pet theories or for things that they want to believe. But in this case, I had nothing whatsoever invested in the initial hypothesis. There is simply a huge blind spot in our reasoning. The "yes" in response to "6, 8, 10" does, in fact, support the hypothesis that the rule is "three even numbers in sequence." The problem is that it supports a very large number of *other* hypotheses too, and that before one can establish that "three even numbers in sequence" is correct, one must rule out these other hypotheses. And yet I failed—failed egregiously, outrageously—to do it. This is *exactly* the same problem that leads people to think that the miraculous recovery of Ms. Liu generates support for belief in the divine power of Falun Dafa.

It is easy to see why our intuitive judgments might be out of whack in this regard. One of the things that rapid cognition does extremely well is pattern recognition. What sets the grandmaster chess player or the experienced doctor or the seasoned firefighter apart is the ability to instantly detect patterns that no one else can see.[9] The human brain is, unfortunately, quite hyperactive in this regard, and tends also to see patterns where in fact none exist. This is called *apophenia* when it reaches pathological proportions, but the underlying tendency is ubiquitous.[10] Most people, for instance, when shown a sequence of random coin tosses or dice rolls, will insist that the sequence is not random—since it contains too many "streaks." Apple experienced a deluge of complaints about the shuffle feature on its iPod from customers who insisted that the random sequence was biased against certain artists.[11] People in general lack an intuitive feel for what randomness looks like, and so are constantly amazed by coincidences that are, as a matter of fact, not particularly improbable. Some psychologists have suggested that this is because, in a natural environment, genuine randomness is somewhat uncommon, and so there is no particular benefit to being able to detect it.[12] A more plausible account is simply that the evolutionary cost of false positives (thinking that there is a pattern when in fact there is none) is much lower than the evolutionary cost of false negatives (thinking that there is no pattern when in fact there is one), and so natural selection has favored a pattern-recognition system that has very high sensitivity and low specificity.[13] In an environment where there is some chance of being eaten by a predator, it pays to treat every rustle in the grass as a potential threat. The cost of getting "spooked" and running away from nothing are much lower than the costs of ignoring some telltale signs and getting torn limb from limb. Thus we tend to get all excited when we see a pattern. If and when we do think "What if I'm wrong?" it is not a thought that occurs to us naturally. It is a cognitive override imposed on us by reason.

¶

My biggest mistake in the 2, 4, 6 challenge was in thinking that because I was *smart,* I was somehow immune to cognitive bias.[14] This is, as it turns out, not true. (In fact, most smart people who read the Falun Dafa email and reject the conclusion do so not because they can spot the error in reasoning, but because of a different bias, *belief bias,* whereby we reject as illogical any argument that leads to a conclusion that we take to be false. In other words, most people reading the email start from the belief that there is no such thing as the divine power of Falun Dafa, and so they reject the argument. Yet many of these same people happen to believe in the divine power of Jesus Christ, and so accept arguments that have exactly the same structure when presented in support of the divinity of Christ. Indeed, the "argument from miracles" figured prominently in Christian theology for thousands of years and, if you can believe what you see on TV, continues to impress many people in the southern United States.)

Keith Stanovich and his collaborators have shown, through an extensive series of studies, that higher intelligence does not make people less susceptible to cognitive biases. The types of cognitive abilities that are measured by intelligence tests are typically *not* those that we associate with rational thought. On the contrary, these tests typically measure intuitive thinking skills (such as the ability to manipulate geometric objects, decipher anagrams, classify words, or categorize items), and they also reward those who are able to respond quickly. These skills are weakly correlated with reasoning ability, and not at all correlated with the ability to avoid cognitive biases. It is interesting to note, however, that once you tell people that their answers are wrong and that they have fallen victim to a cognitive bias, more intelligent people are better at figuring out where they went wrong and at correcting their answers. In other words, intelligence is *useful* when it comes to thinking rationally, but cognitive miserliness—the desire to solve problems with the least effort possible—is independent of intelligence. Intelligence alone does not trigger the override that leads us to question our intuitive judgments. And since we all have the same bugs in our lower-level systems, high-IQ individuals are just as easily tricked as low-IQ individuals.

Stanovich has introduced the term *dysrationalia* to describe "the inability to think and behave rationally, despite adequate intelligence."[15] Everyone knows someone who fits the profile: the retired engineer who becomes a 9/11 truther and spends weeks on end studying the physics of controlled demolition; the farmer who spends the off-season surfing the internet, developing elaborate theories about monetary policy and the perfidy of banks; the secretary who develops an obsessive interest in astrology and insists on doing sophisticated "readings" for everyone she knows; the young mother who starts reading up on pesticides and is soon buying organic everything (and yet continues to nip out for the occasional smoke). Stanovich has argued that our failure to take this sort of irrationality seriously, combined with the fetishization of IQ in our society, has had a number of untoward consequences. The most troublesome is that it has led to the promotion to positions of authority and influence of people who are actually quite irrational and, as a result, make terrible decisions both for themselves and for others.[16]

The best example of this is former U.S. president George W. Bush, who is widely thought to be stupid, despite considerable evidence to the contrary. During the 2004 campaign, when he and John Kerry, his Democratic opponent, were pressed to release their Yale undergraduate transcripts, people were surprised to discover that Bush had graduated with a higher grade point average than Kerry.[17] And yet there can be no doubt that America's first "MBA president" made a series of terrible decisions. In Stanovich's analysis, most of this is due to Bush having adopted a set of flawed decision-making heuristics, all of which led him to put far too much emphasis on his "gut feelings." (For example, he claimed that he was able to get a sense of Russian president Vladimir Putin's "soul" simply from having "looked him in the eye.") Even some of those on his team noted his rather alarming absence of curiosity.[18] He had a particular lack of interest in exploring ideas or opinions that might be inconsistent with his own. He was also a believer in firm decision making, with no second-guessing or doubts. (He prided himself on being "the decider." Asked toward the end of his second term whether he could think of any mistakes he had made as president, he was genuinely stumped.) And finally, there was his habit of praying for guidance (which, on the most probable interpretation, is just a way of bolstering support for one's gut feelings). This is all a recipe for irrational decision making, because it disables the most important mechanisms that we use to counteract confirmation bias.

Like Bush, most cranks and conspiracy theorists are also not dumb, as witnessed by the fact that they are able to develop elaborate theories, along with complex explanations for why their views are not more widely accepted.[19] The problem is that they suffer from an extreme case of confirmation bias. They fail to "think the negative" when it comes to their own views and, for various psychosocial reasons, resist the "check" that the disbelief of others would normally serve in correcting them. One can see this tendency on dramatic display in the movie *Room 237,* which is organized around five different individuals each presenting their personal analysis of the "hidden meaning" of Stanley Kubrick's movie *The Shining.* It's astonishing to listen to people from different walks of life making exactly the same cognitive error, over and over again—but equally astonishing to see how quickly one can be lured into doing the same oneself.

These examples are all fairly harmless. But consider the case of global warming skeptics, who spend untold hours trying to unravel the enormous scientific conspiracy that has tricked us all into believing that human activity is causing changes in the earth's climate. They never stop to ask themselves the simple question, "How could we be increasing the carbon dioxide content of the atmosphere and *not* have it change the earth's climate?" Or consider religion. Even in its most refined variants, any attempt to develop a "rational theology" is inevitably an exercise in confirmation bias. From Aristotle's celebrated five proofs for the existence of God to contemporary arguments for intelligent design, absolutely none of these arguments provide any support at all for what might broadly be described as a "theistic," much less a Christian, worldview. People are so busy trying to make the case for belief in God against the threat of atheism that it never even occurs to them that they need to exclude other hypotheses. Indeed, the Venn diagram for intelligent design arguments looks exactly like the one for the Wason problem. Jumping from "the miracle of life" to "belief in God" is exactly the same as leaping from "2, 4, 6" to "three even numbers in order." There's a gaping hole in the argument, which, unfortunately, most people just glide right past.

Figure 5.2. Intelligent design hypotheses

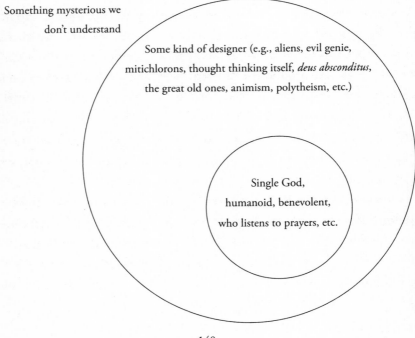

Something mysterious we don't understand

Some kind of designer (e.g., aliens, evil genie, mitichlorons, thought thinking itself, *deus absconditus*, the great old ones, animism, polytheism, etc.)

Single God, humanoid, benevolent, who listens to prayers, etc.

David Hume pointed this out long ago. Even for those who believe in intelligent design, there remains a wide range of possibilities. "A man who follows your hypothesis," he argued, "is able perhaps to assert, or conjecture, that the universe, sometime, arose from something like design: but beyond that position he cannot ascertain one single circumstance; and is left afterwards to fix every point of his theology, by the utmost license of fancy and hypothesis."[20] Given the obvious imperfections in the world, Hume said, the more likely explanation would appeal to some sort of inattention or defect in the creator. Perhaps the world is just a preliminary sketch, carried out by some "infant deity" who "later abandoned it, ashamed of his lame performance." Or it could have been made by a lesser god, "the object of derision to his superiors." It might have been made by an aging, senile deity who died shortly thereafter, leaving the universe to run amok. The possibilities are manifold. More importantly, proponents of intelligent design have not one shred of evidence that could exclude any of these hypotheses. Yet when they demand that we "teach the controversy" over creationism in schools, this is typically not what they have in mind.

This failure to "think the negative" is somewhat exacerbated in our culture by a tendency to view "genius" as the ability to see connections that others don't. That's actually a better working definition of "crazy" than of "genius." Seeing connections is easy—the human mind is wired to see connections and patterns everywhere, even where they don't exist. The trick lies not in seeing connections, but in throwing out the ones that are no good. Albert Einstein may have seen connections that others did not see, but he was also able to say with absolute precision what the testable consequences of his theory were and, most importantly, how that theory could be proven false. It was his ability to "think the negative" that made him a great scientist, not the ability to "think different." Indeed, the central virtue of scientific education—as opposed to merely *technical* education—is the relentless focus on disproof. The scientific method forces us to do something that is, in fact, highly unnatural, which is to think about how we could be wrong: to seek not just confirmation, but disconfirmation.[21]

§

There is a long-standing debate about the uniqueness of Western civilization, and in particular why it gave rise to the scientific revolution, the Enlightenment, and later the Industrial Revolution. There are many theories, but a particularly compelling suggestion is that Aristotle deserves much of the credit—not so much because of the theories he proposed, but because of the theories he *rejected*. At the time that Aristotle began teaching, Plato (and, through Plato's works, Socrates) had already achieved the status of intellectual giants. Their fame and influence extended throughout the Hellenic world. And yet Aristotle began one of his most influential works—now referred to as the *Nicomachean Ethics*—by rejecting the most important idea in Plato's philosophy, namely, the "theory of the Forms." Given a choice between honoring his master and correcting what he saw as his master's mistake, he chose to correct the mistake, on the grounds that philosophy, or the love of wisdom, generates "a sacred duty to prefer the truth to one's friends."[22]

Nowadays we tend to take this sort of behavior for granted, but at the time people found it quite scandalous. Indeed, for hundreds of years philosophy was regarded as an unreliable guide to the truth, not to mention an unsuitable basis for political order, simply because the two greatest philosophers of all time had disagreed with one another. (One of the major projects among philosophers in the Roman Empire, such as Plotinus, was to paper over these differences, in order to cleanse philosophy of this stain on its reputation.)

What Aristotle's rejection of Plato created, however, was a culture of contestation in the Western intellectual tradition. Although Plato had paid lip service to the power of dialogue, there is not much real disagreement going on in his work (Socrates's interlocutors get pummeled into submission far too quickly). With Aristotle, one found dramatic illustration of the idea that intellectual progress could occur by correcting the mistakes of others, so that rather than having to rely on oracles, wise men, or prophets to reveal the truth to us, we could work it out over time, by arguing with one another. The result was a brilliant kluge. As individuals, we have enormous difficulty seeing our own mistakes, much less the biases that lead us into them. People have a powerful inclination to think that "biased thinking on their part would be detectable by conscious introspection,"[23] and yet it isn't. Introspection is far, far less powerful than any of us would have imagined. And unfortunately, the limits of introspection cannot be ascertained through introspection. Thus the most powerful check that we have on our own tendency toward biased thinking is the willingness—perhaps even the eagerness—of other people to correct us.

This is reflected in the fact that, under the right circumstances, *groups* do much better than individuals on tests of biased reasoning.[24] What underlies this, ultimately, is the internal connection between talking and reasoning. If one person happens to get it right, he or she will often be able to explain to the others why it is the right answer, and thereby raise the performance of all. People who get the wrong answer, on the other hand, are less often able to talk others into seeing things their way. This is because the wrong answer is typically a consequence of not having thought the problem through using the resources of explicit, linguistically structured thought, so as soon as you try to explain what you were thinking, the problem with it becomes apparent.

Many of our institutions intentionally sharpen the antagonism between individuals in order to enhance the effectiveness of this kluge. Rather than relying on people's love of wisdom to motivate them to correct others, we associate tangible status rewards with the ability to show others to be wrong. We do so through stylized debates and competitions, such as criminal trials or "peer commentary" on scientific articles. For example, as skepticism about miracles gathered strength in the sixteenth century, the Catholic church began appointing a "devil's advocate," whose job during canonization hearings was to present arguments against the elevation of the proposed individual to sainthood. Since Catholic sainthood to this day requires confirmed reports of at least two miracles after the death of the person, one can see how such an institution would have value. Indeed, it even appears to have had some effect, since the abolition of the devil's advocate in 1983 under Pope John Paul II led to a sharp uptick in the number of canonizations—typically based on accounts of "miracle cures" similar to the one enjoyed by Ms. Liu in Tangshan City.

It is worth noting that these institutional practices of criticism and doubt are not external to human reason. Like the pencil and paper that we use to do mathematical computations, discussion and argumentation with others are part of the machinery of rational thought. Just as thinking is a form of silent talking, reasoning is a form of silent arguing. Our ability to run simulations of these external processes is imperfect and fraught with error. This is why the results of the real thing—actual argumentation—are often superior to the results of its internalized or simulated variant.

It is fortunate that we have other people, because the list of cognitive biases that we have to overcome is formidable. The literature on this has become truly enormous, but here is a partial list, detailing only some of the most important biases:

1. *Optimism bias.* We tend to think that everything will work out for the best, that we have more control over the world than we actually have, and that we are more likable, intelligent, witty, competent, and rational than we actually are. Knowing that half of marriages end in divorce or that 60 percent of restaurants fail within three years does not deter people from getting married or opening restaurants in large numbers.[25] Knowing that all projects go over budget and past deadline does not stop people from assuming that their project will come in below budget and on time. And so on.

2. *Myside bias.* We have—to put it bluntly—self-serving beliefs. An excuse sounds more plausible when it is used to explain our own behavior, not that of others. A distribution seems more fair when it generates a benefit for us while others have to pay the bill. Indeed, a lot of what looks like self-interested behavior is actually—in the mind of the person doing it—completely disinterested behavior but based upon a description of the situation that is completely self-serving.

3. *Framing and anchoring effects.* People will often make completely different decisions depending on how a choice is presented to them (or "framed"). We also tend to be influenced by factors that should have no impact on our decision ("anchors"). For example, it has been shown that the list price of a house has a significant impact on what people take that house to be worth—and that the effect is just as large with professional real estate agents as it is with members of the public at large.[26] Even presenting people with what they know to be random numbers can skew their answers to numerical questions.[27]

4. *Loss aversion.* People care more about losses than (equivalent) foregone gains. For example, if you offer people a 3 percent rebate for using cash instead of a credit card, most will use their credit cards. But if you advertise a lower price along with a 3 percent surcharge for using a credit card, many of the same people will pay cash. (This is a type of framing effect, but it is of such economic significance that it deserves its own category. In particular, it has a huge impact on tax compliance, since people tend to treat tax deducted at the source as a foregone gain and tax owing at the end of the year as a loss.)

5. *Belief bias.* We tend to judge the quality of arguments by whether or not they generate conclusions that we already believe. This makes us incredibly unresponsive to new evidence, different ways of looking at things, and so

on. Consider the following syllogism: "All living things need water. Roses need water. Therefore, roses are living things." Seventy percent of university students consider this an instance of valid reasoning.[28]

6. *Probabilities.* There is an astonishing range of studies showing that people are terrible at dealing with probabilities. We routinely violate simple principles, such as the conjunction rule, which says that two events taken together cannot be more likely than either event taken singly. We treat unlikely events as being more probable if they haven't happened in a while. We also vastly overestimate the significance of small probabilities.[29] More arcane biases involve base rate neglect, whereby we ignore the background probability of an event when assessing new evidence.

What is important to recognize about these biases is that they are all examples of how "thinking with our gut" can lead us astray, or even into making disastrous choices. The only way to correct these biases is through the exercise of reason. Intuition is not only impervious to correction; it is oblivious to its own flaws and limitations. Reason may not be able to overpower these tendencies—indeed, the very idea of a "bias" shows that these flawed decision-making heuristics often intrude into consciousness and corrupt our rational decision-making processes—but it is the only faculty even able to try.

¶

As has been mentioned, we tend to worry about civilization collapsing into barbarism, not the other way around. But what exactly is barbarism? And why does it seem to be the default social arrangement? Thomas Hobbes has been criticized for claiming that the natural state of man—the sort of thing that we get when there are no laws and no government—is "solitary, poor, nasty, brutish and short."[30] If you look at the list, though, and compare it to "failed states" like Somalia, or to the human condition prior to the emergence of the modern state, you can see that he was wrong about only one item on the list. People are certainly poor, they are nasty to one another, there is an incredible amount of violence, and life tends to be short. The only thing Hobbes got wrong was "solitary." People are not solitary in the state of nature; what they are, in fact, is *tribal.* This means that they form small communities or groups bound together by ties of family and friendship ("blood" and "honor"), governed by a powerful in-group code, reinforced through antagonistic and typically violent relations with outsiders. This pattern of social organization describes everything from modern American street gangs to Somali warlords, Albanian clans, and nomadic hunter-gatherer societies throughout human history.[31]

Tribalism is what you get when people act naturally, when they go with their instincts, when they do what *feels right,* both morally and intellectually. This is because we are adapted for living in groups like this, and all of our social instincts support and reinforce this type of social structure. The problem with the arrangement is that it dramatically limits the scope of cooperation. This is why Hobbes claimed that in the state of nature, "there is no place for industry, because the fruit thereof is uncertain: and consequently no culture of the earth; no navigation, nor use of the commodities that may be imported by sea; no commodious building; no instruments of moving and removing such things as require much force; no knowledge of the face of the earth; no account of time; no arts; no letters; no society."[32]

What makes the collective action problems generated by tribalism particularly intractable is that they are not generated by self-interest, narrowly construed. People often engage in antisocial behavior out of a sense of loyalty to their fellow tribe members (or fealty to their god, or commitment to their shared values, or whatever). This is what makes street gangs so hard to combat. People are not just in it for the money. They are genuinely committed to the gang, willing to make huge personal sacrifices in order to support their brothers. They often break the law out of a sense of higher loyalty. The problem is that we have a set of pro-social instincts—to help others, at whatever cost—that are *limited in scope*. We don't want to help any old person; we want to help our brethren, our friends, the people on *our side*. This makes it easy to organize small-scale cooperation within a small group but much more difficult to organize large-scale cooperation across groups. Indeed, it would in many ways be easier getting people to cooperate if they were merely self-interested.

One particularly clear example of this is our taste for vengeance. Human beings appear to be the only primates who exhibit what evolutionary theorists refer to as "altruistic punishment."[33] We are willing to punish people who break the rules or act noncooperatively, even when it is personally costly to do so. Chimpanzees enter into many "I'll scratch your back, you scratch mine" cooperative relationships, but if the other individual fails to reciprocate, they simply end the relationship and refuse to cooperate with that individual again. Humans, on the other hand, will often go out of their way to retaliate, usually at some risk to themselves. Furthermore, uninvolved third parties will sometimes intervene—again, at some risk to themselves—in order to see that the defector makes good or is punished for defecting. There is good reason to think that this propensity is innate, not cultural, simply because it is part of the structure that allows us to acquire and transmit culture in the form of shared rules and institutions. Retributiveness is also quite a visceral, intuitive reaction, which people have difficulty rationalizing.

Now when it comes to organizing cooperation in small groups, retributiveness is clearly advantageous. If you're trying to decide whether to take advantage of someone in a community of merely self-interested individuals, you have to weigh the short-term benefits of free riding against the benefits that you will forego if you get shut out of future cooperative relations. But if you also have to factor in the possibility of retaliation—that some people might track you down and make you suffer, just to get you back for what you did—then it becomes a lot harder to make the case for free riding. This is why, for instance, organized criminal groups can maintain stable systems of cooperation—such as a code of silence—despite their lack of legal authority over members. They are able to operate an entirely decentralized system of punishment.

The big weakness with this system is that it doesn't handle accidents very well. When someone does something wrong then suffers some violence by way of retaliation, we may accept this as a legitimate response. If, however, it is some misunderstanding or accident that leads to an act of retaliation, the person who suffers it is likely to regard it as an act of unwarranted aggression and so respond in kind. This can set off a sequence of tit-for-tat retaliation, in which each new act of "punishment" *compels* the other to respond in kind, creating what we refer to as a "feud." Indeed, if one examines the more famous blood feuds in history, they almost always begin with some alcohol-induced act of violence (or even just insult) that one side took very seriously but that the other side felt should have been excused. As a result, the initial retaliation was not accepted as fair but was instead treated as a provocation, which must be retaliated against. This second retaliation was, in turn, treated as provocation, and so was responded to in kind. Thus the two sides became locked into a pattern of reciprocal violence, of the sort that can last for generations. Indeed, what makes the pattern so difficult to break is that everyone involved feels obliged to continue the feud—that it would be a betrayal of the victims on their side to forgive and forget.

This is a fairly large bug in the human motivational system, because as the number of individuals involved in a cooperative interaction increases, the chances of an accidental defection increase as well.[34] Anyone who has ever worked on a group project or team will know the dynamic. Social pressure can be very effective in small groups, but as the number of people and the anonymity of interaction increase, the chances that everything will fall apart, that the group will collapse into mutual recrimination and paralysis, increases as well. We all know what this sounds like: "If he's not going to help, why should I?" "Let's see how you like it when someone does that to you." "I'll get mine finished just as soon as she finishes hers." These sorts of feelings are often perfectly legitimate, and yet at the same time collectively disastrous. Unfortunately, we have no intuitive feel for when our retributive sentiments are helping out and when they are making things worse.

The only way out of the state of nature involves a rational insight into the structure of the collective action problems we face. Almost every intractable collective action problem involves a conflict between parties, each of which sees itself as good (or as having acted correctly) and its opponents as evil (or as having acted wrongly). This is usually the product of a powerful blend of myside bias, in-group solidarity, and retributivism. And yet this characterization of the problem ("We're good, they're evil") is itself a major source of the problem. It's because each side sees things this way that both refuse to back down. And it's not just that they don't want to back down, it's that they both feel morally obliged to *not* back down.

It's easy to see how collective action problems, by their very structure, encourage this way of thinking. These problems arise when it is possible to create a slight benefit for yourself by creating a larger cost for someone else. Consider a typical "tragedy of the commons," like overfishing. Catching a lot of fish is obviously beneficial for the individual fisherman. But it also creates a cost. By reducing the breeding stock, it reduces the overall fish population, making it difficult to catch as many fish the following year. In extreme cases, it can lead to the complete collapse of the fish stock (as happened with the cod fishery on the Grand Banks off Newfoundland). So why would anyone do this? It's not short-sightedness. It's not that fishermen fail to anticipate that their actions will eventually undermine their own livelihood. It's that each individual was able to capture for himself some of the benefits associated with overfishing, whereas almost all of the costs were transferred onto others. So even though the costs were much greater than the benefits, everyone still had an incentive to produce them.

But when you examine the outcome, it's easy to see how everyone could consider the whole thing to be someone else's fault. After all, if you look at the damage that you suffer, it actually is caused by someone else. So the obvious solution seems to be for the other person to stop what he is doing. If someone were to come along and say "No, *you* need to stop doing it," the natural reaction would be to say "Let him stop first," or maybe "What, are you crazy? If I stop doing it then he gets all the benefit, and I get nothing," or even worse, "No way—not until I pay that bastard back for what he did to me." The problem is that both people say exactly the same thing, and so no one ever stops.

I have heard Newfoundlanders react with outrage—outrage!—at the suggestion that the collapse of the cod fishery was in any way their fault. Why? According to them, it was the Spanish and Portuguese, fishing in international waters, who were to blame. *They* were the ones fishing without quotas, using illegal nets, and so on. When you think about it, Newfoundlanders really had no choice but to take as much as they could. If they had cut back on their catch, it would have just left more for the international fleet. The cod stocks would have collapsed either way; all Newfoundlanders did was try to get their fair share.

That's the story in Newfoundland. But of course, one could undoubtedly go to Spain and Portugal and hear exactly the same story in reverse. They were blameless, it was all the fault of the Canadians, and so on. In a sense, both stories are correct. In a collective action problem, everything bad that happens to *you* is actually someone else's fault. None of this changes the fact, however, that the only way to solve the problem is for everyone, including you, to stop what they're doing, and that means providing a benefit to the very same people who have, in the past, harmed you. This is so contrary to both instinct and intuition that it takes Herculean self-restraint for most people to get out of these problems. First of all, it takes a radical break with our own perspective, in order to see how our actions look to the other person. This typically involves the realization that other people are not evil, but are in fact acting on the same set of motives that we have. The entire language of "good" and "evil" needs to be overcome. Needless to say, this is the sort of insight that only reason can attain. Then, once we have achieved this rational insight into the structure of the problem, we must also impose an override on our intuitions, in order to resist the retaliatory urges that assail us at every level. Most of us are unable to do so, which is why we rely so heavily on kluges in order to achieve large-scale cooperation.

The most important institutional work-around that we have for this is the state.[35] The state promotes cooperation not just by making and enforcing laws, but by exercising a monopoly on the legitimate use of force. It eliminates the disorder and chaos created by private vendettas and feuds by essentially denying individuals the right to private retaliation. Political theorists have long argued that this marks the central difference between the "civil condition" and the state of nature—or, to put it less delicately, between civilization and barbarism. Individuals in the civil condition must renounce the private use of force. This was a major idea in social contract theory, from Hobbes through Locke, and is a principle that is reflected in the basic structure of criminal law in our society.[36] Civil suits involve a conflict between two parties—the plaintiff and the defendant—but criminal cases are always "the state" versus the defendant. Many people find this surprising, because they think that the victim of the crime should be the aggrieved party, not the state. They also find it surprising that, say, the families of Ronald Goldman and Nicole Brown Simpson should have been able to successfully sue O. J. Simpson for the death of their children even though Simpson had been acquitted of criminal charges in the matter. The distinction, however, makes perfect sense. As a result of the civil suit, Simpson was required to pay *compensation* to the families, but he was not *punished*. (Similarly, if you steal something, a civil court can make you give it back, but only a criminal court can punish you, above and beyond that, for having taken it.[37]) Compensation is a private matter between individuals, appropriately dealt with by the civil courts. Punishment is not a private matter, but is rather a public prerogative, and is therefore an issue between the individual and the state. This is a reflection of the fact that individuals in our society are taken to have renounced their right to use force against one another.

If anything deserves to be called the bedrock principle of civilization, this is it. Indeed, one of the major developmental hurdles that societies must overcome is the transition from tribal to hierarchical societies.[38] Even though very advanced systems of cooperation have been organized in tribal societies, there is a clear limit on the level of complexity they can achieve. All major world civilizations have developed only after the subordination of tribal loyalties into a broader, hierarchically organized state that claims a monopoly on the use of force.[39]

The most common mistake that people make when thinking about human sociability is to assume that large-scale civilization is just a scaled-up version of tribal society, able to rely on the same sort of dispositions and instincts. This is not correct. There is a huge developmental hump in the transition from tribal society to the state—one that many societies simply never make it over. The configuration that results at the far end is not natural at all, but involves selective uptake, manipulation, and suppression of our natural impulses. For example, people still have extremely powerful retributivist urges, which never go away and which are never fully satisfied in the civil condition. This is why acts of vigilantism and, more broadly, fantasies about punitive violence and retribution (think of movies like *Death Wish, Dirty Harry, Falling Down,* and *The Brave One*) are ubiquitous in our society. No matter how punitive the criminal justice system, and no matter how widely the net is cast, a large segment of society will never be satisfied. Why? Simply because a civilized society is structurally incapable of satisfying the thirst for vengeance that many people find viscerally compelling.

¶

The most striking feature of collective action problems is the way that people—indeed, whole societies—can get stuck in them. Everyone can see that there is a problem, and in many cases everyone can even agree about what the solution would be. Unfortunately, as long as everyone else is acting in a way that contributes to the problem, no one has any individual incentive to stop. There are many traps like this that societies can fall into. Official corruption, tax avoidance, or even just widespread rudeness are all good examples. Once such a behavior becomes widespread, it is extremely difficult to dislodge. Furthermore, it is in many cases impossible for the society to "evolve" its way out of the problem. Evolution, whether biological or cultural, works through a series of small steps, each of which must constitute something of an improvement over the previous one. In a collective action problem, however, each small step typically makes things worse for the person who takes it. The situation can be improved only if everyone takes a big step. These are the cases in which reason must play a central role. Because it's not possible to try out multiple options in order to see which one is best, we have no choice but to develop the best models of the problem that we can, in order to determine, in the abstract, which one we should choose. We cannot wait and see: we have to try to pick a winner.

One can see here the limitations of the Burke's defense of tradition. Although the mechanism of cultural evolution is extremely powerful in some cases, it is also capable of getting stuck in blind alleys and dead ends. There are times when piecemeal reform will not do, and a complete overhaul is required. Consider the case of police corruption. Once the police start taking bribes, it's incredibly difficult to get them to stop. First of all, whatever rules you may impose, who is going to enforce them? Second, the existence of this secondary income source results over time in lower wages, which means that police officers become dependent upon bribes in order to make ends meet. This makes it difficult for one officer, or even a committed group of officers, to stop taking bribes. Thus the "culture of bribery" becomes self-enforcing, in many cases resulting in government paralysis. There is no obvious way of "evolving" out of it. The only way to fix the problem is to do something dramatic (as in the Republic of Georgia, where in 2005 President Mikheil Saakashvili decided to eliminate corruption among traffic police by firing the entire force—30,000 officers).

Thus there is no one-size-fits-all solution to the question of how social change should occur. There are times when the Burkean faith in tradition, along with the powers of piecemeal social reform, is entirely appropriate. But there are also times when Enlightenment rationalism and radical change are called for. The American political system, for instance, is designed to break up any large concentrations of power. One consequence is that anything other than piecemeal reform is extremely difficult to achieve. Yet the inefficiencies that result from incrementalism tend to accumulate over time.[40] The effects of this can be seen all over. Consider the American tax code, which is extraordinarily byzantine and seems as though it were designed to antagonize the population. While many countries do a complete overhaul of the tax system every decade or so, the United States has gotten along with mere tinkering. The same can be said for health care. It is extremely difficult to see how any incremental process could improve things. Anything less than a complete overhaul will simply lead to increased spending. Yet the American political system is simply not capable of delivering "overhauls" of anything.

Although many Americans manage to persuade themselves that this is one of the virtues of their system,[41] the fact that no other nation in the world has chosen to imitate it speaks volumes. Sometimes big problems require dramatic solutions. This is something that business managers have come to understand. Some organizations can be reformed, but others simply have to be broken apart and put back together along entirely different principles. We need to respect the power of "bottom-up" solutions, but we also need to leave room for radical, sweeping reform in cases where we are mired in muck or locked into a self-reinforcing system of mutual antagonism. So while it's important not to overstate the powers of reason, when it comes to understanding complex systems it's also important to realize that sometimes the only way to move things forward is through big, ambitious plans for reform. Big plans, however, can only be formulated and implemented through the exercise of our rational faculties.

¶

To say that we need to strike a balance between reason and intuition would be to say something true but uninformative. The question is how to decide *when* we should place our trust in nonrational problem-solving mechanisms. Here it is helpful to have a sense of what these different systems are good at and where they struggle. Consider the following as a scorecard for the nonrational parts of our brain.

Things that it's very good at:
Pattern recognition
Tracking movement
Mind reading
Remembering things
Building associations
Seeing the big picture

Things that it can't do:
Count past three
Follow an argument with more than two steps
Consider hypothetical states of affairs
Think strategically
Manage uncertainty
Carry out a long-term plan
Solve large-scale collective action problems

For all its weaknesses, the list of things that only reason can do is quite impressive. Furthermore, the political implications of this analysis are clear. Civilization is not something that arose spontaneously, as an expression of our natural sociability (the way that a hive is to bees). On the contrary, civilization represents the triumph of reason over intuition. It is a precarious achievement, one that is reproduced only because we are able to systematic-ally cultivate and reproduce the controlled processing style of cognition that allows us to preempt and override our more intuitive responses when we judge that these are liable to produce collectively self-defeating out-comes. In this respect, Freud was right in saying that civilization is built upon a partial repression of our instincts. The "natural" form of political authority is just personal loyalty to the ruler. Establishing a system whereby individuals show loyalty to an institution—to the *office* of the ruler, rather than to the *person*—is highly unnatural.

Looking around, it is easy to see that most of the institutional features that make our society decent and livable are unnatural in the same way. The rule of law is achieved only when individuals renounce the private use of force and sublimate their retributivist impulses. A market economy is possible only when individuals abstract from the fairness of particular transactions and evaluate the merits of the system in terms of its aggre-gate effects. Bureaucratic administration is possible only when individuals resist the temptation to use their power to advance the interests of friends and family. The modern welfare state arises when individuals accept that not all collective action problems can be solved through informal sys-tems of reciprocity, that some require the organized enforcement of rules. Multiculturalism and ethnic tolerance are possible only when individuals recognize the cultural specificity of many of their own norms of conduct and so refrain from trying to impose them on others. Each one of these steps is *extremely* demanding, in the sense that it requires both self-control, in order to override the intuitive response, and very abstract, hypothetical reasoning, in order to see the rationale for the institutional arrangement.

The take-home lesson is that in the centuries-old struggle between civilization and barbarism, reason is not a neutral bystander. Certain insti-tutional arrangements are actually "more rational" than others, in the sense that they depend upon people being rational for their reproduction and their merits can be properly assessed only from a rational point of view. This has important implications in the political domain, because it means that certain institutional arrangements can be defended only through appeal to rational arguments and considerations. And thus, to the extent that rationality is squeezed out of democratic political discourse, we may find that a gradual slide into barbarism is the inevitable outcome.

Part II

The Age of Unreason

Holding a rally to "restore" sanity suggests that there was a time, perhaps not long ago, when people were more sane than they are now. But is this so obvious? There is always a temptation to think that the world is getting worse, in every possible way. How can we tell if it's true? Two broad trends should be of concern. First, an unhealthy dynamic is at work in our culture whereby memes that are able to successfully exploit human irrationality seem to prosper—a tendency that is exacerbated by commercial society. Second, influential political movements have arisen, on the left as well as the right, that are explicitly hostile to reason.

6. Has the world gone mad?

. . . or is it just me?

Suppose for a moment that the world were going mad. How would you know? You look around, what do you see? Television is dominated by the raving of lunatics. The public at large is losing the ability to distinguish fiction from reality. Politicians keep repeating the same lies, oblivious to any and all attempts at correction. Banks trip over each other to make loans to people who have no realistic chances of ever repaying. Shoppers cram the malls and consumers buy ever-larger homes and cars, ignoring the environmental catastrophe that lurks just over the horizon. And yet how do you know it isn't just you? Asylums are full of people who think that everyone else is crazy. They wonder how it is possible that others miss the obvious evidence of government conspiracy, or alien abduction, or the signs of divinity in their person. People in cults feel pretty much the same way.

That is why Jon Stewart's Rally to Restore Sanity was a bold move. Accusing your political opponents of being irrational is a difficult charge to make stick, since it raises a number of special philosophical problems. Accusing your opponents of torturing puppies is a straightforward matter—either they did or they didn't; there is a fact of the matter that can be uncovered. Maybe someone can produce a video. Accusing them of irrationality is much trickier. There is no obvious fact that could settle the question; it seems to be just a matter of perspective. One of the most well-established results in the literature on cognitive biases is that people are terrible at distinguishing genuine irrationality from simple disagreement.

As we have seen, our cognitive miserliness often manifests itself in the form of belief bias. When asked to evaluate an argument, to determine whether it is logically valid, we skim it over quickly then simply look at the conclusion and ask whether we think it is true. As a result, logically invalid arguments leading to conclusions that happen to be true ("Roses are living things") will often be judged valid, while valid arguments leading to conclusions that happen to be false will be judged invalid. We have enormous difficulty separating the question of whether a particular piece of *reasoning* is correct from that of whether we agree with the answer it produces. Working this through properly involves a significant feat of abstraction. And because abstraction is cognitively demanding, our default course of action is to attribute faulty reasoning to everyone who disagrees with us.

So for every liberal who thinks that conservatives are crazy, there is a conservative who thinks that liberals are crazy. For every old-timer who thinks that kids these days are crazy, there are a bunch of kids who think that old people are crazy. For every man who thinks that women are crazy, there is a woman who thinks that men are crazy. One might be tempted to conclude from all this that the question of who is rational and who is irrational is undecidable or purely subjective. *Crazy*, as many people in the '60s suggested, may be just another word for "different."

And yet . . . there's crazy, and then there's *crazy*. There does seem to have been a noticeable increase in nuttiness in recent years—particularly in the United States (leading Susan Jacoby to declare this the "age of American unreason"[1]). To pick just one example, the number of Americans who profess to believe in man-made climate change declined from more than 70 percent of the population to fewer than 40 percent over the course of a decade.[2] Rick Perry, the governor of Texas, one of the majority of Americans who don't believe climate science, responded to the searing hot temperatures in the summer of 2011 by declaring three official "Days of Prayer for Rain." All the while the oil wells kept pumping. This was not seen as a major impediment to Perry's run for the Republican presidential nomination. After all, 83 percent of Americans believe that God literally listens to and answers prayers.[3] Perhaps having the government order them to engage in mass prayer does not seem like such a stretch.

And yet how can this be regarded as anything other than a catastrophic failure of the Enlightenment project? That people are still capable of thinking and acting this way—impotently beseeching the gods to solve problems that they themselves have created—is not just an embarrassment to Americans, it's humbling for our species as a whole.

Small wonder that so many Americans have begun to think that political ideology is no longer at the root of their problems. The issue is not that a segment of the population doesn't care about the poor, or has retrograde attitudes toward women, or has become hostile to equality; the problem is that a significant segment of the population is out of touch with reality and is no longer operating within the conventional boundaries of rational argumentation and thought. It is no surprise that commentators have taken to distinguishing the "reality-based community" from the other political constituencies that pepper the American political landscape.

But in order to make these charges stick, something more than just people's impressions will be required. The fact that large segments of the population *seem* to be crazy is not enough to settle the question. Some sort of independent evidence is required. Better yet, we need an explanatory mechanism or model that could show how a problem like this can arise and what sort of factors will exacerbate it.

As it turns out, there is an excellent model available. Understanding it, however, requires looking at some features of our everyday environment in a slightly different light.

❡

Philosophers are sometimes accused of not believing in irrationality—or, more precisely, of claiming that widespread irrationality is a conceptual impossibility.[4] This is a bit of an overstatement. The more general view among philosophers is that attributions of irrationality raise special difficulties because they are *uncharitable*. The problem with uncharitable interpretations is that they make things a bit too easy for the interpreter, to the point where it can undermine the plausibility of the interpretation. Suppose you're watching a baseball game when you overhear your neighbor complaining about what a terrible cricket match it is. The players keep making so many mistakes! Indeed, they seem to barely understand the rules at all. The problem here is obviously not with the players, but with the interpretation. If an interpretation attributes too many mistakes to other people, it suggests that the interpreter may simply be misunderstanding what is going on.

People are, in general, quite difficult to figure out. As we all know, the things that we do and say can be interpreted in many different ways. In order to avoid perpetual misunderstanding, we need some way of distinguishing good interpretations from bad ones. According to one highly influential argument, advanced by the American philosopher Donald Davidson, the way that we do this is by privileging the interpretation that makes the person being interpreted come out sounding the most reasonable.[5] This doesn't mean that irrationality is impossible, it just means that irrationality should be invoked only as a last resort, when all of the other, ordinary interpretations of people's behavior have been exhausted.

This principle was illustrated quite nicely by a satirical headline in *The Onion,* many years ago, which had the usual form: "Area Man Diagnoses Wife with Psychiatric Disorder." The story featured an interview with the "area man," who insisted that his wife came home from work one day and "just went crazy," started screaming and cursing, and eventually threw him out on the street. Reading the story, however, additional details begin to emerge that cast doubt upon his account. It turns out that the man was unemployed, while his wife had just finished working a double shift. He had invited a few friends over to watch the game on TV. An ashtray and maybe a few beers had spilled on the carpet, which she seemed particularly upset about, even though he had every intention of cleaning them up . . .

The joke, obviously, is that his wife started screaming not because she was mentally ill, but because she came home after a hard day at work to find her unemployed husband sitting around with his loser friends trashing the house. It is important to note, however, that none of the additional details that emerge are strictly speaking *inconsistent* with the hypothesis that his wife suffered some sort of an unexpected mental breakdown. Things could have happened in exactly the way that the husband reported. What makes us doubt his interpretation, however, is that as the facts emerge, they begin to suggest a more plausible explanation. Her anger might also have been a reasonable response to her husband's actions. Indeed, what quickly becomes apparent as the article progresses is that the husband's ascription of irrationality in this case was outrageously self-serving.

Davidson's key observation is that when we evaluate two rival interpretations, we have no need to refer to any independent evidence in order to assess their plausibility. We don't need to ask whether the wife had any history of psychiatric illness. What makes the second interpretation ("She got mad because her husband did almost everything possible to upset her") better is simply the fact that it makes her reaction more understandable, which is to say, more reasonable. The problem with ascribing irrationality to people is that it provides too much creative license, allows us to make up a wide range of interpretations consistent with the facts. (This is what allows the husband to select the most self-serving interpretation of his wife's behavior rather than the one in which he is responsible.) In everyday conversation, the way we narrow things down in order to make communication possible is by minimizing the level of irrationality and error that we ascribe to one another.

This is, of course, not to deny that people can be irrational, that they don't have many false beliefs, or that we are not all subject to a wide range of cognitive biases. What it means is simply that the way we go about figuring out what people are up to is by assuming that their beliefs are largely true and their reasoning largely valid. If we didn't do this, we would immediately be overwhelmed by the number of interpretive possibilities. ("He asked for a cup of coffee, but maybe he was confused about the difference between coffee and tea, and what he really wanted was a cup of tea? Or maybe he wanted milk? Or maybe he didn't want anything at all but was merely testing me to see whether I know what coffee is?") Interpretations that hinge on the ascription of irrationality and error to others shoulder a special burden of proof, precisely because of that ascription. This doesn't mean that the burden can't be discharged. It means just that we have to be careful about throwing around these accusations. What we think of as an exposé of the errors made by others can quickly become an indictment of the exposé itself, simply because every time we ascribe an error to another person, we also increase, just slightly, the suspicion that we have misunderstood that person. If our understanding of the world depends crucially upon the claim that everyone else is an idiot, evil, on the take, or part of the conspiracy, then the problem almost certainly lies with our understanding and not with the world.[6]

That said, there can be little doubt that the psychological studies associated with the "heuristics and biases" tradition have succeeded in showing that there are widespread deviations from rationality, particularly in the areas outlined in the previous chapter (confirmation bias, optimism bias, belief bias, etc.). The point is that armchair observation was insufficient to establish this result; the conclusion required a very large number of well-designed studies (and even then, it remains controversial).[7] The fact that ascriptions of irrationality shoulder a significant burden of proof does not mean that they cannot be vindicated. All it means is that when making these kinds of accusations, and trying to make them stick, it is necessary to provide much more in the way of evidence than in the case of ordinary factual claims. Similarly, in order to make the case that our civilization is suffering from a decline in rationality, some reason to believe this must be provided, above and beyond our personal impressions.

¶

The most important thing we have learned about human reason over the course of the past three hundred years is that it is deeply embedded in and dependent upon its environment, both physical and social. First and foremost, many of the shortcuts that our brains use to provide fast solutions exploit regularities and associations that occur only in standard natural environments. Second, many of the rational problem-solving competences we have developed use environmental kluges to overcome the limitations of our evolved cognitive systems. We have, as Andy Clark puts it, built "designer environments" that allow us to enhance the power of the "unaugmented biological brain."[8]

But because of this, it is not difficult to imagine a situation in which people become less rational or the effectiveness of their problem-solving strategies becomes impaired not because of any degradation of their "onboard" resources, but simply through changes in the external environment. Certain environments will naturally be more conducive to effective problem-solving than others. This is obvious when we are trying to do something like solve a math problem while surrounded by loud noise or distracting conversation. There are, however, an infinite number of more subtle ways in which changes in our environment can impair thought.

Many of the intuitive heuristics that we use in decision making depend upon the use of proxies—taking something that is easily observable as a kind of substitute, or stand-in, for something that is not. Changes in the environment can easily lead these heuristics to misfire simply by disrupting the correlation that existed in the environment of evolutionary adaptation. For example, people have a natural aversion to blue food. The presumptive explanation is that, in a natural environment, most food turns blue only when it is moldy or rotten. In the modern world, however, any food can be dyed any color, and so the correlation between "blue" and "unsuitable for human consumption" largely disappears. And yet our minds continue to associate the two. (When margarine was first introduced to the market, dairy farmers pressed for regulations that would have forced manufacturers to dye it blue, precisely to diminish consumer acceptance. Although this initiative failed, in many jurisdictions they did succeed in forcing manufactures to dye it an "unnatural" orange color.)

This reliance on proxies is a ubiquitous feature of our intuitive problem-solving systems. As a result, when the environment changes such that the triggering stimulus is no longer a good proxy for the underlying phenomenon, our intuitive problem-solving heuristics are likely to fail. We have already observed, for instance, that in the environment of evolutionary adaptation, almost the only way to see something happen was for it to actually happen. Thus it made perfect sense for our brains to figure out how common things are by keeping track of the number of times that we have *seen* them happen. The introduction of images drives a wedge between the two, making it possible to see things happen again and again, even when they have only happened once. And yet every time we see an image, our brain unconsciously logs it as an additional occurrence. This means that our intuitions about how often various things occur, and thus about how likely they are to occur again, become extremely unreliable. Unless we are constantly paying attention and exercising a conscious override, we risk being misled. Perhaps the most dramatic example of this is the sharp increase in parental fear of child abduction in the United States, due almost entirely to media coverage and depictions in fiction. The most authoritative study in the United States suggested that in 1999 there were only 115 "stereotypical nonfamily abductions" out of a population of over 70 million children.[9] This is, by any account, a vanishingly small number. Furthermore, rates have since declined, in keeping with the general downward trajectory of crime rates in the United States. And yet parental fear has, if anything, increased.

Similarly, in a world without images, the number of times you have seen someone is a very reliable indicator of how well you know that person, and thus of who is a friend and who is a stranger. Living in a world surrounded by images, however, can lead us to feel as though we are close to people whom we have never met, such as celebrities. (I once mistakenly said hello to the comedian Mike Myers on the street in Toronto. He looked familiar, so I just assumed that he was someone I knew. Passing someone on the street gives you only seconds to decide whether to greet or not to greet, and so not enough time to engage in rational reflection. You have no choice but to go with your intuitive response.) In certain pathological cases, this can lead people to feel closer to strangers than they do to their own friends. In the case of celebrity obsession, one can observe individuals who are unable to exercise the cognitive override required to impose the judgment that, even though *you* may feel incredibly close to them, *they* regard you as just another stranger. If you listen to your "gut," it tells you that you have been friends with this person your entire life. It's only by listening to your "head" that you realize it isn't true. The gut feeling is a straight-up cognitive misfire.

The result is that as our environment changes, as it becomes more unnatural, it makes our fast, intuitive problem-solving strategies increasingly unreliable. This places increasing demands on our rational faculties—increasing our cognitive load, requiring us to pay more attention and exercise greater effort. We find ourselves constantly having to override our natural impulses in order to think things through more carefully. Reason, however, is subject to bottlenecks, and attention is an intrinsically scarce resource. So it is inevitable that as our environment becomes more unnatural, we begin to see a degradation of cognitive performance. This is the basis of Keith Stanovich's comparison of the modern world to a sodium vapor lamp.

If this were the whole story, however, the problem would not be all that significant. Unfortunately, there is one respect in which the sodium vapor lamp analogy is quite misleading. This particular method of making light was invented in order to produce the maximum level of illumination with a given amount of electricity, and it has been adopted primarily because of its low operating cost. The fact that these bulbs generate an unnatural light that tricks the eye into seeing certain colors wrong is entirely incidental to both their function and their spread. If anything, the visual illusion is an irritant, and counts against the widespread adoption of these bulbs (and is one of the factors leading to their current replacement by LEDs). Yet many of the unnatural features of the modern world—the ones that confuse our natural problem-solving heuristics, leading us to make poor decisions—have been invented and become ubiquitous *precisely because* of their tendency to mislead us. The cognitive misfire that they generate is not an accidental byproduct, it is their primary purpose.

There are so many examples of this around us that we have become in many ways inured to them. Consider, for example, something as simple as the cap on a typical bottle of liquid laundry detergent.[10] This is actually a finely crafted artifact, the product of a long process of design and adaptation, a repository of not inconsiderable human ingenuity, all with the specific purpose of misleading the consumer. The typical laundry detergent cap exploits no fewer than three different human frailties, with the intention of tricking us into using too much detergent. First of all, there is the simple fact that the cap itself is outrageously large, potentially holding far more detergent than is needed for a single load. (With the brand that I am currently using, one capful is enough for approximately six loads.) The inattentive consumer will simply assume that one capful equals one load, and proceed on this basis. And even for those who know better, the capful serves as an anchor, systematically biasing us in the direction of pouring out too much detergent.[11]

Second, in order to figure out the correct amount to use, one must actually look down *into* the cap, where it is possible to find a faintly traced line, with a small number 1 beside it. Note that it does not say "single load" or anything to that effect; there are simply three lines, labeled 1, 2, and 3. And rather than the cap's being transparent, so that these interior markings are clearly visible, it is both opaque and dark blue. There are no markings on the exterior of the cap, and the markings on the interior are merely embossed, in the same color, making it impossible to read them under less than ideal lighting conditions, such as one would find in a typical basement where laundry is done. In order to read them, one must actually shine a bright light into the cap. None of this is accidental.

Finally, there is the shape of the cap, which has over the years been redesigned in order to make it much fatter and less tall. As Frances Woolley has noted, this is designed to exploit a very persistent cognitive bias that leads us to underestimate the amount of liquid in short, wide glasses, compared to tall, thin ones.[12] Studies have shown that even experienced bartenders fall victim to this illusion.[13] Everything conspires in a single direction, which is to get people to use too much detergent. Again, this is not an accident. The cap has been crafted and carefully refined over the years in order to achieve precisely this effect. Indeed, those of us who are old enough can remember when the caps were much smaller, and how they gradually got larger and fatter. It is not an exaggeration to say that the cap has evolved in such a way as to better take advantage of the bugs in our cognitive system. (The predictable consequence is that the average person uses far too much laundry soap, leading to unnecessary wear and tear on their clothing.)

The laundry cap is a perfect example of an artifact that is exquisitely adapted for one task, which is to make us stupid. I call objects of this type *deceptors*. Once you start to look around, you can find them everywhere. Pop open the hood of your car, for instance, and you will see plastic casings—boxlike, often with round holes in them—around various components, as well as lining the inside of the hood. In the business they call these *resonators*; their primary function is to transform the sound of the engine, so that drivers like the sound that they hear when they step on the gas.

Some cars even have plastic tubes that feed sound into the passenger compartment at specific frequencies.

During the glory days of the American muscle car, engines made a sound that struck most people as just right—a nice, throaty roar. The demand for higher fuel economy, however, has imposed a number of design constraints on engines that make them less likely to produce the hard revving sound that drivers equate with power or performance. The solution? Change the sound, using the same technology that you can find in any guitar, violin, or cello. When you listen to the sound of the engine in your car, you are basically listening to a musical instrument designed to produce the kind of sound that you *want* your engine to make, not the sound that your engine *actually* makes. It is nothing but a deceptor.

What these deceptors all have in common is that they cause our intuitive problem-solving heuristics to misfire, but in a way that is not accidental to their purpose. They constitute successful designs precisely *because* of the way that they impair our decision-making powers.

¶

Heuristic problem-solving strategies, which rely on easy-to-observe proxies as a stand-in for difficult-to-observe features of reality, work only in what Stanovich refers to as "benign environments," where no one or no thing is trying to gain an advantage over the problem solver.[15] Nature is, for the most part, such an environment, but only because biological evolution is extremely slow. The sloppiness of human cognition creates a lot of ecological niches that other species *could* exploit, it's just that it takes them a long time to arise, and humans are a very recent addition to the planet's fauna. One can nevertheless see the effects in certain species that have evolved adaptations designed specifically to take advantage of human cognitive misfires.

For example, humans, like most mammals, behave altruistically toward their own offspring (feeding them, protecting them from attack, etc.), and there are good evolutionary reasons why such a disposition should have evolved. Yet the mechanism that we use to identify our own offspring is quite rough and ready—we rely primarily upon a set of visual cues, most importantly what are known to psychologists as *neotenous characteristics* but which in ordinary English we simply call "cuteness." Cuteness is a blend of universal characteristics (large eyes, small nose, large head-to-body ratio, hair of a different color, etc.) with some measure of physical resemblance. This tends to evoke caring behavior. Put simply, we look after children because we find them incredibly cute, and we show favor to our own children because we find them cuter than others. This disposition is not particularly discriminatory, as witnessed by the fact that many people are happy to look after other people's kids as well as their own, and find it just as rewarding. But it creates an enormous ecological niche for other animals. Instead of going out and finding your own food, why not trick a human into feeding you, just by being cute?

This sort of parasitism is not unknown in the animal kingdom. Most famously, the cuckoo exploits the magpie by laying its eggs in the magpie nest then letting the magpies do all the work of feeding its chicks. As it turns out, the trigger that generates parental investment in magpies—their equivalent of cuteness—is a combination of the begging cry that chicks make and the sight of their gape. The cuckoo has therefore evolved a particular pattern in its gape, and a more frequent and persistent cry, so that the magpies will be more likely to feed it than they will their own chicks.[16] On a nastier note, cuckoos have also evolved a homicidal impulse, so that the cuckoo chick will try to destroy any other eggs in the nest before they hatch, or it will kill any magpie chicks rather than share a nest with them. Because of a cognitive misfire, one can see the tragic spectacle of magpies going about their business, blithely caring for the monster who just days before snuck into the home, killed the children, and took their place.

Of course, we don't react all that favorably to gaping red gullets and so are not subject to this particular form of exploitation. But if you look at the things that we do react favorably to, and then you look at some of the animal species we surround ourselves with, some uncomfortable parallels to the magpie become apparent. It is not an accident, for instance, that we find dogs and cats particularly cute (consider the expression "puppy-dog eyes," or how much time people can waste looking at pictures of cats on the internet). Dogs are, in many ways, just superneotenous wolves. They have evolved in the direction of preserving juvenile characteristics into adulthood—not just aspects of appearance, but also of behavior, such as barking or playing, which is something that only wolf pups, not adult wolves, do. One can only assume that much of the behavior that we interpret as emotional is also an adaptation that arose precisely as a way of inducing us to care for them.[17]

Clark uses the term *reverse adaptation* to describe this process through which the things around us evolve in response to our own habits of mind and behavior. In the same way that we depend upon elements of our environment in order to reproduce ourselves, some elements of the environment depend upon *us* in order to reproduce themselves. Thus we find ourselves not only with bodies and brains that are adapted to dealing with our environment, but also in an environment that is in many ways— both subtle and gross—adapted to dealing with us. Sometimes this sort of reverse adaptation works to our benefit, but often it does not.

Consider, for instance, the remarkable phenomenon of fruit. It is no accident that, in the religious imagination, the existence of fruit has always been regarded as a sure sign of God's love for his creatures. When you stop to think about it, there is something rather extraordinary about being able to walk into a wild, untamed forest and to find in it, ready-made, these extremely tasty, sweet, nutritious, and colorful foodstuffs, just dangling from the trees or bushes, easy to pick, suitable for holding in the palm of one's hand. It's as though someone out there knew exactly what we like and designed the apple or the blueberry just for us.

Yet part of the reason that fruit seems extraordinary is that we tend to think of ourselves as being adapted to our environment, rather than the other way around. In this case, however, it isn't us that has evolved to eat fruit, it is fruit that has evolved to be eaten by us. Fruit is just another little trick that plants have developed to solve the problem of seed dispersal. Because they can't move, plants need some way to spread their seeds around; otherwise, they wind up competing with their own offspring for sunlight and nutrients. The plant that hits upon a mechanism for getting its seeds somewhat farther away from itself than all the others will enjoy a reproductive advantage. One can find in nature many different mechanisms for achieving this end. Attaching the seed to something light and fluffy that can be picked up by the wind is one of the most popular solutions. Another approach is to hitch a ride on an animal or an insect that does move. Burrs, for example, are seed casings that have acquired the ability to stick to the fur of passing mammals, hopefully to be knocked off some distance from their point of origin. Fruit is a version of the same strategy, except here the objective is to get eaten by the mammal, have the seeds pass through its digestive system unmolested, then get "planted" (and fertilized) some distance from the point of origin.[18] Take an apple, cut it in half, and you can see exactly how the strategy is supposed to work.

With the "fruit" strategy in place, a competition develops between plants, in which the one that is most successful at getting its seeds eaten by mammals will have a reproductive advantage. So while plants are by nature bitter, poisonous, and green, over time some of them developed seed casings that are sweet, nontoxic, and colorful. This doesn't seem so amazing once we realize that the purpose of the entire scheme is to get eaten. Fruit are specifically adapted to satisfy not only mammalian tastes, but even our aesthetic preferences. That's because we are part of their reproductive strategy, and so the more effectively they cater to our tastes, the more likely they are to have offspring that will survive to adulthood. And whatever works, works.

This sort of reverse adaptation to human psychology is not that common in the biological sphere, though. When one looks at the cultural sphere, however, the picture changes entirely. Human culture is also a vast inheritance system, and whether it be in the realm of language, institutions, stories, or even songs, variants compete with one another. In this case, each of these things depends entirely upon us for its reproduction, and so there is a huge amount of reverse adaptation. Consider, for example, children's stories. It is tempting to think that the best ones were invented by some psychological genius who knew exactly how to push our buttons. The reality is much more prosaic. It is that the stories we hear are the result of a ruthless selection process. Each of us gets told literally thousands of different stories when we are young. A few of these stories—for most of us, a very few—will be sufficiently memorable that we will pass them along to our own children. It is useful to think of this as a gigantic competition between stories, in which the way for a story to survive is to get itself memorized and retold (or, in the era of the book, reprinted and repurchased). In such a highly competitive ecosystem, the more memorable stories will be the ones that are maximally effective at exploiting all the quirks of human psychology—in particular, catering to the biases of the "librarian" responsible for organizing and retrieving our memories—often in the most subtle ways possible. It's no accident that the stories you are most likely to pass along are hundreds, in many cases thousands, of years old. The fact that they are old is precisely due to the fact that they are the ones that are most adept at getting themselves reproduced.

If you look around, you can find evolutionary dynamics like this throughout the environment. Take fast food. Every year in the United States, tens of thousands of new restaurants open their doors, each with a menu that is slightly different from everyone else's. Of these, some very small fraction with the right type of menu will become sufficiently popular that they become franchised. In other words, they reproduce. And of the hundreds of new franchise restaurants introduced every year, a handful will become very successful, spread themselves across the country, and perhaps even expand into foreign markets. What is important to recognize is that these restaurants are the outcome of an extraordinarily competitive selection process. While they may cater to the lowest common denominator, we can be certain that their food also appeals to the most powerful human universals of taste. The burger and the french fry have essentially evolved in order to be liked by us (in very much the same way that fruit has evolved in order to be eaten). Indeed, one might even think of the apple as nature's attempt to produce a french fry.[19]

So when we look at the world around us, particularly the elements of the built environment, it is important not to think of it as something that is inert, simply a backdrop to our lives. It is, on the contrary, constantly changing and adapting to us. This raises an important question: Are these processes of reverse adaptation that operate in our culture likely to produce an environment that is more benign or more hostile to the quality of human decision making?

¶

The answer is, I think, easily discerned. Absent conscious guidance, cultural evolution will produce an environment that is more hostile to human rationality. We will wind up with an environment that is increasingly full of deceptors. There are three major forces at work producing this result, which I call *pooling, contagion,* and *pumping: pooling* because once a deceptor is invented, it is difficult to get rid of, and so deceptors tend to accumulate or "pool" in the population; *contagion* because, thanks to their deceptive nature, deceptors are often very good at reproducing themselves; and finally, *pumping* because the creators of these deceptors often use them to "pump" people for money, and so there is an economic incentive to produce them. These three forces conspire to make our environment more hostile over time. Of course, because these are mechanisms that operate in our culture, they are not something that nature does to us. Ultimately, they are things that we do to each other. But because they occur via evolutionary processes, we may not always notice them, and they can be incredibly hard to reverse.

The evolution of fruit is an example of a "nice" environmental adaptation. It is in this respect somewhat unusual, since the overwhelming majority of such adaptations are nasty. One need only compare the relative infrequency of symbiotism in nature, compared to parasitism, in order to see this. Consider the case of viruses. Most people realize that we have evolved adaptations that have arisen in response to viruses—our immune system, for instance. Fewer realize that viruses also evolve in response to us. We are, after all, the environment in which they reproduce. This is actually one of the reasons that we don't have to worry too much about the classic Hollywood movie supervirus, which kills, within hours, everyone with whom it comes into contact. In order to survive, a virus needs to reproduce. Any strain that kills its host too quickly is depriving itself of its own best means of reproduction and dispersal. (This is why, strangely enough, zombie virus movies, like *Resident Evil, 28 Days Later,* or *I Am Legend,* actually make more sense than the "serious" pandemic movies like *Contagion* or *Outbreak.* At least with zombies, you know how the virus gets reproduced.)

With a typical influenza virus, the person who catches it becomes contagious a day *before* she begins to show symptoms. It is precisely because of the delayed onset of symptoms that the virus is able to reproduce itself so successfully (while the person goes about her business, unaware that she is infecting others). By contrast, the SARS virus that caused such a scare in 2002–2003 eventually burned itself out, primarily because it made people sick too quickly. People who caught it already felt incredibly ill by the time they became contagious, and so typically stopped going to work, either staying at home or going to the hospital. Thus the virus was, from an evolutionary perspective, unfit, precisely because it made people sick too quickly. (Many people think that the rate of AIDS deaths has declined in part through the same mechanism—less deadly strains have a reproductive advantage over those that kill the host too quickly, and so the virus is evolving to become less deadly.)

These examples are striking because they show that viruses adapt not just to our physiology, but also to aspects of our social behavior, in order to maximize contagion. As a result of this, we wind up with a huge number of viruses malingering in the population. If they are too deadly, they burn themselves out—people either die or they develop immunity. And so human populations wind up carrying around with them a collection of viruses that have become nothing more than mid- to low-level nuisances.[20] It is common now to talk about "superbugs," which have an evolved resistance to antibiotics. But it is important to realize that almost all of the diseases in circulation are already a type of superbug, selected from among thousands of variants for their ability to exploit us in just the right way, not just dodging our immune system, but getting themselves reproduced without burning out. The problem is that once these extremely well-adapted bugs get added to the population, they very seldom go away, and so we wind up carrying along with ourselves an ever-expanding pool of viruses.

When one looks at things this way, it is discomforting to realize that many aspects of our culture function in the same way. The most obvious example is addictive substances. Addiction is a form of irrational behavior caused by the warp in the way that we evaluate future satisfaction. Certain substances produce a huge initial burst of pleasure, followed by nasty aftereffects, so that over the long term they are harmful. When examined at a distance, we may decide that they are not worth ingesting (smoking, snorting, shooting up, etc.). And yet when the opportunity presents itself, we may find ourselves tempted, because the immediate pleasure looms large while the aftereffects are more distant. And so we reverse ourselves, act against our "better judgment," only to regret the decision later. It is this cycle of commitment, reversal, and regret that is the most characteristic feature of addiction. It persists because of a weakness in the mechanism that we use to implement rational decisions. Things become even worse in cases where the aftereffects can be relieved by ingesting more of the substance (the time-honored trick of drinking to cure a hangover). In this case, regret quickly turns into a craving for more.

Addiction has posed a problem throughout much of human history. And yet, historically, most societies have had to deal with the problems posed by only one, at most two harmful addictive substances. Europeans had alcohol, Asians had opium, Native Americans had tobacco. One of the immediate impacts of international trade was that it globalized these substances—Europeans introduced alcohol to the Americas, and brought back tobacco and coca leaves. In some cases the health consequences were unknown, but in other cases—most notably, opium in Asia—they were not. In each of these cases, once the substance was introduced—the plant and its properties, in the case of opium and coca, or the method of distillation, in the case of alcohol—there was no way to reverse it. The knowledge gets preserved in the culture, and the substance kicks about. Thus each culture winds up carrying about an ever-expanding "pool" of addictive substances, in much the same way that it carries around an ever-expanding pool of viruses. (And in cases of contact between these globalized cultures and indigenous peoples, it is often difficult to say which causes more damage—the sudden exposure to the pool of highly contagious viruses or the exposure to highly addictive substances.)

If you look at the progress of human civilization, there has undoubtedly been some increase in the level of purely internal self-control people are able to exercise. Norbert Elias's brilliant and influential study of the history of table manners is often cited as evidence of this.[21] The upshot of Elias's argument is that the average ten-year-old in our society exercises more self-control than most European adults were even capable of three or four centuries ago. But there are limits to what can be achieved through socialization, simply because the process is subject to biological constraints, whereas the discovery of new ways to exploit human frailty is not.

This is why the avoidance of drug addiction has become a major focus of socialization in our society, and perhaps the most important source of conflict between parents and children. People in the modern world are simply called upon to exercise far, far greater willpower and foresight than anyone ever had to in the past. The advice "don't become an addict" may seem like common sense, yet it is much harder to follow now than it has been at any other time in human history. In the nineteenth century, the only real danger to the North American was that of becoming an alcoholic. Tobacco and coffee were available but were fairly harmless (life expectancy was low, so most people never made it to the age where they might develop cancer from smoking). In the twenty-first century, by contrast, it seems that there is an addictive substance to cater to every possible taste, all widely available in markets both legal and illegal. There are the old stalwarts, alcohol, opiates, cocaine, and tobacco, but also some newcomers, like methamphetamine and fentanyl, and even exotics like khat and betel nut. Then there are refined products, more addictive than the original, like oxycodone and crack. And of course, there is intravenous injection, which delivers a faster "rush" than smoking or snorting, and so is able to more effectively exploit the warp in our temporal attitudes. Some of these substances and practices never rise beyond the threshold of "bad habits," but others can generate florid, life-destroying addictions within a matter of weeks.

These addictive substances are all the cultural equivalents of "superbugs." They are very effective at self-reproduction and highly resistant to eradication. Furthermore, we can expect them to evolve over time, through a combination of both natural and human selection, to become more, not less, addictive. (For example, while there is some debate about whether marijuana should be classified as addictive, marijuana growers are certainly doing their best to make it more so, by selectively breeding plants to increase the concentration of the psychoactive chemical THC.) This is a perfect example of reverse adaptation that is harmful to the human population. Furthermore, the fact that these substances tend to pool in the culture gives us reason to think that over time, our environment will become more hostile. Indeed, it is difficult to think of any time in human history where people have been called upon to exercise as much foresight and self-control—in short, to be as *rational*—as they are today.

As if that wasn't bad enough, people have been working hard to make many other things that we consume as addictive as possible, in some cases by imitating the pattern of stimulation that naturally addictive substances possess. I mentioned in the previous section that fast food is the result of an evolutionary process, one that has not only made fast food tastier, but has also made it difficult to stop eating—a fact that some purveyors gleefully announce, as with the Lay's potato chip slogan "Betcha can't eat just one." If one looks at the pattern of stimulation generated by, say, a tortilla chip, it is front-loaded with pleasure. Indeed, the flatness of the chip is designed to maximize surface area in order to deliver the largest possible load of flavor to the tongue (where the taste buds are located) as quickly as possible. The chip then has a slightly chewy, not particularly appetizing aftertaste, which can easily be eliminated by eating . . . another one! Thus the type of compulsive eating it encourages is not all that different from drinking to cure a hangover.

It's important to realize that addiction is not the same thing as chemical dependency. Addiction is a *psychological phenomenon,* associated with a particular pattern of stimulation. This is why it is not misleading to describe certain foods or activities as addictive. Indeed, the emerging consensus with respect to gambling is that it is also capable of producing a genuine addiction in vulnerable individuals. As Don Ross and Harold Kincaid have observed, when people talk about being "shopaholics" or "sex addicts," this is just an exaggerated way of saying that they really like these activities: "No scientific evidence links intense interest in sex or shopping to the 'classic' drug addictions." But when people say that they are addicted to gambling, they are saying something much closer to the literal truth. Despite the fact that in this case "there is no dependence on exogenous substances," there is nevertheless "strong behavioral and neurobiological evidence that pathological gambling and substance dependence share a common set of features."[22]

It is unsurprising, then, to find that casinos have been evolving over time in such a way as to encourage more and more compulsive behavior among gamblers. The people who run them know that for most gamblers, it's not so much about the money as it is the pattern of stimulation. (This is why, for instance, slot machines have been found to be equally addictive regardless of how low or high the stakes are.[23]) Some games are also more addictive than others—slots are the worst, which is why a typical casino has them lining the entrances, making it more difficult to come and go without succumbing to their lure. (The same principle is responsible for the rack of snack food beside the cashier in the grocery store.) In the casino, everything from the carpets to the lights, the music, and the absence of windows and clocks, not to mention the free food and drinks, is designed to make it as difficult as possible to stop gambling. It is an entire environment designed to undermine self-control, one giant, hyper-complex deceptor.[24]

The problem is that these techniques, once developed, can easily be copied. Indeed, some of the strategies on display in casinos are copied from supermarkets, where consumer behavior has been intensely studied for decades. As everyone knows by now, the entire layout of the standard grocery store is designed not for convenience, but rather to manipulate consumer behavior. This is why the dairy is at the very far end of the store, so that you can't just pop in and buy milk without passing all of the other food. This is why higher-margin items are on the left-hand side as you move down the aisles (most people shop "left," giving those items higher visibility).[25] This is why suppliers have to pay a surcharge to have their items stocked at the end of the aisles, where they will have the highest visibility. Absolutely none of this is done with the goal of enhancing the quality of consumer decision making, much less healthy eating habits. On the contrary: it is designed to maximize revenue to the store.

The newest frontier is the internet, which the advertising model of revenue generation has meant that capturing people's attention (measured in "eyeballs" and "clicks") is the overriding economic imperative. Many people noticed early on that email and messaging can be addictive—the migration of this from computers to phones has generated the familiar sight of people who can't survive five minutes without pulling out their phone and checking their inbox. (Indeed, many people, reading this last sentence, will undoubtedly be seized by the impulse to put down the book and check their messages right now.) Facebook, with its constant status updates, significantly exacerbates this same tendency. Many people are alarmed at how compulsive it can become. Then along came Twitter, which is even worse. And finally, there are video games, particularly those on mobile phones, which have increasingly become a contest to see who can produce the most addictive product. In 2011, the company that made Angry Birds reported that the game had been downloaded over 500 million times and that users were collectively spending over 200 million minutes a day playing it. One might think that with over one billion smartphones in circulation, the fact that so many people are carrying around powerful personal computers would have the capacity to dramatically improve the quality of decision making. Many people are prepared to wax rhapsodically about how their iPhone has become an extension of their mind, allowing them to offload a huge number of cognitive tasks. And the day may still come when companion computers are able to assist us, in real time, to avoid many of the chronic pitfalls of human irrationality. For the moment, however, for every one person who has been helped by the sudden availability of powerful portable computing, there are dozens more for whom the phone has served as nothing more than a source of distraction, and often a gateway to obsessive or addictive behavior.

Taken separately, each of these trends can easily be defended as harmless fun. And yet we need to recognize the global consequences for the individual of producing a built environment in which, in effect, everything is a trap, designed to exploit the frailties of human psychology. We tend to take it for granted that the environments we create will become more *physically* comfortable over time, and yet we fail to summon up much concern over the fact that these environments are constantly becoming more *psychologically* hostile. If we are looking for a reason to think that the world has gone mad—or, to put that in less alarmist language, that there has been a general degradation of rationality in our society—we now have the elements of a theory. As human beings, we depend heavily on our environment in order to reason correctly, but our environment is constantly evolving, undergoing a process of reverse adaptation that favors cultural artifacts that exploit elements of our *irrationality*. And so we have to work harder and harder as time goes by, because our intuitive problem-solving strategies become increasingly inept. And because the cognitive resources needed to override our misfiring heuristics are intrinsically scarce, we find ourselves falling further and further behind.

7. Going viral

Malware of the mind

In the discussion so far, I have been helping myself to what is sometimes called an "epidemiological" approach to human culture.[1] Epidemiology in the strict sense is the study of public health or of diseases in populations. What is crucial about this perspective is that it does not look at the specific etiology of disease, the sort of thing that doctors are interested in: how the patient caught it, what the symptoms are, how it can be cured. Instead, it adopts a broadly statistical perspective, looking at how diseases come and go in populations. From this perspective, things like diet, sanitation, international travel, commuting time, social inequality, and hundreds of other unexpected factors may all turn out to have an important impact on public health that no one would have thought of just by looking at individual cases.

Thinking epidemiologically about culture obviously involves a set of analogies to biological phenomena (such as the comparison to viruses in the previous chapter, or talk about "memes" as units of cultural reproduction—equivalent to "genes" in the biological realm). Some people find this off-putting. With the development of the internet, however, many of these analogies have become irresistible. It is common now to talk about the latest internet "meme," or of a video having "gone viral." The origin of these expressions is quite revealing. The initial extension of the virus metaphor

186

predated the internet, and was used to describe the way in which malicious programs could hijack a computer. The key feature of a biological virus is that it has no way of reproducing without a host. It contains bits of DNA or RNA, which it uses to reprogram the enzymes in a host cell, tricking it into producing copies of the virus. A computer virus works in very much the same way. Early Apple Macintosh computers, for example, were quite vulnerable to viruses, because they were the first machines to use a graphical user interface. When you put a disk in the drive, the computer had to search for and run a small program found on the disk, in order to "mount" it to the desktop. It was easy to rewrite that program, inserting some malicious code that would be loaded into the computer's memory and would cause the machine to copy that same code into the boot sector of any subsequent disk inserted into the machine. The virus metaphor was impossible to resist, since the mechanism of reproduction was almost identical: anyone who stuck their disk into the drive of an infected machine would get infected. If you went on to stick your infected disk into another machine, that one would get infected, and it would go on to infect several other disks. It's pretty obvious why the virus metaphor suggested itself.

Viruses were fairly common even before the internet created new possibilities for transmission. The major contribution made by the internet was the realization that bits of nuisance code could get transmitted not just by infecting the machine, but also by infecting the user. One of the earliest examples of this was the "$250 cookie recipe" email. Back when the internet was young, long before there was such a thing as spam, people nevertheless found themselves receiving multiple versions of nuisance email from friends and family. One of the most common was a story supposedly from a person who had been tricked into purchasing a cookie recipe from the department store Neiman Marcus for $250, and so, in order to avenge himself, was sharing the recipe with as many people as possible. The email began, "This is a true story . . . Please forward it to everyone that you can . . . You will have to read it to believe it . . .," which is typically not an instruction that anyone would feel obliged to obey, except that what followed was a not entirely unbelievable story about why you should forward the email to as many people as possible.

What was noteworthy about the email was that the mechanism through which it was propagated was almost identical to that of a computer virus. Except that now, instead of a bit of malicious code hijacking the computer and tricking it into reproducing the code, this was a malicious email hijacking the *brain of the user* and tricking him into reproducing the email. The mechanisms were so similar that it was impossible to resist the analogy: so people began to talk about "viruses of the mind" or of "wetware" (rather than "software") viruses. This lent force to the epidemiological perspective. For example, people began to realize that the prevalence of a belief, or a "meme," in the population might not be due to the intrinsic credibility of the belief, but simply to the power of its associated reproduction mechanism. Even if only 5 percent of recipients of the cookie-recipe email believed the story, but each one sent it to twenty or more people, then the email could continue to circulate (although eventually the population would develop immunity—those who had been infected once and transmitted it to others would be unlikely to do so again[2]).

Since that time, the contagion metaphor has become ubiquitous, so that we talk about things going "viral" on the internet, or of a "viral" marketing campaign. The term here refers simply to the propagation mechanism—if one person sends a link to two friends, who both send the link to two more friends, and so on, completely obscure videos or web pages can suddenly attract the interest of millions of people, in a completely decentralized way. Calling these *memes* is fair enough, but the term *viral* is sometimes a bit of a misnomer, since it is central to the operation of a virus that it be able to trick its host into reproducing it. In the case of internet videos, there is often no trickery involved. What's striking about real viruses is that—like the cookie-recipe email—they are false yet you can't get rid of them even with concerted effort. (In fact, there's probably someone out there right now reading that very email, thinking, "Wow, I can't believe they charged him $250 for a cookie recipe! I'm going to send this to everyone I know.")

¶

As far as mental viruses are concerned, there is nothing particularly special about the internet. The kind of infections you get there can be found in any human culture—it's just that on the internet, the propagation speed is so high one can see dramatic effects in a very short time. But cultural memes have the same dynamic. In a sense, culture is just a big, slow version of the internet. "Urban legends," for instance, are a lot like chain-letter emails—if they can convince people to retell them, then they can persist forever. And some of them can be quite noxious. Consider, for instance, the *Protocols of the Elders of Zion,* an anti-Semitic tract first published in 1903, which alleges a vast Jewish conspiracy to achieve world domination. Although the original Russian text was exposed as a forgery in the early 1920s, the book has proven almost impossible to get rid of. The primary reason is that if the secret conspiracy alleged in the document was real, then propagating the belief that the document was a forgery would not only be in the interests of the "council of Elders," but also well within its power. So for those who want to believe in it, the document itself provides a plausible explanation for why most other people do not.

This makes the book a perfect instance of those mental viruses belonging to a subgenre known as "conspiracy theories." As we have seen, these all live within the sheltered ecosystem provided by confirmation bias in human judgment. They withstand rational scrutiny because people fail to "think the negative" and so ignore the need to rule out other hypotheses. Furthermore, given that the human pattern detector is calibrated to go off too easily—think of all the patterns people saw in the random song sequence of their iPod shuffle—it's easy to see how these theories could be attractive. Taking in the scope of world events and the trajectory of human development, it is possible that history is just one damn thing after another.

Or it could be the unfolding of some complex plan, orchestrated by a mysterious puppet master. Our *natural* inclination is to think that it is the latter and to ignore completely the need to rule out the former.

Another very common type of mental virus is superstition, particularly of the magical variety. Among Pascal Boyer's studies, some of the most interesting involve his efforts to figure out why some fanciful beliefs capture people's imagination and therefore tend to get reproduced despite their implausibility. The Uduk of the Sudan, for example, believe that certain ebony trees listen to and remember the conversations that people hold in their shade.[3] This is not particularly believable, yet there is something irresistible about it. (In fact, now that I've mentioned it, you will probably never forget it.) Boyer points out that when we are given information about the world, we tend to slot things into a relatively small number of categories, which then provide us with a large number of assumptions about how objects of that type will behave. For instance, when told that a walrus is an animal, even young children will immediately assign to it all of the typical characteristics of an animal (that it must breathe, that it can have babies, or that if you cut it in half it will die). Boyer observed that popular superstitions tend to involve single-point deviations from the standard set of expectations. He tested the hypothesis by putting together a collection of fanciful beliefs, some of them real, some of them invented. Some violated expectations in only one dimension, whereas others violated multiple expectations. He then told these stories to experimental subjects and brought them back a few days later to see what they remembered. The mundane beliefs were easily forgotten, as were those that violated too many expectations. But the ones that involved a single-point deviation from expectations seemed to exercise a peculiar fascination and were more easily remembered.[4]

One can see this structure in many popular superstitions. For instance, ghosts and spirits are taken to be immaterial beings, which gives them the ability to do things like pass through walls. And yet they seldom sink through the floor. Indeed, they are subject to all the usual laws of the universe save one (for instance, they are obviously affected by gravity, otherwise they would be left behind by the earth as it hurtles through space at incredible speed). They are also taken to have all the properties of a standard subject—for example, they remember things that they have seen, they get angry and sad, and so forth. This is, in Boyer's view, what makes these ideas attractive. When a story violates expectations, it attracts our interest, partly just for its novelty value. But if it violates too many expectations, we feel that we don't understand the rules, and so we cannot make any inferences or predictions. It's when a story conforms to all our standard expectations *except one* that we become genuinely intrigued.

From this, it is not difficult to see how superstition evolves into magical beliefs that are, in turn, taken seriously. Getting remembered is the first step on the road to being believed. We all suffer to varying degrees from a problem called *source amnesia,* where we have trouble remembering how we came to know something. To take just one example, almost totally at random, I happen to know that the Polish city of Gdansk was once called Danzig. *How* I came to know that, I haven't the faintest idea. And yet if someone were to say to me "I'm planning a trip to Danzig," I would automatically say, "You probably shouldn't call it that when you get there," despite not having any way of sourcing the information. So if I was living in the Sudan and someone said to me, "I'm going for a picnic under that ebony tree," I might automatically say, "Watch out—some of those ebony trees like to eavesdrop on conversations," without really knowing how I know this. As a matter of fact, I don't really know this, but that doesn't matter so much, because if the person I'm speaking to is a bit credulous, he will now take it to be true, based on my authority.

This may be a bit simplistic. In fact, the central mechanism that turns stories into beliefs is *repetition*. Because our memory retrieval system is based on association, and because repetition builds associations, repetition makes certain ideas spring to mind more readily than others. And because we are used to forgetting exactly how we came to know something or where we learned it, we will often treat a belief that springs to mind as true simply because it springs to mind so easily. The basic set of relationships is very well established in experimental psychology: "The more times one is exposed to a particular statement, the more one is likely to believe the statement to be true. This relationship between repetition and perceived truth is mediated by familiarity; repetition increases familiarity and, in turn, familiarity is used as a heuristic for determining the truth of a statement."[5]

This may be seem innocuous, but it is fraught with consequence. The core mechanism was well understood, implicitly, long before it was demonstrated experimentally. Consider, for example, the dead-on accuracy of Joseph Goebbels's reflections on propaganda. Goebbels said that "propaganda must . . . always be essentially simple and repetitive. In the long run basic results in influencing public opinion will be achieved only by the man who is able to reduce problems to the simplest terms and who has the courage to keep forever repeating them in this simplified form, despite the objections of the intellectuals."[6]

Indeed, one might even *define* an intellectual as "a person who thinks that beliefs should be assessed on their merits." What the epidemiological perspective reveals is that a belief that is deficient with respect to its epistemic merits may nevertheless attract widespread allegiance if it has other, reproductive merits. Such a belief may not be rational, as long as it is *contagious*. Thus if the person who holds the belief feels obliged to "spread the word," or if the idea tends to get stuck in one's head like a pop song, or if the idea just "feels right" because it coheres with an intuition, or if people can't see the problem with it because of confirmation bias, then that idea can enjoy widespread popularity, despite its failure to withstand rational scrutiny.[7]

These are problems that can be found within any culture. There is, however, reason to think that cultural contact and exchange may be resulting in some of the most virulent ideas being transmitted back and forth—like diseases and addictive substances—and beginning to pool within the major global civilizations. These are the superbugs of human culture. One can find the most striking evidence in the development of the "new age" spiritual movement in the United States. Perhaps the most striking feature of this movement—and the part that is most confounding to traditional intellectuals—is that absolutely no attempt is made to unify any of the belief systems that the movement draws upon. Eclecticism is seen as a virtue, so no one really tries to produce a coherent cosmology or worldview. It is a religion without a theology. Walk into any health food store, pick up the local natural living magazine, and you can find ads for crystal therapy, Reiki massage, therapeutic touch, chi energy realignment, aura reading, and so on, all sitting next to one another on the page, with no apparent tension. No one seems to worry about the fact that the people offering to unblock your chi and the ones trying to cleanse your chakras *can't both be right* about what's causing your breast cancer.

The Wikipedia page on "New Age" actually captures the flavor of the movement quite nicely:

> The New Age movement includes elements of older spiritual and religious traditions ranging from atheism and mono-theism through classical pantheism, naturalistic pantheism, pandeism and panentheism to polytheism combined with science and Gaia philosophy; particularly archaeoastronomy, astronomy, ecology, environmentalism, the Gaia hypothesis, psychology and physics. New Age practices and philosophies sometimes draw inspiration from major world religions: Buddhism, Taoism, Chinese folk religion, Christianity, Hinduism, Islam, Judaism, Sikhism; with strong influences from East Asian religions, Gnosticism, Neopaganism, New Thought, Spiritualism, Theosophy, Universalism and Western esotericism.[8]

Again, it seems almost pointless to observe that there is inconsistency here. (How does one combine "elements" of atheism with monotheism and polytheism, without at some point declaring a winner?) The better approach is simply to regard it as a long list of mental viruses, including some of the most contagious and powerful in human history—malware of the mind.

It is certainly no accident that this sort of eclecticism occurs in a movement that privileges intuitive over rational thinking styles. There is a general lesson here for everyone. It has to do with the unusual circumstances in which we find ourselves, living in modern, globalized cultures. In the same way that we are called upon to exercise greater self-control, in order to avoid falling victim to the extraordinary range of addictive substances that are available, we are also called upon to exercise greater rational control, in order to avoid providing an ecological niche for one of these viral thought systems. This is true even for those who adhere to some of the views itemized in the list above. (It is important to realize that, as Boyer points out, even people who are religious are committed to the view that the overwhelming majority of religious beliefs are false, simply because the truth of one religion implies the falsity of all the others. Thus an epidemiological view suggests itself as the most plausible explanation for the phenomenon of religious belief *even for those who are religious.* The only difference between the atheist and the theist is that the latter subscribes to some special story that explains why her own beliefs are exempt from the general principle that all religious beliefs are false.)

One can find an analogous phenomenon on the internet, where particularly virulent bits of malware, like the Blaster worm, can be found in circulation despite being over a decade old. Indeed, it is widely reported that a computer running an unpatched version of Microsoft Windows XP, if connected to the internet, will become infected before the user has a chance to download and install the first security patch.[9] These bits of malware fade away only when operating systems change and eliminate the ecosystem in which they once thrived. Unfortunately for human beings, *our* operating system never changes. We walk around with the same old bugs, vulnerabilities, and security holes, without even being able to implement a patch—all we can do is monitor the traffic and intervene when we see something that is too obviously suspicious. Seen from this perspective, is it so implausible to see analogies between Falun Gong, or the Mormon Church, and a botnet? And is it not reasonable to worry that our mental environment is becoming more and more contaminated all the time?

§

There is one issue that I have not yet said anything about but that must loom large in any discussion of irrationality in our culture. It is the commercial motive. The person who had the brilliant idea of putting mayonnaise on a hamburger or a giant cap on a bottle of laundry detergent or a resonator under the hood of a car was not just trying to make the burger taste better, the detergent easier to pour, or the car more satisfying to drive. He was also trying to make *money*. This is not an accident. The environments that are the most hostile from the standpoint of rationality are those that are the most commercial. If you had to give a child just one piece of advice upon entering a shopping mall, a good suggestion might be "Remember that everything—and by that I mean *everything*—is a trick to take your money." This is, of course, almost the exact opposite of what a natural environment is like, and so it is not unreasonable to expect that it will degrade our cognitive performance.

By now we're all so used to this complaint that we seldom stop to wonder why it must be so. Why does the marketplace seem to be biased against rationality? There is, in fact, a straightforward answer to this, although it is a bit esoteric. It comes from an area of probability theory known as "Dutch book" arguments.[10] One of the big problems that probability theorists have is that, unlike the principles of arithmetic, which most people find quite obvious, the basic principles of probability can be rather unintuitive. Furthermore, some of the logical consequences of these principles produce results that are very surprising, and thus positively counterintuitive.[11] This is not really the fault of the principles, but rather of our intuitions. The bread and butter of the "heuristics and biases" research project was to show that our intuitions about probability and uncertainty are seriously flawed.

In any case, because people find probability theory unintuitive, probability theorists wind up dealing with a lot of skeptics who say, "Why should I reason this way?" or "If this is what rationality requires, then why should I be rational?" This can be a tough question to respond to. After all, you can't *make* someone be rational. The solution that probability theorists cooked up was to show that if you violated any of their fundamental principles, it would be possible for a clever bookie to persuade you to make a bet that you would be guaranteed to lose money on, regardless of how things turned out.[12] The details of the bet would be somewhat more complicated than "heads I win, tails you lose," but the principle would be the same. This is what's called a "Dutch book" (based upon some vague apprehension that the Dutch had pioneered the art of constructing such "books"). Later, as a generalization of this idea, it was shown that if you violated one of the key principles of rational decision theory, you could be turned into a "money pump," allowing an unscrupulous trader to take arbitrarily large amounts of your money.[13] Since this argument is easier to follow, I'll focus on it.

Suppose that you prefer apples to oranges, oranges to bananas, and bananas to apples. Taken as a whole, your preferences violate an important consistency constraint called *transitivity*. You prefer A to B and B to C, but you do not prefer A to C. This actually happens to us all the time, and it's not the end of the world. Our brains are not logic machines, so inconsistency doesn't make smoke come out of our ears. It does, however, make us vulnerable to exploitation. If you are standing around holding a banana, a person could come up to you and offer to trade you the banana for an orange plus a small service charge. Once you get the orange, she could then offer to trade you that for an apple, again with a small service charge. But of course, once you have the apple, she can then trade you that for the banana you started out with . . . plus a small service charge. You have now become a money pump. Unless you change your preferences, this can go on forever, and the service charges will keep adding up. So you might as well just hand over all your money as soon as she walks up to you, and not even bother with the fruit trades.

If hearing the word "service charge" makes this all sound rather familiar, you may suspect that this is actually the business model of many corporations. And you wouldn't be too far off. A lot of the "financial innovation" in the past few decades, at both the retail and the wholesale level, has involved finding new ways to take advantage of human irrationality. This is all motivated by a fundamental asymmetry between rationality and irrationality, which is that the rational can take advantage of the irrational in a way that the irrational cannot take advantage of the rational.[14] If you're not rational, then you are *exploitable,* in the technical sense of the term used by probability theorists (namely, that a rational person can come along and get you to give her all of your money).[15] This is a particularly devastating vulnerability, because it allows other people to take you not just for a little, but for everything you've got. Being rational is of course no guarantee that you won't get suckered (for example, you may still be ignorant, and so enter into trades that are not in your interest). But it does offer a defense against the most extreme form of exploitation, which is that of being turned into a money pump.

Many people manage to maintain something like a consistent set of consumer preferences, and so are relatively immune to exploitation. Yet even when they succeed in maintaining static consistency, they are often dynamically inconsistent. This means that their preferences change *over time* in ways that make them exploitable. This is all because of the warp in the way that we evaluate the future. One could see this quite clearly in the type of financial products that were being sold to consumers, which were the underlying cause of the subprime mortgage crisis in 2008. Subprime mortgages were the leading edge of a relatively new set of essentially despicable business models developed in the late twentieth century, which gave rise to what is known as the "poverty industry."[16] There was a time when businesses—particularly banks—were loath to do business with poor people, simply because poor people were unreliable and didn't have much money. The thing about poor people, however, is that they also tend to have a bigger warp in the way that they evaluate the future. That's partly why they're poor. The consequence, however, is that even though they have less, they can also be much easier to "pump" for money. This is something that drug dealers have known for a long time; eventually mainstream businesses began to realize as well, and clamored for a piece of the action.

Consider, for example, credit cards. Intuition says that lending money to poor people, who may have no job or are always in danger of losing their jobs, is going to be less attractive than lending it to affluent consumers, who have stable jobs and tend to spend a lot more. Yet in certain cases the opposite is true. That's because credit card companies don't make their money from people who pay them back. Although they make some money off the transaction fees they charge, the big money is made when consumers maintain a negative balance on their card and make monthly interest payments. From the credit card company's perspective, prudent, affluent consumers may actually be bad customers.

The same principle is what explains the rise of the "subprime" mortgage market, which precipitated the financial crisis of 2008. As with any loan, the big money is made from people who never pay the principal but just keep making interest payments. The whole idea of subprime mortgages was to lend money to people who did not qualify for "prime" loans because of an impaired credit history, financial insecurity, or just straight-up poverty. The initial thought was that if you made enough of these loans to enough people, the law of large numbers would guarantee you fairly stable returns, simply because no more than a small fraction of them would default in any given year. Once investors began accepting this argument and started wanting to purchase the right to the income stream generated by repayment of these loans, so-called mortgage originators began to employ increasingly clever and aggressive tactics in order to get people to take out the loans.

Lenders had already developed the practice of making interest-only mortgage loans, where the monthly payments covered only the interest charges, making no payment against the principal. These were initially popular with affluent consumers who worked in businesses where they received very large annual bonuses (such as bankers and stockbrokers). They would often want to keep their monthly expenses low but would make large payments against the principal once a year. In theory, however, there was nothing that said you had to pay off the loan at all; you could just keep making interest payments forever. So this was a perfect product to sell to poor consumers. By keeping the monthly payments low—just enough to cover the interest—you could sell loans to people who otherwise would be unable to afford them. You just had to trust that it wouldn't bother them too much when, after making payments for years, they would be no closer to owning the house than they were on day one. And if they stopped making payments, all you had to do was repossess the house and find someone else to take it on.

With these interest-only loans, however, the consumer still had to make the interest payments. The first big innovation in the subprime industry was the adjustable-rate mortgage (or ARM). Rather than charging the person a uniform rate over the term of the mortgage, the ARM would start out with a lower introductory, or "teaser," rate—say, 2 percent instead of 5 percent. But the rate wasn't actually lower. The consumer was typically being charged the 5 percent, it's just that she wasn't being forced to pay the full interest charge. The unpaid amount was being added to the principal, and so the principal on the loan got bigger over time. Initially some effort was made to hide this from the consumer, but over time it was discovered that there was no need. With consumers being sufficiently short-sighted, the total amount paid over the life of the loan mattered very little—the only thing consumers paid attention to were the immediate monthly payments. This led to a huge proliferation of products, including a variety of baroque schemes whereby consumers could purchase "points" that would lower their initial interest rate, with the cost of these points being added to the principal. Almost all of these involved an extremely disadvantageous trade-off between present and future obligations.

These products were defensible on the grounds that a sophisticated, risk-tolerant investor who calculated that the value of a property would rise dramatically in the short term might have some reason to take out a loan of this sort. (Sure, the size of the loan would increase over time, but if the value of the property was increasing at a faster rate, then that wouldn't matter.) The people that the products were sold to, however, were not sophisticated investors, but simply short-sighted consumers who either didn't do the math on what they were owing or didn't care. From the lender's perspective, the objective was to give people loans that they would never pay off—to pump as much money from them as possible, then foreclose and take the property. (This was combined with a set of initiatives aimed at traditional borrowers, designed to deter them from paying off their mortgages, such as easy refinancing terms or even turning the mortgage loan into a line of credit, essentially transforming their home equity into a bank account that they could withdraw from at any time.)

Whatever the theoretical justification for these products, in practice they served as little more than increasingly clever ways of trying to money-pump borrowers. There was a time when people used to put money in the bank in order to help themselves *resist* temptation. Over time the role of banks changed, so that they began to serve as a source of temptation, rather than as a bulwark against it. Instead of helping us to become more rational, they began competing to find new ways to undermine our ability to make sound financial decisions.

§

You can usually tell how old an advertisement is just by reading the copy, in much the same way that archaeologists can date artifacts by noting the geological stratum in which they are found. Most nineteenth-century advertising is extremely discursive, in more ways than one. In a typical print advertisement, not only is most of the space occupied by text, but the text itself is argumentative. It tries to explain, in rational terms, the superiority of the product. Consider, for example, the following advertisement for Fell's Coffee, from 1866:

> The Universal Practice of mixing Chicory and other adulteratives with Coffee, has very much damaged in public estimation, what ought to be the most delicious of Beverages. So effectually have the public been drugged with such mixtures that the true properties have been lost sight of, and many prefer a black and thick infusion to a drink rich in spirit and aroma. General as is the use of Coffee, it is little known that in condensing the vapors extracted from the berry in roasting, a liquor is obtained of the most nauseous taste and of a scent the most unbearable. Under such circumstances it is evidently important that all the gases and fluids extracted by roasting should be carried off as quickly as possible in order to prevent their returning again to the Coffee, which is the case in the confined cylinder. This object is admirably accomplished by the new and patent "Conical Coffee Roaster" as used by Fell & Co., Victoria, in which the berry is directly exposed to the radiated heat, and the vapor extracted carried off instantaneously.[17]

This ad copy is like a small portrait of an earlier age of innocence. By now we are so familiar with the rules of commercial speech that anyone can spot the problems with it. Most obviously, it contains an unflattering portrayal of the very product that it is trying to sell. It violates the basic rule that you never repeat a criticism when responding to it. Who knew that the process of coffee roasting generated a byproduct that is "nauseous" and has an "unbearable" smell? Of course, the ad goes on to explain how Fell & Co.'s technique disposes of this byproduct more effectively than does that of the competition. The assumption being made, however, is that the force of this argument will triumph over the unappetizing associations produced through the use of the words "nauseous" and "unbearable" to describe the "gases and fluids" emitted by coffee beans. This is a sales pitch aimed at the head, not the heart.

During the 1920s and '30s, the introduction of images began to have a noticeable impact on advertising—most obviously, the amount of text shrank as pictures became increasingly dominant. It is also noticeable that a lot more attention was paid to tone and to the rhythm of the words being used. And yet the text remained essentially argumentative, typically consisting of a list of reasons why you should buy the product. Reading an ad was not all that different from listening to someone trying to convince you to buy the product. Consider the following coffee ad, from 1932:

Drink It and Cheer, Drink It and Sleep
Drink what? Sanka Coffee.

Why will you cheer? Because Sanka Coffee is so delicious. Yes, so downright delicious that if you're not absolutely satisfied, we'll return your money.

Why will you sleep? Because 97% of the caffein has been removed from Sanka Coffee. And if coffee keeps you awake— or causes nervousness or indigestion—remember: it's the *caffein* in coffee that does it![18]

One can see some obvious improvements here in the fluidity of the prose. And yet problems remain. The ad contains what looks like, from a modern perspective, too many arguments. (Do you drink it to cheer? Or do you drink it to sleep?) And strangely, it continues the curious practice of drawing attention to problems with the product (it causes "nervousness and indigestion") before attempting to rebut the charges. The reader is being given a lot of credit. Next time she is offered coffee, she may immediately think "indigestion," but she is supposed to go on to think, "Oh yes, but that is caused by caffein, and Sanka has no caffein." In order to get to the positive thought about the product, the consumer must consciously suppress the negative thought that springs to mind unbidden.

After the Second World War, advertisers became significantly more sophisticated. Most importantly, they realized that, in the typical run of cases, the seller could not count on having people's full attention, and that this had important implications for the way that a product should be presented. The Fell & Co. coffee ad is clearly written on the assumption that the prospective consumer will be sitting down, reading through the copy carefully, following the argument, making note of the specific claims being made. In the early twentieth century, advertising copy was still being written as though it were for an audience who could be expected to be paying attention. This all began to change in the 1940s.

Things changed in part because of an increase in the sheer volume of advertising. Consumers became not only less likely to believe what they read, but also more likely to skip past ads or skim through them very quickly. Furthermore, advertisers began to realize that fewer consumers were starting out by reading ads, then going and buying the product based on the information they had received. The development of self-service stores, such as modern supermarkets, created a situation where instead of having to ask someone behind the counter for a specific good, consumers found themselves confronted with a shelf full of unfamiliar products, free to pick their own. In this situation, the most important thing is what they are able to *remember.* Even just recognizing a product name, in the absence of any specific information, can have a powerful (positive) impact on purchasing decisions.

The immediate postwar era is often described as the golden age of the "unique selling proposition." This was largely a consequence of diminished expectations with respect to the consumer. Advertisers realized that most people looking at an ad are not going to read through a big long argument, much less remember it. In fact, you'd be lucky if you could get them to remember just one thing about the product. And so ad agencies began to ask their customers, "If you could tell people just one thing about your product, what would that one thing be?" Companies were encouraged to figure out the unique quality that distinguished their product from its competitors, and to focus all of their energies on that.

It was during this period, in the 1950s, that the coffee industry came up with its most powerful marketing coup: "Give yourself a 'coffee-break'! There's a welcome lift in every cup!"[19] The term "coffee-break" appears between quotation marks because, at the time, it was still relatively unfamiliar. It has, of course, since passed into everyday language, and remains the most effective marketing concept for the product. The suggestion is that drinking coffee is something you do to reward yourself. After working hard, you take a break, and during that break, in order to recharge, you get yourself a cup of coffee. The associations are not just with pleasure and relaxation, but also with accomplishment. No one has ever been able to beat this, which is why the same concept (coffee as a time-out or escape from the pressures of everyday life) is still central to the marketing campaigns of most major coffee-shop chains, including Starbucks. (Supermarket coffee, on the other hand, is usually consumed at breakfast, and so has to be marketed differently.)

The unique selling proposition is still dated, however, by the fact that it persists in giving the consumer a *reason* to purchase the product. The shift to brand marketing in the late twentieth century was based on the discovery that it is not necessary to appeal to the consumer's rationality at all in order for an ad to be effective. You actually don't need to give people a *reason* to buy your product. Brands are about trust, and trust can be cultivated through entirely emotional and intuitive appeals. Thus, increasingly, advertising seeks to bypass the consumer's rationality completely. The most obvious evidence of this is the steady but inexorable decline in the amount of language in advertisement. Language is the vehicle of rational thought, so if you want to bypass reason, cut out the language and stick to pictures. This is why so many ads today feature no text at all, just an image and the company name. Starbucks has even gone so far as to remove the company name from its cups, leaving only its trademark mermaid image on them. Other firms have moved in the same direction, replacing their company names with acronyms (KFC for Kentucky Fried Chicken, H&M for Hennes & Mauritz, RBC for Royal Bank of Canada, etc.).

To say that advertising seeks to bypass people's rational faculties is not to say that people are being brainwashed or programmed to buy things that they don't really want. When advertisers first started using sophisticated psychological techniques, there was a lot of hysteria about "subliminal" advertising, mass hypnosis, the "Manchurian consumer," and so forth.[20] In part this stemmed from an overly credulous attitude toward the boasts of the advertising agencies, who naturally claimed great powers for themselves. The fact that advertising seeks to bypass rationality does not mean that consumers lose their capacity for rational decision making when they make a purchase. It just means that the overwhelming majority of advertising aims to manipulate, rather than to convince. For the most part it just latches onto existing desires that people have—for money, sex, love, attention, status, affirmation, control, and so on—and then pushes us in the direction of thinking that a particular product will help us to satisfy those desires.[21] Often it does so simply by building an association, or even just getting our attention—something that is increasingly difficult to do in the current media environment.

The development of advertising over the course of the twentieth century was, of course, an evolutionary process. It was not the brainchild of some cabal of evil geniuses on Madison Avenue. The kind of advertising that we see around us is there because it is effective. The techniques that work have been discovered one at a time, bit by bit. Because of that, there's not much that can be done about them. No amount of hand-wringing or social criticism is going to change the character of advertising or undermine its effectiveness.[22] (The one thing that has been proven beyond a shadow of doubt is that writing books complaining about the nefarious tactics of advertisers doesn't do a bit of good. Ever since the 1950s, each decade has spawned a new set of books expressing shock and outrage over the insidious new forms of mind control we are being subjected to, which each new generation treats as a revelation. And yet the world keeps turning. Comparing Vance Packard's *The Hidden Persuaders* to Naomi Klein's *No Logo* to Martin Lindstrom's *Brandwashed*, it should be apparent that there is little new under the sun.)

Unfortunately, the standard apologetic for the dominant trends is not much comfort either. Starting with the response to Packard, apologists for the advertising industry have claimed that salvation lies in the new generation. As far back as the 1960s, one can find people arguing that the kids these days are so media savvy that they are immune to the old tricks being played on them by advertisers. Complaining about advertising, the apologists suggest, is something that only old fuddy-duddies do.[23] The kids are, like, way beyond that.

This argument has a tiny bit of truth to it, but it ignores the bigger picture. If people have become more "savvy" these days—although a better word might be "cynical"—this is because they are more likely to treat with suspicion, and therefore to override, the intuitive response that they may have to a product. This is because they know they are being manipulated, by everything from the packaging color and the brand name to the music playing in the store and the ambient lighting. And yet it is important to realize that there is no way of reprogramming the unconscious to discount this or that factor. You cannot just say to your brain, "Ignore the beautiful woman, she doesn't come with the car" and expect it to comply so that in the future, you can rest assured that whatever warm feelings you have about a particular brand of car are based entirely on fuel economy and performance. You have to keep exercising the rational override, every single time.

This is why, no matter how media savvy the kids may be these days, with their Facebook updates and Twitter feeds, they still click on links with pictures of "hot chicks" or "LOLcats" like trained seals. It's as though nothing ever changes. And there's a reason for that. *It's because nothing ever changes.* Or at least not with the adaptive unconscious.

As a result, no matter how savvy we all are, it still takes a conscious effort each and every time we have to override some deleterious response or second-guess some intuitive judgment or "gut feeling" we have. The sheer amount of cognitive effort required to navigate a modern environment without being suckered has increased dramatically. There is reason to think that this grinds us down over time. They say that the average North American is exposed to over 5,000 advertising messages a day. While each message may have its own little trick, the net effect is little short of an all-out assault on reason. It would be unsurprising to discover that this environment resulted in a general degradation of cognitive performance.

¶

In the Mike Judge film *Idiocracy*, Luke Wilson and Maya Rudolph play two average citizens who are enlisted in a cryogenics experiment being conducted by the U.S. Army. Shortly after they are put to sleep, the experiment is discontinued, then promptly forgotten about. The two of them are awakened five hundred years later, in an America that is still recognizable and yet radically transformed. Most significantly, everyone has become an utter and complete idiot. Wilson's first encounter is with an irate citizen sitting in his living room watching a show called *Ow, My Balls* on The Violence Channel, eating congealed fat, which he scoops out with his hand from a large tub, while slurping soda from the built-in dispenser in his La-Z-Boy-style chair. He, like everyone else in this world, turns out to be somewhat difficult to communicate with, since by this time "the English language had deteriorated into a hybrid of hillbilly, Valley Girl, inner-city slang and various grunts." Every time Wilson tries to talk, people just look at him strangely, call him a "fag," tell him to shut up, or threaten to hit him. (The people in this world exhibit one of the traits that has fascinated Judge for years—dating back to his best-known creation, *Beavis and Butt-head*—namely, *impenetrable* stupidity. They are too stupid to know that they are stupid.)

What made people uncomfortable about the film—and what led its distributor and producer, 20th Century Fox, essentially to bury it—was that its image of an intellectually degraded world was, in each case, a recognizable extension of tendencies that are already present in contemporary society. Fox may also have been worried about the reaction of sponsors, because of the broad parody of commercialism throughout the film. One memorable sequence was shot inside a giant Costco store, so large that it had its own internal light rail system to service the thousands of aisles. Every article of clothing or piece of furniture in the movie is branded. The fast food chain Carl's Jr. has taken over the entire food supply with its new slogan "Fuck You, I'm Eating." This is actually not that hard to imagine: the company's current slogan is "Don't Bother Me, I'm Eating," and the chain has provoked consumer ire through its extraordinarily vulgar commercials, including the decision to use the song "Baby Got Back" to promote meals aimed at children. In fact, most of the time the film seems like it's set fifty years in the future, not five hundred.

One of the reasons for the longer time frame, however, is the mechanism that the film posits as an explanation for the degradation. It is none other than the familiar bogeyman of social Darwinists everywhere, namely, overbreeding among the inferior classes. Early on, the movie shows a montage featuring an anxious, overachieving, educated, intelligent couple putting off having children until it is too late. Meanwhile, the couple living in the trailer park down the road have long since become grandparents. The idea is simple: dumb people have more kids, so the population as a whole is getting dumber.

The crass commercialism in the future society is taken to be a product of this general decline in intelligence. In reality, however, the more likely chain of causation would run the other direction. In the real world, at the same time that there has been an obvious coarsening of popular culture, there has also been an *increase* in general intelligence. In the United States, average IQ scores have increased by approximately 3 points per decade, for a total gain in average IQ of just under 22 points between 1932 and 2002.[24] Improvements in nutrition, along with environmental regulation (in particular, dramatic reductions in exposure to lead), are credited with a several-point increase in average intelligence in the American population. So what's making people dumb cannot be a change in biology. It is a change in the culture that is driving the transformation. In other words, it isn't stupidity that causes commercialism, but rather commercialism that causes stupidity. The film gets the explanation exactly backward.

If the argument of this chapter is correct, then the process of reverse adaptation that is driving this process is able to produce not just a coarsening of the culture, but an actual decline in cognitive performance. While none of us may feel particularly dumb or irrational, looking at the world we live in, it's hard to resist the suggestion that we may be. As Robert Cialdini puts it, "More and more frequently, we will find ourselves in the position of the lower animals—with a mental apparatus that is unequipped to deal thoroughly with the intricacy and richness of the outside environment." The irony is that, "unlike the animals, whose cognitive powers have always been relatively deficient, we have created our own deficiency by constructing a radically more complex world."[25]

This is right, except again it is important to recognize that the deficiencies we experience are not just the result of the world becoming more "complex"—as though it were all an inevitable byproduct of technological and social progress. The correct word is *hostile*. Our environment has changed so that the correlations we relied upon in the environment of evolutionary adaptation no longer obtain. This makes it so that our hardwired problem-solving routines, rather than producing answers that are approximately correct, will increasingly provide answers that are exactly wrong. Furthermore, a number of our social institutions encourage this tendency. Doing something to counteract this trend is a political problem of the first degree. Unfortunately, many of our political institutions, far from providing anything like a solution, have become a significant part of the problem.

8. "Dripping wine and blood"

The misology of the modern left

American conservatives seem to take special pride in their ability to drive liberals crazy. Consider the following entirely typical setup. On April 2, 2012, Sarah Palin appeared as a guest host on the *Today* show. She sat for a brief interview with the regular host, Matt Lauer, who proceeded to ask her a series of fairly run-of-the-mill questions. Asked about her support for soon to be Republican presidential candidate Mitt Romney, she said, "Anyone but Obama. I honestly believe that anybody running on that GOP ticket would be infinitely better than what we have today, with these failed socialist policies." A few minutes later, when asked whether she thought the economy was improving, she expressed skepticism. "Maybe for some on Wall Street, but not for the millions still unemployed," she replied.

Lauer, of course, sat there and said nothing. The task of pointing out the inconsistency fell, as usual, to Jon Stewart, who in his evening roundup of the daily news played the two clips back-to-back, then paused for a moment of analysis: "Right, Wall Street fatcats, reaping the benefits of the failed socialist . . . Wait, that doesn't make any *sense*." And of course he's right, it doesn't make any sense. You can't accuse the American president of pursuing a socialist agenda then turn around and criticize him for enacting policies that benefit only Wall Street at the expense of working Americans.

This kind of incoherence is precisely how Palin, even after all these years, continues to drive people like Stewart crazy.

Yet those who take examples like this as a sign of Palin being unintelligent or irrational are missing the bigger picture. Palin was simply following a standard "talking points" strategy, which included a series of phrases—all test-marketed and focus-group studied—designed to build up negative associations around a political opponent. The phrase "failed socialist policies" (or "Kenyan socialism") was, at the time, being used by conservative commentators across the country, often conjoined with the accusation that Obama was only helping his "pals" on Wall Street. Palin actually used the "socialist policies" phrase twice within the space of a few minutes during the *Today* show interview, so it certainly wasn't an accident. The objective was not to present a coherent analysis of the state of American politics, it was simply to repeat a series of key phrases, which would in turn be picked up in media reports and linger in the memory of casual viewers. It didn't have to hang together, because it was intended simply to build up associations, to cultivate the "gut feeling" that there was something dangerous and un-American about the president.

This is part of a conscious and calculated strategy, all based on the discovery—profoundly influential on the American right—that for a vast majority of voters, coherence simply doesn't matter. The objective is to push people's buttons, to appeal to their hearts, not their heads. Consider, for example, the famous "Mama Grizzly" advertisement released by Palin's political action committee in 2010. It is, in a sense, a masterpiece of political manipulation, since it manages to be very powerful without actually saying anything specific. Palin starts out declaring that "this year will be remembered as a year when common sense conservative women get things done for our country." She goes on to describe what she calls "a mom awakening, in the last year and a half, where women are rising up and saying, 'no, we've had enough already,' because moms kinda just know when something's wrong." She then moves on to the image that gave the clip its name:

"I think of the mama grizzly bears, who rise up on their hind legs when somebody's coming to attack their cubs."

All the while, she says nothing at all about what she is opposed to. Instead, she complains about a "fundamental transformation of America" due to "these policies coming out of Washington, D.C., right now," without saying what "these policies" are. (One can see the signs of test-marketing here as well. Republicans say "Washington" rather than "the federal government," because they know that Americans don't have an entirely negative attitude toward "government"—particularly their municipal government, which they often like. So Republicans substitute the term "Washington," which has been shown to have more negative resonance.[1]) Palin promises "common-sense solutions," without saying what these are, or even what problems they are a response to. She ends by asserting that the current situation "isn't right, for our kids and for our grandkids, and we're going to do something about this."[2]

One can understand upon viewing this clip something of the despair that American liberals feel. After all, how do you respond? There isn't anything to respond *to,* because nothing specific has been said. The language is intended to evoke a certain emotional or intuitive response without making any actual claims that could be disputed. Criticizing it is like trying to nail Jell-O to the wall. It's enough to make anyone long for the good old days, when political debate was about issues and politicians staked out clear positions then argued in support of them.

On the other hand, it is a bit rich for the left in America to start criticizing this type of technique and to demand coherence and reasoned debate in politics. After all, the most relentless criticism of "reason" over the course of the twentieth century came from those who were supposedly on the side of progress. Antirationalism was an incredibly powerful current in the 1960s counterculture, and has remained an influential force on the left, particularly in the feminist and the environmental movements, right through to the present day. In many ways, the present irrationalism of the right is simply a consequence of having appropriated left-wing strategy. Before there was "truthiness" on the right, there was "flakiness" on the left, a distinctive intellectual style that became the hallmark of the '60s. Both involve believing what *feels* true, instead of thinking through the evidence and consequences in order to determine whether it actually *is* true.

❡

In 1969, Ayn Rand delivered a lecture entitled "Apollo and Dionysus," based on a rather clever contrast between two events that occurred in the late summer of that year. The first was the launch of the Apollo 11 moon mission in Florida. The second was the famous Woodstock music festival in upstate New York. She had no difficulty presenting these two events as symbols of a "conflict of reason against irrational emotion." On one side of the country were the cool, dispassionate Apollonians, watching their metal rocket streaking up toward the stars, advancing the frontier of human knowledge and exploration. On the other side was the "vanguard of the Dionysian cohorts," literally wallowing in the mud at Woodstock, "made up of wild, rampaging irrationalists, openly proclaiming their hatred of reason, dripping wine and blood." In Rand's analysis, reason was clearly on the side of the individual, while unreason thrived on the passions released by the mob (enhanced by rock music and other intoxicants). Thus the contrast between reason and unreason, in her mind, could be unproblematically mapped onto the distinction between capitalism and communism, market and state, right and left.

While Rand was no doubt correct in the way that she described the alignment of political forces at the time, she made no attempt to explain how it had come about; indeed, she treated it as though it had always been the case. Yet it was not. From David Hume and Edmund Burke in the eighteenth century through to Friedrich Nietzsche in the nineteenth and Martin Heidegger in the twentieth , the most profound critics of rationality have always been men of the right. (Indeed, part of Rand's retelling of the

"Apollo and Dionysus" theme involved distancing herself from Nietzsche, who blamed the Apollonian tendency for much of what was wrong in the world.) The fact that Rand was officially a rationalist continues to make her something of an oddball on the right—for example, her aggressive atheism remains one of the factors that prevents her from being fully embraced by the American conservative movement. This rationalism was actually one of the reasons why she denied that she was a conservative and, before she died in 1982, spoke out against Ronald Reagan for tolerating Christian evangelicals "who are struggling—apparently with his approval—to take us back to the Middle Ages, via the unconstitutional union of religion and politics."[3]

These, however, were thoughts out of season, and it was not long before the two sides reverted to type.[4] Historically, it has been the left that is rationalist and the right antirationalist. "Reason" and "progress" somehow just seem to go together. Although the French Revolution and its aftermath had discredited the Enlightenment project in its classical form, the various socialist movements that sprang up in the nineteenth century were all distinctly rationalist in temperament. This is revealed most obviously in the architectural and planning styles favored by utopians like Robert Owen or Charles Fourier. Both Owen's new model towns and Fourier's workers' cooperatives—*phalanstères*—were laid out with obsessive symmetry, like a formal garden at Versailles. It was as though replacing the aesthetic disarray of traditional workers' housing would correct the social pathologies as well.[5] Even Karl Marx, who was inclined to view the claim to "rationality" of the first Enlightenment as nothing more than bourgeois ideology, nevertheless drew heavily on the authority of science in order to distinguish his "scientific" socialism from the "utopian" versions peddled by, among others, Owen and Fourier. Much of what Marx disliked about capitalism was simply the disorder of an unplanned economy. George Orwell was certainly not wrong when he observed that "the underlying motive of many Socialists . . . is simply a hypertrophied sense of order. The present state of affairs offends them not because it causes misery, still less because it makes freedom impossible, but because it is untidy; what they desire, basically, is to reduce the world to something resembling a chessboard."[6]

What led to the great realignment of the twentieth century—the rise of left-wing antirationalism—was the experience of the Second World War and the subsequent cold war between capitalist and communist powers. Prior to the Second World War, it seemed obvious to most people on the left that capitalism was responsible for all the major ills in the Western world. Even the First World War, despite its apparent political causes, could easily be blamed on capitalism, since the underlying issue was a contest for colonial power. This could be explained by extending the critique of capitalism to a theory of imperialism (as did, for example, V. I. Lenin).[7] The Nazi regime in Germany, however, seemed to defy this pattern of explanation (which is not to say that many did not try; it is just that these accounts failed to produce much conviction). Two distinct evils arose during the Second World War that struck many people as being extremely troubling and not easily explicable as byproducts of mere capitalism or greed.

The first was highly bureaucratized killing. The Nazis were not just killers, but extremely methodical and efficient killers. At the height of the war, every aspect of the procedure in the death camps was carefully administered. There was a system: clothing was removed, sorted into piles; victims were shaved, with the hair being preserved and put to various uses; they were then gassed en masse (far more effective and economical than shooting); later, the teeth of the corpses were examined for gold fillings that could be removed. Everything was itemized, sorted, and exhaustively documented. Someone had obviously put a lot of thought into every aspect of the procedure.

The second major evil was the convergence of science and technology, which was at the time still a relatively recent phenomenon, being used to amplify the capacity to kill. A lot of weapons technology had actually been developed during the First World War—tanks, bombers, flamethrowers, chemical and biological weapons—but not really put to effective use, largely because of social inhibitions. All of these inhibitions came down during the Second World War, and technology became ascendant. Conquerors had always dreamed of wreaking destruction on a vast scale. For the first time in human history, this had become technologically feasible. Furthermore, when the technology was put to use, it was often against civilian populations (not just bombing, but also weapons like the flamethrower, which proved particularly useful at clearing people out of buildings, and thus at taking control of urban areas). And then, of course, there was the nuclear bomb, which brought the powers of destruction to unimaginable new heights.

What these two evils had in common is that they involved an enormous amount of human ingenuity being deployed to solve an essentially technical problem, without any apparent attention to the broader purposes to which it was being directed. The sight of science in the service of *inhumanity* was an enormous blow to the prestige of the Enlightenment and its view that the progress of reason went hand in hand with the betterment of humanity. *At best,* these new evils seemed to indicate that reason and science were neutral in the struggle between good and evil in the world. They certainly showed that reason was not intrinsically a force for progress. Rationality began to seem more like an instrument, a tool that could be used for any purpose, fair or foul.

Even more troubling were the voices claiming that reason was not neutral, but was actually *responsible* for these great evils. The destruction of the Second World War was portrayed as the culmination of the technological impulse, with its underlying hostility to human life and values. This is not so hard to imagine. The scientific method is famous for requiring objectivity and emotional detachment on the part of the investigator. Scientific experimentation also involves extensive manipulation of conditions. When dealing with nature, this is fine, but with people it becomes problematic. "Being objective" can easily be taken to mean "treating people as objects," emotional detachment can translate into indifference to human suffering, and manipulation can take the form of dominance and control.

From this perspective, it is not crazy to think that science might actually involve a non-neutral stance toward the world. Far from being "objective," it might actually be driven by an interest in manipulation and control. Objectification is simply our way of achieving that control. When applied to the natural world, this mentality is what produces environmental devastation. Applied to the social world, it encourages us to treat people in the same way, as objects of manipulation, a population to be managed, repressed, and, if necessary, killed. When applied to the artifacts of human creation, it gives us the concept of the *commodity*, or the tendency to treat everything as just an economic good, susceptible to being bought and sold at the right price. Thus science, technology, bureaucracy, and capitalism all seem to be manifestations of an underlying pathology, namely, the specific form of rationality that prevails in the Western world.

This allegation was made even before the war was over, by two exiled German philosophers, Theodor Adorno and Max Horkheimer, in their 1944 book *Dialectic of Enlightenment*. It became more compelling as the true character of the Soviet regime emerged. People who had hoped that the Industrial Revolution would produce a utopian transformation of society—by freeing mankind from poverty and need—were left with a stark choice between the tawdry commercialism of American consumer society and the bureaucratic nightmare of centrally planned economies. Given a choice between markets and bureaucracy, many found neither particularly desirable. Furthermore, John Kenneth Galbraith argued influentially that the rise of the large, multidivisional corporation within capitalist economies was generating an extension of the planning mechanism that would ultimately produce a convergence between capitalism and communism.[8]

The desire for a third alternative was intensely felt, to escape from what Max Weber had called the "iron cage" of modernity. Increasingly, people came to believe that this cage was constructed by *reason,* and that in order to escape from it, we would have to fundamentally transform our way of thinking about the world. Theodore Roszak coined the term *technocracy* to describe the institutional structure erected on the basis of technical reason—although later it came to be known as simply "the system."[9] In order to fight "the system," it was not adequate simply to rearrange the parts; one needed to undermine the whole, by transforming one's own consciousness.

The most important apostle of this view was Herbert Marcuse, another wartime exile from Germany, a colleague of Adorno and Horkheimer's but one who took a liking to the United States while he was there and decided to stay. He became extremely influential among student radicals in the 1960s. He believed that if we adopted a different orientation toward the world, one that focused on liberation and freedom rather than manipulation and control, it would literally give rise to a new type of science, new bodies of knowledge, governed by entirely different principles and practices: "The liberated consciousness would promote the development of a science and technology free to discover and realize the possibilities of things and men in the production and gratification of life, playing with the potentialities of form and matter for the attainment of this goal. Technique would then tend to become art, and art would tend to form reality: the opposition between imagination and reason, higher and lower faculties, poetic and scientific thought, would be invalidated."[10]

All of this would have been great if it had panned out. Over time, however, it became apparent that merely adopting a new "orientation" toward the world did not produce a brand-new science or a better way of relating to nature or even more successful human communities. Nor did it resolve the tension between "higher and lower faculties." In practice, what these attempts to transcend or overcome reason resulted in was just more authority being granted to our intuitive, heuristic thinking styles, with all of their characteristic weaknesses. The search for a new type of rationality became just another form of antirationalism.

§

It is not an accident that the major players in the twentieth-century critique of rationality were Germans. It would be difficult to overstate just how much the experience of the Second World War undermined the confidence that Westerners had in their own civilization, and nowhere was this more evident than in the nation that was responsible for the greatest excesses. While it is tempting to dismiss Nazism as just a blip, or an outlier, in the larger march of progress,[11] many Germans regarded it as the culmination of several deep tendencies in their society. Furthermore, they were inclined to treat every aspect of their culture—including the Enlightenment conception of reason—as complicit in the crimes that were committed.

Out of this period there emerged what might be thought of as the standard template for late-twentieth-century antirationalism, which one can find repeated again and again throughout the political theory and social criticism of the period. It starts by defining some concept of "technical rationality." This is the bad kind of reason, the sort that is involved in scientific research, economic calculation, assembly-line production, and nuclear weapons manufacture. This is the type of rationality that can tell you the chemical composition of the soup but does not know the flavor; can tell you that humans experience pain but not whether it is good or bad; and knows the price of everything but the value of nothing. The next step is to introduce [*fill in the blank*] rationality. This is the good kind. It is what the child experiences as she contemplates the beauty of a flower; it is what the Samaritan is thinking when he stops to help the wounded stranger; it is what impels us to make love not war. One then recommends that this alternative type of rationality be given priority over the technical variant.

Different people had different names for this second, "good" type of rationality. Horkheimer called it "objective reason"; Marcuse called it "post-technological rationality."[12] Many thought of it as a type of aesthetic judgment, like Adorno's "mimetic reason." There are conservative versions of it as well. George Grant got a huge amount of mileage out of the Heideggerian critique of technology and "technical rationality."[13] Michael Oakeshott's critique of rationalism in politics is organized around a contrast between "technical rationality" and what he calls "traditional rational-ity."[14] The examples can easily be multiplied.

One area where this line of thinking had a particularly powerful impact was in the feminist movement, which emerged in its modern form during the 1960s. There is an obvious temptation to think of the objectivating, dispassionate, technical form of rationality as essentially *male* and to con-trast it with an alternative, feminine form, which would be more inclu-sive, interactive, and compassionate. Needless to say, this characterization plays into a number of traditional gender stereotypes. The suggestion that women are somehow less rational and more emotional than men served for centuries as the standard justification for the exclusion of women from education, employment, and public life generally. Early feminists sought to fight women's oppression by resisting this characterization. For the most part, they were committed to some form of straight-up Enlightenment rationalism. Mary Wollstonecraft began her revolutionary 1792 treatise on the rights of women with the assertion that, when it comes to humanity, "the perfection of our nature and capability of happiness, must be esti-mated by the degree of reason, virtue, and knowledge, that distinguish the individual, and direct the laws which bind society."[15] And since knowledge and virtue naturally flow "from the exercise of reason," it is actually just reason that explains "man's pre-eminence over the brute creation." She went on to assert that as far as women were concerned, the "follies and caprices of our sex," which men point to as evidence of unfitness for autonomy and self-government, are merely "the natural effect of ignorance." In arguing that women are too irrational to be educated, men confuse cause and effect. To the extent that women are irrational, it is *because* they are denied access to education.

The central characteristic of this old-fashioned feminism was that it sought to dissolve gender stereotypes, arguing that it was culture, not biol-ogy, that made women so different from men. Of course, Wollstonecraft was writing at a time when everyone assumed that mankind's domination of "brute creation" was a great thing and that "reason" was an ideal to be aspired to. Women simply wanted to get into the game. But as the ideal of reason became less and less inspiring, the temptation grew to preserve the reason/intuition stereotype and simply celebrate the other half. Perhaps men have their way of thinking about things and women have a different way? The male style has been arbitrarily privileged, simply because men have been running the show. Women will never be able to participate as equals by imitating the male style. They can become equal only by insisting that their own style be recognized as valid. What's more, things might actually be better, since the male style is responsible for all of the long litany of grievances associated with "technical rationality," including, most obviously, war.

One particularly colorful, and not entirely atypical, example of this line of thinking can be found in the work of Mary Daly, a Catholic theologian who broke with the church and its patriarchal traditions with her 1968 book *The Church and the Second Sex,* and later, in *Beyond God the Father.* In this second book, she described her task as one of "breaking down the barriers between technical knowledge and that deep realm of intuitive knowledge which some theologians call ontological reason." One can see here an effective use of the standard antirationalist template, with "ontological reason" being the good type. What is ontological reason? It involves valorizing the "realm of knowledge which is subjective, affective, intuitive."[16] In terms of dual-process psychology, this amounts to a straightforward privileging of our intuitive, heuristic problem-solving systems over the explicit, linguistically mediated, rational system.

One can see already that this is going to be trouble. To make matters worse, two tendencies in the feminist movement pushed even harder in the direction of antirationalism. The first was the view that adversarialism is a "male" pattern of interaction, one that women, who are consensual by nature, need not engage in. So while men were constantly disagreeing with each other, women were supposed to work together, collaboratively advancing the feminist project. (All the stuff about Aristotle rejecting Plato's view was just boys being boys.) But because of this, feminists deprived themselves of one of the most useful kluges in Western civilization, and one of the most powerful checks against confirmation bias. As individuals, we have enormous difficulty thinking the negative. We see patterns all around us, and each new day brings new evidence that confirms our belief in them. Thinking through the hypothetical "What if I am wrong?" is not something that comes naturally. Having other people around whose sole interest lies in doing just that not only serves as an external corrective, it also pushes us to think in a way that our thoughts do not naturally go.

Social criticism is always in danger of tipping over into conspiracy theory. Without the skeptic at the back of the room saying "Why should I believe any of this?" there is little to stop it from going right over the edge. Thus feminists wound up spending inordinate amounts of time discussing the hidden powers of "the patriarchy," along with its ability to control women's bodies and program their minds. Much of this, in retrospect, can easily be categorized as straight-up conspiracy theorizing. It is astonishing, for example, to contemplate the amount of time and energy spent discussing pornography as the cornerstone of women's oppression—all of it completely invalidated by the rise of the internet, which increased the amount of pornography available to the average male by several orders of magnitude and yet led to no demonstrable increase in the oppression of women (and coincided with a decline in the frequency of rape).

The second major problem had to do with a self-radicalizing tendency set in motion by the critique of rationality. Many of the institutions that feminists were hoping to change fell outside the scope of legal regulation. (How does one persuade men to take on more of the burden of household chores? How does one convince more women to become electricians? How can one discourage women from marrying men who make more money than them?) One can change the environment in order to encourage people to make different choices, but ultimately, the decisions that individuals make will be determinative. As a result, change was much slower in coming than many expected. Furthermore, after aggressive experimentation in certain areas like family structure (with the proliferation of communes and collective childrearing arrangements in the 1960s and '70s), there was a period of massive retrenchment, with significant reversion to the old, supposedly "patriarchal" nuclear family.

Some critics responded to this by moving in the direction of pragmatism, concluding that it is more difficult to change the culture than the law, or that the older arrangements between the sexes may have had some unappreciated virtues. But other critics went in the exact opposite direction. Having formulated their "radical" social criticism only to discover that it failed to revolutionize society, they concluded that their original criticism had not been radical enough. With respect to the critique of rationality, many concluded that their mistake lay in thinking that they could criticize technical *reason* while at the same time preserving the same *concepts* used by the technocracy. In order to really change things—in order to revolutionize people's consciousness—it would be necessary to invent a new set of concepts—in effect, a new language—in order to express the ideals and aspirations of the oppressed.

This idea was already present in Heidegger, which is why his work is so difficult to understand. Heidegger felt obliged to invent a new language in which to express himself, one that would be uncontaminated by old assumptions about reason and truth. This suggestion was picked up with a vengeance by many feminists, as well as by theorists in the tradition that came to be known as postmodernism. (This is why it is unfair to characterize the work of postmodernists as "bad writing," despite the fact that a lot of it is actually bad writing. Much of the obscurity is intentional, because it is motivated by this desire to invent a new way of speaking.) One could see this tendency quite clearly in Daly's work, where the language became more unbridled as time went by. In her 1978 book *Gyn/Ecology,* her case for intuition over reason was put in more florid terms:

I have advocated committing the crime of Methodicide, since the Methodolatry of patriarchal disciplines kills creative thought. The acceptable/unexceptional circular reasonings of academics are caricatures of motion . . . Gynocentric Method requires not only the murder of misogynistic methods (intellectual and affective exorcism) but also ecstasy, which I have called *ludic cerebration.* This is "the free play of intuition in our own space, giving rise to thinking that is vigorous, informed, multi-dimensional, independent, creative, tough." It arises from the lived experience of be-ing.[17]

I was an undergraduate when the second edition of this book came out, complete with a "New, Intergalactic Introduction by the Author." Although I was not hostile to either feminism or postmodernism, I remember thinking at the time that her work was really disturbed. (From the introduction: "That year marked my entry into a New Realm of Qualitative Leaping through galaxies of mindspace. I was Moving far out on my Spiraling Intergalactic Voyage, which I Re-Call as beginning *in utero* . . ."[18]) I remember also being quite shocked to find many of my fellow students, not to mention professors, taking it quite seriously. Although Daly herself was an extremist, in many ways her work was, and is, taken very seriously by a lot of people who aren't.[19] This despite the fact that it was really quite crazy, far nuttier than anything the American right has been producing in recent years.

The idea that reason is somehow male has proven extremely difficult to dislodge, and has led innumerable women into thinking that their "intuitions" somehow give them better guidance in life. Fifty years of psychological research, however, has shown that there is surprisingly little difference in the way that men and women reason.[20] There are some very well-confirmed examples of *cognitive* differences between men and women—particularly with respect to visualization, targeting, and certain aspects of memory—

but no differences in *reasoning*. It is not an accident that the differences that do show up are at the level of modular, "built-in" systems. Uniformity of reason, on the other hand, is exactly what one would expect from recognizing the central role that language—in particular, shared, public language—plays in sustaining reasoning practices. It is not all that misleading to think of "reason" as akin to a piece of software that can run equally well on different hardware platforms. There are differences between male and female brains, just as surely as there are differences between male and female bodies. Reason, however, is universal, precisely because much of it lives *outside* our brains. Furthermore, women's intuition turns out to be just as fallible as men's intuition, and women are no more and no less susceptible than men to the standard run of cognitive biases.

¶

Environmentalists sometimes speak as though anyone who ignores the scientific consensus on climate change is completely mad, or in the pocket of the oil industry. And yet there is an element of "too little too late" in the left's holding up science as an unquestioned, unchallengeable authority after having done everything possible to undermine the authority and prestige of science over the course of the past fifty years. Furthermore, there are still many areas where the left feels perfectly comfortable ignoring what scientists have to say. The scientific consensus on global warming is no less comprehensive than the scientific consensus about the importance of childhood vaccination or the harmlessness of certain herbicides or the futility of homeopathic medicine, and yet these opinions are often ignored, or dismissed on the basis of the same kind of conspiracy theories that "climate-change skeptics" use to dismiss research on global warming.

Consider the case of vaccination, which has become a source of enormous anxiety among parents in the granola set. I've known parents to agonize for months over whether to get their child vaccinated. This is actually a perfect example of how acting on the basis of intuition, even motivated by purely altruistic concern for the health and safety of one's child, can produce a collective action problem that makes everyone worse off. Many childhood illnesses are quite dangerous. Vaccines, by comparison, are significantly less dangerous. At the same time, they are also not entirely safe. A child receiving a vaccine has a small but nonzero chance of suffering side effects that can be quite severe. Nevertheless, if you had to compare the potential dangers of the disease to the dangers of the vaccine, it would be a no-brainer: you would get the vaccine. But here is the catch. When you vaccinate your child, not only do you reduce her chances of getting the disease, you also reduce her chances of *transmitting* the disease. Once enough children are vaccinated, it creates what is known as "herd immunity," where a particular virus cannot invade the population because there are not enough carriers. This means that if everyone else is going to be vaccinating their child, it's actually in your interest not to vaccinate your own—that way you avoid the risk of side effects yet you still don't have to worry about your child getting the disease. It's a classic free-rider strategy. The problem is that when too many people do this, it becomes self-defeating, and risks creating an outbreak of the disease.

Not only do parents have a free-rider incentive, but their "gut" also tends to align with it. This coincidence of self-interest with intuition is predictably toxic. Having someone stab your child with a needle and make him scream does not *feel* like the right thing to do. Getting it done is an obvious instance of where a rational override of our intuitive response is required. This override is made difficult by the fact that the dangers of the disease are not just in the future and uncertain, they are tied to a hypothetical. You need to be concerned about more than what is likely to happen—since herd immunity often means that, as a matter of fact, nothing is likely to happen to your child. It's a matter of thinking what *would* happen if everyone acted as you are tempted to act. Making this hypothetical effective in the control of behavior is a challenge for everyone, but it is certainly made worse if one happens to subscribe to an antirationalist ideology that assigns greater authority to one's "maternal instincts" or "gut feelings." That, combined with a bit of paranoia about "big pharma," is enough to tip a lot of people over into the antivaccination camp.

Thus it has always been a struggle getting enough people to vaccinate their children (which is why it is mandatory in many jurisdictions—or mandatory for school attendance). The situation became a lot worse when it was alleged that, beyond the known side effects of various vaccinations, there was also a causal link between vaccination and autism. Although the study that made this allegation was subsequently revealed to be fraudulent, the damage it did was enormous.[21] The "vaccines cause autism" meme is the classic example of a "truthy" claim. Although not actually true, it *felt* intensely true to many parents. The movement achieved enormous influence, culminating perhaps in the appearance of Jenny McCarthy, its unofficial celebrity spokesperson, on *The Oprah Winfrey Show* in 2007. Oprah was subsequently taken to task in a *Newsweek* magazine cover story for providing a platform for a variety of pseudoscience and medical quackery on her show—and the interview with McCarthy was considered one of the most egregious instances.[22] McCarthy, whose son, Evan, may or may not have been autistic, asserted categorically that his condition had been caused by vaccination, and recounted the terrible experience she had: "I said to the doctor, 'I have a very bad feeling about this shot. This is the autism shot, isn't it?'" The doctor dismissed her concerns, the nurse administered the vaccine, and "soon thereafter—boom—the soul's gone from his eyes."[23]

One can understand why Oprah would have been somewhat circumspect in criticizing her guest. Listening to McCarthy talk, two things were immediately apparent. First, she had an extremely strong feeling that what she was saying was true. Second, she believed that her feelings were a reliable guide to what was in fact true. It was precisely because she felt it so strongly that she believed in what she was saying. And since the confidence that a speaker has is often used by the hearer as a heuristic for evaluating the credibility of the speaker's claim, someone who believes something so passionately tends to come across as believable.[24] But this is, of course, a recipe for believing *anything*. Indeed, when confronted with the lack of scientific evidence linking vaccines to autism, McCarthy "replied with all the love that I could muster in my heart": "Who needs science when I'm witnessing it every day in my own home? I watched it happen . . . At home, Evan is my science."[25] Who wants to be the killjoy who points out that Evan is not actually science, and that this is a totally invalid basis for belief? Moreover, how many people would have had the courage to say this in front of an *Oprah* studio audience? The response would have been withering. It's difficult to disparage the belief without at the same time appearing to disparage the sentiment.

And so "heart" wins over "head," with the predictable result that children who might have led healthy, happy lives instead contracted disabling and in some cases fatal illnesses. People who are trying to protect children wind up harming them, simply because they cannot bring themselves to override their "maternal" intuitions.

¶

Some of the antirationalism that was unleashed during the 1960s was intentional, but some of it was not. Perhaps the best example of the latter is the set of ideas associated with the "progressive education" movement. Although many of the basic doctrines date back to John Dewey's writings from the early twentieth century, they became highly influential in the 1960s. My older brother, who started grade one in 1971, got the full-on experience. My parents enrolled him in the new, experimental "open school" in our town. There, every child learned at his own pace, following his own interests. The school had no desks, no set curriculum, and no rote learning. Children organized themselves into groups to work on "projects" based on their interests. The teachers facilitated and made suggestions, but stayed away from anything that resembled traditional instruction. It lasted for a while. At the end of grade two, when my parents realized that my brother could barely read or write and didn't know his multiplication tables, they pulled him out and put him in an old-fashioned school. There, the teachers forced him to learn things that he didn't see the value of, like spelling and multiplication.

The basic idea of an "open school" is still quite familiar, not because many children attend one, but thanks to the popularity of *The Magic School Bus*. *The Magic School Bus* started as a book in 1985 but has since expanded to include over one hundred books, a TV series, and a set of video games, all of which are relentlessly pushed by its publisher, Scholastic, which has special access to the educational market. Parents like it because it's "educational," although they often fail to notice that it subscribes to a very particular educational ideal, one that is firmly anchored in the '60s. The children in Ms. Frizzle's classroom never have to do anything that resembles lessons, and the teacher never gives them any work to do. They don't have to sit in desks; they just roam about, working on projects that interest them, and reporting back to the class if they happen to feel like doing so. They also—in over a hundred books—never spend even one minute studying any of the so-called three R's: reading, writing, and arithmetic (for some reason the kids just come equipped with advanced competence in these areas). All of the learning is experiential. Each book follows a predictable course: after some preliminary chitchat, one of the students will ask a question. Ms. Frizzle will respond by saying, "Let's find out! To the magic school bus!" Everyone then hops on the bus and leaves the school in order to travel back through time to study the dinosaurs, or shrink to the size of a cell and go inside the body, or transform into a bird and migrate, and so on.

It's not an accident that it takes a *magic* school bus to make this pedagogical model work, because in real life it certainly doesn't.[26] Ms. Frizzle's classroom is a type of collective hippie fantasy, not just of how we would like our schools to be organized, but also of what we would like children to be like and how we would like the human mind to function. It would be nice if everything could be learned by seeing and doing, rather than reading books and listening to lectures. It would also be nice if everything that we had to learn was incredibly interesting at the time that we were learning it. And it would be especially great if you could do science without first having to study math, and learn to read without doing any memorization. This is, unfortunately, not the case. The core of formal education involves teaching our brains to function in ways that are highly unnatural, in terms of both our innate biology and our native processing style. And that is necessarily hard and unpleasant.

Learning to think involves forcing (or tricking) your memory into doing things that don't come naturally. It involves figuring out a way to sustain attention for low-stimulus (or "boring") tasks, by avoiding or overcoming distraction. It involves learning to develop external representations of problems in order to work through them systematically. Yet in the background of the "progressive education" ideal is the view that *learning should always be easy.* If students are finding something difficult, or if they are having trouble concentrating, or if they find something too abstract or difficult to remember, it must be a consequence of bad teaching. This is, of course, a tricky area, because sometimes material *is* made more difficult or more boring or less memorable than it should be because of bad teaching. And yet there is also some material that is intrinsically difficult, which there is simply no nice way to learn, from memorizing multiplication tables in early childhood to learning anatomy in medical school.

There is some evidence to suggest that when it comes to thinking rationally, a bit of difficulty may in fact be a good thing. Recall Keith Stanovich's claim that "a large part of education can be viewed as an attempt to develop controlled processing styles that override the fundamental computational bias and thus enable learned rule systems to operate on decoupled representations."[27] The "fundamental computational bias" that Stanovich refers to is our tendency to use the laziest method possible to solve any given problem. Because our heuristic problem-solving systems are extremely rapid and require little attention, our first inclination is always to rely on them. It is often only when we encounter some unexpected problem that we engage our higher cognitive resources. Full-scale analytic thought is reserved for special occasions, when we have exhausted all other options.

Unfortunately, the way that we monitor these lower systems in order to determine whether they are actually doing a good job is based on another heuristic, which psychologists refer to as *cognitive fluency*. Basically, if our intuitive response is fast and effortless, our natural inclination is to treat this as a sign that it is correct.[28] (For example, if it takes you less than a second to recognize someone, you take this as a good sign that you do in fact know this person. If it takes you longer, and you have to look at the person from a few different angles, you take this as a sign that your recognition might not be reliable.) This is a pretty good system from a rough-and-ready evolutionary perspective—it is itself fast and easy, and probably got things right more often than not in the environment of evolutionary adaptation. But it is using a proxy as the basis for its judgment. In the same way that we use a speaker's level of expressed confidence as a basis for judging reliability, in this case we are using the ease with which we have solved a problem as a basis for judging how good our solution is. If our goal is to get things right—not just often enough to survive and reproduce, but actually to get things right—then this is disastrously inadequate.

In one particularly clever experiment, a group of psychologists at Princeton showed just how easy it is to spoof this system.[29] They gave students a set of problems, of the typical sort used to expose cognitive bias—where our intuitive response is incorrect, and so we need to think through the problem rationally in order to get the right answer. The twist was that one batch of students were given the problems printed out in a very clear, easy-to-read font, whereas the other group was given the problems in a difficult-to-read font. There was a significant difference in the error rate between the two groups, with those who received the questions in the more-difficult-to-read format making *fewer* mistakes. This is the opposite of what one might expect. The explanation proposed by the experimenters is that the font impaired their sense of cognitive fluency. It made it *feel* as though the problems were hard to solve, and this in turn led to the intervention of the analytical system. Once the students stopped to think about the problems, however, they could see that the intuitive solution was wrong, and so they initiated an override and produced the correct response.

The lesson to be learned is that *easy* is often the enemy of reason. And yet educators have been told for years that their job is to make things easy for students, or to present things in a way that makes them intuitively accessible. This creates a real danger that teachers may just exploit preexisting cognitive biases rather than teaching students to overcome them. This isn't to say that school should consist of nothing but rote memorization and drills. It just means that there is a strong case to be made for educational conservatism, simply because the pedagogical techniques we inherited are ones that have been subject to development and refinement over the course of thousands of years. There's nothing wrong with tweaking them here and there, but the idea that we should be able to redo schools from scratch, substituting entirely new methods—when we actually understand very little about how children learn—is classic rationalist hubris.[30]

And yet the commitment to easy is so strong that some commentators have even convinced themselves that easy is the new hard. Yale law professor Amy Chua set off an explosive controversy by providing an articulate defense of the "tiger mom" parenting style—making your children practice piano for hours, giving them math problems, denigrating them until they get straight A's, and so on. Chua boasted about her own children never having watched TV, played a video game, or gone to a sleepover. To say that Americans freaked out over this would be to risk understatement. Many felt that it was tantamount to child abuse. David Brooks, however, took a contrary tack. Instead of accusing Chua of being too tough on her kids, he called her a wimp: "Practicing a piece of music for four hours requires focused attention, but it is nowhere near as cognitively demanding as a sleepover with fourteen-year-old girls. Managing status rivalries, negotiating group dynamics, understanding social norms, navigating the distinction between self and group—these and other social tests impose cognitive demands that blow away any intense tutoring session or a class at Yale."[31]

What is astonishing about this response is how exactly wrong it is. The set of skills that Brooks applauds all fall into the category of tribal social instincts. While they may require some cunning and ingenuity, they are not at all "cognitively demanding." They are cognitively complex in the same way that facial recognition is complex—programming a computer to do it would be quite difficult. But that doesn't mean they are demanding or difficult *for us*. Cognitively demanding tasks are ones that require us to override our natural intuitions, in part by maintaining attention over time. Social interaction between teenage girls requires none of this. Indeed, one can see exactly the same management of status rivalries and negotiation of group dynamics in any tribe of chimpanzees.[32] Our civilization is built upon the ability to selectively *override* these primitive social instincts. This requires a great deal of self-control, the kind of self-control that is cultivated by practicing a piece of music for four hours and that is specifically *not* cultivated by hanging out with your friends at a sleepover.

¶

In his 2007 book, *The Assault on Reason*, Al Gore asked a seemingly simple question: "Why do reason, logic, and truth seem to play a sharply diminished role in the way that America now makes important decisions?"[33] The answer, as we have seen, is complex. Part of it has to do with hazardous dynamics at work in our culture—any culture—in which innovations that exploit people's biases have a reproductive advantage over those that do not. One can see this in many different areas, such as the trajectory of advertising over the course of the past century, where the "rational" component was progressively squeezed out by the nonrational. One can see exactly the same trajectory in the political sphere, not just because advertising techniques have been imported into politics, but because both are subject to the same evolutionary dynamics.

What has become clear is that if we let our culture drift, its tendency will be to drift away from rationality. Keeping it on track will require conscious awareness, intervention, and guidance. And yet the constituency most likely to achieve this—the progressive left, those with an interest in using the powers of the mind to improve the human condition—has been hit by a crisis of confidence of unparalleled proportions. The left has not only failed to defend reason against its critics and against the hazardous dynamics within the culture that threaten its supremacy, it has in many cases actively contributed to its decline. Much of this is due to the association of reason with science, science with technology, and technology with warfare, environmental degradation, patriarchy, alienation, and a variety of other ailments. Another large part is due to the explicitly antirationalist ideologies that came out of the 1960s, which were inclined to treat any system of rule-following as inherently oppressive. The final element stems from the utopian impulse and the desire to find revolutionary solutions to social problems, which generates impatience with the slow, steady, uncertain attempts at progress that are all reason has to offer.

Yet while left-wing antirationalism has been virulent, it is also, I would suggest, on the verge of burning itself out. This is because the left, in one form or another, has always been committed to the idea of progress, and progress has always depended on the exercise of reason. Most of the social and economic problems in our society are complex problems that require both ingenuity and collective action to resolve. None of this will happen if we simply follow our gut feelings. Solving collective action problems requires rational insight. Furthermore, the most important institution when it comes to resolving these problems is the state. Thus there is an almost inevitable connection between left-wing politics, support for government, and a commitment to the use of reason to improve the human condition.

9. Run, Forrest, run!

The rise of common sense conservatism

Nineteen eighty was a bad year for the cause of reason in politics. That year saw two major events: first, the election of Ronald Reagan as president of the United States and, second, the launch of CNN, the world's first twenty-four-hour news channel. Both were instrumental in ushering in a new era of irrationalism in politics.

While serving his two terms as U.S. president, Reagan had a number of affectionate nicknames: Dutch, the Gipper, the Great Communicator . . . But to his critics and opponents, he was widely known as the Great Liar. Long before he began to suffer from Alzheimer's disease, or even before he was elected president, Reagan had a way of blurring the line between acting and politics and between Hollywood and real life. He was famous for peppering his political speeches with lines from movies, some of which were spoken by characters that he had played. He once regaled a meeting of the Congressional Medal of Honor Society with a story of the commander of a Second World War bomber who went down with his crewmen instead of bailing out. As far as anyone could tell, he got the story from a 1944 propaganda film called *Wing and a Prayer.*

As these example show, the "lying" accusation was actually a bit wide of the mark. Reagan was not so much a liar as he was a confabulator. The difference is important: confabulators believe what they are saying as they say it, whereas liars know that they are being untruthful. Because of this, confabulation is sometimes described as "honest" or "innocent" lying: confabulators are perfectly sincere in what they are saying, even though they have no reason to believe it.[1] Throughout his political career, Reagan simply invented things whenever it seemed convenient to do so, blending fact and fiction into an undifferentiated haze. By the end of his second term, an entire book had been published documenting his confabulations.[2] Perhaps his most famous began during his campaign for the presidency in 1976, when he started telling the story of the Chicago "welfare queen"—a woman who allegedly had eighty aliases, thirty addresses, twelve Social Security cards, and four husbands, and who had defrauded taxpayers of over $150,000. The story wasn't remotely true, but no matter how often it was debunked by the media, Reagan would just keep telling it.

Now of course, Reagan was hardly the first politician to tell a lie to get elected. The difference was that he didn't seem to be worried about getting caught, and when he did get caught, it didn't seem to affect his behavior. Richard Nixon had been a notorious liar, but he was also notorious for trying to hide his deceptions. And when he did get caught, he looked guilty. Reagan, by contrast, radiated sincerity—mainly because he was being sincere, in his own mind—even when telling a lie that he had been called out on many times. This caused a great deal of consternation in the press. What were journalists supposed to do? Keep calling out the lie every time it was told? It seemed impossible to do so without being seen as partisan. And yet how was the press supposed to perform its traditional role—that of holding power to account—if those in power simply smiled, nodded, and carried on with business as usual? Not only did Reagan continue to lie about the Chicago welfare queen long after being called out, but even worse, Americans didn't seem to care. How could this be?

The short answer is that America was on the cusp of its long-standing love affair with truthiness. Sure, Reagan's story was completely false. But for a great many people, it *felt* true. And because of that, he was able to get away with it. Reagan's lies attained the status of contemporary fables, little morality plays that, while fictional, spoke of deeper truths about American life. What matters is not how things are but how they seem to be, and how that seeming resonates with our most emotional and gut-level responses. David Gergen, who in 1982 worked on Reagan's communications staff, defended his boss in exactly these terms. "Presidential storytelling is a time-honored sort of folk art in American politics," he said. "These stories tend to have a parable-like quality to them; he's trying to tell us how society works."[3]

So perhaps it was not true, as Reagan once claimed, that all the waste in a year from a nuclear power plant could be stored under a desk. But wasn't it true that environmentalists were greatly exaggerating the threat of nuclear power? So there was no Chicago welfare queen. Wasn't it still the case that America's expanding welfare rolls had created a culture of dependency, irresponsibility, and entitlement among the poor? Or consider Reagan's story about the guy who went up to the cashier in a grocery store with an orange in one hand and a bottle of vodka in the other, paid for the orange with food stamps, then used the change to buy the vodka. Couldn't have happened, but that doesn't mean alcoholics aren't abusing the food stamp system.

This is what led to the great discovery, with such fateful consequences for American political culture, that if you found a message that "resonated" and then just kept repeating it over and over again, many people would come to believe it regardless of whether it was true. What Reagan was ultimately able to show is that, even in the political realm, repetition can overpower reality. Of course, this is something that advertisers had known for decades—just by hearing a product name, again and again, people become convinced of its quality—so it was probably just a matter of time before someone applied these lessons to the political realm. Still, it took some nerve to tell bald-faced lies again and again, even after having been publicly corrected.

Recall Goebbels's observation that success will go to "the man who is able to reduce problems to the simplest terms and who has the courage to keep forever repeating them in this simplified form, despite the objections of the intellectuals." Reagan was that man. In his case, however, it didn't seem to require much courage; it was mainly a matter of temperament. As Frank Luntz recalls, "When it comes to repetition, politicians are seemingly addicted to communication variation. Ronald Reagan was the only politician I ever saw who seemed to enjoy saying the same words over and over again as though it was the first time he had ever spoken them."[4]

But Reagan also benefited from some lucky timing. Republicans had realized early on that their candidate could take fairly significant liberties with the truth while on television. Being corrected on-air is extremely unlikely, and so if it does happen, it will probably be in print, a medium with much less reach. (As Peter Teeley, press secretary to Reagan's vice president, George H. W. Bush, explained, back in 1984, "You can say anything you want during a debate and 80 million people hear it." If a fact-check appears in the newspaper the next day, "maybe 200 people read it or 2,000 or 20,000."[5])

Televised debates, however, tend to attract unusually large audiences, and occur rather infrequently. On an average newsday, lying for political advantage was less attractive. But the entire landscape of broadcast television was about to change as Reagan took office, in a way that made disregard for the truth an effective political strategy 365 days a year.

The key event was the launch of CNN, only six months after Reagan's inauguration in 1980. More than any other media outlet, the cable news channel founded by Ted Turner can be credited (or blamed) with the invention of the twenty-four-hour news cycle. The unintended consequence of this was a massive increase in the power of repetition in forming public political opinion. It used to be that a lie, once told, might be repeated only once or twice before being corrected. With a dedicated news channel, however, a lie might be repeated *every fifteen minutes,* for hours and hours, before even being called into question.

The twenty-four-hour news cycle has had a profound influence on how politics functions, thanks to three major developments. The first was speed. Cable news stations, especially networks such as CNN that have stringers, affiliates, and other contacts around the world, are able to cover breaking news in something close to real time. As the news cycle speeds up, the message inevitably becomes compressed. This is the second major development. Television news has always been the "flattest" of the major news media. Compared to print and radio, television works in relatively short video clips, soundbites, and attenuated explanations. And oddly enough, the advent of round-the-clock news only made the situation worse. One might have expected that having every minute of every day to fill, stations would have responded by deepening their coverage, offering more sophisticated reporting with a broader mix of perspectives. But that has not happened. One of the more surprising features of cable news is how few stories get covered on a given day. Typically, fewer than a half-dozen stories get anything resembling substantial coverage, with the lion's share of news being relegated to the text "crawl" that scrolls along the bottom of the screen. What we call "twenty-four-hour news" mostly consists of fifteen minutes of news played on a never-ending loop, with slight variations from cycle to cycle. That is why, even more than speed and compression, the most influential aspect of the twenty-four-hour news cycle is repetition, with the same clips, the same quotes, and the same news copy being read over and over again during the course of a day.

Combined, these factors have had a transformative effect on our political culture. "Pervasiveness and repetition," as George Monbiot has put it, work like a "battering ram" against the rational mind.[6] Once something gets into the news cycle, one can count on it being repeated many, many times. Each time it is repeated, it builds up an association in the viewer's mind. For politicians, this combination of speed, compression, and repetition means that no attack or criticism can go unanswered for any significant length of time. The longer an attack or a lie is left to itself without being disrupted by a response, the more it gets repeated and the sooner it becomes lodged in the public's brain as a fact.

Consider, for example, the strange case of Fox News and ACORN (the Association of Community Organizations for Reform Now), a loose confederation of nonprofit organizations in the United States committed to providing community services in low-income neighborhoods—including voter registration. Fox became convinced that ACORN was stacking the electoral rolls in support of Barack Obama, and so in the two months before the 2008 presidential election, the station aired no fewer than fifty reports associating ACORN with voter fraud (reaching a fever pitch during one three-day period, in which Fox News ran fifteen different reports).[7] Things got even crazier after the election, with Fox commentators accusing ACORN of being a vast criminal conspiracy, of suborning prostitution and murder, of receiving trillions of dollars of government funding, and a variety of other literally crazy accusations. The organization was disbanded in 2010. Nevertheless, the association between ACORN and voter fraud in the popular mind was sufficiently strong that after Obama's re-election in 2012 one poll showed that 49 percent of Republicans believed ACORN had stolen the election for him (despite the fact that the organization no longer existed).[8]

ACORN, of course, was not well equipped to defend itself against this onslaught from the conservative press. Politicians, however, have learned how to prepare themselves. One consequence has been the often-described acceleration of politics in our society. It is not enough anymore for a politician to have a council of advisers who can determine how to respond to an attack. It has become necessary to have a permanent "war room," ready to go into a state of high alert at the slightest alarm. Furthermore, the objective can no longer be to establish the truth; what matters is simply "getting the message out." And when there is barely time to react, there is, needless to say, no time to think, much less time to develop a complex response.

The impact on political discourse has been similar to the effects of the "creative revolution" in advertising. Just as advertisers realized that it's not about the product, it's about the feeling that you get when you think about the product, so campaign strategists and speechwriters decided that political communication is not about what you say, but rather about how you make people feel.[9] The new mantra of political strategy became the idea that elections are a battle for hearts, not heads. And the most effective way to get to people's hearts usually involves bypassing their heads. You need to get their attention, you need to get them to feel something, and you need to give them something that they will remember. The most effective way of doing this is to appeal directly to their intuitions, by saying things that resonate emotionally, that *sound right* or *feel right,* and then just repeat them again and again or, better yet, plant them and let the media do the repetition for you. (Luntz includes "consistency" as one of his cardinal rules of effective communication. But by "consistency," he doesn't mean anything like logical consistency—that is, making it so that the various things you say hang together in a coherent way. What he means by "consistency" is just saying exactly the same thing, again and again, day after day. Or as he puts it, "Repetition. Repetition. Repetition.")[10]

Along with this has come the discovery that effective communication through the media often involves breaking many of the rules that govern everyday conversation and debate. The big discovery, of course, is that if you have the "courage" to persevere (and to ignore "the objections of the intellectuals"), you don't have to tell the truth. But there have been a number of lesser discoveries as well. One of the most significant is that you don't really have to answer questions. Interviews used to consist of a person who asked questions and another who answered them (or at least made some attempt to answer them). Over the past thirty years or so, interviews have become just another opportunity for the person being interviewed to repeat a set of pre-established talking points.

The basic idea behind the talking-point strategy is rather simple. Before being interviewed, politicians will work out (or be given) a set of points that they are supposed to make (or even just phrases that they are to repeat).

When asked a question, their job is basically to free-associate around something that the interviewer has said, in order to find a connection to one of these talking points. Instead of answering the question, the question is simply used as a pretext for saying something else that the person is already intending to say. (As those in the business advise, "Don't *answer* the question—*respond* to the question."[11])

Some politicians are extremely good at this: they can "pivot" to the talking point without it being obvious what they're doing ("Well, I think there's a more fundamental issue, which you're not addressing, which is . . ." or "While my opponent would have you believe that these are important questions, we're trying to focus on the issues that are of genuine concern to Americans, such as . . ."). It will only be afterward, when you think about it, that you'll realize that he or she didn't answer any of the questions. In order to see the underlying machinery at work, you need only listen to someone who is not very good at it. Or listen to what athletes say during "interviews." For at least twenty years now, professional athletes, particularly in team sports, have been effectively prohibited from answering journalists' questions, so all they do is repeat the same dozen talking points ("There's some tough competition out there, they definitely came out swinging, but ultimately this is a team sport, and I think if the guys all pull together, we can still win this one . . .," etc.). This is a little bit different, in that the script athletes are given is a series of platitudinous nonanswers, but the basic principle is the same.

The talking-point strategy puts the journalist in the same tight spot that relentless lying does. There is always the option of calling out the person on their nonresponse, just by saying "You haven't answered the question." But it's very difficult to do this more than once or twice without seeming partisan or making things awkward, so very few journalists will dare to. The people being interviewed know this, and figure that if they just keep responding with more talking points, they can effectively ignore any attempt to get an answer to any question. Every once in a blue moon this turns into a game of chicken, but for the most part journalists tolerate it, and the talking point has thus become the dominant mode of public discussion. This has, in turn, led to a severe degradation of political discourse, because it gives politicians the chance to turn back any demand for *reasons*.

These are, of course, all generic tactics, which could in principle be used by anyone of any political persuasion. They have, however, been taken up much more enthusiastically by the right than by the left. Indeed, one way of understanding contemporary right-wing ideology is to see it as a wholehearted embrace of the new media environment. Conservatives have become the party of all intuition, all the time. This is a political ideology that is perfectly adapted to an environment in which you have ten seconds to make your point, most of the audience is not paying attention, and whatever you say may wind up being repeated hundreds of times.

¶

The core feature of "common sense" conservatism is its hostility to expertise (or what Luntz calls "fancy theories"). This draws upon traditional conservative antirationalism and the critique of liberal "hubris," but also taps into a deep well of anti-intellectualism and anti-elitism, which remain powerful forces, particularly in the United States.[12] The sentiment is perhaps best captured by William F. Buckley's famous line that he would "rather entrust the government of the United States to the first 400 people listed in the Boston telephone directory than to the faculty of Harvard University." Or one can see it on display in the movie *Forrest Gump,* a favorite of American conservatives. The hero of that particular story is a borderline-retarded Southerner who learns a few simple, common sense truths as a child in the 1950s, which then carry him through the tumult of the 1960s—including the Vietnam War—unscathed. Throughout the movie, it is made quite clear that the blame for all of the chaos in American society lies with intellectuals, who are constantly overthinking things and trying to be clever, and thereby lose touch with the simple truths, including the simple moral truths that can guide us all to a good life.[13]

In the early days, there were a few classes of "ivory tower" experts who were still taken seriously. Economists, for instance, were regarded as palatable on the whole, since at least they understood the value of free enterprise. Over time, however, this distinction between "good intellectuals" and "bad intellectuals" broke down, to be replaced by blanket hostility toward any type of theory. One of the most striking things about modern conservatism is the extent to which even right-wing economists have been marginalized within the movement. This was a hard blow for many of them, who for a long time had entertained the expectation that they would be listened to.

In Canada, for instance, many economists were genuinely shocked when the federal Conservative Party made cutting the country's value-added tax (called the GST) the centerpiece of its 2006 electoral campaign, contrary to the advice of almost every economist and tax expert in the country. The GST is a particularly hated tax, simply because it is added on at the cash register for most purchases, and so is highly visible. The Liberal Party of Canada had previously campaigned on a promise to eliminate it, but only the most gullible thought that they were serious. Once in office, the Liberals did the right thing and reneged on the promise. The Conservatives, however, actually carried through (and then, to add insult to injury, repeated the exercise in the following election). This policy was particularly perverse, in that *implementing* the GST had been the centerpiece of a series of pro-market tax reforms introduced by the Conservatives during their previous period of electoral hegemony. Indeed, back in 1991, then prime minister Brian Mulroney suffered an enormous blow to his personal popularity by introducing the GST. His reasons for insisting on it was that value-added taxes are the most economically efficient—far superior to income or sales taxes. In other words, *experts agree* that it is the best form of tax if the goal is to minimize distortions and maximize wealth. Unfortunately, the only way to explain this is with an argument involving several steps and an appeal to at least one hypothetical. It is, in other words, *not common sense,* but rather a product of rational reflection.

In explaining the decision to cut the tax, Prime Minister Stephen Harper's former chief of staff, Ian Brodie, shocked economists again—and provided a terrifying glimpse into the sausage factory of modern politics—by mentioning, almost as an aside, that this important change in tax policy had been adopted without regard for its economic consequences. Their objective at the time, he explained, was to make cutting taxes part of the party's brand, so that voters would associate "Conservative Party" with "cutting taxes." After studying the question, they found that voters had difficulty remembering when their income taxes had been cut, or which party had done the cutting. And so they looked at all the different taxes and chose the one that was most likely to be remembered by voters. They settled on the GST simply because it was the most visible tax. "Despite economic evidence to the contrary, in my view the GST cut worked," Brodie said. "It worked in the sense that by the end of the '05–'06 campaign, voters identified the Conservative party as the party of lower taxes. It worked in the sense that it helped us to win."[14]

In this way, the Conservative Party set about happily undermining one of its own hardest-fought achievements.

After winning that election, the Conservative government went on to pursue a more subtle, indirect strategy for reducing the role of "fancy theories" in politics. One of the difficulties encountered when trying to reduce the size of government is that most of what government does serves a purpose. This is true even in jurisdictions like the United States, where the much-vaunted "checks and balances" in the political system encourage extremely inefficient public spending. If you bring in experts to tell you what "useless expenditures" can be cut, they tend not to be very good at finding any. For example, after U.S. president Barack Obama's first State of the Union address, the Republican selected to provide the rebuttal (Louisiana governor Bobby Jindal) complained about a variety of "useless" spending projects included in the government's economic stimulus package. He singled out for special ridicule the money spent on "something called 'volcano monitoring.'" Commentators at the time jumped on this as a perfect example of truthy politics—Jindal had chosen to criticize volcano monitoring simply because it *sounded* funny, not because it was useless. The point was reinforced a short year later when the Eyjafjallajökull volcano erupted unexpectedly in Iceland, causing massive disruption to commercial aviation throughout Europe and damaging a number of military aircraft. This reinforced the point that volcano monitoring is not only important, but is a perfect example of a public good—precisely the sort of activity that governments *should* be engaged in because private markets will not. As a result, if you bring in a bunch of experts and ask them where to cut "useless" government spending, they will almost certainly conclude that volcano monitoring is a useful public function—thereby contradicting the "common sense" view.

In order to operate, however, there are certain things that experts need, and one of them is *information*. The current vogue in public administration is for so-called evidence-based public policy. Many civil servants are committed to avoiding the administrative overreach that led Western governments of the 1960s and '70s to get involved in a variety of businesses and activities where the state had no comparative advantage (such as intercity busing or coal mining or airline ownership). In the future, it was decided, all major state initiatives would have to be backed up by sound data, proving that the government would actually be able to improve public welfare through a particular initiative. Now, if this is the prevailing attitude, then the best way to "starve the beast" is to deprive it of *data*. Without a source of quality information, it would be impossible to operate on anything other than common sense.

This realization has led to a clear evolution of strategy within the "common sense" movement. You can get only so far by appointing uneducated nonexperts to positions of political power. You still have the problem that the civil service is staffed by highly educated experts, who are never completely under the control of the minister. So the Conservative government in Canada set about attacking the state's internal policy-making apparatus. The first salvo was the decision to make the mandatory long-form census purely voluntary—contrary to the advice of almost all experts, both right and left. Making a census voluntary means that those who fill it out will be a self-selecting group, not a random sample of the population. This essentially corrupts the data, ensuring that it cannot be used as a basis for generalizing about the population.

This was followed by a series of decisions targeting Statistics Canada, the bureau responsible for collecting the data required to make effective policy. When the first big round of public-sector layoffs were announced following the formation of a majority Conservative government in 2011, Statistics Canada was hardest hit, despite no suggestion that the agency was overstaffed.[15] Combined with severe cuts to government science and research institutes, this "amounted to an attempt to eliminate anyone who might use science, facts and evidence to challenge government policies."[16] If, as Stephen Colbert put it, "reality has a well-known liberal bias," then the less anyone knows about reality, the less chance there will be anyone contradicting the homespun wisdom of "common sense" conservative ideology.

¶

If there is one area where the irrationalism of the right is most clearly on display, it is in the area of crime and punishment. Back in the 1980s, the rate of incarceration in the United States was already raising eyebrows. At 200 or so per 100,000, it was twice as high as in most other developed nations. Since then it has skyrocketed to almost 750 per 100,000 (or approximately 1 out of every 100 adults).[17] The United States holds 25 percent of the world's prisoners, despite having less than 5 percent of the world's population. It is also unique in spending more on prisons than it does on police. The situation is completely crazy—so far outside the boundaries of normal behavior that people will undoubtedly look back on the situation in a hundred years and ask "What were they thinking?", trying desperately to understand what kind of collective neurosis could have brought about this state of affairs.

The superficial explanation is to blame it on the American "war on drugs." This of course has *something* to do with it, but is far from a complete explanation (by one estimate, it accounts for only 20 percent of the prison population).[18] Most of it is due to the length of sentences that are handed out and the unusually broad range of crimes that are punished by imprisonment in the United States. Both are a direct consequence of the attitudes toward punishment that have come to prevail within the conservative movement, and the policies that are based on those attitudes. Some of these reflect heightened retributiveness toward the perpetrators of crime. Others reflect a conscious attempt to diminish the role of experts in the punishment process, by eliminating discretion at all levels. The two most important policies are mandatory minimum sentencing, which prevents judges from exercising any discretion in how offenders are sentenced, and the elimination of parole, which prevents officials from within the prison system from exercising discretion.

The reason for this insistence by right-wing legislatures that experts be cut out of the decision-making process is that criminal justice is one area where there tends to be an unusually large disconnect between our common sense ideas and the verdicts of those who actually look at the data and study the question. For example, criminologists know that threatening potential criminals with longer sentences has at best a weak deterrent effect.[19] People who commit crimes typically don't think they will get caught, and so are not thinking about the length of the sentence they might receive. And even if they are, they tend to be more impulsive than the average person, and so they ignore these future considerations. Thus judges, charged with sentencing, tend to have a somewhat different perspective on the matter than does the average person, and are more likely to be aware of the *pointlessness* of handing out extremely harsh sentences.

In 2012, the United States Supreme Court ruled that mandatory life-without-parole sentences for juvenile offenders were unconstitutional. Just to be clear: What these laws had required was that children as young as fourteen involved in serious crimes, often merely as accessories, had to be sentenced to prison for the rest of their natural lives, without possibility of parole. Furthermore, judges were prohibited by law from taking into consideration any extenuating circumstances in handing down these sentences. Given the severity of this punishment, it is extraordinary to think that any legislature should have wanted to eliminate the possibility of judicial discretion. What is more surprising is that at the time that the Supreme Court struck these laws down, a majority of American states (twenty-eight in total) had them on the books. This reflects a widespread impression that judges were being too lenient.

The core problem is that the average person on the street persistently overestimates the effectiveness of punishment. This is a cognitive illusion that is not particularly well known but that causes an enormous amount of mischief, not to mention unnecessary suffering. I happened to learn about it from reading a dog-training manual.[20] The authors were trying to explain why so many owners wind up beating their dogs, even though positive reinforcement—such as giving the dog treats for good behavior— is actually a more effective training strategy. The problem is that the owner's perception of what is working and what isn't working is usually false.

When a dog is trying to perform some new trick, what you typically see will be a series of fairly average performances, along with occasional deviation—every so often you will see a particularly good performance or else a particularly bad one. It is, however, a statistical fact that uncommon events are uncommon, and so an uncommon event is more likely to be followed by a common event than by another uncommon event. This is called *regression to the mean*. As a result of it, an exceptionally bad performance, because it is uncommon, is likely to be followed by an average one, just as exceptionally good performance, because it is uncommon, is likely to be followed by an average one—regardless of whether the bad performance is punished or the good performance rewarded. But if you do start punishing and rewarding, a casual observer is likely to be fooled into thinking that the punishment worked, because performance improved after it was applied, while the reward not only failed, but actually had the perverse effect of encouraging bad performance. The result is an extraordinarily common bias that leads people to overestimate the effectiveness of punishment.[21] Unfortunately, this regression fallacy can be dispelled only by looking at the long-term trend. This is why there is so much disagreement, when it comes to questions of punishment, between the views of experts, who actual study the long-term trends, and the verdicts of common sense.

One can see the same problem with the way that parents deal with their children. Most parents, over time, develop a system for punishing their children, but often have no comparable system of reward. Even more damaging is the fact that many refrain from offering rewards in the mistaken belief that they undermine intrinsic motivation (or that they "spoil" the children). Furthermore, even fairly sensible "child training manuals," such as the popular *1-2-3 Magic,* are heavily biased toward punishment, leading to a system that is all sticks, no carrots.[22]

What makes this regression fallacy especially insidious is the fact that not only is the world organized in such a way as to generate the impression that punishment is more effective, it actually rewards us for thinking that it is. This is something that I know well from my line of work. Like many teachers, I want students to do well. Thus I am disappointed when performance declines, and I am happy when students improve. As a result, giving out low grades tends to be followed by personal satisfaction as students improve, while giving out high grades generates disappointment as students regress to the mean. Daniel Kahneman summed up the situation perfectly when he wrote that "because we tend to reward others when they do well and punish them when they do badly, and because there is regression to the mean, it is part of the human condition that we are statistically punished for rewarding others and rewarded for punishing them."[23]

In other words, the world *conditions* us to prefer punishing people over rewarding them.

This is why "life means life" sentences, or any other legislative restriction that eliminates discretion in the granting of parole, tend to run contrary to the interests and experience of those who work in the criminal justice system. People who have to deal with inmates on a day-to-day basis are more likely to understand the limitations of punishment as a tool for controlling behavior. Being able to offer early parole in return for good behavior is one of the most important carrots that they have at their disposal (the effectiveness of which is amplified by optimism bias, which leads inmates to overestimate their chances of being released). By giving only sticks and taking away all the carrots, common sense conservatism makes it much more difficult for prison wardens to do their jobs.

So we are already biased in the direction of an overreliance on punishment. Compounding the problem is the retaliatory impulse, part of our tribal social instincts, which gives us satisfaction from punishing those who violate social norms. This is, no doubt, a biologically deep-seated phenomenon. One of the features that distinguishes humans from other primates is that we are the only species in which uninvolved third parties will routinely intervene in order to "correct" the behavior of others or punish wrongdoing. In contrast, chimpanzees will often sneak around and do things they're not supposed to do when their superiors in the dominance hierarchy aren't looking; if the individual whose prerogatives are being violated doesn't notice, then the sneaky ones can easily get away with misbehavior—because no one else is going to intervene to stop them.[24]

This is, ironically, one of the traits that is thought to underlie human cooperativeness. Because of the possibility of being punished by a bystander, the opportunities to take advantage of others are significantly reduced. This means that you're also much less likely to be taken advantage of if you do go out on a limb to help someone. Thus punishment plays a central role in making cooperation—or moral behavior in general—possible.

Furthermore, there is good reason to think that the basic structure of punishment is not cultural, but rather is part of the structure that makes culture possible. It's like one of the beams that supports the stage on which the drama of our culture is played out. And if it's an innate disposition, there's good reason to think that it will vary in intensity from one individual to another. In the same way that some people are naturally more sympathetic toward others, there will be some people who have, by inclination, a much stronger retaliatory urge than others.

For people who do have a particularly keen interest in retribution, living in a civilized society imposes much greater hardship than it does for others. This is because of the bedrock principle of the modern state, which is that individuals abandon the right to the private use of force and, in particular, abandon the right to avenge themselves in cases where they are wronged. This authority is instead handed over to the state (the police, the courts, the prison system), which exercises it in a way that seeks to avoid creating the endless cycles of violence and retribution that limit the organizational capacity of tribal societies.

Initially, the frustration created by the abolition of private vengeance was at least partially offset by the transformation of punishment into a public spectacle. The people's thirst for vengeance could be mollified through the public torture and execution of criminals. Until 150 years ago, it was considered normal in European societies to take children to watch hangings, and, before that, to even more gruesome public executions. And Europeans were not particularly bloodthirsty in this regard. For most people, throughout most of human history, violent punishment, torture, and death were regarded as the natural consequence of willful wrongdoing. There's absolutely no doubt that this feels intuitively right to most people. For example, throughout thousands of years of Christian reflection on crime and punishment, there was never any debate about the death penalty, because no one ever seriously considered the possiblity that there was anything wrong with it. It was only with the rise of social contract theory and the idea that the power of the state came from the consent of the governed that people began to wonder why anyone would consent to be ruled by a state with the power to kill its own subjects. Yet even then, it wasn't until the late nineteenth century that anyone took the issue seriously enough to begin pressing for abolition.

Thus the current state of affairs with regard to punishment is highly artificial and involves a huge amount of what Freud called "instinctual renunciation"—in other words, it forces people to override their natural inclinations. Because of this, many people, at a gut level, simply find modern societies to be insufficiently punitive. The abolition of corporeal punishment—flogging and so on—is a large part of this. Much of the endorsement of torture in the United States after the September 11, 2001, attacks was clearly driven by a retaliatory impulse, even among high officials. No one can seriously believe that any intelligence purpose was served by waterboarding Khalid Sheikh Mohammed 183 times. The purpose was obviously to make him suffer. One can see a similar impulse in the quasi-official tolerance of widespread prison rape in the United States (combined with its thinly veiled celebration in popular culture), along with the legalization of certain types of murder (under the rubric of "stand your ground" laws) directed against those who present an intimidating or suspicious aspect.

The common sense conservative desire to get "tough on crime" is therefore driven by a powerful sense of dissatisfaction with the way the criminal justice system operates. Crime in our society is for the most part treated as a social problem—a nuisance—and our policies are aimed at reducing it to the lowest level possible. Because of this, there are several unintuitive features about the way that our justice system works. First of all, the punishments are not as punitive as our "gut" tells us they should be, because experts know that punishment is not nearly as effective as we are naturally inclined to believe. And second, the system is not as retaliatory, simply because retaliation beyond a certain level is incompatible with the civil condition. Thus the objective of "tough on crime" policies is not to reduce the crime rate, it is really just to make the criminal justice system more viscerally satisfying to a certain segment of the population.

This has become fairly obvious in the past few decades, as the crime rate has been declining. In the United States, many of the "tough on crime" measures were taken before the decline, and so it could be argued that they should be continued on the grounds that they are effective. In Canada, however, most of the decline occurred without any particular toughening of the criminal justice system. Thus when in 2011 the Conservative government introduced a series of measures intended to toughen that system further—imposing mandatory minimum sentences, building more facilities in order to accommodate a planned expansion of the prison population—the plan was impossible to justify through reference to its effects, because the crime rate was already at its lowest point in decades and was continuing its steady decline without any such measures in place. From a public policy standpoint, the changes seemed to be punishment for the sake of punishment.

As if to confirm this impression, Public Safety Minister Vic Toews repeatedly emphasized that the government was not going to allow policy to be determined by "statistics" (although on some occasions, he opted for the "alternate reality" approach of simply asserting that crime was increasing, when all the evidence pointed in the opposite direction).[25] He made it clear that the crime rate as such does not matter: "A dangerous person who threatens the safety and security of individuals . . . should not be on the streets regardless of what the crime rate is. That's our focus: to ensure that dangerous people are not on the street."[26] Understood literally, this is crazy talk—Toews is claiming that as long as *any* crime goes unpunished, then the justice system is too lenient. If one follows through on the reasoning, then penalties should be stiffened until the crime rate drops to zero. But of course the point is *not* to follow through on the reasoning. The point is to say that criminal justice policy is going to be based on our visceral reaction to the contemplation of particular criminal acts, not on the "public policy" objective of reducing the number of crimes that occur.

This is why the "debate" over crime is not really a debate: it is occurring outside the framework of rational deliberation. One can see this very clearly in the way that Prime Minister Harper framed the issue. The vast majority of Canadians, he argued, accept the principle of peace, order, and good government, "but there is a minority who don't get it":

> It's one thing that they, the criminals do not get it, but if you don't mind me saying, another part of the problem for the past generation has been those, also a small part of our society, who are not criminals themselves, but who are always making excuses for them, and when they aren't making excuses, they are denying that crime is even a problem: the ivory tower experts, the tut-tutting commentators, the out-of-touch politicians. "Your personal experiences and impressions are wrong," they say. "Crime is not really a problem." I don't know how you tell that to the families of the victims we saw . . . These men, women and children are not statistics. They had families, friends, hopes and dreams, until their lives were taken from them.[27]

Thus the type of people who refer to statistics when debating the issue of crime *are actually a part of the crime problem*. Although they haven't broken the law, they share with the criminals the essential characteristic of "not getting it." Is it any wonder then that sociologists and criminologists who complained about the ineffectiveness of the government's proposed policies didn't get a very serious hearing? The problem was not what they were saying, but simply who they were—ivory-tower intellectuals. As Harper's ever-helpful chief of staff Ian Brodie explained, the criminologists and sociologists did the government a big favor by attacking their policies: "Politically it helped us tremendously to be attacked by this coalition, so we never really had to engage in the question of what the evidence actually shows about various approaches to crime."[28]

What a perfect double dividend. Start by proposing an overly punitive criminal sentencing policy that will do nothing to reduce crime but will pander to the "law and order" constituency, who remain perpetually convinced that system is soft on crime. Then, when the people who do know something about law and order start complaining about the ineffectiveness of the policy, attack them as well, label them a part of the crime problem, and present their opposition as evidence that the system is too soft. Rinse and repeat.

More generally, one can see here how the "post-truth" ethos has expanded beyond the realm of electoral campaigning and public relations to become a governing philosophy and a basis for policy. It's no longer about what the law will *do,* it's about how the law makes us *feel.*

¶

There is one respect in which right-wing antirationalism can be self-limiting. In order to be effective, it must be pursued with at least of modicum of cynicism. The central attraction of common sense conservatism is that it generates successful electoral campaign strategies. But of course, you can't actually *run* a campaign using nothing but intuition and common sense. Conservatives may pride themselves on their opposition to experts making policy on the basis of statistics, but they typically want their election campaigns to be run by experts on the basis of statistics. So behind all the people praising the wisdom of the common folk and demonizing elites and intellectuals, there has traditionally been a core group of very intelligent, well-educated members of the elite. Hence the cynicism: the "assault on reason" has been carried out largely as a ploy, based on a rational calculation that it was a good way of advancing certain political interests.

There is always the possibility, however, that the snake will begin to eat its own tail. It's one thing to glorify the uneducated but then choose highly educated candidates who are good at pretending to be poorly educated. It's something else entirely to put forward candidates who are genuinely uneducated—as the Republicans found out with Sarah Palin (or Christine O'Donnell, the Tea Party–backed candidate for a Senate seat in Delaware, who attracted widespread ridicule by challenging her opponent to specify "where in the constitution is the separation of church and state?"[29]). Similarly, the truthiness that is being served up is intended only for the consumption of prospective voters; it is important that the strategists within the party know where the actual truth lies.

In the wake of the 2012 American election, some evidence began to surface suggesting that the Republican strategists under Mitt Romney's leadership had actually begun to lose touch with reality, to the point where it hindered the effectiveness of their own campaign. In general, Romney and his running mate Paul Ryan stuck quite closely to the "post-truth" playbook, campaigning on a set of positions that bore almost no relationship to their actual views (for example, criticizing Obama for supposedly cutting Medicare, despite themselves wanting to actually eliminate the program). On several occasions, Romney got himself into trouble by picking up talking points from the conservative media, based on "facts" that were demonstrably false. But these were fairly minor bumps on the road.

The real problem that arose was over polling. Campaigns rely very heavily on accurate polls in order to target their efforts, particularly in the United States, where the electoral college system rewards targeted strategies. At some point, Republicans convinced themselves that the mainstream media was involved in a conspiracy to skew public opinion polls in order to overstate support for Obama, based on the vague suspicion that this conferred some kind of advantage on his campaign. And so conservatives developed their own set of parallel "unskewed" polls, which they then tried to push on the media. What surprised many observers was the revelation that insiders in the Romney campaign had begun to take these fantasy polls seriously—that they had begun, in effect, to drink their own

Kool-Aid. This led the campaign to make a number of strategic decisions—about where to send the candidate, in particular—that made no sense to an unbiased observer. The reason they were doing this, it turned out, was that the campaign strategists actually had fantastical beliefs about where the candidate's intervention was likely to be most effective.[30]

Romney apparently went into election night fully expecting to win, and was not just posturing when he told reporters that he had no concession speech prepared. Based on his impression of the rallies late in the campaign, *so* well attended, *so* full of enthusiastic supporters, he was convinced that he had momentum that would carry him to victory. (This is all reminiscent of the joke about the Manhattan socialite who complained about George Bush's election victory: "How it is possible that he won? I don't know *anyone* who voted for him.") People sometimes fail to realize that their own social network is not a representative sample of the population. It's even more essential that candidates realize this, when it comes to the people who attend their rallies. Our intuitions in this area, based on our personal experience, are worth literally nothing. The only thing able to correct these inevitably misleading impressions are the cold, hard numbers that objective polling and statistical analysis have historically provided.

One can see here how the more extreme forms of craziness can become self-limiting in the area of political strategy, insofar as they undermine the basis for rational planning and decision. Because of this, the more troubling forms of common sense conservatism are the more cynical or demagogic ones, where a group of very cunning, intelligent people find ways to manipulate the electorate by appealing to their base urges, then adopt a governing philosophy that is essentially a glorified ratification of the strategies adopted for reasons of political expediency. Consistent antirationalism, by contrast, does have certain inherent limitations, because it tends to undermine its own efficacy.

As a result of the Romney campaign debacle, there have been some calls for a "return to reason" on the right. It is not obvious how far this will go. After all, the central challenge faced by right-wing political parties everywhere—the biggest nut they have to crack—is figuring out how to get a large segment of the population to vote against its own economic interests. Reason is not a particularly reliable ally in this endeavor. Nevertheless, it is possible that the fever of antirationalism has begun to break, in much the same way that it has on the left. What remains in place, however, is the evolutionary dynamic, discussed earlier, whereby "memes" that are able to exploit our cognitive biases survive and prosper. It is easy to see that commercial advertising is *inherently biased* against rationality, for precisely this reason. Various features of our political system, and of electoral competition in particular, exhibit this same bias. No matter what lessons are learned, antirationalism remains a constant temptation, simply because it is incredibly powerful and, when used carefully, incredibly effective. It's also not obvious that criticizing these tendencies is going to have any effect—indeed, there is a huge amount of evidence to suggest that mere criticism accomplishes nothing. If we do really want to change things, we may need to adopt a set of more subtle, more indirect strategies.

Part III

Restoring Sanity

Antirationalism in the political sphere generates
a true dilemma for the progressive: take the high road and
lose, or take the low road and make the problem worse.
Of course, there is a more dire possibility, which is
that you take the low road, make the problem worse,
and still lose. This is, unfortunately, the most likely outcome
of the effort to fight irrationalism on its own terms.
There is, however, a third option. It involves restructuring
the mental environment so that the voice of reason is
more likely to prevail. This cannot be achieved through
individual effort; it necessarily requires collective action.
It calls for a new politics of rationality.

10. Fighting fire with fire

or why you shouldn't wrestle with a pig

In the fall of 1970, Canadian prime minister Pierre Elliott Trudeau found himself facing a dilemma. Prior to entering politics, he was best known as a forceful champion of Canadian federalism against the rising tide of Quebec separatism. At the time, he had presented the choice between federalism and nationalism as a straightforward contest between reason and emotion. Quebec separatism is, and always has been, driven by the ethnic nationalism of so-called *pure laine* Québécois—descendants of the original French colonists, who were conquered by the British during the Seven Years' War (1756–1763) and went on to form a French-speaking minority within the Canadian federation. Nationalism of this form is a classic expression of our tribal social instincts; it creates a powerful sense of community and solidarity by drawing a distinction between "us" and "them." Thus the rapid modernization of Quebec society in the '60s, which brought about substantial collective achievements, came with increased antagonism toward outsiders and growing demands for political independence.

What Trudeau disliked most about this nationalism was its backwardness. "The history of civilization," he wrote, "is a chronicle of the subordination of tribal 'nationalism' to wider interests."[1] And yet he saw clearly that, in contrast to nationalism, "federalism is by its very essence a compromise and a pact."[2] The arguments for federalism were just that, *arguments*. They referred to political principles or long-term interests; they had no gut-level appeal. "Federalism has all along been a product of reason in politics," as Trudeau put it. "It was born of a decision by pragmatic politicians to face facts as they are, particularly the fact of the heterogeneity of the world's population."[3] Thousands of different languages are spoken in the world and there are more than 800 major ethnic groups, yet there are only 160 full-scale states.[4] Insisting that every group have its own state is a recipe for fragmentation and chaos. What sort of a message would it be sending to everyone else in the world if Canadians, despite enjoying practically ideal conditions for mutual toleration (the country is wealthy, industrialized, with two historically liberal cultures and no history of atrocity toward one another) found themselves unable to live together in a shared state?

Defending federalism, in Trudeau's view, meant defending the principle of reason in politics. "Reason before passion" became his personal motto. And yet, over the course of his first term as prime minister, this commitment became increasingly difficult to maintain. Throughout the late '60s, the militant wing of the separatist movement became more and more violent, moving from fairly random robberies and attacks to targeted bombings, most importantly against the Montreal Stock Exchange and the home of the mayor of Montreal. The breaking point came with the kidnapping and killing of the Quebec minister of labor and the kidnapping of the British trade commissioner. Both were taken at gunpoint from their homes—Pierre Laporte, the minister of labor, had been playing catch on the front lawn with his nephew, and was later strangled to death. After the kidnapping, the group responsible released a manifesto, which among other things, referred to Trudeau as "*la tapette,*" which is often translated as "the pansy" but would be accurately rendered as simply "the fag."

This episode illustrated, in the starkest form possible, the conundrum faced by proponents of reason in politics. Violence is, of course, at the furthest extreme from reason when it comes to resolving political disputes.

But what more is there to say when your opponents, given a chance to speak their piece, can't manage much more than to call you a fag? In order for reason to win, you need to have opponents who are willing to engage in rational debate. So what do you do when confronted with a movement that relies not upon reason for its central appeal, but upon a visceral sense of blood and belonging?

Early on, Trudeau had in fact laid out quite clearly what the strategy would be under such circumstances. The solution would be to fight fire with fire: "One way of offsetting the appeal of separatism is by investing a tremendous amount of time, energy, and money in nationalism *at the federal level* . . . Resources must be diverted into such things as national flags, anthems, education, arts councils, broadcasting corporations, film boards."[5] One of the peculiar things about Canada was that, at the time Trudeau came to power, it didn't really have a distinct form of nationalism at the national level. The country was instead the home to two rival national identities, French in Quebec and British in the rest of Canada—the latter based largely on loyalty to the monarchy. For example, there was at the time no national anthem: the French "O Canada" was sung in Quebec, with "God Save the Queen" being sung throughout the rest of the country. The red maple leaf flag had been adopted in 1965 but was still used interchangeably with the Union Jack.

With the conflict between French and English growing more and more intractable, a frustrated Trudeau finally gave up on his old motto, admitting that his faith in reason had been mistaken. "If they want blood and guts," he said, "I'll give them blood and guts."[6] To this end—and with varying degrees of cynicism—he set about creating a new national identity, in part by co-opting traditional French Canadian culture and imposing it at the national level. His efforts began with the aggressive promotion of the national flag (with the Parliamentary Flag Program of 1972, which gave each representative a quota of flags to be distributed to constituents), the designation of "O Canada" as the new national anthem, and the creation of a national holiday (with Dominion Day being renamed "Canada Day"), and which culminated in the repatriation of the Constitution and the adoption of the Charter of Rights and Freedoms in 1982. All of this served to create a new Canadian identity distinct from the British one that had previously been dominant at the national level.

So that is how, in a case of not inconsiderable historical irony, Trudeau—the avatar of pure reason—became the father of modern Canadian nationalism, in all of its most boisterous and vulgar manifestations. One wonders how he would have felt had he seen the closing ceremonies of the 2010 Vancouver Olympic Games, with its giant inflatable beavers, table-hockey players, moose hats, dancing lumberjacks and voyageurs, and Michael Bublé dressed as a Mountie singing "The Maple Leaf Forever." The phrase "What have I done?" might have sprung to mind. And yet, almost forty years after Trudeau made the initial moves, one could see the power of the strategy. Quebec artists essentially boycotted the Olympic ceremonies, refusing to participate in what they rightly anticipated would be an orgy of Canadian nationalism. And yet when the curtain closed, they proceeded to complain about the lack of "French content" in the program. A principled commitment to national sovereignty is all well and good, but no one likes to feel left out of a party. As far as political dilemmas go, the shoe had been moved to the other foot.

¶

Democrats in the United States are used to getting thrashed by the Republicans. They are obviously afraid, and for the most part it shows. Even when taking positions that are clearly supported by a majority of Americans, they hesitate, obfuscate, and fudge. This timidity is one of the things that drives American liberals crazy about their favored party. Consider, for example, that Republicans were willing to impeach President Bill Clinton over a sexual impropriety, whereas the Democrats chose not to pursue criminal charges against former president George W. Bush and his vice president Dick Cheney, despite prima facie evidence of far more serious wrongdoing (most obviously, of having authorized the use of torture, but also of wiretapping without judicial approval).

There is fairly widespread agreement about the reasons for this. Republicans are incredibly good at framing issues and at articulating their views in a way that grabs the attention of both the media and the public. Consider, for example, the way they were able to sidetrack the debate over health care reform in 2009, turning it into a referendum on the desirability of creating "death panels." Sarah Palin set the whole thing off with a simple Facebook post: "The America I know and love is not one in which my parents or my baby with Down Syndrome will have to stand in front of Obama's 'death panel' so his bureaucrats can decide, based on a subjective judgment of their 'level of productivity in society,' whether they are worthy of health care. Such a system is downright evil."[7]

This is, quite literally, crazy talk. The "death panels" in question were entirely a figment of Palin's imagination—no one was ever able to point to anything in the legislation that could be even vaguely construed this way. (The quotation marks in Palin's comment were more like scare quotes, since the passages they marked weren't actually quoted from anywhere or anything.) And yet Palin's allegation managed to completely dominate media coverage of the legislation, crowding out almost all discussion of the actual contents of the bill. As Thomas Frank put it, against the "amplified righteousness" of conservative accusations, these little factual corrections "had as much chance of being heard as a kitten's gentle purring while a freight train roars by ten feet away."[8]

The "death panels" episode was just an extreme example of something that the Republicans are able to pull off routinely, which is to present their own case in a vivid, intuitively accessible way that captures everyone's attention. Even when disconnected from reality, their accusations are enough to put their opponents on the defensive. Part of this is simply through careful choice of terms: "enhanced interrogation" instead of "torture," "tax relief" instead of "tax cuts," "energy exploration" instead of "oil drilling," "Operation Enduring Freedom" instead of "the invasion of Afghanistan," and so on. Democrats try to do the same thing, but Republicans are unquestionably better at it. To take just one small example, Democrats gave their health care legislation the title Patient Protection and Affordable Care Act. The name that stuck, however, was the slightly derisive Republican expression "Obamacare."

The observation that Democrats are terrible at framing is what made George Lakoff, a professor of linguistics at the University of California at Berkeley, an overnight star with the party. What he told the Democrats in his runaway 2004 bestseller *Don't Think of an Elephant!* is that all they need to do in order to win elections is to present their ideas better.[9] In many cases, he argued, Democrats were losing the debates even before getting started, by accepting the way that Republicans were presenting the issues and the terminology that Republicans were using. To cite one of Lakoff's examples, merely using the term "tax relief" constitutes tacit acceptance that Americans are somehow "burdened" by taxes, even though the taxes paid by the overwhelming majority of Americans are only enough to cover a small fraction of the government services they receive.[10] Democrats, he argued, need to learn to pay less attention to the literal meaning of what they are saying and more attention to the emotional resonance that their words have.

The situation that Democrats find themselves in is hardly unique, it is a dilemma faced by intellectuals and eggheads everywhere. There was a particularly nice portrayal of the core problem in the '90s television show *Frasier*. For those who missed it, *Frasier* was a long-running comedy series that constituted essentially an extended portrait of what ordinary people think smart people are like. Superficially, the show was merely anti-intellectual, but deep down it was also quite ideological. (It is no accident that Kelsey Grammer, the executive producer and star of the show, is a politically active far-right Republican.) The show played on the contrast between two lead characters, Dr. Frasier Crane and his brother, Niles, and three "ordinary folks"—their father (a retired policeman), their housekeeper, and the producer of Frasier's radio show. The two brothers, although supposedly both Harvard-educated psychiatrists, were essentially clowns. Over the eleven-year run of the series, not once did either use his supposedly superior intelligence to solve any problem or to do anything remotely clever. Their "intelligence" and education gave them nothing more than a habit of using big words, pretentious taste, and a lack of common sense. (In one particularly memorable scene, Frasier criticizes his housekeeper for having incorrectly dusted the bookshelf—which, like most bookshelves in American homes, contains no books—"You forgot, this *objet* does not face front but rather askew . . . *askew.*") The conservative ideology of common sense was a barely concealed current running throughout the series. Unlike early conservatives, who distrusted intellectuals because they considered them dangerous, *Frasier* suggests that the problem with intellectuals is that they're not actually smart.

In one episode, Frasier becomes the butt of a series of practical jokes played by two new shock jocks hired at the radio station where he hosts an on-air counseling show. They wake him up in the morning and pretend that he's just received an award, or they call him while he's in the bathtub and ask him to describe his effete beauty regimen, all the while broadcasting the conversation to the entire city. After one particularly humiliating episode, which turns him into a public laughingstock, Frasier finally loses his cool. His response is to compose a written "rebuttal," which he plans to read on the air during his own radio show. It begins with a "devastating" quote from de la Rochefoucauld, followed by a quip from Dorothy Parker. His brother, Niles, of course thinks that the rebuttal is deadly. The job falls to their father to explain to them that quoting de la Rochefoucauld is probably going to make things worse, and that the two of them are responsible for bringing this ridicule upon themselves because of their habit of putting on airs and acting as though they're better than everyone else.

American Democrats watching the show must have felt sympathy for Frasier. The relationship between the shock jocks and the pretentious psychiatrist was more than a little reminiscent of the one between American talk radio and Democratic politicians. John Kerry, for example, the Democratic candidate for president in 2004, was relentlessly mocked by the right-wing press for having "nuanced" views on various issues. This quickly turned the word "nuance" into a general term of derision, used like a schoolyard taunt. They called him the "International Man of Nuance," "the Man of a Thousand Nuances," and, with thinly veiled homophobia, "nuancy boy."[11] This wasn't just a pose. Many common sense conservatives actually believe that having nuanced views is a sign of weakness or duplicity. They believe that complaining about "complexity" is nothing more than an excuse made by intellectuals to explain away their unwillingness to take forceful, effective action. Unfortunately, the accusation is difficult to respond to without displaying precisely the characteristic that one is being made fun of for having.

The problem is that some positions are inherently more complicated to explain, and hence involve more nuance, than others. During wartime, for instance, there is always intense pressure on everyone to rally together and show support for the troops. This puts opponents of the war in a tight spot. On the one hand, they typically do not want to see any harm come to their own nation's soldiers. (They are not, in other words, literally cheering for the other side.) At the same time, they believe that the mission is fundamentally unjustified. Thus they necessarily hope that the troops will fail to carry out their central objective, which is to kill people on the other side. In most cases, it is simply not possible to support the troops without supporting, to some degree, the mission, just as it is not possible to oppose the mission without at the same time opposing the troops. The people who run around tying yellow ribbons on trees and hanging banners on overpasses know this full well, which is why they are so aggressive at forcing everyone to pay lip service to the "support the troops" mantra.

People who are opposed to various foreign wars have been trying, at least since the 1960s, to find some way of articulating their position that is direct, pithy, and intuitively appealing. The effort has been without success. (The slogan "Support our troops: Bring them home" is probably the closest anyone has come. I think we can all agree, however, that it doesn't work. Compared to "Kill 'em all and let God sort them out," it sounds confused and contradictory.) In any case, for a huge number of people, war brings out the old friend/foe distinction, polarizing the world into those who are "with us" and those who are "against us."[12] The in-between position, whereby one opposes the war but stops short of supporting the enemy, is a complex construct that can be sustained only at the level of explicit, rational representation. Most people find it profoundly unintuitive, and so treat it as just a "nuanced" way of expressing support for the enemy.

This is why it was a terrible mistake for John Kerry to emphasize his military record when running for president (for instance, by starting his acceptance speech for the Democratic nomination by saluting and saying, "I'm John Kerry, and I'm reporting for duty"). Unlike the Republican John McCain, who was famous for what he did while in the service, Kerry was best known not for what he did while in uniform, but for having been a high-profile opponent of the Vietnam War after having finished his tour of duty. In particular, he testified before the U.S. Senate Committee on Foreign Relations, criticizing not only American policy in Vietnam, but also the conduct of American soldiers. This made him, in the eyes of many Americans, a traitor pure and simple. (A doctored photograph, showing Kerry sitting next to Jane Fonda—who actually was a traitor, in the sense that she traveled to North Vietnam during the war and offered what could only be construed as support for the enemy—revealed quite clearly what mental pigeonhole Kerry was being put in. The fact that the photo was a fake meant nothing in an age of truthiness. So what if the two of them had never sat side by side at a rally? They may as well have, since they were on the same side.)

This is why the infamous Swift Boat ads succeeded. They gave explicit articulation to what many Americans were already feeling in their gut about Kerry. They reminded everyone that while many American prisoners of war were tortured because of their unwillingness to sign statements admitting to war crimes, Kerry went on national television and accused them of precisely that.[13] "I felt betrayed," said one veteran in the ads. "He dishonored his country," said another. Soon Republicans were openly mocking the Purple Heart that Kerry had received for having been wounded in combat (while supporting George W. Bush, the quintessential upper-class coward, who had used his father's connections to avoid having to do a tour of duty in Vietnam).

How is one supposed to respond to this? What exactly is there to be said? Kerry might as well have gone on television and cited de la Rochefoucauld in his defense (perhaps, "*On ne peut répondre de son courage quand on a jamais été dans le péril*").

¶

Here is the central problem faced by progressives: most of their political positions and policy proposals are inherently more difficult to frame than are those of their opponents. Effective framing creates emotional resonance. Consider, for example, one of Frank Luntz's most famous: trying to rebrand "drilling for oil" as "energy exploration." The problem with "drilling for oil" is that is sounds like something bad. First of all, when people think of oil they picture something black and dirty, and probably think of oil spills. Most people also don't use oil in their day-to-day lives, and are only tenuously aware of the connection between oil and the gasoline that they put in their cars. "Drilling" is likely to remind them of the way that oil is extracted and its environmental consequences. "Energy," by contrast, is something that everyone uses, and it carries positive associations. "Exploration" sounds adventurous and progressive and says nothing about extraction, nor does it say anything that will trigger thoughts about the environmental consequences. So this way, when you say "We should cut some of the red tape, so that companies are free to engage in energy exploration," you are saying something that *feels* intuitively correct.

Effective political framing generates the same type of emotional resonance, by appealing to a basic set of social instincts, such as helping friends and family, reciprocity, teamwork, fair dealing, and punishing one's enemies. These ideas can be found in every single human society, throughout all of human history. The problem is that our innate social dispositions are able to sustain only small-scale societies or decentralized tribal federations—which is precisely why people lived this way throughout most of human history. It is only with the rise of the state, within the past 5,000 years, that we have begun to exceed our programming in this regard. The state, however, is a highly artificial construct, created by subordinating and manipulating these social instincts in order to create large, hierarchically integrated institutions.

Much of what we call progress or development consists in finding new ways of resolving the collective action problems that our tribal instincts fail to address or else exacerbate. For example, in a small group, it is possible to punish anyone and everyone who breaks the rules, and therefore to maintain a zero-tolerance attitude toward free-riders. As society becomes larger and less closely knit, it is inevitable that there will be people who break the rules, if only by accident. When we see someone who is lazing about, deriving all the benefits of *our* labor without contributing anything, our natural reaction is one of outrage, combined with a desire to punish the offender, or at least cut him off from those benefits. And in cases where we are not able to single this person out for punishment, then the natural impulse is to withdraw our own cooperation ("If he's not going to help out, then neither am I!").

This is fine, as far as it goes, but the problem is that we respond in exactly the same way regardless of how big the group is. It could be six students doing a class project or millions of people participating in an unemployment insurance scheme. This is why Reagan's "welfare queen" story was so effective—even though it was only a story about a single individual, it made people want to shut down the entire U.S. welfare system. The problem is that with the larger group, there is always going to be someone who takes advantage. If one maintains a zero-tolerance attitude, then cooperation will inevitably break down or collapse in a cycle of mutual recrimination. Maintaining cooperation therefore requires the ability to look at the big picture and to let a few offenses slide—to override our more punitive impulses.

This is the major reason that people cannot be counted on to spontaneously engage in large-scale cooperation. Our punitive impulses, which are actually quite effective at maintaining cooperation in small groups, become an enormous impediment to cooperation as group size increases.[14] Tribal societies typically split up into new groups as the population increases. Our instinctual forms of social behavior produce a basic institutional structure of society that lacks scalability. To the extent that we are able to create more advanced systems of cooperation, it is almost always by supplementing individuals' pro-social instincts with the force of law (or some other hierarchically constituted authority). Thus we encourage people to cooperate of their own volition, but we also threaten to punish those who fail to do so. A *lot* of what government does therefore involves getting people to obey rules that are ultimately to their benefit but that don't correspond to anyone's natural sense of what is right and wrong.

Take a simple example like gun control, which is about as straightforward a collective action problem as you can get. Your chances of getting shot are very strongly correlated with the number of guns out there in the population. At the same time, it never hurts to be better armed than your neighbor. So while the ideal world might be one in which no one has a gun (this is the "cooperative" outcome), an even more ideal world is one in which you have a gun and no one else does. This gives each individual a free-rider incentive to go out and buy a gun. And yet the more people get guns, the more violent and insecure the society becomes. As a result, many people who don't have any particular desire to own a gun will begin to feel like suckers, and so will go out and get one, simply to defend themselves against those who already own one. (In other words, seeing others defect from the cooperative arrangement leads them to defect. This is a perfect example of how the limited scope of pro-social attitudes among humans can lead to an unraveling of cooperation.)

Thus every large-scale outbreak of public disorder in America (such as the L.A. riots, Hurricane Katrina, or even a high-profile school shooting) is followed by a big spike in gun sales. And there is always a constituency prepared to argue that the solution to gun violence is *more guns.* If deranged psychopaths are attacking schools, the solution must be to let students and teachers bring their guns to class so they can fight back. If masked gunmen are attacking movie theaters, people should bring their guns along to the movies. If jihadis are hijacking airplanes with box cutters, the solution must be to let passengers bring their own weapons on board. But this simply turns the collective action problem into a race to the bottom—like turning up your music in order to drown out your neighbor's. A dynamic of this sort is precisely how civilization declines into barbarism.

Getting people to accept the civilized arrangement—strict control of firearms—is tricky, though. First of all, you need to get them to refrain from acting on their narrow self-interest. They need to be willing to forgo the advantages of personal gun ownership. Second, you need to persuade them to trust others to do the same. They need to believe that if they do their part, others will do their part, and so the cooperative outcome—mutual disarmament—really will be achieved. And finally, you need to persuade them to refrain from retaliating when the inevitable violations occur—to stop people from running to the gun shop every time a gun crime is committed.

Gun advocates in the United States have been extremely effective at undermining all three of these conditions. Consider the simple but effective slogan "If guns were illegal, then only criminals would have guns." This suggests that the second condition will not be met—even if ordinary citizens give up their guns, "criminals" will not—so mutual disarmament is not possible: gun control amounts to unilateral disarmament. It also makes an appeal to the retaliatory impulse by tapping into the distinction between ordinary citizens and criminals, posing the issue in terms of "us" versus "them." None of this is contained in the literal meaning of the slogan: when interpreted literally, it is vacuous—if guns were illegal, then everyone who had one would be a criminal, by definition. So it's not about the meaning, it's all about the intuitions that it triggers.

Lakoff's suggestion is that, in response, proponents of gun control need only come up with a better way of framing their opposition to gun ownership. But how exactly is that supposed to work? The visceral reaction that people have to mass murders is clearly ambivalent: it makes some people want to ban guns, but it makes just as many other people want to go out and buy guns. The basic point gun control advocates need to make is that modern, civilized societies have it within their power to achieve something very close to a complete elimination of lethal violence. This point, however, is incredibly hard to make in a way that has visceral appeal. So the best that gun control advocates can do is recite a bunch of statistics, about how low the murder rate is and how rare it is for anyone to be killed by a gun in, say, Germany. Or how much friendlier the police are and how much less likely they are to shoot you if they themselves are not worried about getting shot.

Yet no matter how much data one puts forth, all of it can quickly be undermined by an opponent willing to point to the occasional atrocity committed by a lone gunman, such as the Winnenden school shooting in Germany or the Breivik murders in Norway. In desperation, gun control advocates in the United States have taken to emphasizing the dangers that a gun poses to occupants of one's own home—pointing out how common it is for children to accidentally shoot themselves, or how often burglars or home invaders find and use a homeowner's own gun against him. But this is basically changing the subject, focusing on a private fringe benefit that happens to be more emotionally salient while ignoring the huge cooperative benefit that comes from limiting gun ownership.

Lakoff thinks that the master concept that progressives should be appealing to, in order to frame their policies more effectively, is *empathy*.[15] Schematically, this makes sense. Empathy is clearly an intuitive, nonrational response, as witnessed by the fact that it is nonvoluntary, spontaneously triggered, and most powerfully evoked by visual stimulus. There is a clear evolutionary reason why we have this response; it is designed to motivate parental investment in offspring. But this is why empathy is also notoriously limited in scope—why we feel most strongly the suffering of children, family, and friends, in that order, and then, occasionally, strangers. It is also a notorious feature of empathy that it is triggered only through identification, which is why movies require a sympathetic protagonist and why people respond much more emotionally to stories of individual suffering than they do to statistics about mass murder.

Yet precisely because it is limited in scope—and there are good evolutionary reasons why it must be so—empathy is also notoriously unreliable as a basis for large-scale collective action. One need only look at the manipulations that aid groups must resort to in order to create any sort of sympathy for the starving and impoverished masses in the Third World. Not only must they rely heavily on pictures of single, identifiable individuals—preferably a child, perhaps a woman, but never an adult man—but the victim must be presented in a way that is stripped of any national, political, religious, or often even ethnic markers.[16] Why? Because these markers may disrupt any feeling of identification that potential donors have with the victim. Furthermore, even a suspicion that the victims might have done something to bring the suffering upon themselves is enough to dissolve any feeling of sympathy that most people have. Hence the use of the stereotypical starving child in pleas for charitable donations. And yet precisely because the starving child must be so generic in order for the plea to work at all, campaigns quickly generate "donor fatigue" and the child becomes an object of ridicule (like "starvin' Marvin" on *South Park*). And identification certainly cannot be taken for granted. At one anti–health care reform rally, Tea Party protestors laughed and heaped scorn a man in a wheel-chair suffering from Parkinson's disease, telling him that "if you're looking for a handout, you're in the wrong part of town." Around the same time, Ted Nugent was rallying thousands to his slogan: "Trample the Weak."[17] Empathy may be innate, but so is cruelty.

Given these limitations, how realistic is it to think progressives are going to be able to implement their agenda by appealing to empathy? It's not even obvious that empathy plays that great a role in liberal thinking. Lakoff claims that the basic tenets of liberalism, including individual rights like habeas corpus, are anchored in empathy. This example is particularly ill chosen, since the rights of individuals accused of crimes in America are constantly under attack, precisely because they run counter to so many of our intuitions. The legal protections certainly have a *rational* basis, but it is not at all clear that they have an empathic one. The only way to make sense of the rights of accused criminals is to understand that the person may or may not be guilty. And even in cases where they are, as a matter of fact, guilty, we may not *know* that they are guilty. This is the kind of hypothetical construct that is available only to reason. Lots of people despise defense lawyers, accusing them of defending rapists and murderers. The only way to correct this is by introducing a bit of nuance, pointing out that they are actually only defending people *accused* of rape and murder. Naturally, if you defend people accused of rape and murder, you will wind up defending some people who have actually committed rape and murder. But the point is that we don't know in advance who those people are. If we knew who the rapists and murderers were, we wouldn't need the trial.

This is obviously a subtle point, and so Lakoff suggests instead that liberals should give the argument more visceral appeal by evoking empathy. The natural response is to say, empathy toward whom? Toward criminals? Even if you can duck that accusation and insist that it's empathy for the wrongly accused, there is still the simple and devastating accusation—routinely made by conservatives—that liberals have more empathy for the accused than they do for the *victims* of crime. Furthermore, the unjustly accused are themselves often unsympathetic characters—petty criminals and so forth. The very same traits that led the police to jump to conclusions in their case and assume that they are guilty will tend to make the public unsympathetic to their plight as well. So even if Lakoff's suggestion made sense, it is not obvious that it constitutes good strategy.

Indeed, one of the reasons that legal protections for people accused of crimes need to be so elaborate is that the cognitive biases pushing us in the direction of unjust conviction are so powerful. In other words, it is precisely because of our overzealousness in punishing people that we need to have these protections in place. If you look at cases of innocent people who have been convicted of various crimes, the prosecutors' motivation is typically a mixture of belief perseverance (prosecutors jump to a conclusion, then try to fit all subsequent facts to that hypothesis), confirmation bias (they fail to think the negative, and so don't bother to seek any evidence that would disprove their hypothesis), and punitive zeal (they more strongly want to ensure that "someone pays" for the crime than they want to ensure that the *right* person pays). So we have an elaborate apparatus, starting with the extremely artificial "presumption of innocence," designed to counteract these biases.

It is precisely these biases that make it impossible to "frame" legal protections of accused criminals in an intuitively accessible way. The function of these protections is to counteract and override our intuitive responses to crime, which tend to be retaliatory and overzealous. Thus they are, by their very nature, institutions that can be explained and justified only from a rational point of view. Their sole function is to override our intuitions in order to improve the chances that our justice system will actually mete out something that approximates justice. The same is true of gun control. Ultimately, support for the policy must be based on a *cognitive* insight into the structure of the collective action problem, not a visceral response to the damage caused by gun crime.

When Lakoff suggests that the Democrats need to learn to frame their issues better, there are no doubt some instances where he is right. Democrats do not need to be as hapless as they are. The most famous example is Michael Dukakis's answer, during the second presidential debate with George H. W. Bush, when asked how he would feel about the death penalty if his wife had been raped and murdered. He responded simply by reiterating his opposition to the death penalty, saying, "I don't see any evidence that it's a deterrent and I think there are better and more effective ways to deal with violent crime."[18] This was generally recognized as having been a disastrous response, simply because it was all head and no heart. And yet even without getting emotional, he could have explained that we don't ask the victims of crime to determine criminal justice policy—otherwise, we would still be castrating rapists and quartering murderers in the public square. Victims of crime are obviously more sympathetic than perpetrators, but the hard fact is that their perspective and their accounts are often just as biased and self-serving.[19] The job of the politician is to balance *all* of the interests at stake, including those of society at large, not just pander to one constituency.

One might have thought Democrats would have learned their lesson from this. And yet twelve years later, John Kerry stood by in the presidential debates and let George W. Bush frame the issue of stem-cell research as a contest between "science" and "ethics"—as though stem-cell research was motivated by idle curiosity rather than the desire to cure various terrible diseases. How hard would it have been for Kerry to interject and insist that his support for stem-cell research was also an "ethical" position, perhaps even more ethical, since it gives priority to the needs of real, living and breathing people, instead of just cells in a petri dish?

So there remains a lot of room for improvement in the way that Democrats present their views. At the same time, there are clear limits to how much can be achieved through better framing. Conservatives are able to give their positions gut-level appeal because their political ideology calls for the rejection of any policy proposal that does not have gut-level appeal. Simple solutions to complex problems are easy to sell. The enemies of reason will always have the best slogans. Progressives, however, are calling for a variety of initiatives that are not straightforward. They generally support complex solutions to complex problems. Saying that all they need to do is frame their proposals better is like sending a fighter into the ring with one arm tied behind his back.

¶

Lakoff's emphasis on better framing comes from his more fundamental conviction that morality resides entirely at the level of our intuitions, or that it is fundamentally not rational. This is because he accepts one variant of the '60s critique of "technical reason," which sees it as cold, detached, and amoral. As a result, he thinks there is a basic symmetry between the left and the right—both political orientations are grounded in intuition, not in reason. In Lakoff's view, there is no such thing as a rational politics, because all values ultimately come from the gut. From this perspective, the conflict between progressives and conservatives is essentially a contest between one batch of intuitions and some other intuitions. The problem with the Democrats, therefore, *has* to be that they are not expressing themselves well enough. Lakoff does not take seriously the possibility that some policies might be inherently more difficult to frame in intuitively compelling ways precisely because they are not based on our intuitions, or because they require active suppression of our intuitions in order to be understood. (Jonathan Haidt shares Lakoff's view in this respect, except that he thinks that liberalism comes from a lopsided emphasis on two of the six supposedly innate moral intuitions. This leads him to the conclusion that liberals have to do more than just frame their ideas better: they have to actually embrace a broader range of conservative values.[20])

In the end, Lakoff calls for a "new enlightenment," one based on the supremacy of what he calls "real reason." This is easily recognizable as just another version of the standard antirationalist template, not much different from what one can find in Herbert Marcuse or Mary Daly. Lakoff defines real reason using the standard '60s tropes. It is "largely unconscious and appropriately emotional. It is embodied, and the way it is embodied gives rise to frame-based and metaphorical thought."[21] So far, so familiar. Calling it "reason," though, is a bit misleading. A better word would be *intuition*. Similarly, when Lakoff calls for a "new enlightenment," this is really just a rhetorically misleading way of endorsing the central dogmas of the Romantic counter-Enlightenment. It's not even old wine in new bottles—it's old wine in old bottles with the labels switched around.

Contrary to what Lakoff claims, the idea that reason is neutral with respect to questions of value is extremely dubious. Even David Hume, the father of modern sentimentalism, recognized that our ability to enter into cooperative relations with one another is based upon the *rational* insight that we can all be better off if we follow some mutually agreed-upon rules.[22] This exercise of reason provides the foundation for the state, the market economy, and modern legal orders, as well as "golden rule" moral codes.

Take something as simple as accepting a compromise. Everyone always has a reason to reject a compromise, because everyone thinks that their own view is correct, their own cause is just, or their own values are more important. That gives everyone a reason *not* to compromise. The only way to see one's way toward accepting a compromise is to recognize that because everyone thinks that their own view is correct, no one is likely to back down, and so everyone is better off settling for somewhat less than what they think an ideal arrangement would be. ("He may be evil, but he *thinks* he's good. Furthermore, he thinks that I'm evil, even though I'm good.") This kind of perspective-taking, along with relativization of one's own position, is not accessible to us through intuition. Compromise is always based on a rational insight, and it is respected only by those who are able to veto their first-order impulses. Because of this, there is no way to make compromise viscerally satisfying. Indeed, the enemies of liberalism have been merciless in making fun of the willingness to compromise, always portraying it as a sign of weakness or effeminacy. The only way to sell compromise is to encourage people to assess it from a rational point of view and to recognize the dreary but persistent fact that if everyone always strives to get their own way, the results are likely to be much worse for everyone involved.

Conservatives do have a few issues that are genuinely unintuitive, mainly having to do with the way that capitalism functions. It is difficult to explain why wages bear no relation to how hard a person works or to the value of what the person produces.[23] And it is incredibly difficult to explain why international trade is mutually beneficial and doesn't create unemployment, even if wages in one country are much higher than in the other.[24] Thus protectionism will always have enormous intuitive appeal, because its proponents can tap into our feelings of in-group solidarity. Frustration over the impossibility of explaining these two points to the electorate occasionally generates an outbreak of antidemocratic sentiment on the right.[25]

And yet, by comparison, supporters of modern liberalism have it much worse. Consider, for example, one of the defining ideas of twentieth-century jurisprudence, that there should be a distinction between law and morality. Whenever we see someone doing something that we consider deeply immoral, our immediate reaction is to say that this person shouldn't be allowed to do it. In a small-scale tribal society, where people largely agree about what is moral and immoral, we would get our way. In this type of society, law is basically just the enforcement of morality. With the development of the large-scale bureaucratic state, however, came the gradual acceptance of the idea that not everything that is *wrong* should also be *illegal*. This is partly because people have significant disagreements about what is right and wrong, but also because the law is a blunt instrument, and so trying to regulate certain forms of behavior is likely to do more damage than any good it could create. Thus a person living in the modern world can quite consistently believe that, for example, abortion is immoral and still think that it should be legal. This is central to the idea of individual rights—that people should not be legally prevented from doing a variety of things, including some that are profoundly antisocial. This is, however, a difficult distinction to defend—indeed, it is a quintessentially "nuanced" position. Saying that something should be legal sounds like saying that it's okay to do it. Saying that something is immoral sounds like saying that it's not okay. So which is it?

Thus it is a characteristic feature of many conservative positions, especially in the common sense vein, that they reject any distinction between morality and law. This is why American conservatives are so keen to put up monuments of the ten commandments on courthouse steps, and why they think that homosexuality should be, if not outright illegal, then at least deprived of any legal protection. Fundamentally, the position is not complicated. They think that homosexuality is gross, which leads them to think that it is immoral, which leads them to think that it should be illegal. Intuition doesn't draw any distinctions between these three quite different reactions. Any attempt to drive a wedge between them is seen as simply a load of fancy doubletalk, like supporting the troops but not the mission. The conservative position is, therefore, a hugely regressive political stance— it undoes one of the foundational principles of Western democracy—and yet it is also one that most people find intuitively correct.

One can see here why the "fight fire with fire" response is inherently limited. The Trudeau example, of encouraging federal nationalism to combat provincial nationalism, is something of an exception. It worked—to the extent that it did work—because at either level, nationalism is essentially a trick, designed to make people feel a heightened level of social solidarity toward people who are, in fact, strangers. There is no inherent limit on the level at which the trick can be played. These successes, however, can mislead the friends of reason into thinking that with enough attention to human psychology, anything can be effectively packaged and sold. But this is clearly not the case. The only reason Lakoff thinks it can is that he is a moral noncognitivist, and so doesn't believe that liberal positions are in any way more rational than conservative ones. They just reflect different values, and values are based on gut feelings. Politics, in his view, is nothing but our gut feelings versus theirs.

This way of thinking is one that should make progressives extremely nervous. Apart from the fact that it generates a lot of dubious advice on how to run political campaigns, the major problem is that it essentially ratifies the current climate of irrationalism in the political sphere, making it look like a feature of the human condition, instead of a pathological state of affairs that we have allowed to develop, and that we need to take steps to reverse.

11. Just think harder!

and other unhelpful advice from the Enlightenment

Say what you will about Michael Moore, he has the distinction of being one of the few American liberals to come even close to beating the Republicans at their own game. His films, from *Roger and Me* to *Sicko,* are carefully crafted pieces of political propaganda, designed to amuse and outrage in equal measure. *Sicko,* Moore's critique of the American health care system, contains a number of astonishingly clever set pieces. He starts with the plight of a group of American 9/11 rescue workers who are unable to get health care for various ailments they suffer as a result of volunteering to help at the site of the collapsed World Trade Center buildings. He then contrasts this with the health care facilities provided to detainees at the American prison camp in Guantanamo Bay. (The video he uses to describe these facilities is of politicians and military officials who were obviously reacting against the suggestion that detainees were being abused. Because of this, most of them go overboard describing the lavish facilities and superlative care being provided.) Moore takes the rescue workers to Cuba, in order to get them some of that free U.S. government health care being provided to the accused terrorists. After failing to secure entry to the Guantanamo prison, he decides to take them to a local clinic in Cuba, where they discover that they can refill their prescriptions at a fraction of what they are paying in the United States and that a comprehensive public system of care is available.

The idea that America treats its enemies better than its own citizens—its own 9/11 "heroes"—is a clever way of redirecting a nationalist impulse, which people on the right feel quite keenly. Judging from the number of websites and books attacking Moore and his work, he has managed to make a lot of conservatives crazy, in much the same way Palin makes liberals crazy. And yet there is a clear price to be paid for this rhetorical effectiveness. Inevitably, he winds up cutting a lot of corners. In his *Fahrenheit 9/11,* he devolves into fairly explicit conspiracy-mongering. Even in *Sicko,* where it's not too difficult to find dramatic examples of how the American health care system creates desperation and suffering, a lot of the play is fast and loose. For instance, in his profile of the socialized medicine systems in Canada, France, and the U.K., public health care is consistently described as being "free." Thus the contrast between U.S. health care and public health care systems is presented as a choice between paying for your health care and getting it for free, which makes it seem like a no-brainer. But of course public health care is not free: it is paid for through taxes.

Now there are a lot of things to be said in favor of public health care, particularly universal single-payer systems. Health care winds up costing a lot less when paid for through taxes than when paid for through private insurance, for a number of rather subtle reasons. The United States spends an eye-popping 18 percent of GDP on health care, and yet Americans do not actually consume more health care than people in many countries that spend closer to 10 percent of GDP on health care. In fact, by now the United States government is spending a greater fraction of GDP to deliver health care to just the elderly and the poor than other countries spend to deliver equally good care to their entire populations.[1] In other words, Americans have a catastrophically inefficient way of organizing the delivery of health care. And yet the reasons for this are far too difficult to explain in a movie, much less a movie that aims to be entertaining. It is much easier simply to draw an invidious comparison between "expensive" private health care and "free" public health care.

One can see here the central dilemma that modern liberals face: between taking the "high road" and taking the "low road." What makes it a dilemma, as opposed to just a choice, is that both options seem to involve huge compromises. The problem with the high road is that most of the time it doesn't work. The problem with the low road is that with almost any progressive public policy, it requires misrepresentation, and this can have untoward effects down the line. Much of the dynamic of American liberalism in the past three decades has involved the search for a third option. Success so far has been limited.

⁋

The temptation to bowdlerize the issues is not confined to Moore; it is an inevitable consequence of any attempt to frame complex policy questions in an intuitively compelling way. George Lakoff's take on health care, for instance, is not much more subtle than Moore's. Lakoff sets up the issue by drawing a contrast between "insurance companies," which he regards as essentially evil, and "government," which is concerned with the welfare of citizens: "Insurance companies get their money by denying care, by saying no to as many people in need as they can get away with, while maximizing the premiums they get from the healthy people. Health insurance will always work this way."[2] Health care, by contrast, should be "part of the moral mission of government, where the role of the government is protection and empowerment, which in turn is based on a morality of empathy and responsibility."[3] Thus the "moral bottom line," in Lakoff's view, is a simple choice between a "life-affirming" and a "life-denying" system.[4]

Again, this may be a compelling way of framing the issue. "Life-denying," after all, is just a fancy way of referring to death, and who wants to be on the side of death rather than of life? Many people who have had to settle a claim with an insurance company have come away scarred from the experience, and

American health insurance companies are apparently particularly difficult to deal with, yet it is preposterous to claim that the basic business model of an insurance company is to make money by denying claims. Many insurance companies are actually mutual societies (which is to say, cooperatives), where any money that is not paid out in the form of claims is refunded to policyholders at the end of the year. (Similarly, Kaiser Permanente, which is often portrayed as a big bad corporation, committed to denying health care to as many people as possible, was founded as a cooperative, and the core businesses in the consortium are still run as nonprofits.[5])

Insurance companies create value by pooling risk. Because we have difficulty knowing what our future health care needs will be, there are (significant) advantages to be had from pooling our own health care savings with those of others. Once you get a couple thousand people together, it becomes possible to predict with confidence what percentage of that group will get diabetes, suffer from heart attacks, contract cancer, and so on, and so you know with much greater confidence how much to set aside, and thus what premiums to charge. There's nothing shady about it—it's a straightforward economic benefit. Unfortunately, once you get several thousand people together pooling their health care savings, those same individuals lose whatever incentive they may once have had to seek the most affordable care or to use it only when necessary (after all, "insurance is paying"). Furthermore, people have an incentive to forego insurance when they are young and healthy then sign up for it when they get older or anticipate needing costly care. Thus insurance companies—regardless of whether they are trying to make profits or not—need to have a lot of rules and regulations in order to prevent people from taking advantage of the risk-pooling scheme.

The primary benefit that comes from public health care systems comes from the fact that government has the power to do this much more effectively than private insurers do. It is therefore able to deliver health *insurance*—not health care—at lower cost than a market system does. The important point is that the way socialized medicine works, in countries that have it, is not by abolishing insurance, but rather by having government control the insurance market. It does not consist of governments giving away free health care, as Lakoff and Moore suggest. The way that public health care systems work in Canada, in Australia, and throughout Europe is through control of the (supposedly "life-denying") insurance market.[6] Furthermore, any conceivable transformation of the American system in the direction of universal care would occur through government control of insurance. The ideal system for the United States would be a "single-payer" system like Canada's, where health care delivery is left almost entirely to the private sector, and government simply exercises a monopoly in the health insurance sector. And yet if one were to take Lakoff's "frame" seriously—and treat the central function of insurance as the denial of care—then this would be precisely the nightmare that Sarah Palin envisaged, where a panel of bureaucrats got together to withhold care from those who are deemed insufficiently productive members of society.

In Lakoff's defense, one might say that the advantages of public over private insurance is pretty esoteric stuff, not suitable for framing in any sort of viscerally compelling way. It is inevitable that in trying to put a "human face" on the issue, things will get simplified a bit. The problem is that the way Lakoff and Moore choose to frame the issue is not just simplistic, it is simplistic in a way that undermines the ability to do what ultimately needs to be done to fix the underlying social problem. It is a case where good rhetoric makes for bad policy. This is a dilemma that is often faced by progressive reformers, precisely because the policies that are actually needed to resolve any pressing social problem are almost always very complex, and so cannot be presented in a rhetorically effective way. They can be communicated only rationally, to an audience willing to give them their full attention and to engage in a rational assessment of their merits. If you try that, however, you wind up confronting the *Frasier* problem, of quoting de la Rochefoucauld to a shock jock.

This situation is one that clearly tempts many people to adopt a more cynical strategy, which is to run a campaign that appeals to the heart but then, once elected, rule from the head. All political parties do this type of bait and switch to some degree, and it carries obvious risks of voter backlash if carried out hamhandedly. The greater danger, however, is that it will never be carried out—that policies adopted for rhetorical reasons or because they poll well will actually become the governing policies of the party. The tail will start to wag the dog.

¶

I think by now it is safe to say that Americans overreacted to the terrorist attacks of September 11, 2001. In fact, with the passage of time, one begins to suspect that the devastating success of these attacks—in particular, the number of casualties that the terrorists were able to inflict—will be seen as a one-off, a fluke. After all, even Osama bin Laden didn't expect the towers to *collapse*. That's why he interpreted the outcome of the attacks as a sure sign of the direct intervention of God (on the side of Al-Qaeda, of course).

Terrorism turns out to be a bit harder to pull off than our untutored intuitions might lead us to expect. The Boston Marathon bombing in 2013 may have attracted a huge amount of attention and injured many people, but it actually resulted in only three deaths. This is about the same as the average American school shooting. Inflicting mass casualties is much more difficult than one might imagine.

This is just one of the many correctives to popular perception that Dan Gardner tries to impress upon the reader in his book *Risk: The Science and Politics of Fear.*[7] In general, Gardner thinks that most of the things we're afraid of are vastly overrated. He makes the case with respect to terrorism by pointing to the experience of the Aum Shinrikyo "doomsday" cult in Japan. Here was an organization that had an extraordinary amount of money at its disposal, several well-equipped labs, and as many as one hundred highly trained scientists, working full-time, dedicated exclusively to the task of figuring out how to inflict mass casualties upon the Japanese population, in an attempt to provoke an apocalyptic war. Nevertheless, over the course of seventeen different attacks, using a range of biological and chemical weapons, they never managed to kill more than a few dozen people. The most "successful" was the 1995 sarin nerve gas attack in the Tokyo subway, which killed twelve people and severely injured another forty-two.

Many people found this attack terrifying, yet for Gardner, it was also strangely reassuring. After all, it would be difficult to imagine circumstances more propitious for the success of a terrorist plot—"a fanatical cult with a burning desire to inflict mass slaughter has heaps of money, international connections, excellent equipment and laboratories, scientists trained at top-flight universities, and years of near-total freedom to pursue its operations"[8]—yet they came nowhere near accomplishing their ends.

All of this goes to show that even terrorists who get their hands on biological or chemical weapons (or nuclear material, for that matter) are still a long way away from being able to hurt large numbers of people. Yet in August 2006, 44 percent of Americans told Gallup that they were "very" or "somewhat" worried that they or someone in their family would be a victim of a terrorist attack. This is a phenomenal overestimation of the actual risk. Even before the 9/11 attacks, the thought of terrorism evoked irrational responses. In one particularly famous experiment, published in 1993, a group of psychologists showed that subjects offered flight insurance were willing to pay more for a policy that covered death due to terrorist attack than for a policy that covered death from *any cause* (including, of course, terrorist attack).[9]

Gardner's book is one of many published in recent years that try to show how overblown most popular fears and anxieties are. So what is the solution, according to Gardner? Ultimately, he argues, we simply have to buck up and become more rational: "To protect ourselves against unreasoning fear, we must wake up Head and tell it to do its job. We must learn to *think hard.*"[10] In Gardner's view, the problem is one of reason versus passion, and if reason seems to be losing, then we simply have to try harder to be rational. (Writing books haranguing people, telling them to be more rational, seems to be an important part of the plan.) What he is calling for, in effect, is a revival of the old Enlightenment strategy ("Once more folks, this time with a bit more *effort!*") of evaluating all received opinion at the tribunal of reason and consigning our old biases and superstitions to the dustbin of history.

When compared to Lakoff's "fight fire with fire" strategy, there is much to recommend Gardner's view. Most importantly, he recognizes the fundamental antagonism between what he calls "Head" and "Gut," and sees that in many cases gut is a source of nothing but bad ideas and confused impulses, which only "Head" is able to sort out. For example, if Americans ever want to work out a non-crazy, non-paranoid response to terrorism, they are simply going to have to start thinking about the risks in a more rational way. The United States federal government was once a global leader when it came to the use of cost-benefit analysis to evaluate new public initiatives, but all of this seems to have gone out the window when the issue of security arose. It is difficult to believe that any of the delays and inconveniences imposed on American airline passengers since 2001 would survive a cost-benefit analysis. The decision was made to exempt these security measures from the usual tests—to let the strategy be dictated by fear rather than by any sort of calculation. (Conservatives seem to have no problem with the idea of assigning a dollar value to the lives of workers and consumers when it comes to workplace safety and environmental regulation. Yet they suddenly lose their nerve when it comes to assigning a dollar value to the lives of victims of terrorism.)

Unfortunately, a lot of people are afraid of things that, in the grand scheme of things, are not very dangerous—terrorism being one of them. This is an area where our intuitions are simply wrong. There is no good way of framing that, because we have no intuitive sense of the weakness of intuition. The only way to get to the conclusion is by looking at the statistics in a dispassionate way and saying to people—even the families of the victims—"Your personal experiences and impressions are wrong, terrorism is not really that big a problem." This is why the British slogan "Keep calm and carry on" is so admirable. It's not because it constitutes an adequate policy response to terrorist violence; it doesn't. It's because it recommends an emotional response—not getting agitated and hysterical—that makes it possible to formulate a rational policy response. It encourages a public culture in which the "cool passion" of reason has a chance of being heard.

Unfortunately, it's difficult to imagine that a more rational public culture could be created simply through concerted individual effort to be more rational. We do enjoy the benefits of modern psychology, which gives us a much better sense of where the major pitfalls lie so that we can, in principle, be much more intelligent and self-aware in our quest to eliminate biases in our own thinking. And people certainly have become more disciplined as part of "the civilizing process," not to mention more sophisticated in their reasoning. Yet there are clearly limits to how much we can enhance our onboard resources, not to mention diminishing returns in our attempts at improvement.

In the end, it is a huge exercise in wishful thinking to imagine that just knowing about our biases will make us less likely to fall victim to them. Gardner's book is only one of several that have appeared in recent years by people alarmed by the current climate of irrationalism. Yet they all seem to subscribe to a variant of the view that knowledge will set us free—that just reading books about irrationality will somehow make us less irrational. Christopher Chabris and Daniel Simons, for example, at the end of their lengthy book on the subject of "how our intuitions deceive us," conclude with a little pep talk, encouraging the reader to "think twice before you decide to trust intuition over rational analysis." They go on to make a surprising series of claims for the curative powers of their work:

> There may be important things right in front of you that you aren't noticing due to the illusion of attention. Now that you know about this illusion, you'll be less apt to assume you're seeing everything there is to see. You may

think you remember some things much better than you really do, because of the illusion of memory. Now that you understand this illusion, you'll trust your own memory, and that of others, a bit less, and you'll try to corroborate your memory in important situations. You'll recognize that the confidence people express often reflects their personalities rather than their knowledge, memory, or ability. You'll be wary of thinking you know more about a topic than you really do, and you will test your own understanding before mistaking familiarity for knowledge.[11]

What is strange about this passage is that the authors are making an empirical claim—that knowing about illusions and biases will make people less likely to fall victim to them—and yet offer no empirical evidence in support of it. This is in striking contrast to the rest of the book, which is a meticulous presentation of the empirical research that has established the existence of the major set of cognitive biases. For some reason, when it comes to the question of how to cure these biases, the reader is offered nothing but a profession of faith.

The big question then is whether this claim is true. Does knowledge set us free? Unfortunately, when it comes to our own mind, the answer appears to be no. Just knowing about our biases does not make us less susceptible to them. Indeed, knowledge can easily have the opposite effect, encouraging people to think that they are immune to bias precisely *because* they know so much about it. (There's a strong current of this in Gardner's work.) They fail to appreciate the truly insidious nature of cognitive bias, which is that it's *your own brain* that's doing it to you, so you can't tell by introspection when it's happening.

To the extent that the question has been studied, the results are not encouraging. Brian Wansink, for example, who has conducted extensive research on the contribution that cognitive biases and illusions make to overeating, specifically investigated the question of whether learning about biases makes people less likely to suffer from them. He found that it did not. One of his studies involved the phenomenon that he refers to as *size bias*—an anchoring effect generated by the size of the bowl people are given to serve themselves food. He would bring people into a room with a table laden with snacks, presented in large serving bowls. Participants would each be given an individual bowl, which they could fill with snack food to carry over to their seats. The trick is that some bowls would be bigger than others. Predictably, the people given the larger bowls would eat significantly more.

Wansink decided to try the same experiment on his own students but to warn them in advance about the underlying bias. Here is how he described the plan: "We'll devote a full 90-minute class session just before Christmas vacation to talking about the size bias. We'll lecture to them, show them videos, have them go through a demonstration, and even break them into small groups to discuss how people could prevent themselves from 'being tricked' by bigger serving bowls. We'll use just about every educational method short of doing an interpretive dance."[12] One month later, he invited these same students to a Super Bowl party. They entered a room containing a table laden with snacks. He gave them each a bowl in order to serve themselves. Some of them were given small bowls, some were given larger bowls. The students then went on to exhibit *exactly* the same bias that they had just learned about in class and had spent time thinking and talking about how to avoid.

Part of what made Wansink's experiment work so nicely was a bit of misdirection that he employed. At the end of the snack table, he had students fill out a questionnaire about Super Bowl commercials. (In order to fill it out, they had to set down their snack bowls, which gave him the opportunity to secretly weigh the bowls to see how much food the person had taken.) It was this bit of misdirection that was undoubtedly crucial, because it prevented students from recognizing the setup, and therefore allowed their rational faculties to remain asleep at the switch. This is consistent with Stanovich's observation that intelligence offers no protection against bias, for much the same reason. Once a cognitive override is triggered, both knowledge of our biases and general intelligence are important for helping us to overcome them. The problem is that neither knowledge nor intelligence makes the override more likely to be triggered. People simply can't be expected to be suspicious of everything all the time. Apart from cognitive miserliness—our unwillingness to expend the effort—the limits of human attention do not permit constant vigilance. Furthermore, even if we are in a suspicious frame of mind or likely to be paying attention, all it takes is a bit of distraction to slip one past us.

Thus there is something deeply unrealistic about the old Enlightenment strategy of simply telling people to think harder, to be more critical, to "question authority," and so on. Chabris and Simons end their book by encouraging readers to "take any opportunity you find to pause and observe human behavior through the lenses we've given you. Try to track your own thoughts and actions as well, to make sure your intuitions and gut-level decisions are justified. Try your best to slow down, relax, and examine your assumptions before you jump to conclusions."[13] Now obviously, none of these are bad suggestions, in the sense that it wouldn't *hurt* most people to take a bit more time and think a bit more critically. But we need to be serious about how much can be achieved in this way. There is no basis for optimism that this strategy can do anything to reverse the tide of irrationalism that that confronts us every time we walk out the front door.

When reason steps in to override an incorrect or maladaptive intuitive response, it is an exercise in self-control. The evidence suggests that it is the same system of self-control that we exercise when we prevent ourselves from *acting* in ways that are irrational or contrary to our long-term interests.[14] As such, it is both limited and subject to depletion. (In other words, most people have a self-control "budget," and once they've exceeded it, they become more impulsive until they've had a chance to rest and recharge.) Meanwhile, our environment is constantly evolving in such a way as to put increased demands upon us, requiring us to override our intuitive responses more and more often. In this situation, what kind of a solution is it to tell someone who suffers from cognitive biases simply to think harder? It's like telling someone who is overweight to eat less, or telling an alcoholic to drink less. If he could do that, then he wouldn't have the problem in the first place. The advice is not so much wrong as it is simply unhelpful.

§

The current environment, particularly in the media, creates a genuine dilemma for those who would like to see reason prevail over passion in politics. How do you deal with a political opponent who responds to truth with truthiness, or a social environment in which no one seems to know the difference? The "fight fire with fire" strategy recommended by Lakoff makes sense only under the assumption that all political positions can be translated into pithy, emotionally resonant slogans. In practice, it merely favors extremists, and distorts policy away from what would be best for society toward what can be most easily sold to the electorate. There is no getting around the fact that most moderate, progressive positions are frankly difficult to explain. This is partly because they involve trade-offs between multiple considerations, require collective action, and involve tacit recognition of the limitations of different institutional structures (markets, the state, corporations, legal regulation, etc.).

On the other hand, the "just try harder" strategy recommended by Gardner seems to be no more promising. Trying to engage in rational debate with an opponent who doesn't have any interest in the basic norms of truth is pointless. You can't *argue* with a Rush Limbaugh or a Bill O'Reilly, and if you do, you come off looking like a fool. ("Never wrestle with a pig," as the old saying goes. "You both get dirty, but the pig enjoys it.") Furthermore, the suggestion that the public or the media might respond to exhortations encouraging them to be more rational underestimates the seriousness of the problem. The human capacity to reason is extremely frail and easily exhausted. Our susceptibility to bias and false belief is not an aberration, something that can be blamed on the media. It is certainly not being *helped* by the media at the moment, but the media is only part of a much larger set of forces in our society that are conspiring to produce an environment in which it has become more difficult to carry on a rational debate.

One can see here why a third alternative, which has emerged in recent years in the United States, has considerable merit. The way to respond to right-wing demagogues is not with left-wing demagogues, but with *comedians*. Trying to engage in serious argument with the demagogues is a mug's game: all you wind up doing is elevating their views and debasing your own. Trying to hit back using the same tactics is either ineffective or self-defeating. The solution? Just make fun of them. Reason cannot win in a head-to-head contest against unreason. So when someone is being unreasonable, the best you can do is point out how unreasonable they are, often to comedic effect. This is why satire has always occupied a prominent role in Enlightenment polemic (with Voltaire being the best-known practitioner).

The success of this formula is what explains the most peculiar feature of American politics at the moment, which is that the national political debate is dominated by an exchange between right-wing talk-radio hosts and left-wing comedians. When right-wing demagoguery first started to gather steam, the initial impulse among Democrats was to clone Michael Moore, to have liberal "attack dogs," and to create a liberal talk-radio station (Air America) where liberal political ideas could be presented in more forceful, aggressive ways. The problem is that universal health care, racial tolerance, gender equality, gays in the military, and liberalized immigration don't really lend themselves to hard-hitting, in-your-face presentation. Over time, it became apparent that the more effective response was coming from comedians—from Janeane Garofalo, Al Franken, Jon Stewart, and Stephen Colbert. The reason it worked is that for the most part they would leave liberal political positions out of it and simply focus on the irrationality of the positions being advanced by the right.

Jon Stewart is the most consistent and effective in this regard. Although his show is all about politics, he refuses to engage in political debate with demagogues. He will criticize and make fun of them, but when they try to turn it around and say "Well, what do you propose, smart guy?" he refuses to play along. What they want, of course, is for him to lay out some kind of liberal policy that they can proceed to attack using one of a dozen prepared sound-bites. But Stewart's answer is always "I'm just a comedian. My show is a comedy show. You're the one who claims to be reporting the news or having a serious political debate." The subtext is "If you wanted to have a serious discussion, we could have a serious discussion. But what you do is fundamentally not serious."

The result is a division of labor. The job of wrestling with the pig is taken over by the comedians, which frees up more serious political actors from having to "respond" to every insane allegation made by the right. (For example, when Republican congresswoman Michele Bachmann accuses President Obama of wanting to abandon the U.S. dollar in favor of a "global currency" and therefore introduces legislation in Congress to "ensure that the U.S. dollar remains the currency of the United States,"[15] you don't really want to waste the valuable time of serious people unpacking all the different layers of crazy that went into this particular confection. Just let the comedians handle it.)

This solution, however, remains something of a stopgap. It's better than the sort of deer-in-the-headlights paralysis that dominated the Democratic Party during the Dukakis period, but it does have the effect of turning most of the public debate on political issues in America into a circus sideshow. Furthermore, it is impossible to "restore sanity" through comedic jibes alone (at most one can stem the tide of insanity). The only real solution is to change the environment. A more effective response lies in the recognition that the rapid-fire pace of modern politics, the hypnotic repetition of daily news items, even the preponderance of visual sources of information, are all inimical to the exercise of reason. If it is indeed our objective to "restore sanity," we need to pursue a higher-level strategy, one of restructuring the environment in such a way that the voice of reason has a chance of being heard.

12. Protecting the mental environment

Rethinking the architecture of choice

It is easy to find stories of irrational consumers being taken advantage of by unscrupulous corporations. Take something as simple as the "instant refund" offered by various income-tax preparation companies, such as H&R Block. Why wait for the government to mail you a refund check at the end of the tax year when companies are willing to give you the money right away, as soon as you fill out your return? But of course, it isn't an "instant tax refund"—the government still takes a couple of weeks to mail out the check. What the tax preparation service is actually offering is a personal loan, with the eventual tax refund pledged as security and taken as repayment. If you add up the fees and charges, it quickly becomes apparent that this loan is probably the most expensive you will ever take out, equivalent to an annual interest charge as high as 250 percent. If you really need to buy something right away, you would be several times better off just using a credit card.

The charges on these loans at one point became so exorbitant that governments began to crack down, forcing companies to disclose explicitly the annualized interest rate to consumers. And yet this has only put a slight dent in the business. Companies continue to offer these "instant refunds" and consumers continue to take them. Why? Because of various irrational aspects of consumer psychology: first, the fact that people are impatient and the lure of "instant cash" is great; second, because people mentally classify their tax refund as a windfall gain, and so treat the charges as foregone gains rather than as losses; and, third, because of the simple fact that it is not presented as a loan, so the reasonableness of the fees is not assessed from within that frame.

The story here is a familiar one. We seldom stop to ask, however, why it is always corporations exploiting consumers and not the other way around. After all, if irrationality is a *human* characteristic—that is, if everyone is irrational to a certain degree—then why are there not just as many instances of consumers exploiting irrational corporations? Consider David Phillips, better known as "the pudding guy," who discovered something of a loophole in a Healthy Choice frequent-flier promotion, leading him to buy $3,140 worth of pudding that he cashed in for over 1.2 million air miles. Or consider, as a friend of mine once discovered, that it is possible to arbitrage the menu at Subway. (Instead of ordering a BLT sandwich, she figured out, you can order a veggie sandwich with bacon as an extra and get a BLT for 50¢ less than the menu price.) So it's not impossible for consumers to exploit corporations with inconsistent pricing policies, it just doesn't happen very often.

Similarly, many people took the 2008 financial crisis as a vindication of the idea that stock markets are "irrational"—moved by the "animal spirits" of investors—and therefore in need of stricter regulation. Yet again, if irrationality is a human characteristic, what reason is there to think that legislators are going to be any more rational when drawing up a new set of rules than investors? "If water chokes us," said Aristotle, "what must we drink to wash it down?" And yet there are many cases where speculative bubbles and irrational exuberance have been controlled by central authorities, or where excessive risk-taking has been reduced. Many of the regulations imposed on the banking sector over the course of the twentieth century, such as reserve requirements, have dramatically improved both the stability and the profitability of the banking system.

So how is it that irrationality seems to be so unevenly distributed?

There are, of course, many factors. But if you look carefully at the difference between consumers and corporations, one thing that stands out is that the decisions made by corporations are highly scaffolded (to use Andy Clark's expression).[1] When consumers make decisions about whether to buy something or not, they are relying primarily on the onboard resources of their biological brains. As modern psychology has amply demonstrated, if you take an individual human brain, strip it of all its usual crutches, and put it in an unfamiliar or hostile environment, it will perform pathetically. If you look to the other side of the purchasing decision, however, at the corporation that is doing the selling, what you see is quite the opposite. First of all, the decisions are typically made by groups, or by individuals in consultation with others. Proposals get presented and discussed at meetings or in work groups. The factors going into the transaction will also have been rendered explicit, articulated as part of a long-term cost-benefit calculus. In some cases, teams of sales associates and analysts, working with spreadsheets, will have calculated all of the margins on the sale and projected them into the distant future. In other words, the decision will have been made in a highly structured social environment, with all the assumptions and inferences made explicit and with multiple points of contestation and correction. It is no wonder then that corporate decision making more closely approximates the ideal of economic rationality.[2] It is not because the *people* are more rational, it is because they are operating in an institutional environment that is more conducive to rational thought and planning.

This observation provides a useful point of departure for thinking about the general problem of irrationalism in society. The central limitation of the old Enlightenment view and the set of political strategies that it recommends is that they are completely individualistic. When confronted with large-scale failures of rationality, the most that the Enlightenment view can offer is the recommendation that people think harder. Once we recognize that rationality is highly scaffolded, on the other hand, and that this scaffolding is both external and social, we can begin to conceive of reason as a *social project*. At very least, this should lead us to think more seriously about the consequences of creating an environment that undermines our own rationality. More ambitiously, we might engage in collective action aimed at improving conditions in the social environment, making it more conducive to rational thought.

❡

Sometimes, in order to fix a problem, it isn't really necessary to fix the *problem*. This is the essence of the kluge. When it comes to human irrationality, fixing the problem is often not even an option—we're stuck with the brain that we have—and so we have no choice but to work around it.

To the extent that we are able to achieve something resembling rationality, it is usually because we have good kluges. As productivity expert David Allen put it, "To a great degree, the highest-performing people I know are those who have installed the best tricks in their lives. I know that's true of me. The smart part of us sets up things for us to do that the non-so-smart part responds to almost automatically, creating behavior that produces high-performance results. We trick ourselves into doing what we ought to be doing."[3]

Just as individuals have little tricks that help them to work around their own foibles, so too do societies. There are both individual and collective kluges.

It may seem like a bit of a stretch, but consider the phenomenon of inflation—popularly perceived as a rise in prices, but more strictly defined as a decline in the value of money over time. In principle, there is no reason why inflation should occur. And indeed, orthodox economists of a certain stripe find it irritating precisely for that reason. Consumers also find it annoying, and often take the fact that things used to cost less when they were young as evidence that the world is in a state of moral decline. Yet governments actively promote a moderate inflation rate (central banks usually have a target rate of about 2 percent per year). Why might that be?

The reason is that inflation provides an elegant solution to a number of economic problems caused by our irrational aversion to losses. It is often noted that wages in a market economy are "sticky," which means that they don't change as quickly as some people might like. With most goods, prices move up and down in response to changes in supply and demand. The price of labor, however, does not move about quite so easily, because downward adjustments are extremely difficult. People are happy to get a raise but get extremely upset at the prospect of a decrease in their pay. The underlying phenomenon is *loss aversion*. Promising workers a 5 percent pay increase then reneging and give them only 2 percent will undoubtedly upset them. But this is nothing compared to how they would react if you handed them a 3 percent pay cut. In the first case, the 3 percent loss comes in the form of a foregone gain, whereas in the second case it comes as a straight-up loss. Setting aside the slight complication arising from diminishing returns, it remains the case that people suffer approximately twice the unhappiness from losses as they do from foregone gains of the same magnitude.[4]

This creates something of a problem not just for employers, but for the economy as a whole, because there are occasions when workers *should* take a pay cut (most obviously, when demand for what they produce has declined). Experience has shown, however, that simply cutting wages can create significant disorder, generating labor disruptions, political extremism, rioting, and sometimes even overthrow of a government. This is often irrational, in the sense that there may be no realistic alternative to the wage cut. If there is simply less wealth to go around, people must consume less, and if they are to consume less, they must earn less. Accepting this, however, takes Herculean self-restraint on the part of workers. (It can sometimes be achieved when there is an immediate, simple explanation, such as imminent bankruptcy of their employer. Whenever the explanation gets a bit more complicated, however, people start to reject it in favor of conspiracy theories, all of which have as a common thread the absence of a need for pay cuts.)

Luckily, we have another bit of irrationality that can be used to counteract this first bit of irrationality. When people think about their wages, they tend to put disproportionate emphasis on what economists call their "nominal" wage—namely, the amount that they earn denominated in current dollars. What they should be concerned about, of course, is not the amount of money that they make, but what they can buy with this money—what economists refer to as the "real" wage. So, for example, if the price of everything (food, clothing, transportation, housing, etc.) goes up by 2 percent and workers get a pay increase of 3 percent, then their real wage has increased by only 1 percent. This is the amount that their wage goes up "net of inflation."

Unfortunately—or fortunately, depending on your point of view— workers are generally subject to a *money illusion,* whereby they feel and act as though they are getting 3 percent richer when they get the 3 percent nominal wage increase. This turns out to be an incredibly useful bit of irrationality, because it can be used to do an end-run around loss aversion. It turns out that if you give workers a 1 percent pay increase at a time when inflation is running at 3 percent, they may treat it as a disappointing pay increase, but they don't react the same way that they would to a 2 percent pay cut. Even if they realize, intellectually, that their real wages are going down or that their pay is not keeping pace with inflation, this realization does not trigger the visceral reaction that a cut in nominal wages would provoke.

Because of this, inflation (or currency devaluation) provides a relatively painless way of adjusting wages: you keep paying people the same amount of money, but you make the money worth less. The objective is not to fool people—after all, intellectually, not that many people are fooled, and wage negotiations always take the cost of living or the inflation rate as the benchmark. This work-around merely allows us to fool the dumb part of our brains, so that we are able to accept what the smart part says needs to be done.

Economists who adhere inflexibly to the idea that individuals are perfectly rational have always disliked inflation, because they don't see the need for this psychological kluge. They therefore assume that inflation must have some other (nefarious) motive, such as a desire on the part of government to weasel out of paying its debts. In their view, workers should just suck it up and accept pay cuts when necessary (and if they don't, then the police should go in and crack some heads).

The 2012 crisis in the euro zone—Greece in particular—shows how unrealistic this is, and how heavily all advanced economies rely on the inflation kluge. The central problem in Greece is that wages had risen to unsustainable levels, funded by government borrowing rather than by actual production. Thus Greece found itself in a situation where pretty much everyone in the country needed to take a pay cut. Under normal circumstances, this would have occurred, automatically and almost unnoticeably, through a devaluation in the currency. However, since Greece had joined the euro, it was unable to devalue, leaving it no choice but to lower nominal wages.

The central motivation for wanting to leave the euro would be to create a domestic currency that could subsequently be devalued. From a certain perspective, this makes no sense. There is nothing that can be achieved through currency devaluation that could not also be achieved through direct adjustments in the domestic wage and price levels. The problem is that the latter adjustments are extremely "painful," to the point where they threaten the stability of an entire society.

This example is an instructive one, because it shows very clearly the challenges and options associated with building a more rational society. For over a century, economists have expressed the fervent desire that people be more rational about wages, so that these devices could be dispensed with. They have also, at various times and to varying degrees, convinced governments to deploy significant amounts of force getting people to accept adjustments in wages. Yet what are the chances that people will someday become more rational, so that all this becomes unnecessary?

Inflation, by contrast, offers a solution that is intellectually quite messy but in practice quite tidy. It is essentially an external mechanism that allows us to get much closer to what the ideal of rationality prescribes without actually becoming more rational. It is like the rider jumping down off the elephant in order to rearrange the environment. In my view, external kluges like this provide the best model for thinking about how to enhance the rationality of our decision making. Our challenge is to find more tricks like this, to improve the quality of the political sphere in particular.

¶

When thinking about how to restore sanity, it is useful to go back to the fundamental characteristics of rational thought. It is slow; it requires attention; it is linguistically based, conscious, and fully explicit. Also, because it relies on working memory, it can easily become bottlenecked, and so benefits from externalization—such as having intermediate stages of reasoning written down. It is easy to see how this style of thinking could become entirely hostage to its environment. Consider the simple issue of speed, and the fact that reason is slow. Some ideas or arguments, even rather easy ones, take a good ten or fifteen minutes to explain. And yet outside of the privileged environment of the classroom, it is remarkable how seldom anyone is ever forced to sit and listen to someone else explain something (without flipping the channel, checking for status updates, or interrupting). For some people, the religious sermon is an important exception—except that the range of topics that get covered tends to be quite limited. This means that once a person's formal education is finished, there are very few opportunities to learn new things that can't be communicated in snippets.

Consider, for example, the basic economic argument for free trade. The argument is not particularly complicated, but it is extremely counterintuitive, in part because it shows that trade between nations with radically different wage levels generates no downward pressure on wages in the richer country. David Ricardo worked out the basic analysis in 1817 and it has formed a staple of the economics curriculum ever since. Unfortunately, most people don't take a formal economics class, and so misunderstanding of the basic structure of international trade is practically universal.

In principle, people could go read a book or watch a video and try to figure it out. Yet as Paul Krugman has observed, very few ever do. He regards this as something of a mystery: "Why do policy wonks who will happily watch hundreds of hours of talking heads droning on about the global economy refuse to sit still for the ten minutes or so it takes to explain Ricardo?" He winds up answering his own question, however, when he observes that "teaching the model to docile students is one thing: they get the model in the course of a broader study of economics, and in any case they are obliged to pay attention and learn it the way you teach it if they want to pass the exam. But try to explain the model to an adult, especially one who already has opinions about the subject, and you continually find yourself obliged to backtrack, realizing that yet another proposition you thought was obvious actually isn't."[5]

The problem with adults in everyday social settings is that they are practically unteachable. It is not an accident that Krugman identifies several *social* aspects of the classroom as essential to the proper communication of the argument. It is crucial in developing the argument that the listener accept certain suppositions. The argument also relies upon a simple model that requires decontextualization. Rather than bringing to bear everything that we know about the world—or everything that we think we know about the world—we are asked to put all that on ice, and consider in the abstract the relationship between, say, two people exchanging two goods. This requires what is, for the average person, a heroic level of mental inhibition and self-control (to counteract our fundamental computational bias). The classroom provides scaffolding that significantly diminishes this burden.

The fact that Krugman describes the students as "docile" is only partly tongue-in-cheek. One of the important features of the classroom is that students are not allowed to interrupt. They have to put up their hand in order to ask a question, and even then, the instructor has the prerogative to say "Not now, wait until I've finished explaining this point." This is actually crucial when it comes to developing a sustained argument, but it is highly unnatural and awkward in most other social situations. Anyone who has ever tried to explain Ricardo—or any other vaguely complex argument—at a dinner party, for instance, will know that it is impossible to do so without violating several social conventions. First of all, it requires simply talking too long and too much, and therefore being a "bore." Second, there will always be someone who interrupts, typically to raise a premature objection, make a joke, or raise an issue that is tangential to the central line of argument. There are actually very few "natural" social settings where it is possible to talk for even ten minutes straight without awkwardness. The important thing to recognize is that this serves as a filter on the type of ideas that can be communicated in those settings.

There is one important exception to all of this, and that is the written word. Indeed, for arguments that are longer than about an hour or so, books are invaluable. Consider, for example, the theory of evolution. It also suffers from the problem of being highly unintuitive, primarily because of the age of the earth and the length of time that evolutionary processes have been at work. We all have an intuitive "feel" for how long a year is, a decade, perhaps even a century. When we start talking about billions of years, however, it becomes just a number on the page. We have no "feel" for how long that is, other than the intellectual recognition that it is a very long time. Because of this, our judgments of what is probable and improbable on this timescale are completely out of whack. Most of the "common sense" objections to evolution take the form of what Richard Dawkins calls the "argument from personal incredulity"—namely, "I find this hard to believe, therefore it can't be true."[6] If you scratch the surface of these arguments, however, what you find is that people find it hard to believe because it conflicts with their intuitive sense of what is probable. That's because our intuitive judgments of probability, which are unreliable at the best of times, are completely useless when applied to the question of what might have happened over the course of even a million years, much less four billion.[7]

My guess is that it takes at least an hour to explain the theory of evolution properly (that is, the mechanism of natural selection, along with the most important bodies of evidence that support the theory). Because of this, books play an extremely important role in propagating the theory. To date, no effective substitutes have been found. It is noteworthy, for instance, that for all the popularity of nature documentaries, such as the various BBC series narrated by David Attenborough, they all presuppose the correctness of evolutionary theory but never seek to explain it.[8] In the early days of television, it was assumed that this new technology would serve as a powerful medium for bringing education to the masses. Instead of bringing people to schools, you could bring the school to them, simply by recording and broadcasting lectures. (Much of the same enthusiasm is going on at the moment regarding internet technologies and distance education.) And yet the project failed utterly. Why? Because "school" is more than just a curriculum, it is also a *social setting*.

This is why, when it comes to the cultivation of rationality in society, there can be no substitute for formal education of the traditional sort. Much of what was criticized as authoritarian about old-fashioned educational practices—the teacher's control of the classroom, the organized desks in rows, the reading assignments, problems sets, deadlines, and exams, and finally the assignment of grades—can also be seen as external scaffolding designed to enhance our own deficiencies of self-control when it comes to concentration, planning, and goal attainment. Naturally, some teachers abuse their privileges. But in order to see the advantages of classroom learning, one need only converse for a while with someone who is self-taught. The most common feature of autodidacts is a lack of discipline—a jumpy cognitive style, typically coupled with an inability to sort out good ideas from bad. Confirmation bias is a particularly serious pitfall. One of the advantages of a traditional classroom and curriculum is that it forces you to learn material the way that someone else has organized it, so that you come to understand ideas that you resist as well as ones to which you are initially sympathetic. Teaching yourself tempts people to pick and choose, which may be why autodidacts seem particularly susceptible to confirmation bias and conspiracy theories.

Academics are sometimes accused of wanting to conduct politics on the model of a university seminar. It is important to realize that this is neither feasible nor desirable in a world of interest politics, in which at some point deliberation needs to pass over into action. At the same time, there is a reason why university seminars are designed the way that they are. When people are trying to think, they naturally seek out environments that are conducive to thinking. In order to improve public deliberation, you don't need to make the world over on the model of a classroom. But it should contain some of that model's elements. For example, reason is irremediably *slow* and, because it is linear, requires attention. Yet we often destroy elements of the environment that make this style of thinking possible—sometimes inadvertently, but sometimes thanks to a variety of bad theories about how thinking is done.

Many corporations, for example, have been impressed by the workplace style of "creative" companies, such as advertising agencies, and have sought to reproduce them in various ways. A friend of mine who works at a newspaper was horrified one day when a team of management consultants, charged with promoting "innovation" at the firm, announced that they were going to remove all cubicles and offices, to be replaced by one giant, amoeba-shaped desk that would be shared by everyone in the newsroom. This was intended to break down the "silos" between the different sections and beats at the paper and transform the workday into one nonstop "flowing" conversation. People were to be deprived of personal workspace as well, in order to create a more "fluid" work environment.

While this sort of thing may work well to encourage brainstorming at an advertising agency, a newspaper is a different beast entirely. Advertising and design, with their focus on short, snappy slogans and visuals, are much more heavily weighted toward intuitive thinking styles. Editors and writers, by contrast, need to *concentrate*. The redesigned workspace made this all but impossible. Deprived of his office, my friend on occasion actually took to hiding out in a bathroom stall, in order to get some peace and quiet so that he could read over copy before committing it to print. Within a year the amoeba desk was gone. In this case, the choice was obvious: the new work arrangement basically made it impossible for anyone to work. And yet in many workplaces, less drastic versions of the same set of reforms have been implemented and remain in force. For example, the common rule that employees must keep a clean desk—they are not allowed to accumulate stacks of paper—deprives many people of a very powerful external mechanism for organizing tasks. This restriction may reduce productivity, but not so much that it becomes entirely unfeasible, so the rules may persist despite the cognitive handicap that they impose on workers.

Some of these workplace rules are a simple consequence of bad psychology. Others, though, result from a general cultural trend toward glorifying intuitive thinking styles, along with the "creative" industries in which they are important. There is a failure to recognize that for certain tasks, people require an environment that is almost exactly the opposite. Old-fashioned offices with opaque wooden doors that close may not be particularly glamorous, but if the goal is to create an environment in which employees are able to concentrate on one task for more than a minute, they have considerable merits.

¶

In May 2012, New York City mayor Michael Bloomberg announced that he would take the unusual step of banning the sale of sugared drinks in bottles or cups larger than 16 fluid ounces. The measure was introduced in an attempt to combat the growing problem of obesity in the United States (approximately two-thirds of the American population is overweight, one-third of the population obese).[9] Although many factors contribute to the poor quality of the American diet, consumption of soda is one of the most obvious. The average American drinks 216 liters of soft drinks per year, almost twice the average consumption of people in any other country in the world. One liter of Coca-Cola contains 112 grams of sugar, or 433 calories.[10] Drinking 216 liters of Coke every year adds an impressive total of 24 kilograms of extra sugar to one's diet.

Critics were quick to pounce on Bloomberg's proposal, complaining about big brother, the nanny state, and the death of liberty, while at the same time observing (inconsistently) that the regulation was toothless, since there is nothing to stop a person from buying two 10-ounce sodas rather than the prohibited 20-ounce bottle. Of course, if people were perfectly rational and they really wanted to drink 20 ounces of soda, this is what they would do. Yet a substantial body of psychological research shows that the idea underlying the ban on large sodas is sound, because of our tendency to engage in what Brian Wansink calls "mindless eating."[11] People don't usually start with a clear concept of how much they should be eating and then buy that much. They tend, rather, to eat what is put in front of them. Because of this, serving size has an incredibly powerful anchoring effect. At the time that Mayor Bloomberg announced his plans, the *smallest* drink you could buy at several fast-food chains in New York was 20 ounces, so the change in anchor brought about by the policy would have been quite significant.

Wansink has in fact done a large number of experiments on portion size, with results that all lean in the same direction. In one typical exercise, he gave adults attending a meeting a bag of M&M's on the way in. Some were given a half-pound bag of candies, others a one-pound bag. Those with the larger bags ate, on average, twice as much as those given the smaller bag (thereby consuming an extra 264 calories). In a second experiment, he gave more bags of M&Ms to two groups. The bags all contained 200 M&Ms, but for one group the candies were divided into 20 smaller bags, containing

10 each. The rest just got the 200 in a single bag. The group that had only one bag to open ate, on average, almost twice as many candies as those who had to open both the large and the portion-sized smaller bags.

The results on serving size and cognitive bias are incredibly consistent. If you give people food in a large package, they prepare more of it, serve more of it, and eat more of it. People will often leave some food behind on their plate, but they tend to calculate this as a fraction of the total amount served. Thus the amount that they eat is not an absolute quantity. If you give them a larger plate with more food on it, they eat more.[12]

Furthermore, these psychological effects are far more powerful in determining how much people eat than any nutritional information that is available to them. According to Wansink, as he researched the question, "it became clear to me that education—as defined by most experts—was not the answer . . . Clearly labeling calories and serving sizes is a good idea. But we have to be realistic about how much impact it will have on behavior. Most research shows that—outside of an artificial lab situation—labeling influences only a small minority of consumers."[13]

Indeed, an earlier New York City initiative that required all chain restaurants to clearly post the calorie count of every item on their menu had only a modest effect on consumer behavior.[14] In cases where it did lead to a significant difference in the number of calories consumed, this was typically because the obligation to post calorie information led restaurants to change their menus. (It is noteworthy that several restaurants preferred to withdraw certain items from their menu rather than admit publicly how many calories were in them. Also, it should be noted that there is some evidence to suggest that a simpler labeling scheme, in which foods are given green, yellow, and red stickers, depending upon how unhealthy they are, may be more effective.[15])

It is important to recognize that when people talk about an "epidemic of obesity," what they are really talking about is an epidemic of irrationality. Of those who are overweight, a significant fraction express a desire to lose weight, and large numbers actually attempt to do so, through diets and exercise plans of various sorts. At any given time, more than 40 million Americans are on a diet of some type or other. The problem is that they are unable to carry through on their intentions. People resolve to eat better and to exercise more, but they systematically fail to do so, primarily because of the "warp" in the way that we evaluate the future. Diabetes and heart disease are distant concerns, whereas food tempts us right here and now.

When it comes to accounting for this epidemic, it seems obvious that human beings have not changed: it is our environment that has changed. And it is not just that a greater variety of foodstuffs and food additives are available. It is that we live in an environment that systematically exploits every conceivable type of cognitive bias in order to undermine our self-control, in order to get us to eat more. Unfortunately, the traditional advice given to people tends to put all of the emphasis on individual will-power. This is based on the mistaken idea that self-control is located some-where "inside the head." The self-controlled person is usually seen as one who has a capacity to exercise tremendous willpower, not as one who is able to organize his life in such a way that he is not called upon to exercise tremendous willpower. This is extremely misleading. As often as not, what looks like willpower is actually the result of more or less well-orchestrated attempts by individuals to arrange their lives in ways that *economize* on willpower, by avoiding situations that call for its exercise.

Looking inside someone's office, their kitchen pantry, their bedroom, or even on their computer desktop, what one sees is an entire structure of cognitive and volitional scaffolding, a "system" that this person uses in order to accomplish (with varying degrees of success) routine tasks. Many aspects of the way that this environment is organized are intended to facilitate self-control.[16] People who are good at environmental manipulation try to organize their affairs in such a way as to make certain activities easier and others harder. Is the TV set in the bedroom or in front of the exercise equipment? Is the beer in the fridge or in the basement? Is the alarm clock beside the bed or across the room?

Wansink is one of the few who is aware of the importance of this, and so instead of the "New Year's resolution" model of self-control, he recommends instead that we "reengineer our personal food environment to help us and our families eat better."[17] The emphasis on environment is central. Some of the manipulations that he recommends are clever and quite subtle. He notes, for instance, that the size of plates and bowls has increased over the past few decades and that this has been shown to encourage overeating.[18] (When one knows that an appropriate-sized portion of meat is the size of a deck of playing cards and a single serving of pasta is the size of a tennis ball, it becomes apparent that most of the tableware sold in North America is far too large.) A simple remedy is just to buy smaller plates and bowls—from an antiques store, if necessary.

Unfortunately, not everyone is in a position to build themselves a little cocoon, a carefully controlled environment designed to keep the temptations of the outside world at bay. Furthermore, constructing such an environment takes considerable foresight. It also requires us to overcome the optimism bias that leads us to overestimate, time and time again, our own self-control. In other words, the type of personal qualities required to build the right kind of designer environment are precisely the qualities that are in short supply, which the environment is intended to correct. So it's difficult to get the whole project off the ground. Here we can see the central weakness in the idea of achieving self-control by engineering a "personal food environment." It limits us to the set of changes that we are able to make *as individuals*. It thereby neglects an incredibly powerful resource that we have available to help us, namely, *other people*.

§

One of the most unnatural features of modern urban environments is that we are constantly surrounded by strangers. This is not at all like the environment of evolutionary adaptation, and it can have all sorts of untoward effects. For example, a relative of mine discovered, after moving out of Toronto to live in a small town, that she became a far less aggressive driver. It wasn't because of the calming effects of the peaceful small-town lifestyle. It was because it dawned on her one day—much to her horror—that everyone in town knew what car she drove, so if she was spotted speeding through a school zone or accelerating into a yellow light, everyone would know it was her. The result was that she acted far less impulsively when she drove.

Of course, these systems of social control are precisely why many people find small-town life oppressive. It's one thing to have neighbors commenting on your driving, something else entirely to have them keeping tabs on your sex life. It is important to recognize, however, that all of this social structure can also serve as a self-control mechanism for the individual. Did my friend find it oppressive, having to drive more courteously? On the contrary, she described it as helping her to be the type of person that she wanted to be.

There is, in this respect, some truth to the conservative complaint about the way liberals seek to destigmatize various forms of failure, such as drug addiction, adultery, divorce, or long-term unemployment. The standard liberal argument is that these things are often not the person's fault, so society should not add insult to injury by making the person feel bad about it. And there is, of course, something right about this: some people are genetically predisposed toward alcoholism or drug abuse, women get abandoned by the fathers of their children, economic crises can throw millions out of work through no fault of their own, and so on. There is, however, a self-control dimension to each of these problems as well. Many people who are genetically predisposed toward alcoholism nevertheless avoid becoming addicted. Many women know, at some level, that the man they are with is unreliable, and so refrain from having children with him. The irony is that by reducing the level of social stigma associated with failure, liberals may inadvertently make it more difficult for people to exercise the self-control required to achieve these outcomes. That's because the stigma serves as an important piece of scaffolding; it gives people one more incentive to avoid becoming addicted, or a "cheater," or a deadbeat parent, or unemployed.

319

These cultural influences, however, pale in comparison to broader structural changes that are undoubtedly increasing the space of individual liberty but that at the same time tend to undermine self-control. Consider a simple vice like staying up late. One of the most peculiar trends in the United States has been a decrease in the average number of hours that people sleep (more than 30 percent of the population aged thirty to sixty-five report less than six hours per night of sleep on average), combined with growing complaints about tiredness.[19] Although some of this can be ascribed to longer work hours and commute times, it remains the case that Americans in this age group still manage to watch, on average, well over two hours of television per day. This suggests that for many people, staying up late may be a self-control problem.

As someone who is always staying up late, I can attest that poor self-control is a major factor. At two o'clock in the afternoon, when I am at work struggling to stay awake in the middle of some boring meeting or research presentation, I always resolve to go to bed earlier. It seems to me then that pursuing my late-night activities (which consist almost entirely of surfing the internet and playing video games) is far less important than being well rested and productive at work. And yet somehow, at midnight, faced with the prospect of turning off the computer and actually going to bed, I find myself remembering one more site that I haven't checked, or wanting to make it to just one more save point, or wanting to stay on the server just until the next map change. The "greater good" of being well rested at work seems like a distant concern, easily overwhelmed by what-ever mildly stimulating thing I happen to be doing at the moment.

I'm old enough to remember a time when going to bed was much, much easier. First of all, there was no internet, and there were no video game consoles. Even TV, that great time sponge, used to stop at a certain point, sometime around midnight. I can't remember the number of times I watched the national anthem all the way through to the end, until the station actually switched off and went to the test pattern. At about the same time, bars and restaurants would all close, the subway would shut down and buses would stop running. There was a clear message in all of this: "Time to go to bed." This message was also quite easy to comply with, because there was almost nothing else to do. The only other option was to read a book, which is usually a good way of falling asleep anyhow.

Since that time the world has changed to a remarkable degree: stores are open at all hours, the internet never sleeps, entertainment is available at any time, in any form. Each one of these changes has resulted in an expansion of choice and, in some respects, personal freedom. Yet it has also created an environment that is more taxing, by transferring the burden of self-control from society to the individual. In the same way that the twenty-four-hour beer store is a mixed blessing to the alcoholic and legalized casinos are a burden for the problem gambler, twenty-four-hour television—or, worse, the internet—can easily become a curse for the insomniac. It is therefore perfectly natural when we look at the way the built environment is organized to consider the implications that it has not only for freedom of choice, but also for self-control. Furthermore, we might reasonably choose *not* to make certain changes, precisely because they would undermine self-control to an unacceptable degree.

¶

Judging by the hysterical reaction to Bloomberg's proposed soda ban, we have a long way to go before the "mindful reengineering" of the food environment that Wansink calls for can occur in the public sphere. Just recently I was in the Philadelphia airport, drinking a cup of coffee, when I thought it might be nice to have a chocolate bar to go with it. I got up and poked my nose into a few shops, where I discovered, to my surprise, that it is no longer possible to buy a regular-sized chocolate bar anywhere in the departures area of the Philadelphia airport. The only thing being sold were the outrageous new "king-sized" bars, which are about twice the size of the old-fashioned ones. I felt like a bit of a naif, but I was actually somewhat

321

shocked that in the midst of all the public debate about obesity and portion size, the food industry would go ahead and not only upsize chocolate bars, but actually stop selling the smaller ones.[20]

I have no idea whether it was the retailers or the manufacturers behind this, but faced with this kind of uncooperative behavior, many people will naturally want to see increased legal regulation. The central objection, however, to legal regulation of things like portion size is that it is an exercise in legal paternalism. A law is considered paternalistic when it stops you from doing something not because the activity causes harm to someone else, but because it is not good for *you*. Mandatory motorcycle helmet laws are the stock example. If you ask, "Why am I being forced to wear a helmet?" the answer will be "It's for your own good." (Whenever the justification for a law includes the phrase "for your own good," that's a clear sign that it is paternalistic.) The problem with such laws is that they raise the obvious objection, "If it's for my own good, then why do I need to be forced?"

The most influential arguments against paternalism were provided by the nineteenth-century philosopher John Stuart Mill. In *On Liberty,* Mill argued that there is something problematic about the way the state substitutes its own judgment for that of the individual when deciding what is good for that person. In order for the law to be worthwhile, it would have to be the case both that the person is actually making a mistake about where her own good lies and that the state is in a better position to judge the issue correctly. This is, Mill argues, rather unlikely, since "with respect to his own feelings and circumstances, the most ordinary man or woman has means of knowledge immeasurably surpassing those that can be possessed by any one else."[21] What is presented as a case of a person making an *error* is therefore more likely to be just a case of two people having a *disagreement.* With respect to motorcycle helmets, for instance, some people obviously think that personal safety is extremely important. Other people may not be so concerned with personal safety, but may think that looking cool is extremely important. So they may choose not to wear a helmet simply because they don't value safety that highly. (And who's to say that they are wrong? Maybe they are desperate to start a family, and looking cool is the only way to attract a mate.)

Modern studies of cognitive bias, however, present a challenge to Mill's argument. If our mistakes were random and unpredictable, then it's true that the state would have a hard time second-guessing an individual's own judgment. For every one or two times that officials got it right, there would be a half-dozen times they got it wrong, so the net effect would be negative. The whole idea of cognitive *bias*, however, is that people make systematic errors in their reasoning, errors that are, as a result, highly predictable. This means that when dealing with irrationality, paternalistic legislation may actually be able to produce a net benefit.

Looking around, it's easy to see that a lot of rules and regulations currently in place are paternalistic. Consider the case of restaurant inspectors. Where I live, inspectors give restaurants a grade of green, yellow, or red (on a sign that each restaurant is obliged to post in the front window), where green indicates a pass, yellow indicates some minor infractions, and red means that there are major food safety or hygiene violations. And yet it is noteworthy that when the inspectors give a restaurant a red grade, the restaurant is forced to shut down until it can demonstrate that the problems have been resolved.

Why shut down the restaurant? One would think that just posting the red sign in the front window would be enough. If people still wanted to eat there knowing that there were serious health infractions on the premises, shouldn't that be their business? Closing down the restaurant seems to be a clear violation of the prohibition on paternalistic uses of state power.

The problem is that potential customers are subject to a number of cognitive biases and misfires, so if we didn't give inspectors the power to close down the restaurant, too many people would make decisions that they would later regret. First of all, people don't take germs and toxins as seriously as they should. Our natural heuristics classify certain things as "gross" and generate a disgust reaction that make us unwilling to eat them. But this is an extremely coarse-grained system, and it is useless at detecting a number of common food toxins (including various dangerous strains of *E. coli*). So people are likely to say "the food looks fine" or "the food tastes great" and infer on that basis that it is safe to consume. They are also likely to exhibit optimism bias, and so assume that *they* are less likely to be affected ("I have a strong stomach"). Finally, and most importantly, they are often *hungry* by the time they arrive at the restaurant. So while they may see the red sign on the way in, they are also likely to assign too much value to eating right *now* and too little concern to the repercussions of that decision the following day.

So we have a paternalistic rule in place, not so much because some bureaucratic busybodies want to impose their standards on others, but because we can all see that the rule prevents us from making a rash or intemperate decision. It protects us from our own irrationality. What makes this type of paternalism different from the kind that Mill criticized is that we are subject to a restriction not just for our own good, but for our own good *as we ourselves conceive it both before and after the fact* (or our own good as we would conceive it if we sat down and thought about it sometime when we weren't hungry). The reason we need the law—the external scaffolding—is because our conception of the good is not always sufficient to govern our behavior, and hence can fail us at the point of decision.

It is, of course, important not to get too enthusiastic about paternalistic institutions. The willingness of courts to strike down paternalistic legislation in the twentieth century is one of the major reasons that we now enjoy many of the freedoms that we do, particularly in the area of sexuality. At the same time, it is important to recognize that relatively small manipulations—which generate only very slight interferences with individual liberty—can have large effects when it comes to promoting the overall good. For example, in states that have an "opt-out" system for organ donation, rates of organ donation typically exceed 90 percent, whereas in states that have an "opt-in" system, rates seldom exceed 20 percent. There is no reason to think that this reflects a difference in values between these different countries; it is entirely a product of the default rule. In one case, it is a bit of a hassle to donate your organs; in the other it is a bit of a hassle to *not* donate your organs. As Cass Sunstein and Richard Thaler have pointed out, since *any* system will need to have a default option, we may as well make the most beneficial option the default one.[22]

Sunstein and Thaler introduce the term *choice architecture* to describe "the context in which people make decisions."[23] Because people are influenced by a huge range of factors, changing the choice architecture can lead to huge shifts in the actual choices that people make, even without significantly altering the incentives. For example, some pension plans in the United States require workers to fill out some paperwork in order to enroll. A surprisingly large number of workers fail to do so, even when it means forfeiting matching contributions from their employer. They just never get around to it. If the system is rearranged so that participation in the plan is the default and those who want to opt out must complete the paperwork, then far more workers participate. In a sense, it is absurd for people to leave hundreds, often thousands of dollars on the table just because they can't be bothered to fill out some forms. But they do it all the time.

Sunstein and Thaler initially called this manipulation of default rules *libertarian paternalism,* on the grounds that it constituted *no* interference with individual liberty whatsoever. They later relented, and decided to call it *nudge paternalism.* A nudge, in their view, "is any aspect of choice architecture that alters people's behavior in a predictable way without forbidding any options or significantly changing their economic incentives. To count as a mere nudge, the intervention must be easy and cheap to avoid."[24]

The key idea here is that a nudge does not "significantly" alter people's economic incentives—or, one might be incline to say, "objectively," because at the point of decision it does alter their incentives in a significant way: it changes their behavior! Filling out paperwork is a type of cost—not always an economic one, but still a cost. It is both time-consuming and psychologically taxing. So an opt-in system essentially discourages people from joining by imposing a paperwork requirement on them. Changing the system to opt-out reassigns the cost. It just doesn't seem like a big deal, because it is so insignificant compared to the amount of money at stake. Nevertheless, if it weren't a real cost, then reassigning it would make no difference to peoples' decisions.

So what Sunstein and Thaler are really recommending is that we organize our external choice environment in such a way as to make our irrationality "a remedy unto itself" (as Hume put it). We are too short-sighted to care enough about our retirement *and* we are too lazy to do paperwork. By making it so that we have to do some paperwork in order to reduce our retirement savings, we use one form of irrationality to cancel out the other one. Laziness becomes a cure for shortsightedness.

Mayor Bloomberg's proposed soda ban is an example of nudge paternalism. It doesn't actually stop anyone from drinking large quantities of soda (especially since many American restaurants offer free refills). But if it ever comes into effect, it will change behavior in three ways. First, the anchoring effect of the smaller cup will lead people to drink less, by changing their perception of how much normal human beings drink. Second, while they can always go and get more soda, they will often be too lazy to get up, and so will stop drinking once they have finished their 10 ounces. And finally, in cases where someone really does have a powerful thirst, and so buys two 10-ounce sodas, it will raise the cost slightly, by eliminating the volume discount that large portions enjoy.

Of course, a more straightforward approach is simply to impose a tax on sugared drinks (something that is being contemplated in various parts of Europe, such as France). This is a very attractive tax for a number of reasons, including the fact that it is incredibly easy to specify what products should be subject to it (unlike, say, a tax on "deep-fried" food, which is more difficult to define). This might seem like old-fashioned paternalism, but in reality it's not all that different from nudge paternalism. The only difference is that instead of increasing the "psychological cost" of drinking too much soda, it increases the economic cost.

Thus nudge paternalism is, in a sense, a case of old wine in new bottles. What is new is the attention to the choice environment, along with the recognition that the way a choice looks to an objective observer may be very different from the way that it looks to someone actually confronting the choice.

¶

Greater attention to these elements of choice architecture, with an eye toward helping people to make what they themselves acknowledge to be the right choices, has the potential to greatly improve the performance of our cognitive system. There is a useful analogy to be drawn between the way that social institutions should be organized and the way that technology is designed. When it comes to computers and other electronic gadgets, a very sophisticated discussion has arisen around the idea of making interfaces "user friendly." It is generally recognized that if engineers and programmers are left free to design the interface, it will be quite logical but, precisely for that reason, user *unfriendly*. It will be unintuitive. The user will have to look things up in a manual in order to figure out how to get it to work. It will put excessive demands on working memory, by requiring the user to memorize commands. Figuring it out will require explicit learning and the development of expertise.

The ideal interface is one where the user never has to consult a manual, because she can simply guess how it works. Building such an interface requires a thorough understanding of human cognitive biases, limitations, and quirks. It will use visual memory or gestures instead of sequences of linguistic symbols, in order to avoid the limitations of working memory. It will tap into the associations that people already have from interacting with the world, in order to help them guess how to get various things done in the virtual environment. It will be organized in such a way that a person will get the results that she desires by doing what feels intuitively right or what is easiest.

Social institutions should be user friendly in exactly the same way: they should transform our weaknesses and biases into strengths. Unfortunately, most are not. Many are designed to work contrary to the individual's interests—they are user-*hostile,* in the sense that they try to trick people into doing the wrong thing. Even in the public sector, where the incentive to take advantage of the user is at least diminished, almost no attention is paid to the choice architecture. Most of these institutions are user-*unfriendly,* in the sense that they are designed by technocrats without regard for the limitations of the typical user. Of course, unfriendly is better than hostile. Nevertheless, a lot more could be done to enhance the efficacy with which individuals can interact with these institutions.

Within the field of design, there been a long-standing emphasis on the relationship between human cognitive systems and the built environment, with a relentless focus on structuring the environment in such a way as to amplify our abilities, to make us more capable and more effective in our interventions. Under the rubric of "cognitive design," an extremely sophisticated discussion has developed about ways of making our biases work for us, rather than against us. The consequences of this can be seen all around. It is an astonishing thing to watch a four-year-old sit down in front of an iPad and figure out on her own how to work the interface. This is truly the pinnacle of good design. We might dream about a day when an equally concerted effort is made to improve our social institutions, in order to achieve the same effortless integration. The ideal would be a world in which we work together to create environments that make us smarter, instead of environments that makes us dumber, not just with the objects that we manipulate but with the institutions with which we interact.

13. Small steps to a saner world

The Slow Politics Manifesto

When thinking about how to create a more hospitable environment for the exercise of reason, it is important never to forget the value of a good kluge. We often have a choice between *forcing* ourselves to act rationally and *tricking* ourselves into acting rationally. The former is usually better for our self-esteem, but the latter is often more effective. (Compare: I have a bad memory. One evening, I come across a paper that I need to bring to the office the next morning. What do I do? I could try to make myself remember to bring it, through some kind of memory exercise or conditioning. Or I could just take the paper and lean it against the front door, so that when I leave for work in the morning it will be in my way. I do the latter—it works much better. It is the perfect example of what David Allen is referring to when he talks about the "smart part of you" setting things up so that the "not-so-smart part of you" responds correctly.[1])

This insight becomes even more important when we realize that reason is subject to a budget constraint. People can only handle being rational so much of the time. This means that it is important to pick our battles, both as individuals and as a society. We can spend only so much time and energy overriding our intuitions and impulses before we run out of steam. So if there are some situations that would require a huge amount of self-control to power our way through without error but that can as a whole easily be avoided, we are far better off just avoiding them. Mohandas Gandhi, for example, used to demonstrate his capacity for sexual abstinence and marital fidelity by sleeping between two naked young women. Most men, to the extent that they are able to achieve marital fidelity, do so by *avoiding* situations in which they find themselves lying in bed between two naked young women. It is not obvious that the latter strategy is in any way inferior.

We can often achieve the outcome that reason recommends by turning our own irrationality against itself. Instead of buying a bunch of snack food then trying not to eat it, just don't buy it. Suddenly, the fact that you're too lazy to walk to the corner store—in itself a failure of self-control—becomes an indirect means of exercising self-control.

§

Consider the eternal problem of race in America. This is an area where liberals have expended a huge amount of energy, insisting that people adopt a more rational basis for their evaluation of individuals. And yet it is hardly an exaggeration to say that all of our social instincts are "groupish," in particular our tendency toward in-group bias. This means that liberals, in demanding universalism with respect to race, commit themselves to making—and recommend to others—a huge investment in overriding their intuitive responses and natural biases. This can create an enormous amount of psychic tension.

The philosopher Iris Marion Young provided a classic formulation of the liberal demand: "Unconscious racism, sexism, homophobia, ageism, and ableism occur not only in bodily reactions and feelings and their expression in behavior, but also in judgments about people or policies. When public morality is committed to principles of equal treatment and the equal worth of all persons, public morality requires that judgments about the superiority or inferiority of persons be made on an individual basis according to individual competences."[2]

Without disagreeing with the basic sentiment expressed here, I think it's important to recognize is that Young is basically demanding that people stop using an entire part of their brain. Our heuristic reasoning is powered by pattern recognition and association. When applied to social interaction, this makes us natural stereotypers. When we see people, we classify them automatically and without conscious thought. This primes us to remember certain things, feel certain ways, and expect certain actions. Some of these associations are positive; some are inevitably negative. When they are negative, you get all the "isms" on the list that Young rattled off, and more.

Because of this, the difference between people who are racist (or sexist, or homophobic, etc.) and people who are not racist is typically not that the former engage in stereotyping while the latter do not. Everyone engages in stereotyping; the only difference is how far people go to suppress or override it. A lot of energy has been invested by psychologists in showing that even people who do not have overtly racist attitudes nevertheless have underlying racist sentiments and reactions, which they are constantly having to suppress. (There are some very fine-grained experimental methods that demonstrate this quite clearly. When people are suppressing a thought it slows them down, so if you show them a picture, followed by a word-selection task, you can tell by reaction time when they are vetoing their initial impulse.[3])

Thus the demand that evaluation of persons should be done "on an individual basis according to individual competences" is extremely difficult to live up to, depending on the circumstances. In a work environment, where a manager has ample opportunity to observe the capacities and performance of an individual employee over time, it is relatively simple. But in a job interview, when a manager has ten minutes to assess a potential applicant, it becomes a great deal more difficult. When someone brushes past you on the street, it is impossible.

In one respect, this news is depressing. There is a long-standing debate about whether racism is something natural or whether it is taught. What has been demonstrated without a doubt is that the way people divide into groups, generating both heightened solidarity within the group and antagonism toward people outside the group, is about as innate as things get and is highly resistant to change. Even if you put people together who are almost completely identical or who are deprived of the usual markers of status and identity, they will find some kind of difference, then use it as a basis for invidious comparison. And while reason may tell us that these divisions are arbitrary, our gut is able to invest powerful emotional significance in them. This lends support to the view that people are, if not naturally racist, then at least naturally ethnocentric.

That's the bad news. The good news, however, is that while in-group bias is both innate and psychologically powerful, the characteristic that we zero in on, when distinguishing in-group from out-group, *appears to be unspecified.* What psychologists have found, again and again, is that our sense of group membership is remarkably easy to manipulate and can easily be evoked by traits that individuals themselves know to be inessential. Even just giving people a group label, like "X" or "W," can be enough to do the trick.[4] Group identity and classification seems to be driven not by characteristics that are "important" in some absolute sense, but by whatever characteristic is most *salient* at the time of judgment.

This suggests that, despite the powerful in-group bias, people are not naturally racist. (From an evolutionary perspective, why would they be? There were no different races in the environment of evolutionary adaptation, since there was no interaction between people from geographically distant populations.) People will be racist only if race is made salient when it comes to the formation of groups. If you give them some other basis of identification (e.g., Cubs fans versus White Sox fans), then they may no longer be racist. Certain differences, such as speaking a different language, will always be difficult to ignore, and so possess intrinsic salience. But racial differences are not of this sort. This creates the possibility of spoofing the in-group solidarity system, just by distracting it from racial differences and feeding it some other basis of classification.

Psychologists Robert Kurzban, John Tooby, and Leda Cosmides conducted a series of experiments that demonstrated this in a particularly clever way.[5] They showed participants a series of videos of people speaking, then gave them a surprise memory test afterward, asking them to match sentences to the picture of the person who said it. By looking at the pattern of mistakes, one can discover how people "encode" or classify individuals. For example, a person may not be able to remember exactly who said a particular sentence, but may remember that it was a woman. Thus if there were four male and four female speakers, subjects would be more likely to confuse what one woman said with what another woman said, rather than with what a man had said.

What the investigators found was that, barring other criteria, test subjects had a strong propensity to classify speakers not only by gender and age, but also by race. But this could be overwhelmed by the simple expedient of giving some speakers grey T-shirts and others yellow ones. With this manipulation, subjects looking to find a coalitional pattern among the speakers quickly learned to ignore race and to focus on shirt color. What is striking is that they continued to encode speakers just as strongly by gender, but once they began to notice shirt color and to suspect that shirt color determined which group the speaker belonged to, they began to pay a lot less attention to the race of the speaker. This suggests that when people fixate on race, they are actually not all that interested in race; what they are really interested in is group membership, and they are picking up on race because it seems like the most salient cue. Give them some other, more salient cue, and they will fixate on that.

There is a classic *Star Trek* episode that illustrates the principle quite nicely.[6] It begins with the USS *Enterprise* rescuing a refugee from an unexplored planet whose inhabitants have an unusual pigmentation pattern that makes one side of their body black and the other side white. Shortly after the rescue, a second spaceship shows up, containing a law enforcement official from the same planet, who demands the right to extradite the refugee, accusing him of fomenting rebellion on their home planet. The two bicker and fight, and over time it becomes apparent that they are bitter enemies, from two different social classes in their world that have been at war for ages. Each one insists that he has nothing in common with the other, much to the consternation of the crew of the *Enterprise,* who can see no difference between them. Finally, the official explains what he thought would have been obvious to everyone with eyes to see: that while he is black on the *left* side and white on the *right,* his enemy is black on the *right* side and white on the *left.*

What makes this little twist so effective is that as soon as he points it out, you (the viewer) realize that it's obvious. It's not even a small difference—it's actually quite a large difference, one that you've been staring at for over forty minutes without noticing. But because we tend to think in black/white racial terms, color is the only thing that is *salient* to us, and so all we saw were people who were half black, half white.

There is a very astute insight here into the psychology of race. What matters is not so much the differences between individuals but which differences we choose to invest significance in. This is the good news on race. It suggests that the best way to overcome race may simply be to distract people from it. If there is nothing else to attract people's attention, the set of physical characteristics that distinguish race will be regarded as significant, but this can be overcome by reducing the salience of these characteristics. There is probably nothing we can do to stop people from classifying others into groups and developing animosity toward those whom they regard as belonging to an out-group. Yet even if we are unable to change this basic feature of human psychology, we can develop an effective work-around, by manipulating the environment so that people classify each other in ways that are less socially pernicious. For example, instead of allowing people to fixate on inherited features of individuals—such as skin color—we could encourage them to focus on arbitrary or symbolic features—like hair style. The advantage of hair style is that it can easily be changed, and so does not translate into permanent disadvantage for any class of individuals.

This may explain why the military and sports teams have been far more successful at creating racial integration than many other institutions in American life. What distinguishes both of them is that they cultivate very intense, particularistic loyalties. There is good reason to think that these forms of group identification simply crowd out the other ones based on race. This can be far more effective than asking people to subscribe to some universalist ideal, one that forces them to overcome or suppress their "groupish" instincts.[7]

From this perspective, the real problem in America is not so much racism as it is race *consciousness*. (Indeed, to any non-American, the most oppressive feature of intercultural relations in America is not that people are racist, but just that they talk and think incessantly about race, even worse than the way the English talk and think incessantly about class.) And yet this feature of American culture seems to be one that everyone, white and black, conservative and liberal, is involved in a giant conspiracy to sustain and reinforce. This is because most Americans who are progressive on the subject believe that racism must be overcome directly, and that this can only be done by increasing sensitivity and awareness of racial differ- ence. A lot of progressive black politics has done the same, by rejecting the older ideal of a "color-blind" society and insisting upon the recognition and affirmation of a positive black identity. This winds up being an inadvertent recipe for the reproduction of racism. Even though the intention is to cre- ate a positive group identity, its dominant effect is to make race *salient* as a basis of group identity, which means that it will also, inevitably, become a locus of negative valuation for some.[8]

¶

None of this discussion so far speaks to the problem that sparked the initial demand for a return to reason, and that is the epidemic of craziness that seems to have swept over the American political landscape. This is of course a problem not just for Americans, but for people all around the world. It remains the case that most people think of the United States as the world's leading democracy. Although they may not choose to imitate many of the specific features of American democratic institutions, the prestige of democracy around the world is very much tied up with the performance of the American system. When this political system proves demonstrably incapable of keeping charlatans, conspiracy theorists, and religious fanatics out of political power, this is a huge blow to the prestige of democratic systems as a whole.

To see the problem that this creates, consider the situation in China, where plenty of people have very reasonable concerns about the possible consequences of democratization and whether it would be, on the whole, good for their country. Defenders of the existing system, such as Zhang Weiwei, put the argument in exactly these terms: "Despite its well-known strengths, liberal democracy as an institution has been seriously eroded by such persistent problems as demagoguery, short-termism, simple-minded populism, the excessive influence of money and the role played by special interests . . . the Chinese system of meritocracy makes it inconceivable that anyone as incompetent as America's George W. Bush or Japan's Yoshihiko Noda could ever get to the top."[9] The more degraded and corrupt American democracy becomes, the more difficult it becomes to argue for democracy—even if many of the conditions in the United States are a consequence of unusual features of that particular political system, which need not be imitated elsewhere.

Contemporary apostles of democracy often like to wax rhapsodically about the origins of Western civilization in Athens during the classical period. They point to democracy as one of the preconditions for the great flowering of science, art, philosophy, and mathematics that occurred during that period. They often forget to mention that the great philosophers of ancient Athens—Socrates, Plato, and Aristotle—were quite hostile to democracy. Their central objection to popular rule was that they regarded it as unstable. The figure that they feared most was that of the *demagogue,* the unscrupulous individual who could gain power by appealing to the emotions and prejudices of the people. For Plato in particular, it was this vulnerability to demagoguery that was the fatal flaw in democratic political systems.

From this perspective, it is more than a bit disconcerting to observe that modern democratic politics, particularly in America, has devolved into all demagoguery all the time, and that members of the pundit class—from David Brooks to Margaret Wente—have been mining contemporary psychology to argue that this is not just an aberration or even a problem, but that it is simply the human condition. If people are nothing more than a bundle of emotions and prejudices, what harm could there be in appealing to these emotions and prejudices as a way of getting elected? And besides, if your opponent is doing it, what choice do you have?

This line of argument has made it difficult to see the current situation as a problem, and even more difficult to start looking for solutions.

One of the reasons that modern democracies are able to survive despite this epidemic of demagoguery is that they have a wide range of institutions that insulate political decision making from direct democratic control (all of which were absent in ancient Athens). The biggest difference is that our democracy is representative, rather than direct, which means that citizens only choose leaders; they do not (except in exceptional circumstances, such as referenda) vote on policy. Beyond this, the mere fact of having written laws, applied impartially, which are time-consuming and difficult to change, lends stability to the system. Then there is the institution of judicial review, which permits unelected judges to strike down legislation that is deemed to involve misuse of state power—either because it violates individual rights or because it fails to respect the division of powers within a federal system. There are many other, less obvious arrangements as well. Almost every democracy has moved to an arrangement in which the central bank operates with almost complete independence from the government of the day. This is important because the central bank is often called upon to pursue unpopular policies, such as maintaining high interest rates to control inflation. That would be very difficult to do if central bank decisions were subject to direct popular or legislative control. There is no justification for this arrangement other than the recognition that if the public did have control over the central bank—as various populist movements have at various times demanded—they would make terrible decisions.

Thus it is important to recognize that modern democratic political systems involve a delicate compromise between, on the one hand, the desire for public control of decision making and, on the other hand, the need for rational, coherent policy. Democracies need to be democratic, but they also need to *work,* in the sense that they need to produce a state that effectively discharges its responsibilities. Thus they have a variety of institutional features that allow them to function even when the democratic public sphere is completely degraded. They do so largely by shifting power and control away from elected representatives toward experts. Even in the United States, where this is difficult to do, one can find examples all over. The most obvious is the enormous role that the Supreme Court has played in making decisions that, in most other democracies, would be left to the legislature. But one can see it in other areas as well, such as the amount of autonomy that government agencies have or the increased use of cost-benefit analysis in public decision making.

If one looks, for example, at the record of regulatory decision making by the Environmental Protection Agency in the United States, one can see that it tracks very closely the level of *public concern* over various hazardous substances. The problem is that the level of public concern bears very little relationship to how hazardous various substances actually are.[10] To pick just one example, the public cares very little about radon gas in their homes, despite the fact that it is the second leading cause of lung cancer (after smoking). It is certainly far more dangerous than second-hand cigarette smoke. The problem is that, unlike cigarette smoke, it is colorless and odorless, and is therefore difficult to get anyone to worry about. Experts, however, consider it a serious problem. Thus the requirement that all new environmental regulations pass a cost-benefit test winds up giving greater authority to expert judgment and diminishes the impact of public pressure.

So one solution to the problem of demagoguery is simply to have less democracy, and to hand decisions over to experts. This solution has certain advantages (indoor radon gas levels are more likely to be checked) but many well-known disadvantages. A more attractive solution is to improve the quality of democratic deliberation, or at least to provide preconditions for more rational debate. As a matter of fact, many of the complex and arcane procedures involved in democratic decision making are designed to do just this.

As we have seen, one of the most important features of reason is that it is slow. This is true not only of the operations of individual brains, but also of the social processes of contestation and dialogue that serve as a check on individual bias. Thus one way in which democratic institutions enhance the quality of decision making is simply by slowing down the process. The most obvious example of this is bicameralism—the practice of having two legislative bodies, the "house" and the "senate," both of which must pass a bill before it becomes law. In Canada, where the Senate is unelected and almost never vetoes legislation, there is an obvious question as to what purpose it serves. (And so political parties on the left and right, which tend to be more populist in orientation than parties in the center, want to either abolish it or see its members be elected.) Yet the existing Senate serves an important purpose in the mere fact that it slows down the legislative process. (This is why it is often called the chamber of "sober second thought.") With two legislative houses and a complicated process whereby bills have to go back and forth between them, undergoing multiple "readings," both legislators and the public at large have a chance to go through things carefully, to think about and debate the consequences of a bill. Furthermore, the slowness of the procedure gives the public a chance to mobilize around the issue, for debate to occur. So even if the second chamber does nothing to make the legislative process more democratic, it can nevertheless make it more *rational*.

Popular democratic theory, however, puts a huge amount of emphasis on the practice of voting and comparatively little emphasis on argumentation and debate. One of the glaring deficiencies of the American political system, for instance, is that the president is never forced to engage in debate with other legislators and is never forced to answer any question he doesn't want to answer. In the British parliamentary system, the prime minister has to show up in the House of Commons when it is in session and defend the policies of the government. He or she is there treated like any other member of Parliament, and thus jeered, heckled, and challenged by members of the opposition. For this reason, and despite how degraded the spectacle has become over time, "question period and debate institutionalize doubt and scepticism in the political system."[11]

The American president, by contrast, is like an elected monarch. Once a year he gives a speech to the House of Representatives, but no one has a chance to challenge anything he says to his face, and it becomes a national incident if the assembled legislators fail to show the utmost deference and respect. Apart from that, the only time that the American president has to answer questions is at press conferences. This is a disastrous arrangement, because it means that almost all public communication between the president and legislators is filtered through the media (and is therefore biased in the direction of talking points, sound-bites, and all the other tricks politicians use to get the media to say what they want them to say). If a reporter misbehaves or asks too difficult a question, or presses an issue too far, then she simply won't be called on again, and may not even be invited back. Furthermore, the president is under no obligation to take questions if he doesn't want to. Ronald Reagan, during his final two years in office, all but stopped holding press conferences. This was at a time when there were serious questions about his mental competence, and yet Americans had no way of assessing his state of mind. In retrospect, there seems to be little doubt that, had he been forced to enter a "parliamentary bear pit"[12] every week the way the British prime minister is, he could not have survived his second term in office.

In January 2010, House Republicans took the unusual step of inviting President Obama to address their caucus retreat in Baltimore, after which the president spent over an hour responding to questions *directly from legislators.* Two things about this were noteworthy. First, Americans from one end of the country to the other were astonished by the lucidity of the exchanges. What they were used to seeing was the president and the members of Congress exchanging barbs through the media. Seeing the president able to respond to questions *directly* was a revelation. Second, there was the fact that President Obama completely eviscerated his opponents—to the point where Fox News cut off the live broadcast, in order to save the Republican Party from further embarrassment. The major reason is that most of the Republican legislators did what they were accustomed to doing, which is use their questions as an opportunity to spout talking points. They didn't realize that this only works as a media tactic; it doesn't work in a face-to-face exchange with a political opponent, particularly one who can take as much time as he likes to respond.

Because it went so badly for them, Republicans never invited Obama back. Therein lies the central problem with the American presidential system: this kind of exchange is *optional.* In most other democracies, this kind of exchange is institutionalized as a requirement. As it stands, the American political system simply lacks any mechanism to force the president and legislators to explain themselves or their actions *to one another.* This makes the "norm of truth" very difficult to enforce, and in turn encourages the slow descent into truthiness. The point is that irrationalism is not an inevitable consequence of the modern condition; it is in many respects a consequence of the institutions we have chosen. Furthermore, it's not that difficult to think of institutional changes that would increase the role of reason in American political discourse. The problem is that people haven't been thinking about this question because they fail to see how the exercise of reason depends upon its environment. Al Gore's book *The Assault on Reason,* for example, contains the usual complaints about the media but has nothing at all to say about how American political institutions are organized. It simply doesn't occur to Gore that if the government were held accountable by the *opposition,* rather than just the media, and if political debate occurred among legislators with the status and authority to challenge each other, then a lot of the problems he is complaining about would be diminished.

Parliamentary democracies are, of course, not immune to many of the same problems that have bedeviled the American system. In particular, there has been a huge decline in the cognitive content of "question period" or "question time." Much of this was precipitated by the introduction of television cameras, which encouraged legislators to shift away from argumentation and debate toward short, emotional sound-bites—the sort of thing that plays well on television. This, however, is not impossible to remedy. The obvious recourse is simply to remove the television cameras. Short of that, there are already multiple restrictions on what the cameras can record and how the footage can be used. One could simply add the restriction that broadcasters are not allowed to reproduce segments of less than one minute in length. Similarly, the British system that requires submission of questions in advance is demonstrably superior because it diminishes the temptation to go for "gotcha" questions and allows for the preparation of more intelligent responses.

§

Criticizing the American political system has, unfortunately, become something of a mug's game, simply because the deficiencies are all mutually reinforcing, and so no matter how much sense it would make to change one thing or another, nothing is going to get fixed. Campaign finance reform might be a good idea, as would an end to the gerrymandering of electoral districts, but it's difficult to see any plausible sequence of events that could lead to that outcome. In order to change these things, you would need to elect a president and a *lot* of legislators intent on changing them, and that's unlikely to happen, precisely *because* of existing campaign finance arrangements and gerrymandering. This is why some Americans have begun to argue seriously for a constitutional convention that would look at reforming American institutions from the ground up—simply because there is no path that leads from the existing institutional arrangements to a better set through incremental change. But of course, there is no path that leads from the existing institutional arrangement to a constitutional convention either, so the whole discussion is pie in the sky.

There are, however, a few tweaks that are not entirely outside the realm of possibility that could lead to a slight increase in the sanity of public discourse in America. For example, while the media has its shortcomings throughout the world, broadcast news in America is especially bad, and it's difficult to say exactly why. The insistence on providing saturation coverage of sensational but ultimately unimportant stories has become almost perverse in its intensity. More subtlely, American journalists have a peculiar habit of interviewing each other rather than independent experts, making the entirely media universe something of closed loop. When discussing the federal budget, for instance, they will often put together panels consisting entirely of lobbyists and other journalists. It is relatively rare to see an actual economist (with the exception of Paul Krugman, who typically appears in his capacity as a *New York Times* columnist, not as an economist). This seems to be just a part of the culture of American journalism—public television is nearly as bad as private—and it's difficult to see what could be done about it.

There are some other more obvious problems. The creation of straight-up propaganda networks like Fox News in America has done enormous damage to the quality of democratic discourse in that country. Many people blame the abolition of the Federal Communications Commission's

"Fairness Doctrine" in 1987, under President Reagan, for setting this process of degeneration in motion. This rule had required broadcasters, both radio and television, to inform their audience about matters of public interest, and specified that "coverage of these issues must be fair in the sense that it provides an opportunity for . . . contrasting points of view."[13] This doctrine was, over the years, unpopular with both the left and right, depending on the tenor of discussion in the media. It seems clear, however, that a lot of current right-wing talk radio, as well as Fox News, could not operate as it currently does without the abolition of this rule.

Because of this, Democratic legislators periodically attempt to revive the rule, prompting outrage among conservatives. And there are some obvious problems with it. Not only is the rule exceedingly vague, but it encourages the type of "opinions on the shape of the earth differ" reporting that makes it difficult to hold people to account for lying. Most other developed countries, by contrast, have narrower rules that focus specifically on lying and misrepresentation. The European Parliament, for instance, has passed a resolution specifying that "news broadcasting should be based on truthfulness, ensured by the appropriate means of verification and proof, and impartiality in presentation, description and narration."[14] In the United Kingdom, the Broadcasting Code requires that "news, in whatever form, must be reported with due accuracy and presented with due impartiality." Canada has a rule (enforced by the Canadian Radio-television Communications Commission) that simply prohibits the intentional, repeated broadcast of "false or misleading news." This type of constraint is more easily defended than the Fairness Doctrine, since it is closer in spirit to the laws governing false advertising. And yet the Canadian rule is strong enough to have so far prevented Fox News from expanding into that market.

Many of the problems with news networks are similar to the ones posed by political advertising, which constitutes a huge challenge to the quality of democratic discourse but which is very difficult to do anything about. Typically, attempts to limit advertising focus on controlling the amount of money that can be spent (through spending limits and constraints on donations, which have, in effect, now been completely abolished in the United States). Another approach might be to focus on the impact that political advertising has on the rationality of public discourse. The most obvious and uncontroversial reform would be to hold political advertising to the same "false advertising" standards that ordinary commercial advertising is expected to satisfy. Companies are subject to fairly strict rules when it comes to the claims that they make in their advertisements—even statements that are true and yet misleading may be prohibited. Political advertising, on the other hand, is basically subject to no constraints. Certain practices, such as editing a recording of one's opponent's speech, removing words in order to change the meaning of a sentence, are so obviously deceptive that it is difficult to believe they are legal in any jurisdiction. The telling of obvious lies could also be restricted. Of course, in the United States the constitutional straitjacket (in particular, the extremely broad way that the Supreme Court has been interpreting the First Amendment) would prevent any such changes, but that doesn't mean that other democratic societies should be forced to follow the American lead.

It doesn't take any fancy theory of human psychology to see how a prohibition on outright falsehood could be salutary. Indeed, many people are surprised to discover that political advertising is held to a lower standard than commercial advertising.[15] There are other, more subtle changes, however, that could also enhance the rational character of political communication. For example, one could prohibit the use of images, music, and sound effects in political advertising—making it so that the ad could feature only the candidate talking.[16] This would make it more difficult to bypass the audience's rational faculties. Such changes would no doubt be challenged as a violation of "freedom of speech," which is why it is important to emphasize that they do not actually restrict *speech*.

One could also take measures aimed at eliminating certain "voter suppression" techniques.[17] Negative advertising, for example, is often intended to create disgust with the political system and thereby reduce voter partici-pation. It works in part because it leads more of one's opponents' support-ers to stop voting than it does one's own. But of course, when all sides do it, it just leads to an overall decline in voter turnout. A relatively simple way to address this problem is to make voting mandatory, as it is in Brazil, Australia, Argentina, and many other countries. Failure to vote is, after all, a free-rider strategy for anyone who enjoys the benefits of living in a democratic society, so it doesn't violate any important principles to prohibit it. By making voting mandatory, certain forms of political advertising that are not really aimed at communicating but rather have the strategic intent of discouraging participation would be rendered ineffectual.

It is still unclear what the long-term impact of the internet on the quality of political discourse will be. This is partly because the technology is changing so quickly and partly because the impact on traditional media—newspapers in particular—is yet to be determined. Twitter, of course, because of the limits it imposes on message length, is completely inimical to rational debate. It encourages the verbal equivalent of slap fighting. The incredible "need for speed" that Twitter imposes is also catastrophic from the standpoint of rationality. So the fact that journalists and pundits now spend hours every day tweeting and reading tweets cannot be a good thing.

Blogs have much more potential, and obviously have become an important element of the political culture. It is, however, interesting to observe that no blog or media site hoping to maintain a rational debate can get by without active censorship of "trolls"—people who post comments simply with the goal of provoking other people. This doesn't violate any-one's freedom of speech, because of course the trolls can always go and post somewhere else. A more subtle problem is caused by paid commentators. Many newspaper and magazine sites, for instance, are essentially crippled by staffers working for the major political parties, who are given a series of talking points then instructed to comment on all news stories and opinion pieces on all major media outlets. They are like trolls, in the sense that they are not interested in engaging in discussion with the other commentators, but they are seldom outrageous or inflammatory. The net effect is just to flood the comments on these sites with junk and to sidetrack serious discussion. This dramatically diminishes the value of the internet as a tool for political discussion and debate. Bad talk drives out good, and so the only people left on the site are those who are too naive to realize that they're arguing with paid political hacks.

Furthermore, the resurgence of text-based communication caused by the internet may end up being just a consequence of bandwidth limitations. As it gets easier to move more and more data, the importance of video is steadily increasing. (So now, instead of just blog posts and comments, people upload videos, prompting others to upload "response" videos, and so on.) The move to the more visual medium has exactly the impact on the quality of discourse that one would expect. It is entirely possible that the past ten years will be looked back on as the "golden years" of public discourse, precisely because of the technological limitations that left us with no choice but to type out long messages to one another and to leave written comments on blogs.

§

The protestors who threatened to turn the Rally to Restore Sanity into a rally to restore politeness were right about several things. The decline of rationality in public life bears more than a passing resemblance to the decline of civility, which has been ongoing for more than forty years. As time goes by, people seem to get ruder and ruder, while popular entertainment becomes more and more vulgar. The problem with this decline is that it is almost entirely a cultural phenomenon, which makes it very difficult to reverse. You can blame the media, but obviously the media is just a part of a much broader trend. The problem is that, in the competition for attention, being rude (or vulgar) is a way of getting noticed. In order for it to work, however, you need to be ruder than everyone else. Everyone else, of course, is not about to stand idly by and let you steal all the attention. They will respond in kind. The result is a classic race to the bottom, where the level of rudeness gets steadily ratcheted up over time. But what can be done about it? Complaining about this or that egregious instance is completely self-defeating, because it gives the offenders precisely the attention that they crave. And it's not the type of thing that can be legislated against. Courtesy is maintained by informal social norms. Once those norms begin to erode, it is very difficult to see how the process can be halted.

This problem—how to stop or reverse long-term cultural decline—is one that traditional conservatives used to worry about (and religious conservatives still do). Common sense conservatives, by contrast, tend not to worry at all (perhaps because vulgarity is the way that "real people" talk), and in public discourse, it is conservative commentators who have been pushing the level of rudeness to new depths (not to mention making violent rhetoric increasingly mainstream).

Rationality is also maintained by a system of informal norms. These include not only a commitment to the cooperative search for the truth, a willingness to accept the force of the better argument, and a recognition of the possibility of reasonable disagreement, but also more fine-grained norms, such as the willingness to listen to others (sometimes at length), the ability to focus on a single topic, and the ability to move on when disagreement becomes intractable. Rationality is not hardwired. Indeed, when isolated from one another, we are not particularly good at reasoning. But as even Jonathan Haidt acknowledges, "if you put individuals together in the right way, such that some individuals can use their reasoning powers to disconfirm the claims of others, and all individuals feel some common bond or shared fate that allows them to interact civilly, you can create a group that ends up producing good reasoning as an emergent property of the social system."[18]

What happens, though, when people begin to act in ways that undermine the "common bonds" that make good reasoning possible? One can see the erosion quite clearly in the political world, where a dynamic has set in that seems to undermine rationality just as steadily as the competition for attention has undermined civility in popular culture. In this case, what drives the process is ultimately a competition for votes. People have found all sorts of highly effective strategies for winning votes that, unfortunately, violate the basic norms of rational discourse.

This rising demagoguery poses a serious challenge to the political system: it may help to win elections, but it degrades democracy and impedes the ability of the state to develop rational policy, not just in response to crises (such as the 2008 financial crisis or the longer-term crisis of global warming), but even with respect to the everyday business of government (such as maintaining infrastructure or keeping schools open and staffed). Both politicians and campaign strategists have been acting as though the democratic system can't be broken. This is obvious in the case of campaign tactics that involve suppressing voter turnout, but is equally true of strategies that involve willful violation of the norms of truth and civil dialogue. This recklessness may be due to the belief that democracy is nothing more than the expression of the individual liberty of citizens and therefore needs no special "ethic" in order to survive. But that is clearly not the case. Democracy involves a finely balanced set of institutions that evolved over the course of hundreds of years. Maintaining this balance requires an enormous amount of self-restraint on the part of everyone involved. It is not at all obvious that it can survive in a system of no-holds-barred electoral competition.

When people enter into a competitive interaction, there is a temptation to think that any conduct at all can be justified on the grounds that "it helps you win"—and that refraining from doing something that might help you win is either stupid or naive. But this is not true in every area of social life. The mere fact that an interaction is competitive does not mean that anything goes. All staged competitions—and democracy, like sport, is a carefully staged competition—are governed not only by explicit rules, but also by an implicit "code" that puts constraints on how far people can go to win. Even warfare, perhaps the most extreme form of competition, is governed by rules. Granted, this code of honor in warfare has been significantly eroded over the course of the past century. Yet the fact that it ever existed at all—despite the lack of any serious legal enforcement—gives the lie to the idea that people are incapable of restraining themselves in competitive interactions. Even when people are trying to kill each other, they are still capable of respecting informal norms that limit the destructiveness of that competition.

This sort of code is, of course, much easier to destroy than it is to build. One of the most serious objections to the American use of torture in the "global war on terror" is that it violated the spirit, if not the letter, of a set of norms about the treatment of prisoners that had been painstakingly built up over time. In much of American public discourse, the mere fact that "lives were at stake" was taken to be sufficient to justify the most outrageous behavior. It took Christopher Hitchens, the most vocal British supporter of the war, to remind people that it is possible to act honorably even when lives are at stake. In a memorable exchange with Bill O'Reilly, he observed that "in the Second World War the British had a special prison for captured Nazi spies. And you were fired in that prison if you even raised a hand or you even threatened violence. This was a time [when] London was being bombed every single night."[19]

The American decision to prosecute the war on terror without honor was not an unfortunate necessity, forced on them by circumstances. It was a decision. The same can be said for the choice, made by many of the same people, to fight elections without honor, by engaging in every sort of demagoguery possible. The decline of honor is a huge loss to the political system. And like the decline in military honor, it's not obvious what can be done to fix it once it's broken. Informal norms are by their nature unenforced, and often unenforceable. People are willing to follow these rules as long as everyone else does, and so when one person stops, the rest may quickly follow. Getting *everyone* to go back can be an enormous challenge, even if they can all see that they would all be better off that way.

Part of the problem, in the case of the political system, is that people have talked themselves into the view that the outcome is not actually that damaging and that "all demagoguery all of the time" is a perfectly natural way for a democracy to function. The argument of this book is intended, at the very least, to undermine that notion. But when it comes to repairing the damage, there is no quick fix.

§

It should go without saying that writing books about the decline of reason is not the sort of thing that is likely to slow the decline of reason. It is simply preaching to the choir. Anyone who makes it to the end of a three-hundred-page book on the subject is obviously not part of the problem. Furthermore, the project of reversing the trend is too big and too complicated for any one person to accomplish much. The work itself, as Burke put it, requires the aid of many minds. It requires above all collective action, in order to bring about the social conditions that make rational politics possible. I will end, therefore, not with a set of proposals, but with a manifesto, a call to action for those wanting to improve the mental environment. If we can have a Slow Food Manifesto, it seems perfectly reasonable that we can also have a Slow Politics Manifesto:

> Our era, which began and has developed under the banner of
> the Enlightenment, first invented liberal democracy, then took
> it as its political ideal.

> But we have become enslaved by speed, and have all suc-
> cumbed to the same insidious virus: Fast Life, which disrupts
> our habits, impairs our concentration and forces us to con-
> sume information in ever-smaller packets.

To be worthy of the name, we *Homo sapiens* should rid ourselves of speed before it reduces us to a species in danger of
extinction.

A firm defense of quiet, rational deliberation is the only way
to oppose the universal folly of Fast Life.

Our defense of reason must rest on three pillars. First, we
must better *understand* the conditions that make it possible.
Second, we must *deliberate* about how to improve those conditions. And finally, we must engage in *collective action* aimed
at bringing about those improvements. Only in this way can
we banish the degrading effects of Fast Life.

In its frenzied competition for attention, Fast Politics has
changed our way of making decisions, making us prey to
demagogues. This threatens our democracy and our way of
life. Slow Politics is now the only truly progressive answer.

Politics should be about cultivating intelligence rather than
demeaning it, building on experience rather than going with
our gut feelings. What better way to set about this than an
international exchange of experiences, knowledge, projects?

Slow Politics promises a better future.

Slow Politics cannot succeed as an individual endeavor. It is
an idea that needs many committed supporters who can help
turn this into an international movement.[20]

Epilogue

There is much that was right in the old conservative critique of the French Revolution. The philosophers of the first Enlightenment overestimated the power of the unassisted, unaugmented, isolated, individual intellect, and therefore dramatically underestimated the contribution to civilized conduct made by social institutions and culture handed down over the course of generations. While these traditions may have encoded many ancient prejudices, they also carried a fair share of ancient wisdom. The fact that this came as a surprise to anyone was due to a fundamental misunderstanding of how human reason operates and, in particular, of the peculiar genius that we show for colonizing the surrounding environment in order to augment our computational capacities.

Consider something as simple as multiplication, an elementary mathematical operation that most children master by age eight. We tend to think of it as "part of math," and therefore as an operation that the brain is able to perform all on its own. And yet a minimally competent grade-school student in our society would qualify as a mathematical genius by the standards of the ancient world. This is not because children have gotten smarter; it's because we have better *tools* for thinking. Think about what would be involved in doing multiplication as a citizen of the Roman Empire. What is XCVIII times CCCXIV? Trying to perform multiplication on numbers represented in this way is a bit of a head-scratcher. To the extent that we are able to do it, it's because we can convert them to Arabic numerals: 98 times 314 is a problem that most of us know how to solve.

One can see here the superiority of the Arabic system: you can line up numbers so that each order of magnitude is in its own column. The Roman and Arabic systems are much more than just notation for writing things down and remembering them. They are also an external technology that we use to manipulate numbers and perform computations. And because of the expressive superiority of the Arabic system, our computational abilities were augmented. Our biological brains received an "upgrade" from this particular bit of culture—one that we now take for granted simply because it is ubiquitous and acquired at an early age.

We are surrounded by these sorts of upgrades, in every area of social life. We are unaware of them only because they work so well, leaving us free to forget about them. Traditional conservatives were therefore right to argue that we should be cautious when it comes to making changes in our social institutions and cultural heritage. In the same way that cultural upgrades make us smarter, they also give us greater foresight, enhance our self-control, and, most importantly, make us more cooperative. The combination of hierarchical social organization and market integration have allowed us to create systems of cooperation that vastly exceed anything found in nature. And yet it is far too easy to take this all for granted, and therefore to inadvertently destroy systems that we actually need in order to get along.

Consider the case of the market. One of the most unfortunate episodes in the history of the Soviet Union was the number of people who were tried and executed as "saboteurs." The evidence under which they stood accused was sometimes that while there was a shortage of certain goods in some parts of the country, there was a surplus of those same goods elsewhere. It was assumed that such a ridiculous state of affairs could only be the result of internal enemies, working to undermine the revolution.[1] With the benefit of hindsight, it is easy to see that the function of moving goods from areas of surplus to areas of scarcity is performed by speculators hoping to take advantage of arbitrage opportunities. Having just abolished the market and criminalized speculation, communist revolutionaries failed to realize that they would need to create a replacement for this feature. They had simply taken it for granted that if there was too much of something in one place and not enough of it in some other place, some reasonable person would move it from the first place to the second. They did not realize that this is, in fact, an extremely difficult organizational accomplishment. Because it had been resolved so smoothly and effortlessly by the market, they assumed that it came about spontaneously, and so failed to plan for its replacement. It was only after abolishing the market that they realized what a valuable function it had been performing.

So there is considerable substance in the old conservative critique of the rational, planned society, and of social engineering more generally. Rationalist excesses often stem from a misunderstanding of how the relationship between individual and society works. Wanting to abolish capitalism in order to have "the community of associated producers" decide how the economy should be run is a lot like wanting to abolish the tyranny of written numbers so that the people can be free to do math "in their heads." The external mechanism is not just a frill: it is an essential piece of technology that allows us—in the narrow sense of the term—to accomplish something that we would otherwise not be able to accomplish.

And yet while all of this is correct, it is important not to get too carried away by the insight. The image of the central planner sitting at his desk with a sharpened pencil and slide rule surveying the entire economy and calculating the optimal production and allocation of resources turned out to be a disastrous illusion. The calculations are simply too complex to be done even by the most powerful computer. "Central planning" is precisely the kind of rationalist utopia that people criticize when they complain about social engineering. The market, with its decentralized, chaotic network of independent producers haggling over prices and percentages, turns out to be much more effective. And yet it is important to recognize that the market is not fundamentally different from central planning, in the sense that it does not seek to achieve some completely different objective. It is actually just an indirect way of achieving the optimal production and allocation of resources that socialist planners had always dreamed of.[2] It is a kluge that we adopt as part of a *rational* commitment to extending the scope of human cooperation in such a way as to improve the welfare of each individual. It is, in other words, implemented in the service of the *same* rational utopia that communists sought to achieve. It is simply a case of reason achieving its objectives by hook, rather than by crook.

It is important to recognize, however, that respecting social institutions and showing deference to aspects of inherited culture is not at all the same thing as "going with our gut." Indeed, the major function of many of these institutions is precisely to help us exercise restraint in overcoming our intuitive, gut reactions. This is obviously true of traditional marriage, but equally true of our criminal justice system, our social safety net, our environmental laws, and even the taxation system. Conservatives, unfortunately, seem to have lost track of this insight.

This is why the current climate of antirationalism is so entirely misguided. It's all well and good to have a mountain of psychological research detailing the different ways in which we routinely fail to think and act rationally. But the obvious practical implication is not that it's okay to be irrational: it's that we need to work a lot harder at becoming rational, and that where we fail, we need to develop systems and strategies that insulate us from the consequences of these failings. It is important to remember that rationality is not some alien set of rules imposed on us from on high; it is, rather, the basis of human freedom and autonomy. It is the set of rules that we follow when we want our beliefs to correspond to reality, when we want to avoid failure in the pursuit of our objectives, and when we want to agree on principles for living life in common. It is through the exercise of reason that we have been able to escape from the social conditions that prevailed throughout 99 percent of the history of our genus—that of small-scale societies ruled by superstition, threatened by violence, living at or near the subsistence level.[3] So while it is important not to have any illusions about the power of human reason, it is just as important not to have any illusions about the alternative.

Whether our society has actually become "less rational" over the past few decades is difficult to say. People were pretty crazy in the past as well. The world that I grew up in was subject to the constant threat of nuclear annihilation, based on a great-power rivalry that would be difficult to describe as entirely sane. Furthermore, people have been complaining about the decline of public discourse for decades—stridently since the dawn of television[4]—and yet the sky has not fallen. What I have tried to show, however, is that there is the potential for a hazardous dynamic to develop in the way that cultural systems as a whole are reproduced, with irrational memes pooling in the population in much the same way that viruses and addictive substances do. In order to avoid civilizational decline, we need to be concerned not only about changes at the institutional level, but also about these tendencies within the culture.

All of this is exacerbated, of course, by the rise of a political movement explicitly committed to assigning intuition priority over reason. Furthermore, unlike the "irrational left," which has been almost entirely excluded from political power in Western democracies, the "irrational right" has actually enjoyed significant electoral success. Many people are rightly pessimistic about the possibility of changing this, particularly in the United States. There are so many different institutional failures in American society right now, all of them mutually reinforcing, that it does seem difficult to picture a way forward. It is no accident that there has been a huge resurgence of interest in Isaac Asimov's *Foundation* novels among American liberals. These books speak to the question that has been troubling many: What is the responsibility of intellectuals, faced with a civilization in irreversible decline that has no interest in listening to intellectuals? Asimov's answer, unfortunately, is to secede from society, let everything collapse, then spend the next thousand years putting things back together.

With any luck, we will be able to do better than that. At very least we—friends and allies of the Enlightenment—must change our tactics and give it a second try.

Acknowledgments

Most of my books have been rather solitary endeavors, but in this case I have benefited enormously from conversations and comments from a number of extremely knowledgeable, brilliant, talented people. First and foremost, I would like to thank Andrew Potter, to whom this book is dedicated. Most of the argument of this book was worked out with Andrew, and it was initially planned as a co-authored work, a follow-up to *The Rebel Sell,* which we wrote together in 2004. When we first started working on this book, Andrew was living in Toronto, with a somewhat boring job that left him plenty of free time to write. Shortly after we worked out the argument, and even sketched out the table of contents and the first draft of an introduction, he was offered what I like to think of as a "grown-up job" as managing editor of the *Ottawa Citizen.* He moved to Ottawa, and hasn't had more than fifteen minutes to collect his thoughts since (much less write a book). So I wound up writing it up myself. I nevertheless owe an enormous debt to Andrew for his contributions—beyond just working out the ideas, some of it was written by him (material drawn from a magazine article we co-wrote, "Retrouver la Raison," *Nouveau Projet,* 1 [2012]).

I have also benefited enormously from conversations over the years with David R. Olson, and even more from his detailed comments on the manuscript. Psychology is not my field, and so the opportunity to converse with an expert, especially one as eminent in his field as David, was absolutely invaluable. Most importantly, he took pains to impress upon me that not every study is credible and not everything that gets published in a psychology journal is true. If I manage to come across as less than entirely credulous, David deserves much of the credit. Nevertheless, as is inevitable in a work such as this, I simplify a number of very complex issues. I am aware of this, and would just like to emphasize that this is despite David's efforts, not due to them.

I would also like to thank Joel Anderson for introducing me to the "extended mind" hypothesis and convincing me of its importance, as well as working with me on a number of academic projects, including a co-authored paper, "Procrastination and the Extended Will" (published in Mark White and Chrisoula Andreou, eds., *The Thief of Time* [Oxford: Oxford University Press, 2010]). The importance of kluges is something that Joel impressed upon me, particularly through his paper "Neuroprosthetics, the Extended Mind, and Respect for Persons with Disability," in Marcus Düwell, Christoph Rehmann-Sutter, and Dietmar Mieth, eds., *The Contingent Nature of Life: Bioethics and Limits of Human Existence* (Heidelberg: Springer, 2008). He has also used the manuscript of this book twice in his courses, and so he has served not only as an able critic, but as a conduit for the comments of his students at the University of Utrecht.

As far as the manuscript is concerned, I have benefited from comments and discussion with Idil Boran, Dominic Martin, Terrence Heath, June Clark, Jennifer Petrela, Andreas Petrela Paiement, Simone Chambers, Jocelyn Maclure, and Russell Hoy. I have also benefited enormously from conversations over the years with Ronald de Sousa, Kyle Menken, and Benoit Hardy-Vallée. For research support I would like to thank the Social Sciences and Humanities Research Council of Canada and the Pierre Elliott Trudeau Foundation. And finally, I would like to thank my editor at HarperCollins, Jim Gifford, as well as Doug Richmond, for putting in a larger-than-usual amount of work editing the book. The first drafts of it were pretty rough; to the extent that it hangs together better now, it is largely due to their efforts. Noelle Zitzer and Stephanie Fysh also provided invaluable assistance in the preparation of the final manuscript, and special thanks are owed to Priscilla Tang for compiling the index.

Notes

Introduction

1. This was Stewart's original title. He later merged it with comedian Stephen Colbert's "March to Keep Fear Alive," to make the "Rally to Restore Sanity and/or Fear," which strikes me as a less effective title.

2. "Stephen Colbert," interview, A.V. Club (January 25, 2006), http://www.avclub.com/articles/stephen-colbert,13970/ (accessed May 9, 2013).

3. Glenn Kessler, "Euthanasia in the Netherlands: Rick Santorum's Bogus Statistics," The Fact Checker, *Washington Post* (February 22, 2012), http://www.washingtonpost.com/blogs/fact-checker/post/euthanasia-in-the-netherlands-rick-santorums-bogus-statistics/2012/02/21/gIQAJaRbSR_blog.html (accessed May 9, 2013).

4. The confusion here is between *involuntary* and *nonvoluntary,* where *nonvoluntary* refers to cases in which an explicit statement, either for or against, is lacking. For a survey of the facts regarding euthanasia policy in the Netherlands, see L. W. Sumner, *Assisted Death: A Study in Ethics and Law* (Oxford: Oxford University Press, 2012), pp. 187–89.

5. Harry Frankfurt, *On Bullshit* (Princeton: Princeton University Press, 2005), p. 1.

6. Laura Penny, *Your Call Is Important to Us: The Truth about Bullshit* (Toronto: McClelland & Stewart, 2005).

7. When pressed to justify the strategy, the Conservatives defended their claim on the grounds that their cap-and-trade plan was revenue neutral while the NDP proposal was supposed to bring in revenue and could therefore be labeled a "tax." Following this logic, the Liberal carbon tax proposal, put forward during the 2008 election campaign, was not actually a carbon tax, since it was intended to be revenue neutral (the tax on carbon was to be offset by cuts in income tax).

8. Tim Harper, "Conservatives Sentence Tom Mulcair to Death by Talking Point," *Toronto Star* (September 18, 2012).

9. John Bryden, "Speaker Urged to Stem Tide of Partisan Vitriol in House of Commons," *Winnipeg Free Press* (October 22, 2012).

10. Frank Luntz, *Words That Work: It's Not What You Say, It's What People Hear* (New York: Hyperion, 2007), p. 211.

11. David Brooks, *The Social Animal: The Hidden Sources of Love, Character, and Achievement* (New York: Random House, 2011), p. xiv.

12. Jonathan Haidt, *The Righteous Mind: Why Good People Are Divided by Politics and Religion* (New York: Pantheon, 2012), p. 156.

13. Haidt, *The Righteous Mind,* p. 114.

14. Apart from their deep involvement in racial animus, concepts of purity are often very closely tied to social status hierarchies. See Elliot Turiel, *The Culture of Morality: Social Development, Context, and Conflict* (Cambridge: Cambridge University Press, 2002), pp. 173–74.

15. Haidt, *The Righteous Mind,* p. 1.

16. Haidt, *The Righteous Mind,* p. 88.

17. Haidt, *The Righteous Mind,* p. 224.

18. Pierre Manent, *An Intellectual History of Liberalism,* translated by Rebecca Balinski (Princeton: Princeton University Press, 1995), pp. xv–xvi.

19. This is according to an estimate by the Center for Public Integrity (Caitlin Ginley, "On Financial Reform Bill, 52 Percent of Lobbyists Worked in Government," Center for Public Integrity [June 10, 2010], http://www.publicintegrity.org/2010/06/10/2656/financial-reform-bill-52-percent-lobbyists-worked-government/ [accessed June 18, 2013]).

20. As Thomas Frank observed, "under the urging of this trumped-up protest movement, the Republican Party proceeded to *win a majority in the U.S. House of Representatives*; in the state legislatures of the nation it *took some six hundred seats* from the Democrats; as of this writing it is still *purging Republican senators and congressmen* deemed insufficiently conservative and has even succeeded in *having one of its own named as the GOP's vice-presidential candidate*" ("To the Precinct Station," The Baffler, 21 [2012]).

21. Thomas Frank, *Pity the Billionaire: The Hard-Times Swindle and the Unlikely Comeback of the Right* (New York: Picador, 2012), p. 186.

22. In 2004, George W. Bush's campaign undertook an extensive polling exercise in order to determine which issues made voters most angry. See Sasha Issenberg, *The Victory Lab: The Secret Science of Winning Campaigns* (New York: Random House, 2012), p. 140.

23. Michel Foucault, *Madness and Civilization: A History of Insanity in the Age of Reason,* trans. Richard Howard (New York: Vintage, 1988).

24. For a selection, see Dan Ariely, *The Upside of Irrationality: The Unexpected Benefits of Defying Logic at Work and at Home* (New York: Harper, 2010); Malcolm Gladwell, *Blink: The Power of Thinking without Thinking* (New York: Little, Brown and Co., 2005); Leonard Mlodinow, *Subliminal: How Your Unconscious Mind Rules Your Behavior*

(New York: Pantheon, 2012); and Matthew Hutson, *The 7 Laws of Magical Thinking: How Irrational Beliefs Keep Us Happy, Healthy, and Sane* (New York: Penguin, 2012). Following the conventions of modern publishing, it is the subtitles that tell the tale.

25. For a discussion of this, see Joseph Heath, *Filthy Lucre: Economics for People Who Hate Capitalism* (Toronto: HarperCollins, 2008), pp. 44–48.

26. Ole Rogeberg, "Taking Absurd Theories Seriously: Economics and the Case of Rational Addiction Theories," *Philosophy of Science,* 71 (2004): 263–85.

27. One can find a typical expression of this in Margaret Wente's column in the *Globe and Mail,* where she often makes an invalid inference from the fact that people get emotional when talking about politics to the conclusion that people's political views are determined by their emotions. For example, "When it comes to politics, most of us react with our paleomammalian brain. We only think we're basing our preferences on reason. The neuroscientific evidence is overwhelming that we form our opinions first, then find the facts to back them up" ("The Amygdala Election," *Globe and Mail* [March 29, 2011]).

Chapter 1

1. Keith Stanovich, *Rationality and the Reflective Mind* (Oxford: Oxford University Press, 2011), pp. 106–7. The original formulation of the problem is in Hector J. Levesque, "Making Believers out of Computers," *Artificial Intelligence,* 30 (1986): 85.

2. Called "serial associative cognition" or "impulsively associative thinking" by Stanovich (*What Intelligence Tests Miss: The Psychology of Rational Thought* [New Haven: Yale University Press, 2009], p. 181).

3. David Hume, *The Philosophical Works*, Vol. 4 (Boston: Little, Brown & Co., 1854), p. 220.

4. This formulation is from Robert Brandom, *Making It Explicit: Reasoning, Representing, and Discursive Comment* (Cambridge, MA: Harvard University Press, 1998).

5. Gladwell, *Blink,* pp. 5–6.

6. Harold Garfinkel, *Studies in Ethnomethodology* (London: Polity, 1984), p. 33.

7. Keith Stanovich, *Who Is Rational? Studies of Individual Differences in Reasoning* (Mahwah, NJ: Lawrence Erlbaum, 1999), pp. 32–33.

8. Monica Bucciarelli, Sangeet Khemlani, and P. N. Johnson-Laird, "The Psychology of Moral Reasoning," *Judgment and Decision Making,* 3 (2008): 121–39.

9. Stanovich, *Who Is Rational?,* pp. 165–79.

10. For an overview, see Nelson Cowan, *Working Memory Capacity* (New York: Psychology Press, 2005).

11. For general discussion, see Alan D. Baddeley, *Working Memory, Thought, and Action* (Oxford: Oxford University Press, 2007).

12. Jonathan St. B. T. Evans, *Hypothetical Thinking: Dual Processes in Reasoning and Judgement* (New York: Psychology Press, 2007), p. 174.

13. Mariano Sigman and Stanislas Dehaene, "Brain Mechanisms of Serial and Parallel Processing during Dual-Task Performance," Journal of Neuroscience, 28 (2008): 7585–98. See also James T. Townsend, "Serial vs. Parallel Processing: Sometimes They Look Like Tweedledum and Tweedledee but They Can (And Should) be Distinguished," Psychological Science, 1 (1990): 46–54.

14. See Kenneth J. Gilhooly, "Working Memory and Reasoning," in Jacqueline P. Leighton and Robert J. Sternberg, eds., *The Nature of Reasoning* (Cambridge: Cambridge University Press, 2004), pp. 54–56.

15. Jonathan St. B. T. Evans, "In Two Minds: Dual-Process Accounts of Reasoning," *Trends in Cognitive Science,* 7 (2003): 454–59. I use the term *dual process* rather than *dual system* in reflection of the fact that things are actually a lot more complicated than the term *dual system* suggests. For example, see Keith Stanovich, "Distinguishing the Reflective, Algorithmic, and Autonomous Minds: Is It Time for a Tri-Process Theory?" in Jonathan St. B. T. Evans and Keith Frankish, eds., *In Two Minds: Dual Processes and Beyond* (Oxford: Oxford University Press, 2007).

16. Jonathan St. B. T. Evans, "The Heuristic-Analytic Theory of Reasoning: Extension and Evaluation," *Psychonomic Bulletin and Review,* 13 (2006): 382.

17. Andy Clark, *Being There: Putting Brain, Body, and World Together Again* (Cambridge, MA: MIT Press, 1997), p. 227.

18. Daniel C. Dennett, *Consciousness Explained* (Boston: Little, Brown and Co., 1991), p. 215.

19. This is not a joke. Pocket Fritz, which runs on a mobile phone, has won several tournaments and has achieved a grandmaster rating of 2898.

20. Ulrich Schwalbe and Paul Walker, "Zermelo and the Early History of Game Theory," *Games and Economic Behavior,* 34 (2001): 123–37.

21. Adrianus Dingeman de Groot, *Thought and Choice in Chess* (The Hague: Mouton, 1965), pp. 335–36; de Groot, "Intuition in Chess," *International Computer Chess Association Journal,* 9 (1986): 67–75. On compression in the visual representations using in heuristic search, see Christopher F. Chabris and Eliot S. Hearst, "Visualization, Pattern Recognition, and Forward Search: Effects of Playing Speed and Sight of the Position on Grandmaster Chess Errors," *Cognitive Science,* 27 (2003): 645. I am bowdlerizing somewhat—this was actually known before the advent of chess-playing computers.

22. This is how the designers of the system put it. See Chrilly Donninger and Ulf Lorenz, "The Chess Monster Hydra," *Field Programmable Logic and Application,* 3204 (2004): 927.

23. Jonathan Evans writes, "What typically happens is that an expert recognizes a situation as of a kind encountered previously and rapidly retrieves a scheme that provides

a solution . . . The application will involve some explicit reasoning (sometimes mental simulations to check feasibility of solutions) but the key to intelligent action is the automatic retrieval process" ("Dual-Processing Accounts of Reasoning, Judgment, and Social Cognition," *Annual Review of Psychology,* 59 [2008]: 267). Also see Gary Klein, *Sources of Power: How People Make Decisions* (Cambridge, MA: MIT Press, 1998), p. 15, where he calls this "recognition-primed" decision making.

24. Jonathan St. B. T. Evans, "How Many Dual-Process Theories Do We Need? One, Two, or Many?" in Evans and Frankish, eds., *In Two Minds,* p. 35.

25. Compare to Richard Dawkins's evolution of "biomorphs" (*The Blind Watchmaker: Why the Evidence of Evolution Reveals a Universe without Design* [New York: W. W. Norton, 1996], pp. 57–59).

26. Neil Shubin, *Your Inner Fish: A Journey into the 3.5-Billion-Year History of the Human Body* (New York: Random House, 2009), p. 192. The discussion of the hiccup that follows is from Shubin.

27. William Hirstein, *Brain Fiction: Self-Deception and the Riddle of Confabulation* (Cambridge, MA: MIT Press, 2005), p. 31.

28. Hirstein, *Brain Fiction,* p. 32.

29. Albert Yonas, A. Gordon Bechtold, Daniel Frankel, F. Robert Gordon, Gerald McRoberts, Anthony Norcia, and Susan Sternfels, "Development of Sensitivity to Information for Impending Collision," *Perception and Psychophysics,* 21 (1977): 97–104.

30. Michael McCloskey, Allyson Washburn, and Linda Felch, "Intuitive Physics: The Straight-Down Belief and Its Origin," *Journal of Experimental Psychology: Learning, Memory, and Cognition,* 9 (1983): 636–49.

31. A phrase borrowed from Jerome H. Barkow, Leda Cosmides, and John Tooby, eds., *The Adapted Mind: Everyday Psychology and the Generation of Culture* (Oxford: Oxford University Press, 1992). Note that I am rejecting their view, as well as that advanced by Keith Stanovich, *The Robot's Rebellion: Finding Meaning in the Age of Darwin* (Chicago: University of Chicago Press, 2005), pp. 63–68.

32. John Tooby and Leda Cosmides, two of the most influential proponents of "evolutionary psychology," describe the human mind as "an intricate network of functionally dedicated computers, each activated by different classes of content or problem, with some more general-purpose computers embedded in the architecture as well" ("The Psychological Foundations of Culture," in Barkow, Cosmides, and Tooby, eds., *The Adapted Mind,* p. 94). One can see the problem in the final clause. Why would a few "general-purpose computers" be added to the mix? Why is there no sign of evolution having produced a "general-purpose computer" anywhere else in nature?

33. See Derek Bickerton, "Resolving Discontinuity: A Minimalist Distinction between Human and Non-human Minds," *American Zoologist,* 40 (2000): 862–73.

34. Mark Hauser and Elizabeth Spelke, "Evolutionary and Developmental Foundations of Human Knowledge: A Case Study of Mathematics," in Michael S. Gazzaniga, ed., *The Cognitive Neurosciences,* Vol. 3 (Cambridge, MA: MIT Press, 2004).

35. Tooby and Cosmides, "The Psychological Foundations of Culture," pp. 108–12.

36. And by "designed" I mean "adapted."

37. Dennett, *Consciousness Explained,* p. 210.

38. For the former, see Allan Pavio, *Mental Representations: A Dual Coding Approach* (Oxford: Clarendon, 1986), pp. 53–83; on the latter see Ian Hacking, *Why Does Language Matter to Philosophy?* (Cambridge: Cambridge University Press, 1975).

39. See Mark Richard, *Propositional Attitudes* (Cambridge: Cambridge University Press, 1990) for discussion.

40. Elizabeth S. Spelke and Sanna Tsivkin, "Language and Number: A Bilingual Training Study," *Cognition,* 78 (2001): 45–88.

41. This has to do with the importance of recursion for grammar. See Marc D. Hauser, Noam Chomsky, and W. Tecumseh Fitch, "The Faculty of Language: What Is It, Who Has It, and How Did It Evolve?" *Science,* 298 (2002): 1569–79.

42. As Margarita Azmitia puts it, "There is wide agreement that self-regulation emerges from other-regulation" ("Expertise, Private Speech, and the Development of Self-Regulation," in Rafael M. Diaz and Laura E. Berk, eds., *Private Speech: From Social Integration to Self-Regulation* [Hillsdale, NJ: Lawrence Erlbaum, 1992], p. 101). See also Janet Wilde Astington, "The Developmental Interdependence of Theory of Mind and Language," in N. J. Enfield and Stephen C. Levinson, eds., *Roots of Human Sociality: Culture, Cognition and Interaction* (Oxford: Berg, 2006), pp. 179–206.

43. Lev Vygotsky, *Mind in Society: The Development of Higher Psychological Processes* (Cambridge, MA: Harvard University Press, 1978), p. 24. See also David Bakhurst, *The Formation of Reason* (Oxford: Wiley-Blackwell, 2011), pp. 153–54.

44. For a more nuanced account, see Laura E. Berk, "Children's Private Speech: An Overview of Theory and the Status of Research," in Diaz and Berk, eds., *Private Speech.*

45. Alexander Luria, as reported in Karl Levitin, *One Is Not Born a Personality: Profiles of Soviet Education Psychologists,* translated by Yevgeni Filippov (Moscow: Progress Publishers, 1982), p. 118.

46. Roy F. Baumeister, E. J. Masicampo, and Kathleen D. Vohs, "Do Conscious Thoughts Cause Behavior?" *Annual Review of Psychology,* 62 (2001): 341–42. For a developmental perspective, see Philip David Zelazo and Douglas Frye, "Cognitive Complexity and Control: II. The Development of Executive Function in Childhood," *Current Directions in Psychological Science,* 7 (1998): 121–26.

47. As Katherine Nelson puts it, "Language (and logic) are public constructions with private ramifications. Among the ramifications is the possibility of using language

as a cognitive representational level with greater analytic power than any prior nonsymbolic representation system" (*Language in Cognitive Development* [Cambridge: Cambridge University Press, 1996], p. 15).

48. See Hauser, Chomsky, and Fitch, "The Faculty of Language." There is still a "chicken and egg" question of whether recursion came first, enabling natural language, or vice versa. My preference is, obviously, for the latter order of explanation. The connection between language, recursion, and mathematics is more obvious to those familiar with the so-called Peano axiomatization of arithmetic, particularly the definition of number in terms of the "successor" function.

49. As Andy Clark writes, "This power of computational transformation constitutes a neglected virtue of linguistic practice. It reveals language as the ultimate upgrade: so ubiquitous it is almost invisible; so intimate, it is not clear whether it is a kind of tool or an added dimension of the user. But whatever the boundaries, we confront a complex coalition in which the basic biological brain is fantastically empowered by some of its strangest and most recent creations: words in the air, symbols on the printed page" ("Magic Words: How Language Augments Human Computation," http://www.nyu. edu/gsas/dept/philo/courses/concepts/magicwords.html [accessed May 9, 2013]).

50. Michael Dummett, *Truth and Other Enigmas* (Cambridge, MA: Harvard University Press, 1978), p. 117.

51. Dummett, *Truth and Other Enigmas*, pp. 116–17.

52. See Janet Shibley Hyde, "The Gender Similarities Hypothesis," *American Psychologist*, 60 (2005): 581–92.

53. These two lists are from Evans, *Hypothetical Thinking*, pp. 14–15, slightly modified.

54. Evans, *Hypothetical Thinking*, p. 110.

Chapter 2

1. "The Temple of Reason," in Isaac Kramnick, ed., *The Portable Enlightenment Reader* (New York: Penguin, 1995), pp. 168–71.

2. Leo Gershoy, *The Era of the French Revolution, 1789–1799* (Princeton, NJ: D. Van Nostrand, 1957), p. 160.

3. Stephen Jay Gould and Elizabeth S. Vrba, "Exaptation: A Missing Term in the Science of Form," *Paleobiology*, 8 (1982): 4–15.

4. Like many stories coming out of Nigeria, this may be a hoax, but see Addy Dugdale, "Nigerian Man Builds Working Helicopters from Junk," *Gizmodo* (October 22, 2007), http://www.gizmodo.com.au/2007/10/nigerian_man_builds_working_he/ (accessed May 9, 2013). True or not, it nevertheless provides an excellent illustration of a kluge.

5. Dennett, *Consciousness Explained*, p. 210.

6. Gary Marcus, *Kluge: The Haphazard Construction of the Human Mind* (Boston: Houghton Mifflin, 2009).

7. Marcus, *Kluge,* p. 21.

8. Marcus, *Kluge,* p. 45.

9. For discussion of these and other weaknesses of memory, see Christopher Chabris and Daniel Simons, *The Invisible Gorilla: How Our Intuitions Deceive Us* (New York: Broadway, 2009), pp. 61–79.

10. Pascal Boyer, *Religion Explained: The Human Instincts That Fashion Gods, Spirits, and Ancestors* (New York: Basic Books, 2001), p. 223.

11. Dennett, *Consciousness Explained,* p. 259.

12. Dennett, *Consciousness Explained,* p. 220.

13. The term *scaffolding* in psychology is more commonly associated with the work of Jerome Bruner. See, for example, David Wood, Jerome S. Bruner, and Gail Ross, "The Role of Tutoring in Problem Solving," *Journal of Psychology and Psychiatry,* 17 (1976): 89–100. Clark uses the term in a slightly different sense, to refer to ways in which "we solve problems by 'piggy-backing' on reliable environmental properties" (*Being There,* p. 45). The central difference from Bruner is that there is no sense in Clark's use of the term that the scaffolding will some day be taken down.

14. Again, see Cowan, *Working Memory Capacity* and Baddeley, *Working Memory, Thought, and Action.* It is interesting to compare the discussion of working memory in psychology with the discussion in computer science of the Von Neumann bottleneck in the architecture of standard computer systems.

15. Eyal Ophir, Clifford Nass, and Anthony D. Wagner, "Cognitive Control in Media Multitaskers," *Proceedings of the National Academy of Sciences,* 106 (2009): 15583–87.

16. "The main conclusion from the studies of multitasking is that virtually nobody does it well: As a rule, it is more efficient to do tasks one at a time rather than simultaneously" (Chabris and Simons, *The Invisible Gorilla,* p. 32).

17. Timothy Wilson, *Strangers to Ourselves: Discovering the Adaptive Unconscious* (Cambridge, MA: Harvard University Press, 2004), p. 24.

18. See Henry K. Beecher, *Measurement of Subjective Responses: Quantitative Effects of Drugs* (New York: Oxford University Press, 1959) and George Ainslie, *Picoeconomics: The Strategic Interaction of Successive Motivational States within the Person* (Cambridge: Cambridge University Press, 1992), p. 103.

19. Daniel Simon and Christopher Chabris, "Gorillas in Our Midst: Sustained Inattentional Blindness for Dynamic Events," *Perception,* 28 (1999): 1059–74. The video is available online, but once you've been told about the gorilla, it's impossible not to notice it. See also Simon and Chabris, *The Invisible Gorilla.*

20. See Stanovich on the importance to rationality of "cognitive decoupling," separating our

hypothetical representations from our primary representation of the world (*Rationality and the Reflective Mind,* pp. 48–52).

21. Clark, *Being There,* p. 191.

22. Does that make us ectologs?

23. Gerd Gigerenzer, *Gut Feelings: The Intelligence of the Unconscious* (New York: Penguin, 2007), p. 11.

24. William Easterly, *The White Man's Burden: Why the West's Efforts to Aid the Rest Have Done So Much Ill and So Little Good* (New York: Penguin, 2006), p. 282. See also James Scott, *Seeing Like a State: How Certain Schemes to Improve the Human Condition Have Failed* (New Haven, CT: Yale University Press, 1998), p. 227.

Chapter 3

1. For discussion of this analogy, see George Basalla, *The Evolution of Technology* (Cambridge: Cambridge University Press, 1989).

2. Peter J. Richerson and Robert Boyd, *Not by Genes Alone: How Culture Transformed Human Evolution* (Chicago: University of Chicago Press, 2005); also Basalla, *The Evolution of Technology,* p. 3.

3. Edmund Burke, *Reflections on the Revolution in France* (1790; Oxford: Oxford University Press, 1993), p. 170.

4. For an overview, see Frank Cunningham, *Theories of Democracy: A Critical Introduction* (Oxford: Routledge, 2002) and Ian Shapiro, *The State of Democratic Theory* (Princeton, NJ: Princeton University Press, 2003).

5. Thomas Jefferson, letter to James Madison, September 6, 1789, in *Thoughts on War and Revolution: Annotated Correspondence,* edited by Brett F. Woods (New York: Algora, 2009), p. 93.

6. See Jürgen Habermas, "'Struggles for Recognition in the Democratic Constitutional State," in Amy Gutmann, ed., *Multiculturalism: Examining the Politics of Recognition* (Princeton, NJ: Princeton University Press, 1994), p. 132. Note that conservatism is a child of the Enlightenment, as is romanticism.

7. It is worth noting that our intuitions are often even worse in these situations. Dietrich Dörner, in *The Logic of Failure: Recognizing and Avoiding Error in Complex Situations* (New York: Basic Books, 1996), presents a nice experiment showing how the introduction of a five-minute delay between cause and effect in a simple task can make it impossible for most people to figure out the relationship (p. 130).

8. Laura E. Berk, "Why Children Talk to Themselves," *Scientific American* (November 1994): 78–83.

9. Reported in Terrence Deacon, *The Symbolic Species: The Co-evolution of Language and the Brain* (New York: Norton, 1998), p. 244.

10. Deacon, *The Symbolic Species*. It has been suggested that laughter in humans is a vestigial trace of these primate vocalizations, since it is contagious across individuals in much the same way that ape vocalizations are, and is also very difficult to suppress.

11. Clark, *Being There*, p. 191.

12. Baumeister, Masicampo, and Vohs, "Do Conscious Thoughts Cause Behavior?" p. 351.

13. It also appears to be subject to depletion. See Roy E. Baumeister, Ellen Bratslavsky, Mark Muraven, and Dianne M. Tice, "Ego Depletion: Is the Active Self a Limited Resource?" *Journal of Personality and Social Psychology*, 74 (1998): 1252–65.

14. Lynn T. Kozlowski, "Pack Size, Reported Cigarette Smoking Rates, and Public Health," *American Journal of Public Health*, 76 (1986): 1337–38.

15. For more extensive discussion, see Joseph Heath and Joel Anderson, "Procrastination and the Extended Will," in Mark White and Chrisoula Andreou, eds., *The Thief of Time: Philosophical Essays on Procrastination* (Oxford: Oxford University Press, 2010).

16. For more extensive discussion of these and other collective action problems, see Joseph Heath, *The Efficient Society: Why Canada Is as Close to Utopia as It Gets* (Toronto: Penguin, 2001), p. 69.

17. David Gauthier, *Morals by Agreement* (Oxford: Oxford University Press, 1986).

18. Plato, *The Republic*, Book 2, in *Complete Works*, Vol. 2, translated by B. Jowett (New York: Tudor Books, 1937), p. 46. It is worth noting that this is not the theory that Plato accepts, because it does not show the *intrinsic* worth of just acts.

19. Gresham M. Sykes and David Matza, "Techniques of Neutralization: A Theory of Delinquency," *American Sociological Review*, 22 (1957): 664–70.

20. Donald R. Cressey, *Other People's Money: A Study in the Social Psychology of Embezzlement* (Glencoe, IL: Free Press, 1953).

21. David Sally, "Conversation and Cooperation in Social Dilemmas: A Meta-analysis of Experiments from 1958 to 1992," *Rationality and Society*, 5 (1995): 58–92.

22. This term is from Richerson and Boyd, *Not by Genes Alone*, p. 214, but I am using it in a different sense than they do.

23. This is the biggest problem with Frans de Waal's widely celebrated work (e.g., *Primates and Philosophers: How Morality Evolved* [Princeton, NJ: Princeton University Press, 2006]). De Waal catalogues a series of pro-social behaviors among chimpanzees and suggests that the underlying mechanism might account for cooperation among humans as well. He glosses over the fact that chimpanzees are incapable of large-scale cooperation (that is, they are unable to support tribal groups larger than about one hundred). Thus whatever pro-social tendencies we share with them, they must *not* provide an adequate account of human sociality; otherwise, we would see large-scale chimpanzee societies as well. See Robert Boyd and Peter J. Richerson, "The Evolution of Reciprocity in Sizable Groups," *Theoretical Biology*, 132 (1988): 337–56.

24. Richerson and Boyd, *Not by Genes Alone,* p. 230. See also Robert Boyd, Peter J. Richerson, and Joseph Henrich, "Cultural Evolution of Human Cooperation," in Robert Boyd and Peter J. Richerson, *The Origin and Evolution of Culture*s (Oxford: Oxford University Press, 2005), p. 265.
25. Benjamin J. Kaplan, *Divided by Faith: Religious Conflict and the Practice of Toleration in Early Modern Europe* (Cambridge, MA: Harvard University Press, 2007), pp. 62–63.
26. Edward Shils, "The Study of the Primary Group," in Daniel Lerner and Harold D. Laswell, eds., *The Policy Sciences: Recent Developments in Scope and Method* (Stanford, CA: Stanford University Press, 1951), p. 64. See also David Wong, *Natural Moralities: A Defense of Pluralistic Relativism* (Oxford: Oxford University Press, 2006), p. 142.
27. Benedict Anderson, *Imagined Communities: Reflections on the Origin and Spread of Nationalism* (London: Verso, 1983).
28. Carl Schmitt, *The Concept of the Political,* translated by George Schwab (Chicago: University of Chicago Press, 1996).
29. Richerson and Boyd, *Not by Genes Alone,* pp. 231–35.
30. Karl P. Schuessler and Donald R. Cressey, "Personality Characteristics of Criminals," *American Journal of Sociology,* 55 (1950): 476–84; Gordon P. Waldo and Simon Dinitz, "Personality Attributes of the Criminal: An Analysis of Research Studies, 1950–65," Journal of Research in Crime and Delinquency, 4 (1967): 185–202; David J. Tennenbaum, "Personality and Criminality: A Summary and Implications of the Literature," *Journal of Criminal Justice,* 5 (1977): 225–35.
31. Christopher R. Browning, *Ordinary Men: Reserve Police Battalion 101 and the Final Solution in Poland* (New York: HarperCollins, 1992).
32. Stanley Milgram, *Obedience to Authority: An Experimental View* (New York: Harper & Row, 1974).
33. Craig Haney, Curtis Banks, and Philip Zimbardo, "Interpersonal Dynamics in a Simulated Prison," *International Journal of Criminology and Penology,* 1 (1973): 69–97.
34. Donald L. McCabe, Linda Klebe Treviño, and Kenneth D. Butterfield, "Cheating in Academic Institutions: A Decade of Research," *Ethics and Behavior,* 11 (2001): 219–32.
35. McCabe, Treviño, and Butterfield, "Cheating in Academic Institutions," p. 222.
36. Christopher Hitchens, *God Is Not Great: How Religion Poisons Everything* (New York: Hachette, 2007), pp. 15–36.
37. This is what undoubtedly explains the phenomenon, described most influentially by Antonio Damasio, *Descartes' Error: Emotion, Reason, and the Human Brain* (New York: Penguin, 1994), that people who suffer brain damage that results in emotional deficits also lose certain capacities for rational decision making and control. Many people have taken this to show that reason is a sham and that our emotions are doing all the work. This is too hasty. What it shows is that reason does not have its own dedicated systems,

but rather uses various parts of the brain, including parts that belong to older, non-rational systems, in order to get its work done. In other words, Damasio's work suggests that reason is an exaptation.

38. Jonathan Baron, *Rationality and Intelligence* (Cambridge: Cambridge University Press, 1985), p. 168.

39. This formulation is from Jonathan Wolff, *Ethics and Public Policy: A Philosophical Inquiry* (Oxford: Routledge, 2011), p. 79.

Chapter 4

1. Gladwell, *Blink,* p. 48.

2. Nalini Ambady and Robert Rosenthal, "Half a Minute: Predicting Teacher Evaluations from Thin Slices of Nonverbal Behavior and Physical Attractiveness," *Journal of Personality and Social Psychology,* 64 (1993): 431–41.

3. Jerome S. Bruner and Mary C. Potter, "Interference in Visual Recognition," Science, 144 (1964): 424–25. For general discussion of the phenomenon, see Baron, *Rationality and Intelligence,* pp. 163–66.

4. As Christophe Chabris and Daniel Simons point out, even Gladwell's famous example of the art experts detecting the forged statue has obvious problems. There are many, many examples of forgeries that fooled all the experts until they were discovered by scientific analysis, such as radiocarbon dating or X-ray imaging. See Chabris and Simons, *The Invisible Gorilla,* pp. 232–34.

5. We appear to rely upon the sensation of "cognitive fluency" or ease in order to determine whether we need to engage System 2 reasoning. For an overview, see Daniel Kahneman, *Thinking, Fast and Slow* (New York: Farrar, Straus and Giroux, 2011), pp. 59–70. Even being in a good mood tends to make people "less vigilant and more prone to logical errors" (p. 69).

6. Aphorism slightly modified from Stuart Sutherland, *Irrationality* (London: Constable, 1992), p. 270.

7. Stanovich, *Rationality and the Reflective Mind,* p. 83.

8. Clark, "Magic Words."

9. Brooks, *The Social Animal,* p. 219.

10. Brooks, *The Social Animal,* p. 219.

11. Brooks, *The Social Animal,* p. 244.

12. Brooks, *The Social Animal,* p. 246.

13. Brooks, *The Social Animal,* p. xvii.

14. Azar Gat, *War in Human Civilization* (Oxford: Oxford University Press, 2006), pp. 11–35. Also Christopher Boehm, *Hierarchy in the Forest: The Evolution of Egalitarian*

Behavior (Cambridge, MA: Harvard University Press, 1999). The phrase "wife capture" is from Boyd, Richerson, and Henrich, "Cultural Evolution of Human Cooperation," p. 367.

15. Stanovich, *The Robot's Rebellion,* p. 11.

16. Dacher Keltner, *Born to be Good: The Science of a Meaningful Life* (New York: W.W. Norton, 2009); Robert Wright, *The Moral Animal: Why We Are the Way We Are* (New York: Vintage, 1995); Frans de Waal, *Good Natured: The Origins of Right and Wrong in Humans and Other Animals* (Cambridge, MA: Harvard University Press, 1996).

17. Evans, *Hypothetical Thinking,* p. 19.

18. Stanovich, *The Robot's Rebellion,* p. 31.

19. This observation of baby jackdaws is attributed to Konrad Lorenz by Ken Binmore, *Natural Justice* (Oxford: Oxford University Press, 2005), p. 16. Binmore does not provide a reference, and I have been unable to locate any. The story is not implausible, though; one can find accounts of similar observations of "misfires," including one by Lorenz involving jackdaws, in Niko Tinbergen, *The Animal in Its World* (Cambridge, MA: Harvard University Press, 1972), pp. 98–99.

20. Amos Tvesky and Daniel Kahneman, "Availability: A Heuristic for Judging Frequency and Probability," *Cognitive Psychology,* 4 (1973): 207–32.

21. Dan Gardner, *Risk: The Science and Politics of Fear* (Toronto: McClelland & Stewart, 2008), pp. 66–68.

22. Robyn M. Dawes, *Everyday Irrationality: How Pseudo-scientists, Lunatics, and the Rest of Us Systematically Fail to Think Rationally* (Boulder, CO: Westview, 2001), p. 207.

23. A classic discussion is Paul Slovic, Baruch Fischhoff, and Sarah Lichtenstein, "Facts versus Fears: Understanding Perceived Risk," in Daniel Kahneman, Paul Slovic, and Amos Tversky, eds., *Judgment under Uncertainty: Heuristics and Biases* (Cambridge: Cambridge University Press, 1982).

24. Kathryn A. Braun-LaTour, Michael S. LaTour, Jacqueline E. Pickrell, and Elizabeth F. Loftus, "How and When Advertising Can Influence Memory for Consumer Experience," Journal of Advertising, 33 (2004): 7–25.

25. Stanovich, *The Robot's Rebellion,* p. 134. See also Cosmides and Tooby, "The Psychological Foundations of Culture," p. 73, and Roger Shepard, "The Perceptual Organization of Colors: An Adaptation to Regularities of the Terrestrial World?" in Barkow, Cosmides, and Tooby, eds., *The Adapted Mind.*

26. Gerd Gigerenzer, Peter A. Todd, and the ABC Research Group, *Simple Heuristics That Make Us Smart* (Oxford: Oxford University Press, 2003).

27. Stanovich, *Who Is Rational?* p. 190.

28. Stanovich, *Who Is Rational?* p. 193. It is worth noting that this is a complete repudiation of John Dewey's very influential educational philosophy.

29. Timothy D. Wilson and Jonathan W. Schooler, "Thinking Too Much: Introspection Can Reduce the Quality of Preferences and Decision," *Journal of Personality and Social Psychology*, 60 (1991): 181–92.

30. United States Department of Agriculture, "Profiling Food Consumption in America," *Agriculture Fact Book, 2001–2002*, http://www.usda.gov/factbook/chapter2.htm (accessed June 23, 2013).

31. Daniel T. Gilbert and Timothy D. Wilson, "Miswanting: Some Problems in the Forecasting of Future Affective States," in Joseph P. Forgas, ed., *Feeling and Thinking: The Role of Affect in Social Cognition* (New York: Cambridge University Press, 2000), pp. 178–97.

32. Itamar Simonson, "The Effect of Purchase Quantity and Timing on Variety-Seeking Behavior," *Journal of Marketing Research*, 27 (1990): 150–62.

33. Timothy D. Wilson and Daniel T. Gilbert, "Affective Forecasting: Knowing What to Want," *Current Directions in Psychological Science*, 14 (2005): 131–34.

34. Robert Frank, *Luxury Fever: Weighing the Cost of Excess* (Princeton, NJ: Princeton University Press, 2000), pp. 79–83.

35. George Ainslie, *Breakdown of Will* (Cambridge: Cambridge University Press, 2001). See also Howard Rachlin, *The Science of Self-Control* (Cambridge, MA: Harvard University Press, 2009).

Chapter 5

1. William Dowell, "Interview with Li Hongzhi," *Time* (May 10, 1999).

2. Boyer, *Religion Explained*, pp. 71–75.

3. The additional claims, that the woman became young and beautiful and that Master Li is superior to Jesus Christ, both strike me as gratuitous embellishments. After all, we have it on good authority that Jesus Christ brought a man back from the dead. Can Master Li do that?

4. Kahneman, *Thinking, Fast and Slow*, p. 173.

5. Thomas Gilovich, *How We Know What Isn't So: The Fallibility of Human Reason in Everyday Life* (New York: The Free Press 1991).

6. Emily Pronin, Daniel Y. Lin, and Lee Ross, "The Bias Blind Spot: Perceptions of Bias in Self versus Others," Personality and Social Psychology Bulletin, 28 (2002): 369–81.

7. Peter C. Wason, "On the Failure to Eliminate Hypotheses in a Conceptual Task," *Quarterly Journal of Experimental Psychology*, 12 (1960): 129–40. I have since had the opportunity to try the test out on the author of a widely used textbook on critical reasoning. (Philosophers tend not to read psychology, so he was unfamiliar with the test.) He failed, although not quite as egregiously as I had. It occurred to him that they might also be odd numbers, but he didn't manage to escape the assumption that they were ascending in increments of two.

8. There is a debate about whether this should be called "confirmation bias," because in principle, any of the questions being asked could be attempts at disconfirmation. What is striking about the task is that people fail to generate and test what they take to be false hypotheses. For the broad reading of confirmation bias, see Raymond S. Nickerson, "Confirmation Bias: A Ubiquitous Phenomenon in Many Guises," *Review of General Psychology,* 2 (1998): 175–220. For critique and a discussion of the controversy over the correct interpretation of this task, see Evans, *Hypothetical Thinking,* pp. 34–35.

9. Klein, *Sources of Power.*

10. With respect to vision, psychologists refer to the phenomenon as *pareidolia,* defined as "the human mind's tendency to promiscuously perceive meaningful visual patterns in randomness" (Chabris and Simons, *The Invisible Gorilla,* p. 155). This is why the faces of Jesus or the Virgin Mary show up so often on people's toast or in misshapen potatoes or what have you. As in so many cases, what distinguishes the pathological from the normal is not that the underlying tendency is different, but that the pathological individual is unable to inhibit it.

11. Stephen Levy, *The Perfect Thing: How the iPod Shuffles Commerce, Culture, and Coolness* (New York: Simon & Schuster, 2006), pp. 190–96.

12. Jonathan Evans writes, "It is clear from psychological research that we have very poor intuitions about random events, but it could be argued that true randomness is rarely manifest in the natural word and that we were designed by evolution to detect patterns in noisy environments" (*Hypothetical Thinking,* p. 152).

13. This is an idea known as *error management theory;* see Martie G. Haselton and David M. Buss, "Error Management Theory and the Evolution of Misbeliefs," *Behavioral and Brain Sciences,* 32 (2009): 522–23. The idea is that if errors can occur in several different dimensions and the fitness consequences of error are different in these different dimensions, then evolution may not favor a system that minimizes errors overall; it may instead produce a system that produces many errors but skews them into a dimension in which the cost is lower. My favorite example of this is the bias in male perception of female attractiveness. Given a very brief glimpse or indistinct image of a woman, men almost always err on the side of overestimating her attractiveness (relative to their own assessment after more careful inspection). One can think of some plausible evolutionary reasons why this might be so. (Music videos, incidentally, are relentless in their exploitation of this bias.)

14. As Stanovich writes, "We found that across a wide range of cognitive biases, the tendency to magnify the biases of others and minimize our own was not attenuated by high intelligence . . . If anything, the tendency was increased by high intelligence, not because the more intelligent subjects were in fact less biased but instead because they tended to assume that they would be less biased" (*Rationality and the Reflective Mind,* p. 135–36).

15. Stanovich, *The Robot's Rebellion,* p. 163.

16. There is also the problem of compartmentalization. As Jonathan Baron has observed, "The public pronouncements of Nobel Prize winners on matters outside their fields seem to vary enormously in the extent to which rational thinking was involved" (*Rationality and Intelligence,* p. 191).

17. Michael Kranish, "Yale Grades Portray Kerry as a Lackluster Student," Boston.com, June 7, 2005, http://www.boston.com/news/nation/washington/articles/2005/06/07/yale_grades_portray_kerry_as_a_lackluster_student (accessed June 23, 2013). The typical liberal assumptions are well articulated by Susan Jacoby, *The Age of American Unreason* (New York: Vintage, 2009), who starts by comparing John Kerry to John Kennedy, "both scions of wealth and privilege, both recipients of the best possible American and international education, both epitomizing cosmopolitanism," then laments the fact that Kerry "spent much of his campaign in a doomed effort to make himself look and sound more like an average Joe" (p. 283). She goes on to suggest that with George W. Bush, "there cannot be anyone in the country who believes that Bush's brain would have gotten him anywhere near Yale . . . without his family name and connections" (p. 284). But this is just to say that Bush, like Kerry, was a "scion of wealth and privilege."

18. David Frum, "Bush Is Incurious and Dogmatic but He Is Still the Right Leader," *Financial Times* (September 27, 2005) (accessed June 23, 2013).

19. For some reason, being an engineer seems to make people particularly vulnerable to dysrationalia. This may explain why engineering schools—not madrasas—seem to be the largest breeding grounds for future terrorists.

20. David Hume, *Dialogues Concerning Natural Religion,* ed. Bruce McEwen (1779; Edinburgh: William Blackwood, 1907), p. 79.

21. There is a classic psychology experiment that shows how important this task is. Subjects were asked to draw balls from an opaque urn containing some mixture of red and blue balls and to guess whether the majority were red or blue. The tendency was for subjects to settle on an initial hypothesis rather quickly, after which *all* subsequent draws simply reinforced belief the hypothesis, regardless of what color the balls were. If they started out thinking "blue," then they would mentally note each new instance of blue as confirmation, while each instance of red would be discounted. They would do the exact opposite if the initial guess was "red." Thus mixed evidence tends simply to reinforce previous belief, whatever that belief may be. See Gordon F. Pitz, "An Inertia Effect (Resistance to Change) in the Revision of Opinion," *Canadian Journal of Psychology,* 23 (1969): 24–33. One can see the obvious relevance of this in many areas, such as the history of medicine.

22. Aristotle, *Nicomachean Ethics,* edited by Roger Crisp (Cambridge: Cambridge University Press, 2000), p. 8.

23. Stanovich, *Rationality and the Reflective Mind,* p. 112.

24. Results on group deliberation are mixed. For an overview, see Cass R. Sunstein, *Infotopia: How Many Minds Produce Knowledge* (New York: Oxford University Press, 2006), pp. 57–64.

25. Restaurant failure rates are often overstated. There have been some attempts recently to correct that. See H. G. Parsa, John T. Self, David Njite, and Tiffany King, "Why Restaurants Fail," *Cornell Hotel and Restaurant Administration Quarterly,* 46 (2005): p. 310.

26. Kahneman, *Thinking, Fast and Slow,* p. 124.

27. Amos Tversky and Daniel Kahneman, "Judgment under Uncertainty: Heuristics and Biases," *Science,* 185 (1974): 1124–31.

28. For discussion, see Keith Stanovich, *Decision Making and Rationality in the Modern World* (Oxford: Oxford University Press, 2009), p. 108.

29. See Jeffrey S. Rosenthal, *Struck by Lightning: The Curious World of Probabilities* (London: Granta, 2005).

30. Thomas Hobbes, *Leviathan,* edited by Richard Tuck (1651; Cambridge: Cambridge University Press, 1996), p. 89.

31. See Boehm, *Hierarchy in the Forest*; see also Benoît Dubreuil, *Human Evolution and the Origin of Hierarchies: The State of Nature* (Cambridge: Cambridge University Press, 2010).

32. Hobbes, *Leviathan,* p. 89.

33. Ernst Fehr and Simon Gächter, "Altruistic Punishment in Humans," *Nature,* 415 (January 2002): 137–40.

34. Because of this, "the capacity for reciprocity to maintain cooperation decreases geometrically as the group size increases" (Nathalie Henrich and Joseph Henrich, *Why Humans Cooperate: A Cultural and Evolutionary Explanation* [Oxford: Oxford University Press, 2007], p. 51).

35. Some people may have wanted me to say "the market" here rather than "the state." I assign priority to the state not to downplay the significance of the market, but merely as a reflection of the fact that the state always comes first. There has never been, nor could there ever be, an instance of the spontaneous emergence of a market economy— it must always be institutionalized through law. That having been said, the market is clearly the second-most important kluge ever developed when it comes to extending the scope of human cooperation. On this, see Paul Seabright, *The Company of Strangers: A Natural History of Economic Life* (Princeton, NJ: Princeton University Press, 2004).

36. Hobbes, *Leviathan,* pp. 214–16; John Locke, *Second Treatise of Government,* edited by C. B. Macpherson (1690; Indianapolis: Hackett, 1980), p. 47 (§88), p. 67 (§130).

37. This is something of a simplification. For more general discussion, see Kenneth W. Simons, "The Crime/Tort Distinction: Legal Doctrine and Normative Perspectives," *Widener Law Journal,* 17 (2008): 719–32.

38. Boehm, *Hierarchy in the Forest*.

39. Francis Fukuyama, *The Origins of Political Order* (New York: Farrar, Straus and Giroux, 2011).

40. Steven M. Teles, "Klugeocracy: The American Way of Policy," New America Foundation, (December 12, 2012), http://www.newamerica.net/publications/policy/kludgeocracy_the_american_way_of_policy (accessed June 18, 2013).

41. Peter Baker, "Hip, Hip—If Not Hooray—for a Standstill Nation," *New York Times* (June 18, 2011).

Chapter 6

1. Jacoby, *The Age of American Unreason*.

2. The frequency of extreme weather events in recent years has since driven the rate up to over 50 percent.

3. Cathy Lynn Grossman, "Poll: 83% Say God Answers Prayers, 57% Favor National Prayer Day," *USA Today* (May 4, 2010).

4. See Stanovich, *Decision Making and Rationality*, pp. 95–124; also Stanovich, *The Robot's Rebellion*, p. 155. The article that served as the focus of much discussion was L. Jonathan Cohen, "Can Human Irrationality Be Experimentally Demonstrated?" *Behavioral and Brain Sciences*, 4 (1981): 317–70

5. Strictly speaking, that maximizes the ascription of true beliefs. See Donald Davidson, "On the Very Idea of a Conceptual Scheme," *Proceedings and Addresses of the American Philosophical Association*, 47 (1973–1974): 5–20.

6. Joseph Heath, "Problems in the Theory of Ideology," in William Rehg and James Bohman, eds., *Pluralism and the Pragmatic Turn: The Transformation of Critical Theory; Essays in Honor of Thomas McCarthy* (Cambridge, MA: MIT Press, 2001).

7. E.g., Gigerenzer, *Gut Feelings*.

8. Clark, *Being There*, p. 191.

9. This is the NISMART-2 study conducted by the U.S. Department of Justice: David Finkelhor, Heather Hammer, and Andrea J. Sedlak, "Nonfamily Abducted Children: National Estimates and Characteristics," *NISMART: National Incidence Studies of Missing, Abducted, Runaway, and Thrownaway Children* (Washington, D.C.: U.S. Department of Justice, Office of Justice Programs, Office of Juvenile Justice and Delinquency Prevention, October 2002), http://www.missingkids.com/en_US/documents/nismart2_nonfamily.pdf (accessed May 11, 2013).

10. This example is taken from a brilliant discussion by Frances Woolley, "Over-selling Soap," *Worthwhile Canadian Initiative* (December 2, 2010), http://worthwhile.typepad.com/worthwhile_canadian_initi/2010/12/the-news-item-dominated-the-

new-york-times-most-popular-list-for-weeks-for-your-dishwashers-sake-go-easy-on-the-detergent.html (accessed May 11, 2013).

11. See the discussion of anchoring effects in chapter 5.

12. Original observation by Jean Piaget, *Six Psychological Studies* (New York: Random House, 1967).

13. Woolley, "Over-selling Soap."

14. Stanovich, *Rationality and the Reflective Mind*, p. 21.

15. N. B. Davies, *Cuckoos, Cowbirds and Other Cheats* (London: T. & A. D. Poyser, 2000), pp. 104–5.

16. Brian Hare and Vanessa Woods, *The Genius of Dogs: How Dogs Are Smarter Than You Think* (New York: Penguin, 2013), pp. 119–21.

17. Mary F. Wilson and Anna Traveset, "The Ecology of Seed Dispersal," in Michael Fenner, ed., *Seeds*, 2nd edn. (New York: CABI, 2000).

18. This is why there is something suspicious about people who claim not to like fast food. Of course, there is no question that some are able to *cultivate* a distaste for it—often by channeling the disgust they feel for the social class of the average fast-food customer. But to deny that hamburgers, pizza, or burritos speak to you at some level seems to me little more than an attempt to deny one's essential humanity. Seeing them as the outcome of an incredibly competitive evolutionary process is central to understanding their appeal.

19. This is one of the theses central to Jared Diamond's highly influential book about European contact with the Americas, *Guns, Germs, and Steel: The Fates of Human Societies* (New York: W. W. Norton, 1997). Diamond argues that Europe and Asia had essentially been swapping diseases for centuries, resulting in both populations sharing an incredibly large pool of viruses and having high levels of acquired immunity. The Americas, in part because of their north–south geography, didn't have the same exchange of diseases, and so had a relatively small stock of viruses and very little immunity. Europeans had centuries to adapt to the viruses they carried with them. When this entire batch of highly contagious viruses was introduced all at once into the Americas, the result was the complete extinction of the indigenous population in certain areas.

20. Norbert Elias, *The Civilizing Process*, Vol. 1 (Oxford: Blackwell, 1969).

21. Don Ross and Harold Kincaid, "Introduction," in Don Ross, Harold Kincaid, David Spurrett, and Peter Collins, eds., *What Is Addiction?* (Cambridge, MA: MIT Press, 2010), p. ix.

22. Wolff, *Ethics and Public Policy*, pp. 52–53.

23. See Natasha Dow Schüll, *Addiction by Design* (Princeton, NJ: Princeton University Press, 2012).

24. For general discussion, see Ron Larson, "Core Principles for Supermarket Aisle Management," *Journal of Food Distribution Research*, 37 (2006): 107–11.

Chapter 7

1. Dan Sperber, *Explaining Culture: A Naturalistic Approach* (Oxford: Blackwell, 1996).

2. On November 11, 1995, the *Globe and Mail* newspaper printed the email and recipe, treating it as fact.

3. Boyer, *Religion Explained*, p. 69. Also Wendy James, *The Listening Ebony: Moral Knowledge, Religion, and Power among the Uduk of Sudan* (Oxford: Oxford University Press, 1988).

4. Boyer, *Religion Explained*, pp. 79–82. The experiments were conducted in collaboration with Justin Barrett.

5. Alison R. Fragale and Chip Heath, "Evolving Informational Credentials: The (Mis) Attribution of Believable Facts to Credible Sources," *Personality and Social Psychology Bulletin*, 30 (2004): 227. See also Hal R. Arkes, Catherine Hackett, and Larry Boehm, "The Generality of the Relation between Familiarity and Judged Validity," *Journal of Behavioral Decision Making*, 2 (1989): 81–94; see also Scott A. Hawkins, Stephen J. Hoch, and Joan Meyers-Levy, "Low-Involvement Learning: Repetition and Coherence in Familiarity and Belief," *Journal of Consumer Psychology*, 11 (2001): 1–11.

6. Joseph Goebbels, *The Goebbels Diaries*, edited by Louis P. Lochner (London, 1948), entry for January 29, 1942, p. 22, cited in David Welch, *The Third Reich: Politics and Propaganda*, 2nd edn. (London: Routledge, 2002), p. 26.

7. Intelligent, well-educated people, it should be noted, are perfectly capable of succumbing to belief contagion. There are academic versions of urban myths—ideas that get published in refereed papers but for which each paper cites some other paper that repeats the claim, which cites some other paper, and for which no one ever seems to have an original source. The most famous of these is the "Eskimo words for snow" myth, according to which the Inuit have a huge number of different words for snow. It turns out they don't, but this didn't stop some of the most prominent intellectuals of the twentieth century from claiming that they do. See Laura Martin, "'Eskimo Words for Snow': A Case Study in the Genesis and Decay of an Anthropological Example," *American Anthropologist*, 88 (1986): 418–23.

8. "New Age," *Wikipedia*, http://en.wikipedia.org/wiki/New_Age, accessed May 7, 2012. Unsurprisingly, the entry is not very stable, and has since been modified several times.

9. Matt Loney, "Study: Unpatched PCs Compromised in 20 Minutes," *CNET News* (August 17, 2004), http://news.cnet.com/2100-7349_3-5313402.html (accessed May 11, 2013).

10. For an overview, see Menachem E. Yaari, "On the Role of 'Dutch Books' in the Theory of Choice under Risk," in D. P. Jacobs, E. Kalai, M. I. Kamien, N. L. Schwartz, P. Hammond, and A. Holly, eds., *Frontiers of Economic Theory: The Nancy L. Schwartz Memorial Lectures, 1983–1997* (New York: Cambridge University Press, 1998).

11. Most notably, Bayes' rule, which seems to say something quite substantive and controversial about how we are committed to evaluating new evidence but which is actually

just an elementary consequence of the definition of conditional probability. See Stanovich, *Decision Making and Rationality*, pp. 53–55.

12. Frank P. Ramsey, "Truth and Probability," in *The Foundations of Mathematics and Other Logical Essays* (London: Routledge and Kegan Paul, 1931), pp. 156–98.

13. Donald Davidson, John McKinsey, and Patrick Suppes, "Outlines of a Formal Theory of Value," Philosophy of Science, 22 (1955): 140–60.

14. Which is not to say that the irrational have no response. They may have the advantage of being able to make more credible threats, because, being crazy, they might carry out the threat even after it has failed to achieve its desired effect. The rational are usually bluffing—once the threat has failed, they see no reason to carry it out, and so no one believes them in the first place. So if the irrational are *exploitable* by the rational, we might say that the rational are *extortable* by the irrational.

15. Fredrick Schick, "Dutch Bookies and Money Pumps," *Journal of Philosophy*, 83 (1986): 112–19.

16. For more extensive discussion, see Heath, *Filthy Lucre*, p. 260.

17. *Cariboo Sentinel* (Aug. 27, 1866), p. 1, http://historicalnewspapers.library.ubc.ca/view/collection/cariboosent/date/1866-08-27#1 (accessed July 5, 2013).

18. Advertisement for Sanka Coffee, *Good Housekeeping* (June 1932), p. 128, http://retro-ads.net/v/1930s/Food/1932_SankaCoffee.jpg.html (accessed May 11, 2013).

19. Advertisement by Pan-American Coffee Bureau, reproduced in Jim Heimann, ed., *All-American Ads: 50s* (Köln: Taschen, 2001), p. 627.

20. For more extensive discussion, see Joseph Heath and Andrew Potter, *The Rebel Sell: Why the Culture Can't Be Jammed* (Toronto: HarperCollins, 2004), p. 206.

21. Heath and Potter, *The Rebel Sell*, pp. 208–9.

22. There was a time when consumer opposition to advertising might have stemmed the tide. Inger L. Stole, *Advertising at War* (Urbana: University of Illinois Press, 2012), argues that it was the success of domestic propaganda during the Second World War that really broke the back of popular resistance. But since, the die has been cast.

23. For example, see James Twitchell, *Lead Us into Temptation* (New York: Columbia University Press, 1999), p. 23.

24. James R. Flynn and Lawrence G. Weiss, "American IQ Gains from 1932 to 2002: The WISC Subtests and Educational Progress," *International Journal of Testing*, 7 (2007): 209–24. See also James Flynn, Are We Getting Smarter? Rising IQ in the Twenty-First Century (Cambridge: Cambridge University Press, 2012).

25. Robert B. Cialdini, *Influence: The Psychology of Persuasion* (New York: HarperCollins, 1984), p. 277.

Chapter 8

1. Luntz, *Words That Work,* p. 279.

2. The video can be found in a variety of places, including Palin's PAC: http://www.sarah-pac.com/videos (accessed July 5, 2013)

3. Ayn Rand, "Sanction of the Victims," in *The Voice of Reason: Essays in Objectivist Thought* (New York: Penguin, 1989), p. 156.

4. For interesting discussion of the American trends, see Gordon Gauchat, "Politicization of Science in the Public Sphere: A Study of Public Trust in the United States, 1974 to 2010," *American Sociological Review,* 77 (2012): 167–87, showing that "conservatives began the period with the highest trust in science, relative to liberals and moderates, and ended the period with the lowest" (p. 167).

5. This is a style that subsequently became known as "high modernism." See Scott, *Seeing Like a State,* pp. 88–90.

6. George Orwell, *The Road to Wigan Pier* (Orlando, FL: Harcourt, 1958), p. 179.

7. V. I. Lenin, *Imperialism: The Highest Stage of Capitalism* (1916; Moscow: International Publishers, 1970).

8. John Kenneth Galbraith, *The New Industrial State* (Princeton, NJ: Princeton University Press, 2007).

9. Theodor Roszak, *The Making of a Counter Culture: Reflections on the Technocratic Society and Its Youthful Opposition* (New York: Doubleday & Co., 1969).

10. Herbert Marcuse, *An Essay on Liberation* (Boston: Beacon Press, 1969), p. 24.

11. See Steven Pinker, *The Better Angels of Our Nature: Why Violence Has Declined* (New York: Penguin, 2011), pp. 191–92.

12. Herbert Marcuse, *One-Dimensional Man* (Boston: Beacon Press, 1964), p. 239.

13. George Grant, *Lament for a Nation: The Defeat of Canadian Nationalism, rev. edn.* (Montreal: McGill-Queen's University Press, 2000).

14. Michael Joseph Oakeshott, *Rationalism in Politics and Other Essays* (Indianapolis, IN: Liberty Press, 1991), pp. 3-13.

15. Mary Wollstonecraft, *The Vindications: The Rights of Men and the Rights of Women,* ed. D. L. Macdonald and Kathleen Sherf (1790, 1792; Peterborough, ON: Broadview, 1997), p. 117.

16. Mary Daly, *Beyond God the Father: Toward a Philosophy of Women's Liberation* (Boston: Beacon Press, 1973), p. 39.

17. Mary Daly, *Gyn/Ecology: The Metaethics of Radical Feminism,* 2nd edn. (Boston: Beacon Press, 1990), p. 23.

18. Daly, *Gyn/Ecology,* p. xi.

19. At the time of writing, Google Scholar showed that *Gyn/Ecology* had over 2,300 academic citations. That is a lot.

20. Eleanor Emmons Maccoby and Carol Nagy Jacklin, *The Psychology of Sex Differences* (Stanford, CA: Stanford University Press, 1974), pp. 98–110; Alan Feingold, "Sex Differences in Variability in Intellectual Abilities: A New Look at an Old Controversy," *Review of Educational Research*, 62 (1992): 61–84.

21. Fiona Godlee, Jane Smith, and Harvey Marcovitch, "Wakefield's Article Linking Vaccination and Autism Was Fraudulent," *British Medical Journal*, 342 (2011): 64–66.

22. Weston Kosova and Patrice Wingert, "Live Your Best Life Ever!" *Newsweek* (May 29, 2009).

23. See "Mothers Battle Autism," Oprah, http://www.oprah.com/oprahshow/Mothers-Battle-Autism/ (accessed May 13, 2013).

24. Chabris and Simons, *The Invisible Gorilla*, pp. 103–15.

25. Jenny McCarthy, *Mother Warriors: A Nation of Parents Healing Autism against All Odds* (New York: Penguin, 2008).

26. David Olson, *Psychological Theory and Educational Reform: How School Remakes Mind and Society* (Cambridge: Cambridge University Press, 2003), pp. 16–19.

27. Stanovich, *Who Is Rational?* p. 193.

28. Valerie A. Thompson, Jamie A. Prowse Turner, and Gordon Pennycook, "Intuition, Reason, and Metacognition," *Cognitive Psychology*, 63 (2011): 107–40.

29. Adam L. Alter, Daniel M. Oppenheimer, Nicholas Epley, and Rebecca N. Eyre, "Overcoming Intuition: Metacognitive Difficulty Activates Analytical Thought," *Journal of Experimental Psychology: General*, 136 (2007): 569–76.

30. For an excellent discussion, see Olson, *Psychological Theory and Educational Reform.*

31. David Brooks, "Amy Chua Is a Wimp," *New York Times* (January 17, 2011).

32. Frans de Waal, *Chimpanzee Politics: Power and Sex among Apes*, rev. edn. (Baltimore, MD: Johns Hopkins University Press, 1998).

33. Al Gore, *The Assault on Reason* (New York: Penguin, 2007), p. 1.

Chapter 9

1. Hirstein, *Brain Fiction*, p. 19.

2. Mark Green, *To Err Is Reagan: Lies and Deceptions from the President* (San Francisco: Foundation for National Progress, 1987).

3. Michael Barone and Jodie T. Allen, "The 'Great Communicator' or the 'Great Prevaricator,'" *Washington Post* (October 10, 1982).

4. Luntz, *Words That Work*, p. 13. He goes on to say, "His message never wavered, and that was the major reason he sustained personal credibility even though a majority of Americans opposed many of his policies during his administration" (p. 13).

5. Fay S. Joyce, "2 Approaches to a Candidate's Image: Showing the Message or Speaking It," New York Times (November 1, 1984).

6. George Monbiot, "Advertising Is a Poison That Demeans Even Love—and We're Hooked on It," *The Guardian* (October 24, 2011).

7. Eric Boehlert, "Fox News' ACORN Fanatics Still Won't Address GOP's Widening 'Voter Fraud' Scandal," *Huffington Post* (February 10, 2012), http://www.huffingtonpost.com/eric-boehlert/fox-news-acorn-fanatics-s_b_1932745.html (accessed December 19, 2012).

8. "National Opinion on Libya, the Norquist Plan and Obama's Reelection," Public Policy Polling (December 4, 2012), http://www.publicpolicypolling.com/pdf/2011/PPP_Release_National_1204.pdf (accessed December 19, 2012).

9. Frank Luntz quotes this a lot (e.g., *Words That Work,* p. 18), crediting it to Warren Beatty.

10. Luntz, *Words That Work,* p. 11.

11. "Staying on Message with the Media," Moveon.org, http://www.moveon.org/team/training/Staying_on_Message_with_the_Media.doc (accessed May 30, 2012).

12. Classically described in Richard Hofstadter, *Anti-intellectualism in American Life* (New York: Vintage, 1963).

13. As Thomas Frank has observed, this way of thinking divides the world into two classes, ordinary people and "intellectuals": "Either you're a productive citizen, or you're some kind of snob, a university professor, or an EPA bureaucrat. Compared to the vivid line separating intellectuals and productive members of society, all other distinctions fade to nothingness" (*Pity the Billionaire,* p. 92).

14. John Geddes, "Ian Brodie Offers a Candid Case Study in Politics and Policy," *Maclean's* (March 27, 2009).

15. Allan Gregg, "1984 in 2012: The Assault on Reason," speech to the Faculty of Public Affairs, Carleton University, Ottawa, September 8, 2012, http://www.ipolitics.ca/2012/09/08/1984-in-2012-the-assault-on-reason-speech/ (accessed May 14, 2013).

16. Gregg, "1984 in 2012."

17. Roy Walmsley, *World Prison Population List,* 9th edn. (London: International Centre for Prison Studies, 2011).

18. William J. Stuntz, *The Collapse of American Criminal Justice* (Cambridge, MA: Harvard University Press, 2011), p. 48.

19. See Paul H. Robinson and John M. Darley, "Does Criminal Law Deter? A Behavioral Science Investigation," *Oxford Journal of Legal Studies,* 24 (2004): 173–205.

20. The Monks of New Skete, *The Art of Raising a Puppy* (New York: Little, Brown & Co., 1991).

21. Norman Miller, Donald C. Butler, and James A. McMartin, "The Ineffectiveness of Punishment Power in Group Interaction," *Sociometry,* 32 (1969): 24–42.

22. Thomas W. Phelan, *1-2-3 Magic,* 3rd edn. (Glen Ellyn, IL: Parentmagic, 2003).

23. Daniel Kahneman, "Biographical," Nobelprize.org (2002), http://www.nobelprize.org/nobel_prizes/economics/laureates/2002/kahneman-autobio.html (accessed May 15, 2013).

24. Ernst Fehr and Urs Fischbacher, "Third-Party Punishment and Social Norms," *Evolution and Human Behavior,* 25 (2004): 63–87; Katrin Riedl, Keith Jensen, Josep Call, and Michael Tomasello, "No Third-Party Punishment in Chimpanzees," *Proceedings of the National Academy of Sciences,* 109 (2013): 14824–29.

25. "Crime Agenda Fuels High Costs," *The StarPhoenix* (Saskatoon, January 17, 2013).

26. Canadian Press, "Crime Rate Debate Won't Stop Tory Push: Toews," CTV News (February 22, 2011), http://www.ctvnews.ca/crime-rate-debate-won-t-stop-tory-push -toews-1.610672#ixzz20nWdyFvH (accessed May 15, 2013).

27. Prime Minister Stephen Harper, remarks at the 6th Annual Gala and Fundraiser for the Canadian Crime Victims Foundation, Vaughan, Ontario, June 6, 2008, http://pm.gc .ca/eng/media.asp?category=2&id=2145 (accessed May 15, 2013).

28. Geddes, "Ian Brodie Offers a Candid Case Study in Politics and Policy."

29. Evan McMorris-Santoro, "Christine O'Donnell: Where in the Constitution Is the Separation of Church and State?" *Talking Points Memo* (October 19, 2010), http:// tpmdc.talkingpointsmemo.com/2010/10/christine-odonnell-where-in-the-constitution -is-the-separation-of-church-and-state.php (accessed May 15, 2013).

30. Alexander Burns, "The GOP Polling Debacle," *Politico* (November 11, 2012), http:// www.politico.com/news/stories/1112/83672.html (accessed June 18, 2013); Noam Scheiber, "The Internal Polls That Made Mitt Romney Think He'd Win," *New Republic* (November 30, 2012), http://www.newrepublic.com/blog/plank/110597/exclusive-the-polls-made-mitt-romney-think-hed-win# (accessed June 18, 2013).

Chapter 10

1. Pierre Elliott Trudeau, *Federalism and the French Canadians* (Toronto: Macmillan, 1977), p. 156.

2. Trudeau, *Federalism and the French Canadians,* p. 191.

3. Trudeau, *Federalism and the French Canadians,* p. 195.

4. James D. Fearon, "Ethnic and Cultural Diversity by Country," *Journal of Economic Growth,* 8 (2003): 195–222.

5. Trudeau, *Federalism and the French Canadians,* p. 193.

6. John English, *Just Watch Me: The Life of Pierre Elliott Trudeau: 1968–2000* (Toronto: Alfred A. Knopf, 2009), p. 199.

7. Sarah Palin, "Statement on the Current Health Care Debate," Facebook (August 7, 2009), http://www.facebook.com/note.php?note_id=113851103434 (accessed June 15, 2012).

8. Frank, *Pity the Billionaire,* p. 97. His remark is actually made in the context of Republican claims about small business and job creation, but the point is a general one.

9. George Lakoff, *Don't Think of an Elephant: Know Your Values and Frame the Debate* (White River Junction, VT: Chelsea Green Publishing, 2004).

10. George Lakoff, *The Political Mind: A Cognitive Scientist's Guide to Your Brain and Its Politics* (New York: Penguin, 2008), pp. 236–38.

11. Mark Steyn, "John Kerry Is All Tied Up in Nuances," *Telegraph* (March 2, 2004). "Nancy boy" is an older term for a homosexual, something that would have been well known to Steyn's British readers.

12. Carl Schmitt, *The Concept of the Political*, translated by George Schwab (Chicago: University of Chicago Press, 2007).

13. There is a good discussion of this in Luntz, *Words That Work*, p. 87.

14. This is an extreme difficult point to grasp. One cannot overstate the importance of Boyd and Richerson, "The Evolution of Reciprocity in Sizable Groups," in clarifying this point.

15. Lakoff, *The Political Mind*, p. 47.

16. On this, see the interesting discussion by Craig Calhoun in "A World of Emergencies: Fear, Intervention, and the Limits of Cosmopolitan Order," *Canadian Review of Sociology*, 41 (2008): 373–95.

17. Ted Nugent, "Trample the Weak, Hurtle the Dead," *Washington Times* (June 24, 2010), cited in Frank, *Pity the Billionaire*, p. 188.

18. Halford Ross Ryan, "The 1988 Bush-Dukakis Presidential Debates," in Robert V. Friedenberg, ed., *Rhetorical Studies of National Political Debates: 1960–1992*, 2nd edn. (Westport, CT: Greenwood, 1994), p. 160.

19. Roy F. Baumeister, *Evil: Inside Human Violence and Cruelty* (New York: W. H. Freeman, 1997), pp. 46–47.

20. Haidt, *The Righteous Mind*, pp. 305–9.

21. Lakoff, *The Political Mind*, p. 119.

22. David Hume, *A Treatise of Human Nature*, edited by L. A. Selby-Bigge, 2nd edn. (1739–40; Oxford: Clarendon, 1978), p. 477.

23. As Friedrich Hayek put it, "the manner in which the benefits and burdens are apportioned by the market mechanism would in many instances have to be regarded as very unjust *if* it were the result of a deliberate allocation to particular people" (*Law, Legislation and Liberty*, Vol. 2 [London: Routledge & Kegan Paul, 1976], p. 64).

24. For my own attempt, see Heath, *Filthy Lucre*, pp. 103–5.

25. Bryan Caplan, *The Myth of the Rational Voter: Why Democracies Choose Bad Policies* (Princeton, NJ: Princeton University Press, 2007).

Chapter 11

1. Simon Rogers, "Healthcare Spending around the World, Country by Country," *Guardian* (June 30, 2012), http://www.guardian.co.uk/news/datablog/2012/jun/30/healthcare-spending-world-country (accessed December 20, 2012).

2. Lakoff, *The Political Mind*, p. 56.

3. Lakoff, *The Political Mind*, p. 68.

4. Lakoff, *The Political Mind*, p. 67.

5. Specifically, the Kaiser Foundation Health Plan and the Kaiser Foundation Hospitals are nonprofits.

6. There is only one significant example of government-provided care, which is the NHS in the U.K. But this is not a particularly attractive model, precisely because it gets the government too much involved in the provision of care.

7. Gardner, *Risk.*

8. Gardner, *Risk*, p. 296.

9. Eric J. Johnson, John Hershey, Jacqueline Meszaros, and Howard Kunreuther, "Framing, Probability Distortions, and Insurance Decisions," *Journal of Risk and Uncertainty*, 7 (1993): 35–51.

10. Gardner, *Risk*, p. 342.

11. Chabris and Simons, *The Invisible Gorilla*, p. 241.

12. Brian Wansink, *Mindless Eating: Why We Eat More Than We Think* (New York: Bantam, 2006), p. 69.

13. Chabris and Simons, *The Invisible Gorilla*, p. 242.

14. Roy F. Baumeister, Todd F. Heatherton, and Dianne M. Tice, *Losing Control: How and Why People Fail at Self-Regulation* (San Diego, CA: Academic Press, 1994).

15. Matt Yglesias, "Bachmann Introducing Bill to Ban Use of Made-Up Global Currency," ThinkProgress (March 29, 2009), http://thinkprogress.org/yglesias/2009/03/26/192285/bachmann_introducing_bill_to_ban_use_of_made_up_global_currency/ (accessed May 16, 2013).

Chapter 12

1. The argument developed here owes an enormous debt to Andy Clark's brilliant paper "Economic Reason: The Interplay of Individual Learning and External Structure," in John N. Drobak and John V. C. Nye, eds., *The Frontiers of the New Institutional Economics* (San Diego, CA: Academic Press, 1996).

2. Clark, "Economic Reason," p. 271.

3. David Allen, *Getting Things Done: The Art of Stress-Free Productivity* (London: Penguin, 2001), pp. 85–86.

4. Kahneman, *Thinking, Fast and Slow*, p. 284.

5. Paul Krugman, "Ricardo's Difficult Idea," http://web.mit.edu/krugman/www/ricardo.htm (accessed May 16, 2013).

6. Dawkins, *The Blind Watchmaker*, p. 38.

7. The irony here, as Dawkins points out, is that we have intuitions governing a relatively short time frame precisely because our brains are the product of evolution.

8. The exceptions are two pieces on the subject of Charles Darwin's life and work.

9. Centers for Disease Control and Prevention, "Adult Obesity Facts" (August 13, 2012), http://www.cdc.gov/obesity/data/adult.html (accessed May 16, 2013).

10. The average person, at an average activity level, should be consuming somewhere between 2,000 and 2,500 calories total per day.

11. Wansink, *Mindless Eating.*

12. This has been known for a long time. See Paul S. Siegel, "The Completion Compulsion in Human Eating," *Psychological Reports,* 3 (1957): 15–16; Andrew B. Geier, Paul Rozin, and Gheorghe Doros, "Unit Bias: A New Heuristic That Helps Explain the Effect of Portion Size on Food Intake," *Psychological Science,* 17 (2006): 521–25.

13. Wansink, *Mindless Eating,* p. 203.

14. "New York's Calorie Counting," *Economist* (July 28, 2011). See also Bryan Bollinger, Phillip Leslie, and Alan Sorenson, "Calorie Posting in Chain Restaurants," NBER Working Paper No, 15648, National Bureau of Economic Research (January 2010), http://www.nber.org/papers/w15648 (accessed June 18, 2013).

15. Douglas E. Levy, Jason Riis, Lillian M. Sonnenberg, Susan J. Barraclough, and Anne N. Thornsdike, "Food Choices of Minority and Low-Income Employees," *American Journal of Preventative Medicine,* 43 (2012): 240–48.

16. See Heath and Anderson, "Procrastination and the Extended Will."

17. Wansink, *Mindless Eating,* p. 204.

18. Wansink, *Mindless Eating,* p. 68.

19. Committee on Sleep Medicine and Research, Board on Health Sciences Policy, *Sleep Disorders and Sleep Deprivation* (Washington, D.C.: National Academies Press, 2006), p. 58.

20. For a general discussion of the food industry, see Michael Moss, *Salt Sugar Fat: How the Food Giants Hooked Us* (New York: Random House, 2013).

21. John Stuart Mill, "On Liberty," in *The Basic Writings of John Stuart Mill* (1869; New York: Random House, 1992), p. 79.

22. Richard H. Thaler and Cass Sunstein, *Nudge: Improving Decisions about Health, Wealth, and Happiness* (New York: Penguin, 2008).

23. Thaler and Sunstein, *Nudge,* p. 3.

24. Thaler and Sunstein, *Nudge,* p. 6.

Chapter 13

1. Allen, *Getting Things Done,* p. 86.

2. Iris Marion Young, *Justice and the Politics of Difference,* new edn. (Princeton, NJ: Princeton University Press, 2011), p. 136.

3. This is the core phenomenon in the famous Stroop effect. See Colin M. MacLeod, "Half a Century of Research on the Stroop Effect: An Integrative Review," *Psychological Bulletin,* 109 (1991): 163–203. For applications of similar techniques to the study of racial attitudes, see Jennifer A. Richeson and J. Nicole Shelton, "When Prejudice Does Not Pay: Effects of Interracial Contact on Executive Function," Psychological Science, 14 (2003): 287–90.

4. Marilynn Brewer, "In-Group Bias in the Minimal Intergroup Situation: A Cognitive-Motivational Analysis," *Psychological Bulletin,* 86 (1979): 317.

5. Robert Kurzban, John Tooby, and Leda Cosmides, "Can Race Be Erased? Coalitional Computation and Social Categorization," *Proceedings of the National Academy of Sciences,* 98 (2001): 15387–92.

6. The episode is "Let That Be Your Last Battlefield" (1969). It is sometimes compared, unfairly, to Dr. Seuss's *The Sneetches* (New York: Random House, 1964).

7. Gat, *War in Human Civilization,* p. 135.

8. Roy Baumeister writes, "In the history of the world, increased recognition of differences between groups has led more often to conflict and violence than to peaceful cooperation and sharing. America is now making a dangerous gamble on the opposite result" (*Evil,* p. 79).

9. Zhang Weiwei, "Why China Prefers Its Own Political Model," *Europe's World* (Spring 2013), http://www.europesworld.org/NewEnglish/Home_old/Article/tabid/191/ArticleType/ArticleView/ArticleID/22086/language/en-US/Default.aspx (accessed May 14, 2013).

10. Cass Sunstein, "Cognition and Cost-Benefit Analysis," Journal of Legal Studies 29 (2000): 1059–1103.

11. C. E. S. Franks, *The Parliament of Canada* (Toronto: University of Toronto Press, 1987), p. 156.

12. Franks, *The Parliament of Canada,* p. 156.

13. This is from the FCC's 1974 formulation. See John Corry, "Why the Fairness Doctrine Is Still Important," *New York Times* (September 15, 1985).

14. Council of Europe, Parliamentary Assembly, Resolution 1003 on the Ethics of Journalism (1993), http://assembly.coe.int/documents/adoptedtext/ta93/eres1003.htm (accessed December 21, 2012).

15. Amy Sullivan, "Truth in Advertising? Not for Political Ads," *Time* (September 23, 2008).

16. A similar suggestion has been made by Ronald Dworkin, *Is Democracy Possible Here? Principles for a New Political Debate* (Princeton, NJ: Princeton University Press, 2006), p. 151. This is followed by a detailed discussion of the legal implications of such a restriction in the American context—specifically, whether it would be unconstitutional.

17. Stephen Ansolabehere and Shanto Iyengar, *Going Negative: How Political Advertisements Shrink and Polarize the Electorate* (New York: The Free Press, 1995).

18. Haidt, *The Righteous Mind*, p. 90.

19. "O'Reilly Debates Christopher Hitchens about Coerced Interrogation, Water-Boarding," *The O'Reilly Factor*, Fox News (January 12, 2009), http://www.foxnews.com/story/0,2933,479839,00.html (accessed May 16, 2013).

20. Hat tip to Folco Portinari, author of the Slow Food Manifesto (December 10, 1989): http://www.slowfood.com/about_us/eng/manifesto.lasso (accessed May 16, 2013).

Epilogue

1. János Kornai, *The Socialist System: The Political Economy of Communism* (Princeton, NJ: Princeton University Press, 1992), p. 272.

2. Heath, *Filthy Lucre*, pp. 158–63.

3. Gat, *War in Human Civilization*, p. 4.

4. Neil Postman, *Amusing Ourselves to Death: Public Discourse in the Age of Show Business* (New York: Penguin, 1985).

Index